KANT ON FREEDOM AND SPONTANEITY

Spontaneity – understood as an action of the mind or will that is not determined by a prior external stimulus – is a theme that resonates throughout Immanuel Kant's theoretical and practical philosophy. Though spontaneity and the concomitant notion of freedom lie at the foundation of many of Kant's most pivotal theses and arguments regarding cognition, judgment, and moral action, spontaneity and freedom themselves often remain cloaked in mystery, or accessible only via transcendental argument. This volume brings together a distinguished group of scholars who explore the nature of freedom and spontaneity, the arguments Kant offers surrounding these concepts, and their place in Kant's larger philosophical system. The collection will appeal to scholars interested in any aspect of Kant's philosophy, especially those who hope to gain a deeper insight into these fundamental Kantian ideas.

KATE A. MORAN is an Associate Professor of Philosophy at Brandeis University. She is the author of *Community and Progress in Kant's Moral Philosophy* (2012) and a number of essays on Kant's moral and political philosophy.

KANT ON FREEDOM AND SPONTANEITY

EDITED BY
KATE A. MORAN
Brandeis University

CAMBRIDGE
UNIVERSITY PRESS

CAMBRIDGE
UNIVERSITY PRESS

University Printing House, Cambridge CB2 8BS, United Kingdom

One Liberty Plaza, 20th Floor, New York, NY 10006, USA

477 Williamstown Road, Port Melbourne, VIC 3207, Australia

314–321, 3rd Floor, Plot 3, Splendor Forum, Jasola District Centre, New Delhi – 110025, India

79 Anson Road, #06–04/06, Singapore 079906

Cambridge University Press is part of the University of Cambridge.

It furthers the University's mission by disseminating knowledge in the pursuit of education, learning, and research at the highest international levels of excellence.

www.cambridge.org
Information on this title: www.cambridge.org/9781107125933
DOI: 10.1017/9781316421888

© Cambridge University Press 2018

This publication is in copyright. Subject to statutory exception and to the provisions of relevant collective licensing agreements, no reproduction of any part may take place without the written permission of Cambridge University Press.

First published 2018

Printed and bound in Great Britain by Clays Ltd, Elcograf S.p.A.

A catalogue record for this publication is available from the British Library.

Library of Congress Cataloging-in-Publication Data
NAMES: Moran, Kate A., editor.
TITLE: Kant on freedom and spontaneity / edited by Kate Moran,
Brandeis University, Massachusetts.
DESCRIPTION: 1 [edition]. | New York : Cambridge University Press, 2018. |
Includes bibliographical references and index.
IDENTIFIERS: LCCN 2018013120 | ISBN 9781107125933 (hardback) |
ISBN 9781107565890 (pbk.)
SUBJECTS: LCSH: Kant, Immanuel, 1724-1804. | Liberty. | Spontaneity (Philosophy)
CLASSIFICATION: LCC B2798 .K223643 2018 | DDC 123/.5092–dc23
LC record available at https://lccn.loc.gov/2018013120

ISBN 978-1-107-12593-3 Hardback

Cambridge University Press has no responsibility for the persistence or accuracy of URLs for external or third-party internet websites referred to in this publication and does not guarantee that any content on such websites is, or will remain, accurate or appropriate.

For Paul Guyer
With fond appreciation for his scholarship, mentorship,
and friendship

Contents

List of Contributors	*page*	ix
Acknowledgments		xi
List of Abbreviations		xii
Introduction		1
Kate Moran		

PART I SPONTANEITY: PURE CONCEPTS OF THE UNDERSTANDING, IMAGINATION, AND JUDGMENT — 11

1	Kant on Imagination and Object Constitution	13
	Rolf-Peter Horstmann	
2	Pure Understanding, the Categories, and Kant's Critique of Wolff	30
	Brian A. Chance	
3	Transcendental Idealism in the B-Deduction	48
	Michael Rohlf	
4	Kant's *A priori* Principle of Judgments of Taste	66
	Jennifer Dobe	

PART II THE INNER VALUE OF THE WORLD: FREEDOM AS THE KEYSTONE OF KANT'S MORAL PHILOSOPHY — 87

5	Guyer on the Value of Freedom	89
	Patricia Kitcher	

viii   *Contents*

6   Kant, Guyer, and Tomasello on the Capacity to Recognize
    the Humanity of Others   107
    Lucas Thorpe

7   Does Kantian Constructivism Rest on a Mistake?   137
    Julian Wuerth

8   Moral Realism and the Inner Value of the World   155
    Frederick Rauscher

PART III FREEDOM AS AUTONOMOUS WILLING:
KANT'S SENSIBLE AGENT   169

9   On the Many Senses of "Self-Determination"   171
    Karl Ameriks

10 Inclination, Need, and Moral Misery   195
    Kate Moran

11 Religion and the Highest Good: Speaking to the Heart
    of Even the Best of Us   214
    Barbara Herman

PART IV FREEDOM ON A BOUNDED SPHERE: KANT'S
POLITICAL PHILOSOPHY   231

12 Right and Ethics: A Critical Tribute to Paul Guyer   233
    Allen Wood

13 From Justice to Fairness: Does Kant's Doctrine of Right
    Imply a Theory of Distributive Justice?   250
    Michael Nance and Jeppe von Platz

Postscript: Nature and Freedom in Kant's Practical Philosophy   269
Paul Guyer

Bibliography   295
Index   305

Contributors

KARL AMERIKS is a professor emeritus at the University of Notre Dame and held the McMahon-Hank Professorship in Philosophy there.

BRIAN A. CHANCE is a professor of humanities at the Oklahoma School of Science and Mathematics and affiliate faculty member in philosophy at the University of Oklahoma.

JENNIFER DOBE is an assistant professor in philosophy at Grinnell College.

PAUL GUYER is Jonathan Nelson Professor of Humanities and Philosophy at Brown University.

BARBARA HERMAN is Griffin Professor of Philosophy and professor of law at the University of California, Los Angeles.

ROLF-PETER HORSTMANN is a professor emeritus in philosophy at the Humboldt University.

PATRICIA KITCHER is Roberta and William Campbell Professor of Humanities at Columbia University.

KATE MORAN is an associate professor of philosophy at Brandeis University.

MICHAEL NANCE is an assistant professor of philosophy at University of Maryland, Baltimore County.

JEPPE VON PLATZ is an assistant professor of philosophy at the University of Richmond.

FREDERICK RAUSCHER is a professor of philosophy at Michigan State University.

MICHAEL ROHLF is an associate professor of philosophy at the Catholic University of America.

List of Contributors

LUCAS THORPE is an assistant professor of philosophy at Boğaziçi University.

ALLEN WOOD is Ruth Norman Halls Professor of Philosophy at Indiana University Bloomington and Ward W. and Priscilla B. Woods Professor emeritus at Stanford University.

JULIAN WUERTH is an associate professor of philosophy at Vanderbilt University.

Acknowledgments

Early versions of many of the essays in this volume were presented at the "Nature and Freedom in Kant" conference at Brown University in October 2013. Mike Nance, Fred Rauscher, Jeppe von Platz, and Jennifer Uleman deserve special thanks for organizing the conference. Marie Johansen and Joana Rolfes provided invaluable assistance with web design and administration, respectively. Funding for the conference was provided by the Office of the Dean of the College, Brown University; the Cogut Center for the Humanities, Brown University; the German Academic Exchange Service (DAAD); the Franklin J. Matchette Foundation; the Goethe-Institute; the Consulate General of the Federal Republic of Germany in Boston; the Department of Philosophy, Brown University; and the Department of Philosophy, University of Pennsylvania. Many thanks to Jacob Caldwell for his assistance in preparing the final manuscript.

Abbreviations

The following abbreviations are used in this volume to refer to Kant's texts. Page citations refer to *Kants gesammelte Schriften*, Berlin-Brandenburgische Akademie der Wissenschaften (formerly: Königlich Preußische Akademie der Wissenschaften), Berlin: Walter de Gruyter (1900–). Only references to *KrV* refer to the "A" and "B" pages of the first and second editions; all other references list volume and page number of the Prussian Academy edition of Kant's works, e.g.: *GMS* 4:420. All translations are taken – unless otherwise stated – from the *Cambridge Edition of the Works of Immanuel Kant*, Cambridge University Press.

AA	*Akademie-Ausgabe (Academy Edition)*
Anth	*Anthropologie in pragmatischer Hinsicht (Anthropology from a Pragmatic Point of View)*
Collins	*Moralphilosophie Collins (Lectures on Ethics Collins)*
DfS	*Die falsche Spitzfindigkeit der vier syllogistischen Figuren erwiesen (The False Subtlety of the Four Syllogistic Figures)*
EaD	*Das Ende aller Dinge (The End of All Things)*
GMS	*Grundlegung zur Metaphysik der Sitten (Groundwork of the Metaphysics of Morals)*
GSE	*Beobachtung über das Gefühl des Schönen und Erhabenen (Observations on the Feeling of the Beautiful and Sublime)*
Herder	*Praktische Philosophie Herder (Lectures on Ethics Herder)*
HN	*Handschriftlicher Nachlass (Notes and Fragments)*
IaG	*Idee zu einer allgemeinen Geschichte in weltbürgerlicher Absicht (Idea for a Universal History with a Cosmopolitan Aim)*
Jäsche	*Logik Jäsche (Lectures on Logic Jäsche)*
KpV	*Kritik der praktischen Vernunft (Critique of Practical Reason)*
KrV	*Kritik der reinen Vernunft (Critique of Pure Reason)*
KU	*Kritik der Urteilskraft (Critique of the Power of Judgment)*

List of Abbreviations   xiii

MAM	*Mutmaßlicher Anfang der Menschengeschichte (Conjectural Beginning of Human History)*
MAN	*Metaphysische Anfangsgründe der Naturwissenschaft (Metaphysical Foundations of Natural Science)*
Mrong	*Moral Mrongrovius (Lectures on Ethics Mrongrovius)*
Mrong II	*Moral Mrongrovius II (Lectures on Ethics Mrongrovius II)*
MSI	*De mundi sensibilis atque intelligibilis forma et principiis (Inaugural Dissertation)*
NF	*Naturrecht Feyerabend (Lectures on Natural Law Feyerabend)*
Prol	*Prolegomena zu einer jeden künftigen Metaphysik (Prolegomena to Any Future Metaphysics)*
RezSchulz	*Recension von Schulz's Versuch einer Anleitung zur Sittenlehre für alle Menschen (Review of Schulz's Attempt at an introduction to a doctrine of morals for all human beings regardless of different religions)*
RGV	*Die Religion innerhalb der Grenzen der bloßen Vernunft (Religion within the Boundaries of Mere Reason)*
RL	*Metaphysische Anfangsgründe der Rechtslehre (Doctrine of Right)*
SF	*Der Streit der Fakultäten (The Conflict of the Faculties)*
TG	*Träume eines Geistersehers (Dreams of a Spirit Seer)*
TL	*Metaphysische Anfangsgründe der Tugendlehre (Doctrine of Virtue)*
TP	*Über den Gemeinspruch: Das mag in der Theorie richtig sein, taugt aber nicht für die Praxis (On the Common Saying: That May be True in Theory, but It Is of No Use in Practice)*
V-Anth	*Vorlesungen über Anthropologie (Lectures on Anthropology)*
Vigil	*Metaphysik der Sitten Vigilantius (Lectures on Ethics Vigilantius)*
WA	*Beantwortung der Frage: Was ist Aufklärung? (An Answer to the Question: What is Enlightenment?)*
WDO	*Was heißt: Sich im Denken orientiren? (What Does It Mean to Orient Oneself in Thinking?)*
ZeF	*Zum ewigen Frieden (Toward Perpetual Peace)*

Introduction

Kate Moran

Spontaneity – understood as an action of the mind or will that is not determined by a prior external stimulus – is a theme that resonates throughout Immanuel Kant's theoretical and practical philosophy. Though spontaneity and the concomitant notion of freedom lie at the foundation of many of Kant's most pivotal theses and arguments regarding cognition, judgment, and moral action, spontaneity and freedom themselves often remain cloaked in mystery, or accessible only via transcendental argument. Kant never addresses spontaneity head-on in any of his published texts, but this fact belies its importance in Kant's system.[1] It is a hallmark of rational agency and condition of the rational agent's ability to cognize and act.

In the theoretical sphere, questions regarding spontaneity pertain especially to the pure concepts of the understanding and, in particular, the spontaneous act through which the cognizing subject applies these concepts. This spontaneous act underlies nothing less than the possibility of human cognition and, by extension, Kant's notion of the self and the transcendental apparatus that characterizes his critical philosophy. Spontaneity is closely related to Kantian notions of "thinking" (as opposed to intuiting), "understanding," "apperceiving," and "judging" (see Pippin 1987:450). Though the set of questions that may be raised about Kant's notion of spontaneity in this context is vast, several themes emerge as being of central concern. In particular, how shall we interpret Kant's account of the acts of understanding and imagination through which the subject synthesizes cognition? What is the nature and origin of the pure concepts of the understanding? How shall we interpret Kant's notoriously difficult

---

[1] Kant does discuss spontaneity in the L₁ Metaphysics lectures; curiously the discussion drops out of later lectures.

arguments regarding the application of these concepts in the Transcendental Deduction? And how might we understand judgment more generally, especially when it is extended to include the faculty that underlies disinterested judgments of taste?

Though it would be a mistake simply to equate Kant's notion of epistemic spontaneity with practical spontaneity or moral freedom, there are obvious similarities between the theoretical and practical spheres. The central similarity is that rational choice, like cognition, is unexplainable in terms of prior, sensible influence (Allison 1996: 132). In the practical sphere, then, the mystery of spontaneity manifests itself as a series of questions about the nature of rational agency and, ultimately, about moral freedom, or autonomy. Kant makes it clear that the moral law is the law of freedom. But already in this statement we confront a number of puzzles about freedom and its relationship to the moral law. Just how should we understand the type of freedom at issue in this claim? Is it a capacity rationally to set and pursue ends (including non-moral ends)? Or is it best understood as the capacity to act in accordance with self-imposed laws? Beyond this, there are a number of questions about the precise role that freedom plays in Kant's argument for the moral law. Is freedom a value that ought to be protected or even, in a sense, maximized? Or is it better understood as a property of the will that makes unique demands – especially regarding universality – on its subject?

Questions regarding the freedom of moral subjects become even more complex when we take into account the fact that autonomous moral agents are also sensible agents, subject to inclination and desire. This fact generates a series of questions about the moral challenges that the embodied rational agent confronts. How, for example, shall we understand Kantian notions of virtue and virtuous struggle? And how should we interpret the ultimate unification of sensibility (understood in terms of happiness) with freedom (understood in terms of virtue) in Kant's concept of the highest good?

Finally, freedom also constitutes the basis of Kant's political philosophy. Kant claims that his universal principle of right is based upon "the innate right of freedom," and this naturally generates a series of questions about the type of freedom at issue in Kant's argument. Is it the same type of freedom referred to in his ethical philosophy? And how does a system of right emerge from freedom? Further, what are the implications of this principle of right for embodied agents who unavoidably live together on a bounded sphere? For example, what, if any, system of distributive justice is prescribed by this commitment to freedom in political theory?

Introduction

OVERVIEW OF THE VOLUME

Part I   Spontaneity: Pure Concepts of the Understanding, Imagination, and Judgment

In Chapter 1, Rolf-Peter Horstmann examines what Kant calls the "transcendental function" of imagination. Since Kant repeatedly characterizes both the understanding and the imagination as faculties of synthesis, the imagination's precise role is not always obvious from the text. Is the imagination simply to be identified with the understanding? Or might it be in some sense distinct from the understanding, while still functioning under the guidance of the understanding? Or might the imagination have a role to play in cognition that is wholly distinct from that of the understanding? Horstmann argues that the imagination has the task of differentiating from among the totality of a subject's sense impressions those that comply with general conceptual rules, and those that are not subject to these rules. The challenge in delineating imagination's role in this respect is to show how the imagination can have a role distinct from that of the understanding. Nevertheless, Horstmann argues that we pay a steep price for simply subsuming imagination under the understanding. Specifically, it becomes difficult to explain how it is possible that – already at the level of receptive sensibility – material is available that is fit for the synthesizing activities of the understanding. His chapter thus defends an interpretation according to which imagination has an *apprehending* function. On this account imagination transforms mere "sensations" or impressions – nonindividuated and unstructured psychological events – into what Kant calls "perceptions," i.e., conscious, contentful representations that constitute the material out of which intuitions are synthesized.

In the next chapter, Brian Chance continues this investigation into cognition by considering the origin and nature of the pure concepts of the understanding, or the categories. Contrary to the view that *a priori* intuition provides content to the categories that is constitutive of their being categories, Chance argues that the categories are products of the understanding alone and introduce a purely intellectual content into cognition. To advance this claim, Chance examines the differences between Kant's conception of the understanding and the conception of the understanding endorsed by Wolff and his followers. Specifically, he argues that Kant's assertion in the *Inaugural Dissertation* of a "real use" of the understanding in is an overt rejection of the Wolffian conception of the understanding as the capacity to render distinct content that is already present in sense and a catalyst for the issues raised in the 1772 Herz Letter that Kant does not fully address until the first *Critique*. In defense of his reading, Chance also argues that Kant borrows the language he uses to describe the categories from the Wolffian tradition. For the sense in which Kant affirms the purity of the understanding is precisely the sense in which Wolff and his followers deny it. And since Kant also identifies this purity with the understanding's spontaneity, Chance argues that there is a deep continuity between Kant's rejection of the Wolffian account of the understanding and his rejection of the Wolffian account of reason.

With a discussion of the categories in place, the volume proceeds to consider Kant's argument in the second edition of the transcendental deduction (the B-Deduction). In Chapter 3, Michael Rohlf argues that the B-Deduction is part of Kant's argument for transcendental idealism in the first *Critique*. Rohlf begins by arguing against the common assumption that the argument for transcendental idealism is contained within the Transcendental Aesthetic. He then develops his interpretation of the B-Deduction's role. In particular, Rohlf argues that section 26 of the B-Deduction is intended to prove that our representations of space and time are singular. Building on Beatrice Longuenesse's interpretation of section 26 (Longuenesse 1998: chapter 8) – according to which space and time, as formal intuitions, are first generated by a transcendental synthesis of the imagination under the synthetic unity of apperception – Rohlf further argues that the formal intuition of time supplies the "bare representation of unity as applied to time." Crucially, Rohlf argues, this is a condition of assigning schemata to categories and applying these categories to empirical representations.

Spontaneity is central not only to Kant's account of cognition, but also to his account of judgments of taste. In metaphysics lectures from 1794, for example, Kant remarks that "the beautiful arts are such that they do not coerce approval from people, but rather leave their judgment free, so that their approval is given spontaneously. In them no rules can be despotically prescribed, they are rather a free play of the imagination..."[2] But this description leaves open a question about what the principle of taste is, and how it is possible. In Chapter 4 Jennifer Dobe argues that the experience of beauty begins in a feeling of pleasure that we perceive as both free and as arising from a shared human nature. Dobe thus contributes to the

---

[2] *Metaphysik K₃*, XXVIII 815–16, following Guyer's translation in the Cambridge edition of the *Critique of the Power of Judgment*.

Introduction 5

longstanding debate about what the principle of judgments of taste is. She argues that the principle, and thus the basis of these judgments, is our shared cognitive nature, according to which our imaginations are attuned to our understanding's need for unity.

Part II The Inner Value of the World: Freedom as the Keystone of Kant's Moral Philosophy

Part II of the volume examines the role of freedom as a foundational component in Kant's moral philosophy. In Chapter 5, Patricia Kitcher considers Kant's notion of freedom, its relationship to the formula of humanity, and the relationship of the formula of humanity to the highest good. Though Kitcher thinks freedom and the formula of humanity do serve to demonstrate the moral law's bindingness, she rejects the idea that freedom can be defined in terms of the capacity to set ends, or that freedom itself is an end that Kant's moral philosophy enjoins us to pursue. Instead, she advances a novel interpretation of Kant's claim that "we must necessarily lend to every rational being that has a will also the idea of freedom" (*GMS* 4:448) by looking at Kant's remarks about how it is that we can regard others as rational thinkers in the first *Critique*. Ultimately, Kitcher argues, this interpretation explains the bindingness of the moral law and, by extension, provides an argument for the duty to promote the happiness of others that does not depend upon thinking of happiness as intrinsically valuable.

In Chapter 6, Lucas Thorpe considers a series of questions about how agents recognize freedom in – and ascribe freedom to – other individuals. Thorpe considers three central questions: First, what does it mean, from a Kantian perspective, to be "human" in a morally-relevant sense? Various answers have been offered in response to this question – including, for example, the view that it is a capacity for agency that constitutes the capacity for humanity, or, alternately, that it is a capacity for morality that constitutes this capacity. Thorpe offers a novel amendment to the second view – that "to be 'human' in the morally relevant sense is to have the capacity for morality, and that this involves: (a) the capacity to recognize others as ends rather than merely as means and (b) the capacity to enter into relations of ethics community with us." This answer, however, leaves open a series of questions about how we go about ascribing moral status to others, and what justifies our doing so when we do. In response to these sorts of questions, Thorpe defends a view he calls "moral reliablism," which includes two components: first, that agents have quasi-perceptual

6 KATE MORAN

ability to pick up on various types of social affordances, in particular the ability to engage in ethical interaction. Second, the view includes a normative claim that we should assume that this capacity is reliable as a postulate of pure practical reasoning. Thorpe draws on recent research in developmental psychology to support his view.

The next two chapters consider how Kant's claims regarding freedom function in his argument for the moral law itself. In Chapter 7, Julian Wuerth presents a positive interpretation of Kant's strategy for arguing for the categorical imperative. Wuerth calls this strategy the "elimination of sensibility process," according to which Kant systematically eliminates the offerings of sensibility in order to isolate the teachings of pure reason. The chapter then applies the findings of this discussion to an assessment of Kantian constructivist strategies in ethics, especially the constructivism of Christine Korsgaard. Wuerth points to some problems with a number of constructivist systems, and then argues that Korsgaard's constructivism, for all of its virtues, does not respect Kant's distinction in kind between reason and sensibility and in the end falls short as an interpretation of Kant's argument.

In Chapter 8, Frederick Rauscher considers Kant's claim in the Collins lecture that "freedom is the inner worth of the world" (*Collins* 27:344) and argues against a realist interpretation of this assertion. On a realist conception, value would be a property of humanity independent of both the empirical moral agent and the transcendental conditions for moral agency as such. The chapter advances several arguments to show that such a value property either could not exist, or would be unknowable to the moral agent. Rather than an intrinsic property, Rauscher argues that value is merely a formal ordering imposed by reason upon nature. To say that humanity has absolute value is simply to say that, in the order that pure practical reason imposes on the ends of rational agents, humanity has a higher place than any other end. Just as the value of contingent ends of empirical moral agents is simply their place in those agents' subjective ordering of ends, so humanity as a necessary end for all rational agents is simply the place of humanity in pure practical reason's objective ordering of ends.

Part III   Freedom as Autonomous Willing:
Kant's Sensible Agent

The volume proceeds to consider the complexities of the embodied Kantian moral agent – an agent who is simultaneously subject to inclination yet capable representing the moral law. In Chapter 9, Karl Ameriks

Introduction 7

argues for a middle path between two extreme but common objections to the *Groundwork*'s account of moral self-legislation as autonomy. The first of these argues that to speak of the moral law as rooted in self-legislation is to be too ambitious, overly subjective, and to ignore the essentially receptive character of reason. According to this objection, the focus on self-legislation suggests a failure on Kant's part to recognize reason as a capacity that appreciates reasons to act given to the subject by what is essentially outside of it. The contrasting second objection stems from a worry about what can appear to be an overly close connection drawn between morality and freedom as autonomy. Here the critic objects that the emphasis upon the "nomos" of autonomy in the *Groundwork* is too restrictive, and in a sense overly objective, insofar as it makes our actions appear so thoroughly law-oriented that it seems to leave open only two alternatives for agents: They can either be forced by reason to follow the moral law or forced by natural necessity to fail to follow the moral law. In contrast to Kant's own later works, such an account does an injustice to our faculty of free choice, or at least our ability to act in ways more complex than these two narrow options. In his chapter, Ameriks steers a middle course between the Scylla of subjectivity and the Charybdis of lawlike freedom, arguing that the transition from section II to section III in the *Groundwork* can be read as providing an account of autonomy defensible against both of these objections.

The volume then begins to consider a series of questions prompted by the observation that human agents are autonomous, and yet simultaneously subject to inclination and desire. In Chapter 10, Kate Moran considers the attitude that autonomous agents ought to take toward inclination. Kant himself often describes inclination as the antagonist of moral willing and virtuous struggle, even suggesting at one point that "to be entirely free from [inclination] must ... be the wish of every rational being" (*GMS* 4:428). Moran argues that this assertion – and others like it – are often misunderstood as a wholesale indictment of inclination. She offers an analysis of the text that demonstrates that Kant's concern is not with inclination as such, but with inclination as a source of need and neediness. The chapter continues to consider Kant's conception of neediness, and his account of the ideal stance toward inclination – something he calls independence. Though independence is an impossible ideal for free, yet sensible, agents, it is nonetheless an informative ideal. In particular, the ideal serves as a standard against which one can measure the ways in which agents fall short of complete independence. Moran offers a sketch of the

8 KATE MORAN

"moral misery" that agents experience when need gains ascendancy over freedom.

In Chapter 11, Barbara Herman examines Kant's discussion of religion and the highest good in Kant's *Religion within the Boundaries of Mere Reason*. In other texts, Kant's arguments regarding the highest good revolve around a pair of concerns: that human beings can never will well enough to deserve happiness, and that desire for the highest good is not consistent with good willing. But in the *Religion*, Herman argues, Kant's main concern is with the corrosive moral anxiety that arises in even the best of us faced with a propensity to evil whose source is the heart, not the will. Kant argues that this anxiety can be resolved by adopting the narrative of overcoming in Christian theology, using the son of God as a prototype or typic for a reformation of moral sensibility. Religion provides a perspective of infinite time, without risking antinomy, and a notion of sacrifice and gift that allows us to draw past bad willings, as well as our potential for moral lapse, into a narrative of improvement that redeems them. The chapter concludes with a discussion of the end of the ethical community in the *Religion*. Since Kant sees an ongoing threat to human goodness arising from the ways we pursue separate purposes, the solution is a union around a common principle: an ethical community, understood as a kind of church. Herman thus finds in Kant an argument that human nature might require something contingent, namely religion of a certain sort, if the highest good, and so the freedom of which we are capable in this life, is to be realized.

Part IV Freedom on a Bounded Sphere: Kant's Political Philosophy

The fact that human agents are free also lies at the basis of Kant's political philosophy. The next two chapters in the volume consider Kant's argument for the principle of right, and the implications of this principle. In Chapter 12, Allen Wood argues against the view that Kant's principle and duties of right are based in his ethics. He argues instead that right and ethics have distinct foundations, but that both are part of morals (*Sitten*) and are unified through their shared conception of obligation, namely, conformity to universal laws. Over the course of his discussion, Wood advances several arguments against the view that ethics serves as the foundation for right in Kant's thought. In place of that view, he argues that the only foundation for Kant's principle of right is a question about what can justify coercion. The answer to this question, Wood argues,

Introduction

simply involves the formal consistency of freedom according to a universal law. But he argues that this does not transform imperatives of right into hypothetical or pragmatic imperatives. Rather, the rightful authority rests upon a rational response to the categorical command of reason.

In Chapter 13,Michael Nance and Jeppe von Platz explore the political implications of the innate right to freedom in Kant's *Doctrine of Right*. In particular, they ask whether the innate right to freedom implies a theory of distributive justice. To answer this question, they investigate Paul Guyer's argument that Kant's theory of property in the *Doctrine of Right* implies a Rawlsian conception of distributive justice (see Guyer 2000b). Guyer's argument for this conclusion is that Kant's theory of property implies a contractualist theory of distributive justice that, in turn, implies that the distribution of property rights must be fair to all affected by it, and that this fairness is secured only by something like Rawls's second principle of justice, the difference principle. Nance and von Platz question each stage in this argument. In the first place, they argue that Kant holds a *conventionalist*, though not necessarily a contractualist, view of property rights. They next argue that if the contractualist ideal is interpreted in terms of what is *acceptable* to each member of society, this yields a principle of mutual advantage. If, on the other hand, contractualism is interpreted as placing moral constraints on the terms it is permissible to offer other members as terms of society, then this yields a principle of formal equality. Neither strategy yields the difference principle. Nance and von Platz thus conclude that Kant's *Doctrine of Right* is compatible with, but does not require, a variety of principles of distributive justice.

Postscript: Freedom and Nature

All of the contributors to this volume have been inspired by Paul Guyer's groundbreaking work on Kant's philosophy. In the postscript to the volume, Guyer considers another difficult Kantian question: Given his emphasis on freedom and spontaneity, how does Kant intend to bridge the gap between freedom, on the one hand, and nature, on the other? Guyer argues that Kant advances a thesis regarding the unity between a morally perfect world and the natural world as early as 1781, in the *Critique of Pure Reason*. Nevertheless, in *The Critique of the Power of Judgment* (1790), Kant claims that this third *Critique* is needed in order to bridge the "incalculable gulf fixed between the domain of the concept of nature, as the sensible, and the domain of the concept of freedom, as the supersensible" (*KU* 5:176). Guyer argues that the third *Critique* does not mark a shift in Kant's conception of the relationship between freedom and nature. Indeed, throughout the critical decade, Kant continues to argue for a bridge between freedom and nature. Guyer examines three of these bridges: First, though it may on its face seem as though a good will is all that is required by morality, Kant's ethics actually demands actions of agents who are embodied and active in the natural world. In particular, Kant is concerned with agents' freedom to set and pursue ends, and that this capacity be preserved and promoted. Second, though the decision to make the moral law one's fundamental maxim may seem to be a purely noumenal matter belonging to a free, autonomous will, it is both reflected in nature and affected by nature. Third, Guyer argues that Kant's ultimate view of the highest good is that the "moral world" that represents the object of morality is something that can only be realized in nature. All of these features of Kant's moral theory demonstrate that while freedom and spontaneity are indeed hallmarks of his philosophical system, they nevertheless act upon nature, and are affected by nature.

PART I

Spontaneity: Pure Concepts of the Understanding, Imagination, and Judgment

CHAPTER 1

Kant on Imagination and Object Constitution

Rolf-Peter Horstmann

The claim put forward in this chapter is that Kant's theory of the process of the constitution of an object of cognition relies heavily on his belief that productive or transcendental imagination plays a central role, but in the end, he does not succeed in giving a convincing account of what this role consists in. In order to substantiate this claim, I will discuss some basic features of his epistemology under the perspective of how imagination can fit in.

A familiar way to characterize the gist of Kant's epistemological message is to start with his formulation of the supreme principle on which all synthetic judgments are founded (i.e., on which the possibility of the objective validity or the truth of a synthetic judgment is founded), and according to which "Every object stands under the necessary conditions of the synthetic unity of the manifold of intuition in a possible experience" (*KrV* A158/B197). The claim, obviously, is that objects *as objects of cognition* (not as objects, e.g., of thought or imagination or as formed matter) depend on the conditions under which they can be experienced, and this leads to another formulation of the same principle which says: "The conditions of the possibility of experience in general are at the same time conditions of the possibility of the objects of experience" (*KrV* B197). Because Kant defines experience as empirical cognition (*KrV* B147) and thinks of cognitions in terms of judgments, this statement can be translated into the claim that an object of cognition, i.e., an object about which I can make an empirical judgment, has to be such that it conforms to the conditions of empirical judgment, i.e., it has to be such that it can be addressed by a judgment.

What, then, are the conditions of an empirical judgment? First, one has to notice that the phrase "conditions of an empirical judgment" is short-hand for the longer formulation "conditions of the objective validity of an empirical judgment." Thus, the question is: What are the conditions of the objective validity of an empirical judgment? Kant's answer is well known:

13

Whatever else might be involved in the formation of an empirical judgment, there are two conditions that are the most basic: (1) there has to be something or other that is or at least could be "given" through the senses and that conforms to the requirements Kant puts forward for what he calls an "intuition" and (2) there have to be concepts available that can capture what is "given" as an intuition. These two demands for Kant are both eminently plausible and totally uncontroversial because they express what he rightly takes to be implied in our normal understanding of the term "empirical judgment": Every empirical judgment has to have a non-conceptual content, i.e., a "given" object it is *about* (otherwise a judgment is just either a mathematical or a conceptual truth or a Kantian principle of the understanding) and a conceptual form, i.e., it must connect concepts in a way that yields a judgment. Given that this understanding of what is required for an empirical judgment is right (and Kant never doubted this), then it makes sense to think with Kant of such a judgment as the result of a process of transformation of non-conceptual content into conceptual form. If one is inclined to identify the realm of intuitions with the domain of "the non-conceptual," and if one thinks of "the non-conceptual" and "the conceptual" as a complete alternative (*vollständige Disjunktion*), then the question as to the conditions of the objective validity of empirical judgments seems to require an answer to the different and systematically prior question as to the details of the transformation process of non-conceptual "stuff" into conceptual representations. And indeed, Kant himself points in the direction of this question when he declares that the problem one has to solve in any attempt to analyze the conditions of an empirical judgment consists in explaining "how subjective conditions of thinking [i.e., concepts] should have objective validity, i.e., yield conditions of the possibility of all cognition of objects [i.e., non-conceptually "given" intuitions]" (*KrV* A89 f./B122). Now, it seems that Kant himself can and does establish a link between the non-conceptual and the conceptual in a very prominent passage without relying on imagination at all (but only on sensibility and understanding). The passage I have in mind is what Kant, in the second edition of the *Critique,* refers to by the name of a metaphysical deduction.[1]

---

[1] There is a lot of guesswork over more than 200 years as to why the metaphysical deduction is supposed to be a deduction, what makes it metaphysical, and even where exactly it is located. Kant is of no help because he nowhere cares to give even a hint to an explanation of what he means with this term. Though there has never been a general agreement as to what the metaphysical deduction is about, it is safe to say that nobody would object to Guyer's formulation according to which "the so-called metaphysical deduction is meant to establish that the categories are the conditions of the *possibility* of cognition of objects" (Guyer 2001:318).

Here in the metaphysical deduction Kant can be seen as offering in two famous sentences a very straightforward answer as to how it comes about that non-conceptual content can get conceptual form by invoking just two faculties, i.e., sensibility and understanding. Kant can be understood to say that what brings about the transformation of what is rooted in non-conceptual sensibility into the conceptual form of a judgment is the understanding alone.

However, even if one agrees with the view that the metaphysical deduction successfully establishes a link between the conceptual and the non-conceptual elements involved in the formation of an empirical judgment by insisting on the necessary contribution of (conceptual) rules of the understanding in the act of object constitution about which (empirical) judgments can be rendered, one cannot avoid the impression that this success is based on our willingness to accept a premise that is argued for by Kant neither in the metaphysical deduction itself nor elsewhere in the "clue"-chapter. This premise concerns the organization of the matter that is unified by the activity of the understanding into representations of objects, i.e., it concerns the manner in which, according to Kant, sensible representations have to be present to the mind in order to count as representations out of which the understanding can form representations of objects. Quite obviously the metaphysical deduction implicitly presupposes that the sensible representations the understanding operates synthetically on are such that they *can* be unified into object representations. This again presupposes that a manifold of sensible representations can be unified into intuitions because the sensible representations the understanding is working with are intuitions. But why and how is this presupposition justified? Why is it that we have to think of sensible representations as unifiable into intuitions, and how does it come that – if they are unifiable this way – they can lead to representations of objects? These questions have to be taken seriously, not so much because of worries concerning the soundness of the argument of the metaphysical deduction, but for a substantial reason. Kant has to avoid the impression that for him objects of cognition are based on random collections of sensible representations the understanding happens to single out as intuitions arbitrarily in the endeavor to unify them according to its unifying rules. This is so because otherwise he would have to give up on his very reasonable claim that it is not enough for an empirical object of which we can have knowledge to be grounded in whatever sensible representations happen to be around, but that there has to be an inherent affinity between those sensible representations that end up as intuitions out of which an object of cognition can be formed. In other words, there must be more to sensible representations than just the fact of their occurrence in the mind if they are to qualify for representations out of which "given" intuitions can arise that can be united into the representation of an object. This means that Kant has to concentrate more closely on the details of what is happening on the sensibility side of object formation up to the point where intuitions start to play a role. And this is exactly what Kant is doing by invoking imagination in both versions of the "deduction" chapter (though the first version is much more detailed with respect to imagination than the second and follows a different strategy).

However, when it comes to the role imagination is supposed to play in his account, a lot remains obscure. The first thing to worry about is why and how Kant wants to draw a distinction between imagination and the understanding at all. The background to this worry is the following: Kant obviously thinks of imagination as a faculty whose synthesizing activity in the process of the constitution of an object of cognition is subject to and guided by rules that in the end reflect the demands which flow from the unity-providing faculty of apperception, and which are founded in the necessary unity of apperception, i.e., the unity of (self-) consciousness.[2] These rules are the categories and the synthesizing activity is directed toward items that are given by sensibility. At the same time, Kant thinks of the understanding as a faculty that by exercising a synthetic activity on what is given by sensibility has to employ the very same categorical rules as imagination does in transforming intuitions into units of reference for concepts, i.e., into objects of cognition. If imagination and understanding perform the same tasks under the same regulatory constraints on the same material provided by sensibility, why and how are these faculties to be distinguished?

Does this mean that in the end one is better off to follow Kant's own practice in the years after publication of the first edition of the *Critique* and to downplay the role imagination plays in the process of object cognition? Although such a move is quite tempting and presumably will not find much resistance from many current Kant scholars, it might well go with a price Kant himself, for very good reasons, has not been prepared to pay. This price consists in the inability on Kant's part to explain how it comes that already on the receptive level of sensibility material is available that is fit for the synthesizing activities of the understanding if there were no different synthesizing faculty, i.e., his so-called "imagination," involved.

[2] Cf. e.g., *KrV* A124.

If this is right, then there must be a difference between the performance attributed to imagination in producing intuitions on the one hand, and representations of objects on the other. In order to see why this is so, and to show that Kant has been very well aware of this problem lurking on the side of the organization of sensible material, one has to go back and look again at his analysis of how the representation of an object of cognition comes about.

The view attributed here to Kant concerning the constitution of an object of cognition is that of a process which leads from sense impressions or sensations to the representation of a full-blown cognitive object, i.e., an object about which objectively valid judgments can be made. This process contains two distinguishable stages. The first goes from sense impressions to representations of individual items (undetermined objects), i.e., intuitions; the second from intuitions to conceptual representations of (determinate) objects. Both classes of representations, intuitions and concepts of objects, are constituted in that they are products of some activities of the representing subject. From what was discussed earlier, it is quite likely that the second stage, from intuitions to concepts, is not really of interest for someone who attempts to secure imagination as a self-standing and independent status within Kant's conception of object formation. This is so because what is going on at this stage is definitely dominated by the understanding in that the understanding provides the rules (rooted in the transcendental unity of apperception), without which the necessary unity of an object of cognition would not be possible. At this stage, imagination has the thankless task to do whatever is necessary to support the understanding in the endeavor to "bring a transcendental content," as Kant calls it in the metaphysical deduction (*KrV* A79/B104), into a manifold of intuitions, thereby giving, so to say, the spatio-temporal stability and determinateness necessary for an object that can be referred to by a concept to an otherwise rather instable conglomerate of perceptions in an intuition. The understanding achieves this determination by somehow forcing imagination, which is used to deal with material given in sensibility under space-time conditions, to act synthetically in an object-constituting way, i.e., to perform a "transcendental action" (*KrV* A102, B154) or to fulfill its "transcendental function" (*KrV* A123).

This second stage of the process, from intuition to representation of an object Kant is picturing, is based, in any case, on two assumptions: (1) The synthetic activity of the understanding is restricted to object constitution; the understanding cannot do anything else other than bring together representations (whether they are intuitions or concepts) into representations of objects, i.e., into representations that are determined by the (categorical) rules necessary for *thinking* a given manifold as objectively unified or for *taking* a suitable manifold as being united in the representation of an object. (2) The synthetic activity of imagination is not restricted to object constitution, i.e., imagination can bring together sensible representations in ways that result in complex representations of as yet undetermined objects which do not qualify as representations of cognitive objects. These two assumptions, together with the explicit goal of the second stage to provide the details of the process of cognitive object constitution, lead to the quite sensible assessment that at the second stage imagination is of no interest for its own sake but has to be addressed only in its function as the servant of the understanding.[3] And this might have been a reason for Kant to downplay the role of imagination in contexts where he is primarily interested in pointing out the achievements of the understanding.

However, although assumption (2) already shows that within the two-stage scenario, imagination at the second stage might have a lot more to do than just synthesizing items under the spell of the understanding, it is primarily the first stage, from sense impressions to intuitions, which is in need of imagination, as exercising an activity that is different from that of the understanding and not restricted to synthesizing alone. Why is that so? The short answer to this question is: Because there is a difference between the emergence of a representation that has the status of an intuition and the formation of a representation of a cognitive object, with the result that not every intuition has to be a representation of an object. Before this assertion can be substantiated, one has to look in more detail at what is going on at the first stage of object constitution, i.e., on the way from sense impressions or sensations to intuitions.

According to Kant, sensations are the ultimate building blocks of representations of objects, i.e., for Kant the phenomenology of object constitution has to start with sensations (*KrV* A19 f./B34). Sensations are taken by him to be affections of what he calls "sensibility" (*Sinnlichkeit*), and because he knows of two kinds of sensibility, i.e., outer and inner sense, he distinguishes between affections of the outer and the inner sense. Although it is not quite clear how to interpret this distinction,[4] it is at any

---

[3] This does not mean, at all, that this second stage has no relevance for the success of Kant's epistemological enterprise. On the contrary, questions concerning the details of his account as to how we are supposed to transform intuitions into conceptual representations of objects have been raised ever since the publication of the first *Critique*.

[4] This is due to the obscurity connected with the conception of self-affection discussed by Kant himself extensively in sections 24 and 25 of the B-Deduction.

Kant on Imagination and Object Constitution

rate clear that he wants sensations to be affections of the organs of the (five) senses, and thus physiological events. Sensations as physiological events are, as Kant rightly points out, "for us nothing" (*KrV* A120) if they are not conscious states of a subject or "connected with consciousness" (*KrV* A120). As conscious states, sensations have a content, i.e., they represent qualities like colors, shapes, sounds, etc., and occur sequentially in time. These content-filled representations Kant calls "perceptions" *(KrV,* B147). They are the material out of which *we* form intuitions, and imagination (and not the understanding) is supposed to be active in this forming process.[5] Given that there are indeed these three elements, i.e., sensation, perception, and intuition involved in this process, and that these elements form a constitutive sequence such that sensations make possible perceptions and perceptions ground intuitions, the process seems to be divided into two phases, the first leading from sensations to perceptions, the second from perceptions to intuitions. The question as to the role of imagination in this process, then, is: In which of these phases and in what manner is it involved? Is imagination operative in both phases, and, if so, in the same or in a different manner? Or is it at work in only one of these phases? The following remarks intend to tentatively reconstruct aspects of what Kant takes to be the phenomenology of the constitution of intuitions (not of cognitive objects!) guided by the ambition to uncover a couple of features unique to imagination.

One could be tempted to expect already, during the first phase, i.e., at the very beginning of the way from sensation to perception, a genuine function for imagination as a subjective synthesizing faculty. This is so because there has to be some explanation as to how the process goes on that transforms the purely physiological event of a sensation into a content-full conscious mental representation, i.e., a perception. This process has to involve an activity of the representing subject if one does not want to maintain either of two (within the Kantian framework) rather implausible hypotheses concerning the essential characteristics of sensations: The first would be that there is no need for a process because bare sensations already have representational content, the other that bare

---

[5] In both versions of the deduction, it is not quite clear how exactly Kant wants us to understand the relation between sensations, perceptions, and intuitions. Sometimes he writes as if an intuition is just a collection of different perceptions, which in turn are conscious sensations (see earlier references), and sometimes one has the impression that he wants perceptions to be the intentional correlate only of intuitions, which would mean that intuitions are the constitutive basis of perceptions or that they make perceptions possible (*KrV* B160, B164). This confusing ambiguity extends into later parts of the first *Critique* as well. Cf. the *Anticipations of Perception*, (*KrV* B207 ff.).

sensations are causally efficacious in that they are the causes of perceptions. While the first hypothesis would be hard to reconcile with Kant's convictions as to the non-representational character of sensations, the second would violate his view as to the passivity of sensibility. If the transformation process cannot be explained by relying on peculiarities of bare sensations (like having representational content or being causally efficacious) then, it seems, what remains is to have recourse to some mental activity of the subject. So, why not think of imagination doing this job of transforming sensations into perceptions? Imagination within the Kantian framework is, after all, intimately connected with non-conceptual activities at the level of sensibility and is even said to be "a necessary ingredient of perception itself" (*KrV* A120fn.).

However, it might be objected that this suggestion does not look very promising as long as one tends to think of imagination as a faculty whose exclusive task consists in synthesizing individual items into more complex wholes. If imagination could indeed do nothing else other than synthesizing, then surely enough it would be a very implausible candidate for playing a role in the transformation process from sensation to perception. This is so because what is needed here is not a faculty whose activity consists in synthesizing but rather a kind of discerning faculty. What is required here is something like an interpreting faculty that can somehow manage to individuate sensations which are stipulated as featureless items by giving them discriminable representational content, thereby elevating sensations to perceptions. Such a faculty would provide qualitatively distinguishable individual perceptions which, according to Kant, "by themselves are encountered dispersed and separate in the mind" (*KrV* A120). This seems to imply that such a faculty has not much to do with a connecting activity. And if the exclusive function of imagination is to provide connections then, it seems, it is not fit for this transformational task from sensation to perception because there is no connecting, no synthetic activity involved.[6]

There are two ways to counter this objection. The first is to doubt that it really is the case that for Kant imagination is restricted to its connecting function, i.e., that it can do nothing other than putting given elements, perceptual or otherwise, together. The second is not to doubt

---

[6] Unfortunately, as far as I can see, Kant nowhere tells us how he would like to explain the transformation of sensations into perceptions. Maybe he would give an interpretation that relies on the conditions an item has to fulfill in order to become included (*aufgenommen*) into the unity of consciousness. One could read his remarks on *KrV* A108 ff. and A121 fn. as pointing in this direction.

Kant on Imagination and Object Constitution

that imagination is restricted to acts of connection but at the same time to claim that Kant conceives of synthesis of imagination not as a simple and uniform, but as a complex activity.

I take this second way to be unconvincing because of what Kant explicitly says about synthesis (e.g., *KrV* A77 ff./B102 ff., A97, A101, A116, B130). However, there is no textual obstacle to proceed on the assumption – underlying the first way suggested earlier to overcome the objection – that the activities of imagination are *not* restricted to the performance of acts of synthesizing, and hence that imagination *can* be involved in non-synthetic activities. If imagination can play a role in the transformation of sensations into perceptions, then it does have an autonomous occupation that distinguishes it from the understanding in the process of creating representations of objects based on intuitions because this occupation is not meant to be a synthetic one. It might also have a genuine function within Kant's two-stage model of object formation in the domain in which *we* form intuitions out of perceptions, i.e., in the second phase of the first stage. In terms of the two-stage model imputed here to Kant, this means: If imagination is to have a genuine function and if it cannot figure as a self-standing activity at the second stage (because at this stage it would exercise a synthetic activity under the spell of the understanding), then it has to get assigned a genuine role in either one or both phases of the first stage, i.e., in the transition from sensations to intuitions. Because this transition, or at least a part of it, is the main achievement of what Kant calls "apprehension," it is especially with respect to its apprehending function that imagination can be expected to lead a life of its own, independent of any direct interference from rules of the understanding.

What, then, is happening on the level of apprehension? The apprehending mind, we are told, "is to bring the manifold of intuition into an image" (*KrV* A120). In order to do this, it must "antecedently take up the impressions into its activity, i.e., apprehend them" (*KrV* A120), or it has – to quote another formulation – "first to run through and then to take together" (*KrV* A99) a manifold of perceptions. However, this process of taking up impressions (which I take to be perceptions), though quite understandably conceived by Kant as taking place antecedently to the acts of running through them and taking them together, cannot be the beginning of the whole process from sensation to an image because there still is the step from sensation to perception which is unaccounted for if apprehending starts with perception. How is one to conceive of this step (the first phase of the first stage previously mentioned) or, in Kant's words, how do sensations become "modifications of the mind in intuition" (*KrV* A97)?

Maybe it helps to discuss this question by looking a bit more closely at a concrete example. Assume that I, by chance, fall into a swimming pool filled with cold and rather dirty water. What is my situation as to the sensations with which I am confronted? I guess I will have millions of sensations, i.e., physiological occurrences that result from affections of all my five senses. These are, as purely physiological events, no modifications of the mind, though they are definitely changes in my bodily state. In order to make them modifications of the mind I have to transform (some of) them into individual episodes of which I am conscious, i.e., into perceptions. Thus, immediately after falling into the pool I cannot but become aware, in a very rapid succession in time, of a lot of things, each of which is a disparate item. I have somehow to notice that there is that feeling of coldness on my skin, that I have the optical impression of darkness, that I have the taste sensation of brackish water, that there is a muffled sound around, etc. How am I to account for this transformation from an all-encompassing non-individuated and unstructured physiological event into single episodes which I can distinguish from one another, thereby making them items which can be "encountered dispersed and separate in the mind" (*KrV* A120)? Obviously, it is more than likely that one will introduce an activity that has to accomplish this transition. An activity in Kant's map of the mental is based in a faculty. Because this activity at work in the transition is supposed to be part of the cognitive process, it must be related to one of the cognitive faculties. These are sense, imagination, and apperception (*KrV* A94, A115). Sense by definition is not the right candidate for a transitional activity because it can only passively receive data; it is the faculty of receptivity. Apperception is no good candidate either because just by itself it only provides the form of unity to whatever is such that it can be connected. It might be objected that already the very concept of an individual item that can be distinguished from other items presupposes the possibility to view this item as a unit, thus making it dependent on the apperceptive activity in its categorizing function. Though this is right, it does not make apperception the material source of perceptions; it just accounts for their singularity.[7] Hence

---

[7] This means that apperception in its so-called original (*ursprünglich*) state is not confined to, in the end, conceptual, i.e., categorizing operations, but has initially only the much more basic function to provide numerical identity or "unity in the time-relation of all perceptions" (this term is used here in its first edition meaning as referring to conscious impressions!). This is nicely confirmed in a passage from the beginning of the *Analogies of Experience* in the first *Critique* which states: "In the original apperception all this manifold, according to its time relations, is to be unified; because this says its

the only candidate left for the transforming activity within the Kantian taxonomy of cognitive faculties is imagination.

Admittedly, there is not that much in Kant's texts by virtue of which one can claim that a reasoning along the lines pointed out here is part of his considered view as to the transition from physiological states to perceptions of individual sensations that can count as a manifold out of which intuitions are formed. However, granted that one were allowed to attribute to him such a reasoning, he would be in the position – to use a rather daunting English metaphor – to kill two birds with one stone. On the one hand, he would have gained the means to address a problem and to point to its solution, which inevitably arises for every causal theory of perception that starts with physiological episodes in the shape of sense impressions as the ultimate building blocks of perception, i.e., the problem of individuating these impressions. On the other hand, he would be able to give us an argument as to why he wants to think of imagination as a self-standing and irreducible faculty without which cognition would not be possible. A stance on imagination, as suggested by the previous reasoning, would imply that the task of imagination – at least in its productive function[8] – does not solely consist in synthesizing items into wholes. It would hold the activity of imagination responsible for providing a representational material which first of all makes synthesis possible by creating individual and discernible units (perceptions).

Although a reasoning like the one sketched a moment ago – irrespective of whether Kant really would subscribe to it or not – might be a way to secure the faculty of imagination an albeit rather fragile autonomy against the faculties of sense and apperception, it could be objected that it is by no means sufficient to demonstrate the independence of imagination from the understanding. It could well be that imagination does the job of transforming physiological states into individual perceptions, i.e., content-full unities of which I am conscious in a way that somehow involves the rules of the understanding. After all, perceptions are meant to have characteristics that make them suitable for playing the role of a manifold out of which

---

[original apperception] transcendental unity *a priori* under which everything stands what is to belong to my (i.e., my unified) cognition and thus can become an object for me" (*KrV* A177/B221).

[8] Whether Kant thinks of reproductive imagination as a capacity that can do anything other than synthesizing is not quite clear. On the one hand he takes it to be a rule-guided synthetic activity (e.g., *KrV* A100), and on the other he wants it to be active in providing representations of objects without their presence (*KrV* A100).

intuitions can be formed, which in turn can function as the material on which the understanding performs its synthetic activity which leads to the representation of an object. Thus, the very fact that they are necessary elements in the constitution of object representations seems to submit them to the very same rules that are operative on the level of intuitions. If my imaginative processing of sensations would lead to conscious episodes that in no way could fit together, e.g., if I had sometimes an acoustic perception of colors or a tactile perception of smells, whereas at other times my acoustic perceptions would contain feelings of pressure and my optical perceptions would shift between having as their content noises and tastes, then these perceptions could not become elements of an intuition, i.e., a manifold that can be brought together in an intuition. Hence, imagination must somehow transform physiological events "in the right way." And, is it not the case that "the right way" has to be defined in terms of object-constituting synthetic rules, which would mean that in the end imagination becomes again dependent on the understanding?

However, this objection is not really convincing because it appears to be self-defeating. Already the notion of "the right way" obviously makes sense only in contrast to other ways. And if there are other ways in which imagination can perform the transformational task at hand, then this seems to imply that just the opposite from being dependent is the case: The very fact that imagination could do differently, i.e., could act in such a way that there would be no chance to get the resulting perceptions into an intuition shows that it is a self-standing and independent faculty that (presumably within certain limits) is free to do whatever it wants. It is not that difficult to come up with examples that make it likely that imagination indeed acts in ways that do not aim at providing materials for the formation of intuitions, i.e., that do not result in providing items which then can function as elements out of which intuitions can be formed. Think of sexual episodes: Obviously, in these episodes there are present many or "a manifold" of sensations "accompanied by consciousness," i.e., perceptions which, however, are so diverse that they cannot be unified into an intuition which could become the basis for the representation of an object. Viewed from this perspective, that there are options of acting available to imagination, the fact that imagination can and does, but by no means has to create perceptions that meet the standards of the understanding, indicates that it is not constrained by the rules of the understanding. Rather, it seems, it is up to imagination to "decide" whether it conforms to the demands connected with what the understanding needs in order to form representations of objects. The only rule it has

Kant on Imagination and Object Constitution   25

to obey, as Kant points out quite explicitly (*KrV* A99), is the rule of sensibility, i.e., that it has to let perceptions form a sequence in time.[9]

If one agrees that it is acceptable to attribute to Kant the idea that imagination has some sort of "freedom" from the rules of the understanding, at least at the initial phase of the first stage of gathering elements for creating a representation of an object, a quite natural thing to ask is whether this "freedom" extends to the second phase of this stage as well, i.e., to the phase from perception to intuition. Remember that both phases of this stage are conceived of as involving a mental activity (namely imagination) in its capacity to operate exclusively on the level of sensibility, which is meant to imply that this activity is not assumed to be subject to conceptual rules but is supposed to operate in a non-conceptual way. Here, in the second phase, the task no longer consists in arriving at perceptions but to create out of perceptions intuitions. Kantian intuitions have to be understood as unified collections of perceptual data of which I am conscious. Therefore, the task imagination has to perform now in this second phase consists in actively going through (*durchlaufen*) the perceptions at hand in order to select those that qualify for bringing about an intuition of an as-yet-undetermined object.

How does this selection process work? According to the reconstructive picture suggested here, the following is the case: Imagination finds itself confronted with a large number of perceptions, only some of which are such that they can be connected into the unity of an intuition. Thus, to turn again to phenomenology, in any given situation I will have some sound perceptions, some color and shape perceptions, and different smell and taste perceptions, all of them ordered in time without having any reason, to use Kant's words, "to summon to the subsequent [perceptions] a perception from which the mind did move on to another [*eine Wahrnehmung, von welcher das Gemüt zu einer anderen übergegangen, zu den nachfolgenden herüberzurufen*]" (*KrV* A121). In order to bring some object-representation-enabling structure into this ordered sequence of inhomogeneous perceptions, imagination has to pick out those that are of the right kind, i.e., those that fit together into the unity of an intuition. If, e.g., I were conscious of a colored sound perception accompanied by a tactile smell perception and followed by an optical perception of a taste,

---

[9] To think of (productive) imagination as having some degree of "freedom" while performing in what was called earlier "the first phase of the first stage," the act of transforming physiological events into perceptions helps to connect Kant's considerations regarding imagination in the first *Critique* to what he says about imagination in the third *Critique*.

there would be no way for imagination to make them fit together into an intuition; and even if my perceptions were not that strangely "non-objectifiable" as these synesthetic perceptions are but would comply with the "normal" sense distribution (colors are perceived by the optical sense, tastes by the gustatory sense, etc.), it could still very well be the case that they cannot mesh with one another into a single intuition. Just think of the perception of a color in front of you and the almost simultaneous perception of a sound in the far distance. Actually, the very possibility of becoming conscious of different sensations as individual events depends on the inherent independence of perceptions from intuitions. A perception is in its own right more than just an ingredient of an intuition, or, in other words, I can have a perception without thereby automatically having a (maybe incomplete) intuition. Hence, imagination has to seek out the right kind of perceptions, i.e., those that can be used in the process of constituting a unitary intuition.

Imagination acting in this selective capacity is guided by just a single criterion: It is guided by whether a perception can be integrated into a unity of an intuition, i.e., a unity that is compatible with what Kant calls (in section 18 of the B-Deduction) the "objective unity of apperception." The phenomenologically sound assumption behind this move on Kant's part is the idea that only those collections of perceptions can have the unity of an intuition that do not interfere with my being able to think of myself as an identical subject. If any collection of perceptions would in principle qualify for the status of a unitary intuition then, as Kant rightly points out, "I would have as multicolored, diverse a self as I have representations of which I am conscious" (*KrV* B134). This shows that the demand for unity in connection with an intuition is not immediately related to the demand for the unity of an object based on the category "unity" in the table of categories. That an intuition has to have a specific unity is due directly to the demands connected with the possibility of a unified and identical self. Therefore, the unity of an intuition is not owed to an object-constituting concept and is no conceptual ingredient provided by the understanding.[10]

If imagination brings about intuitions by starting with perceptions and uniting (some of) them in the manner just sketched, can it be called "free" or "independent" or "autonomous" in the same way as it was in the process of transforming physiological events into perceptions? Obviously not. Whereas in the latter case imagination can be said to be "independent"

---

[10] The distinction between unity as an object-constituting concept (a category) and unity as an achievement and characteristic of apperception is pointed out nicely by Kant in *KrV* (B131).

or "autonomous" because there appears to be no interference at all from either apperception or the rules of the understanding in the transformational process, and it can be termed "free" because it is free to follow either no rule at all or rules that are exclusively its own, imagination in the former case is definitely restricted in its activities by the demands, though not of the understanding but of apperception concerning unity. Though being subject to the conditions under which the unity of the self, i.e., apperception is possible is without doubt a constraint on imagination's "freedom," it is a much less rigorous constraint than the restraints that come with being subject to the requirements of the understanding. If one were to call the freedom imagination enjoys in the context of the production of perceptions "absolute" freedom, one can think of imagination's freedom in the process of forming intuitions as a "relative" freedom. But even in this state of relative freedom, imagination would be completely independent of the operations of the understanding, and in this sense, autonomous.

That there is a difference between being dependent on apperception alone and being dependent on the rules of the understanding (perhaps together with apperception) shows not just in the different degrees of freedom connected with these dependencies. It also shows in the results of the activities of imagination. Whereas, in the process of uniting a manifold of perceptions into an intuition, all that imagination has to achieve is intuitive unity; in contrast, it has to accomplish objective unity or the unity of an object when acting in the service of the understanding. Kant very sensibly makes it quite clear – at least in the A-deduction – that there is a fundamental difference between an intuition and the representation of a cognitive object (*KrV* A124). An intuition being just a unified collection of perceptions which somehow fit together (can be brought under an apperceptive unity) has to be such that the understanding might be able to use it as material for creating a general representation (i.e., a concept) of an object. Or, to put it a little bit metaphorically, an intuition has to contain the promise of an object. In order to become the representation of an object an intuition has to be treatable or, so to say, manageable by the understanding, that is to say it has to be accessible to categorization. This accessibility condition is not fulfilled by a single intuition but presupposes what Kant somewhat vaguely calls "a manifold of intuition."[11] Otherwise one would never get to a general representation

---

[11] There is a well-known ambiguity in Kant's use of the term "manifold of intuition": On the one hand, this term refers to the manifold of perceptions out of which a single *intuition* is formed.

of an object (of cognition). In other words: Kant, by insisting on the difference between an intuition and the representation of a (cognitive) object, does account for an attitude which indeed has a solid basis in the phenomenology of perception, i.e., the attitude that many, if not most of the intuitions we have, do not end up in representations of objects. It is just those intuitions that can give rise to reproductive and recognitive activities that make a representation of an object possible. These activities, though they involve imagination *"in its transcendental function"* as well, are subject to the categorical rules of the understanding and start their work on the next, the second stage of the long way from sensation to the representation of an object whose concept can function as a predicate in a judgment. Here in the second stage, which begins with intuitions, conceptual elements in the shape of the categories have their debut, and imagination loses both freedom and autonomy. Fortunately, Kant does not abandon imagination to this sad fate. According to him, imagination happily regains far away from cognitive processes a new and authentic life in aesthetic contemplation. It took Kant a couple of years before he found the right means for this resurrection of imagination in the shape of a theory of taste.

Let me highlight at the end what I take to be the most interesting positive points that result from ascribing to Kant the model of cognitive object formation outlined so far. These are mainly two, the first one relates to an aspect essential for every systematic account of object formation in cognition, the second relates to Kant's special presentation of such an account. The systematically interesting point is the following: Every theory of cognitive object formation, as far as it bases object formation on perception and thinks of perceptions as having semantic content, has to somehow answer the question as to how this semantic content comes about. There are many answers around, both from the philosophy and the psychology of perception, which, rather vaguely, connect the origin of semantic content to brain activities and neuronal processes and try to establish in this way a direct link between physiological events (brain activities, neuronal processes) and semantic content. What these theories fail to provide is an account of the conditions that have to obtain for an item to be able to have a semantic content. At the least, one has to expect that such an item can be distinguished from other items and that it has a

---

On the other hand, he seems to refer, with this expression as well, to the manifold aspects a single *object* can have when given "in intuition." In this second use the term "intuition" designates a mode of awareness of an individual object, in the first, a distinct entity.

specific singularity that is such that there is a one-to-one correspondence between the item and its semantic content. Thus, the systematically interesting lesson to be learned from Kant's approach is that a theory of perception based on sensory input first of all has to account for the distinctiveness and singularity of what psychologists nowadays call "percepts" before it can be of any help for a theory of cognitive object formation.

This leads directly to the second point that can be seen as a positive result of attributing to Kant the model of object formation outlined here. In the beginning, it was said that there always have been and still are serious worries about whether and how the faculty of imagination can be acknowledged as a constitutive and self-standing factor in Kant's attempt to somehow bring together conceptual and non-conceptual elements in his conception of an object of cognition, as outlined in the first *Critique*. This, however, seems to be an ill-founded worry if one is prepared to follow the suggestions put forward here. Rather, it shows that imagination has in a certain sense to carry the main burden in the laborious process to make, out of amorphous and unstructured physiological sense-impressions, representations of full-blown cognitive objects. In this process, imagination in the initial sensory stages plays a surprisingly autonomous role and reveals an admirable and almost unrestrained range of creative activities whose rules (if there are any) are unknown to us. It is only in the later, conceptual stages of this process that imagination has to succumb to foreign demands and to follow the categorical rules of the understanding. All this confirms quite nicely Kant's assessment of imagination according to which it is "a blind, though indispensable function of the soul without which we would have nowhere any cognition at all" (*KrV* A78/B103). So, ultimately Kant was right to insist on the essential role imagination has to play, even in purely epistemological contexts, and why this is so can be explained by going back to his view on cognitive object formation elaborated here. It cannot be denied that he himself, in the course of time, became somewhat reluctant to highlight this role as clearly as he did in the first edition of the *Critique*. Yet, this reluctance seems to be rooted not so much in doubts about imagination's function as in the complexities connected with imagination's activities. It surely does not indicate that Kant changed his general view in a fundamental way.[12]

---

[12] This chapter is a very condensed version of a much longer piece that is scheduled to appear in 2018 under the title *Kant's Power of Imagination*, with Cambridge University Press. The version printed here owes many thanks to Dina Emundts, Eckart Förster, Gary Hatfield, and Sally Sedgwick for helpful comments.

CHAPTER 2

Pure Understanding, the Categories, and Kant's Critique of Wolff

Brian A. Chance

The importance of the pure concepts of the understanding (i.e., the categories) within Kant's system of philosophy is undeniable.[1] They provide the basis not only for the synthetic *a priori* cognition of nature articulated in the Analytic of Principles of the first *Critique* and the *Metaphysical Foundations of Natural Science*, but also for the claims about the supersensible that Kant argues are the proper objects of rational belief in all three *Critiques*, *Religion within the Boundaries of Mere Reason*, and the essays "On the old saying that it may be good in theory, but it is of no use in practice" and "What Real Progress Has Metaphysics Made in Germany since the Time of Leibniz and Wolff?"

As I hope to make clear in this chapter, the categories are also an essential part of Kant's critique of Christian Wolff, whose system of philosophy dominated German philosophy in the eighteenth century.[2] In particular, I shall argue that Kant's development of the categories (as well as their forerunners in the 1770 *Inaugural Dissertation*) represents a decisive break with the Wolffian conception of the understanding and that this break is central to understanding the task of the Transcendental Analytic. However, this break is not merely that Kant affirms while Wolff and his followers deny a sharp distinction between sensibility and the understanding, which is the aspect of Kant's rejection of Wolff that scholars have frequently noted.[3] Rather, this break concerns differences in their views about the understanding itself. For while Wolff conceives of the understanding as a mental capacity to extract and make distinct content already present in the senses, Kant conceives of the understanding in its "real use" as a capacity to produce purely intellectual content.

---

[1] Throughout this chapter, I shall use the terms "pure concepts of the understanding" and "categories" as synonyms. For an intriguing argument against this practice, see de Boer 2016.

[2] For a general discussion of this dominance, see Beck 1969:276–305. The most extensive discussion of Wolff's influence during the early part of this period is still Ludovici 1737.

[3] See, e.g., Wolff 1963:15f. and Laywine 1993:104f.

30

Pure Understanding, the Categories, & Critique of Wolff   31

In the *Inaugural Dissertation*, then, Kant affirms what he will subsequently call the spontaneity of the understanding, and it is this aspect of his break with Wolff that I wish to focus on in this chapter.[4] Appreciating this aspect of Kant's break with Wolff is not merely relevant to a proper understanding of the *Inaugural Dissertation*, however, but also, as I hope to show, for Kant's views in the first *Critique*. For the intellectual concepts whose existence Kant affirms in the *Inaugural Dissertation* are the forerunners to the pure concepts of the understanding he introduces in the *Critique*, and Kant's comments about the nature of these concepts have tended to suggest one of two mutually inconsistent readings. The first, which I shall call the *intellectualist reading*, is that the categories are products of the understanding alone that introduce a purely intellectual content into what is given both in sense and in *a priori* intuition.[5] The second, which I shall call the *sensibilist reading*, is that while in part products of the understanding, it is not the understanding but *a priori* intuition that supplies the *content* of the categories and that this content is *constitutive* of their being categories.[6] To take but one example, Kant claims that his "analysis of the entirety of our a priori cognition into the elements of the pure cognition of the understanding" will show that the concepts of the understanding "belong not to intuition and to sensibility, but rather to thinking and understanding," but also that it is only the "a priori manifold of sensibility" whose existence has been established by the Transcendental Aesthetic that "provide[s] the pure concepts of the understanding with a matter, without which they would be without any content [and] completely empty" (*KrV* A65/B89 and A77/B102).

---

[4] Cf. *KrV* A51/B75.

[5] See Kemp Smith 1918: lil, 182f., and 195f.; Paton 1936 (vol. 1): 259; Wolff 1963:60, 71, 130, and 177; Guyer 1987:97–100; Guyer 2010:121 and 125–9; and Tolley 2012. Each attributes a purely intellectual origin to the categories, although some would not endorse the further claim that the categories are purely intellectual concepts, as opposed to, say, identical to what Kant calls the "functions of judgment."

[6] See Allison 2004, Waxman 2005, and Longuenesse 2006. Allison holds that "a reference to sensible intuition (though not to a particular type thereof) is an *essential component* of the *very concept of a category* for Kant, whereas it is completely alien to the concept of a logical function" (2004:156, my emphasis); Waxman holds that the "manifold [of sense] and its synthesis have to be added to the logical functions [of judgment] before these concepts [i.e., the pure concepts of the understanding] can arise" and that these concepts cannot "be deprived of their relation to the manifold and its synthesis without thereby ... reverting to their purely logical, nonobjective character as forms of judgment" (2005:28); and Longuenesse holds that "all that remains" of the categories absent pure intuition are the logical functions of judgment and that they "become categories ... only when the understanding's capacity to judge is applied to sensible manifolds" (2006:151). See also Waxman 2008:181–4 and Greenberg 2001:138.

32   BRIAN A. CHANCE

Comments of this latter sort thus represent a serious challenge to the intellectualist reading of the categories, and it is here that I believe a more detailed understanding of the nature of Kant's break with Wolff is especially helpful. For the account of the understanding Kant rejects in the *Inaugural Dissertation* has much in common with the account of the understanding's role in relation to the categories suggested by passages such as *KrV* A77/B102, and the account of the understanding he endorses in the *Inaugural Dissertation* has much in common with the account of the understanding's role in relation to the categories suggested by passages such as *KrV* A65/B89. Moreover, once the nature of Kant's break with Wolff in the *Inaugural Dissertation* is made clear, it is easy to see that much of Kant's subsequent terminology in the *Critique* serves to emphasize this break. For when Wolff and his followers deny the possibility of purely intellectual concepts, they do so by denying the possibility of what they call a "pure understanding"; and the pure understanding is, of course, precisely what Kant proposes to analyze in the Transcendental Analytic.[7] Moreover, when Kant describes the understanding as the "ability to bring forth representations itself" and then glosses this ability as the "*spontaneity* of cognition," he is asserting of the understanding precisely what Wolff and his followers deny when they assert that there can be no pure understanding (*KrV* A51/B75).

The structure of this chapter is as follows. In Section 1, I elaborate on the details of the Wolffian account of the understanding and, especially, the Wolffian denial of a pure understanding. While my focus is on Wolff, I also briefly discuss these views as they are found in Gottsched, Baumgarten, and Meier. In Section 2, I then consider the two main phases of the pre-critical Kant's rejection of the Wolffian account, beginning in his 1762 essay *On the False Subtlety of the Four Syllogistic Figures*, and the relationship between this rejection and the questions announced in the famous 1772 Herz letter. Together, these sections constitute an indirect defense of an intellectualist reading of the categories. In Section 3, I turn to a direct defense of this reading by considering Kant's comments about the understanding and the categories in the *Critique*. In the first part of that section, I elaborate on the ways in which the terminology of the *Critique* suggests that Kant is continuing to position himself against the Wolffian denial of a pure understanding that he targeted in the *Inaugural Dissertation*. In the remainder of that section and against the background of the previous two, I discuss the passages that support the intellectualist reading

---

[7] Cf. *KrV* A65/B90.

Pure Understanding, the Categories, & Critique of Wolff   33

and attempt to show how the many passages that appear to support a sensibilist reading can be made consistent with it.

1   The Wolffian Account of the Understanding

Wolff and his followers discuss the understanding in their writings on logic, empirical psychology, and rational psychology. At the most basic level, they conceive of the understanding as one of the mind's many cognitive capacities, all of which are grounded in its fundamental power of representation.[8] These capacities are examined in detail in empirical psychology, and one of the main goals of rational psychology is to show how they are all grounded in the mind's power of representation. For its part, the subject matter of logic is continuous with empirical and rational psychology insofar as logic examines our mental capacities, but it is also separate from both insofar as its focus is on the use of these capacities to cognize truth and not on them merely as such.[9]

In their various discussions of the understanding, Wolff and his followers consistently characterize it as the capacity to distinctly represent the possible.[10] To unpack this characterization, however, we must first say something about what Wolff means by "distinctness" as well as the cognate term "clarity."[11] Both are properties of thoughts, and both are defined in terms of the relationship between a thought and its object. A thought, which Wolff defines as an "alteration" or "effect" of the mind of which we are conscious, is clear just in case it allows us to recognize its object and distinguish our thought of it from thoughts of other objects and is

---

[8]   For a discussion of this as well as the difference between a capacity (*Vermögen*) and a power (*Kraft*) in Wolff's psychology, see Dyck 2014:32–4.

[9]   See, for example, Wolff's *Discures praeliminaris de philosophia in genere*, §§88–91. Empirical and rational psychology are two of the five traditional divisions of metaphysics in the Wolffian tradition, the other three being ontology, cosmology, and natural theology.

[10]   For Wolff's characterization, see his *Vernüfftige Gedanken von Gott, der Welt und der Seele des Menschen, auch allen Dinge überhaupt* (hereafter *Deutsche Metaphysik*), §277. Wolff sometimes describes the understanding as merely the capacity to think the possible, but in the *Deutsche Metaphysik*, §284 and the subsequent *Der vernüfftigen Gedanken von Gott, der Welt und der Seele des Menschen, auch allen Dinge überhaupt, anderer Theil, bestehend aus ausführlichen Anmerkungen*, §90 he makes clear that this broader meaning is not the proper one. Wolff's *Psychologia empirica*, §275 gives a slightly different definition: "Facultas res distinct repraesentandi dicitur *Intellectus*." What is most important for our purposes, however, is that the understanding (*Verstand* or *Intellectus*) is associated with distinct cognition. Gottsched *Erste Gründe der gesamten Weltweisheit* vol. 1, §1 and §915; Meier *Metaphysik* §626; and Baumgarten *Metaphysica*, §624 all follow Wolff in this regard.

[11]   As Wolff makes clear in the Preface to the *Vernüftige Gedanken von den Kräften des menschlichen Verstandes und Ihrem Gebrauch in Erkänntnis der Wahrheit* (hereafter, *Deutsche Logik*), these distinctions are influenced heavily by Leibniz's "Meditationes de Cognitione, Veritate et Ideis."

34 BRIAN A. CHANCE

otherwise obscure.[12] Thus, I can have a thought of an object simply by looking at it or recalling it in memory, but for my thought of it to be clear I must also be able to distinguish it from other objects, i.e., to identify it as a cup, or a book, or my cat. As Wolff puts it, thoughts are clear when "we know very well what we think and can distinguish them [i.e., the thoughts in question] from others."[13] More generally, he writes that clarity arises through the "observation of a difference in what is manifold," while obscurity arises through the lack of such observation.[14]

Similarly, a thought is distinct just in case it contains clear representations of the parts of its object in virtue of which it is that object and no other. Wolff introduces distinctness by observing that we are sometimes able to "determine the difference in what [i.e., the object] we think and when prompted can thus convey it to others."[15] As becomes apparent in Wolff's example, the "difference" in question is anything that distinguishes the object of the thought from some other objects. Thus, "when I think of a triangle and a square, I can determine the difference of the triangle and square, and when someone asks me in virtue of what I distinguish these figures from each other and from all others, I can name this difference."[16] As Wolff puts it, thoughts "always encompass a plurality" and distinctness arises "when our thoughts are clear with respect to their parts or the manifold which is to be encountered in them."[17]

When Wolff and his followers characterize the understanding as the capacity to distinctly represent the possible, then, the feature of our mental landscape they mean to pick out is our ability to discriminate objects or kinds of objects according to criteria that we ourselves recognize and, at least in principle, can articulate. And, as Wolff emphasizes, this somewhat technical conception of the understanding is grounded in a garden variety colloquial one:

> Thus when a person can tell us nothing about a thing, despite being able to imagine it, that is, when he has no distinctness in his thoughts (§206), we generally say that he has no *understanding of it* or he does not *understand* it; whereas when he can tell us what parts of the thing he represents, we say that he has an *understanding of it* or that he understands it. At times we quite explicitly present distinctness as the reason someone has not understood something, such as when we say, "How can he say that?

---

[12] *Deutsche Logik* 1.2 and *Deutsche Metaphysik* §194. I cite the *Deutsche Logik* by chapter and section number.

[13] *Deutsche Metaphysik*, §198.   [14] *Deutsche Metaphysik*, §201.   [15] *Deutsche Metaphysik*, §206.

[16] *Deutsche Metaphysik*, §206.   [17] *Deutsche Metaphysik*, §207.

> He understands nothing about it," even though we know that he perceives the thing and can imagine it.[18]

Thus, to understand something is not merely to correctly categorize it, either as a particular or a kind, but to do so with an awareness of what makes the categorization correct; and having this awareness is simply what it means to have a distinct concept of whatever one has categorized. Moreover, just as a distinct representation is the product of the understanding, an indistinct representation, whether clear or obscure, is the product of the lower cognitive capacities of perception (*Wahrnehmung*) and imagination (*Einbildungskraft*).

Importantly, however, Wolff also believes it is impossible for human beings to make their concepts completely distinct and, hence, that these concepts will always have some connection to perception and imagination. And while it is perhaps not surprising that this would be true of our concepts of things that are uncontroversially encountered only in experience, it is also true of more abstract concepts, such as our concepts of numbers. For these concepts, according to Wolff, are all reducible to our concept of unity (*Einheit, Unitas*), and abstract though it may be, Wolff holds that this concept is still confused.[19] Moreover, the terminology in which Wolff chooses to express this point is that of purity and impurity. In the *Deutsche Metaphysik*, for example, he writes that the understanding is "pure" when it is "separated from the senses and imagination" and impure when it is "still connected" to them or, what is the same, when "indistinctness and obscurity are still to be found in our cognition."[20] Similarly, in the *Psychologia Empirica* he writes that the understanding is "said to be pure if no sort of confused and no sort of obscure thing is mixed into the concept of the object which it has" and impure "if there are in the concept of the object things that are perceived confusedly or completely obscurely."[21] And in both, he asserts quite clearly that our understanding is "never completely pure."[22]

Moreover, the nature of Wolff's rejection of the possibility of a pure understanding makes clear that even our fundamental ontological concepts

---

[18] *Deutsche Metaphysik*, §277, emphasis in original.
[19] In §314 of his *Psychologia Empirica*, for example, he writes, "In the doctrine of numbers we suppose no primitive notion, except that of unity, and so there is no need for any confused concepts [*notio*] to be supposed, *except that of unity*" (my emphasis).
[20] Wolff, *Deutsche Metaphysik*, §282. Cf. *Psychologia Empirica*, §313.
[21] Wolff, *Psychologia Empirica*, §313.
[22] Wolff, *Deutsche Metaphysik*, §284. Cf. *Psychologia Empirica*, §315, the heading of which is "why our understanding is never completely pure."

36   BRIAN A. CHANCE

are ineluctably tied to sense and imagination. For when Wolff discusses our concepts of numbers in the *Psychologia Empirica*, he does so because he believes these concepts are the closest approximation we as human beings have to pure concepts. Thus, he writes that algebraic formulae "serve to illustrate the pure understanding" but that they do so despite the fact that "the notions corresponding to them are not completely of the sort that the pure understanding requires."[23] If even these concepts are ineluctably connected to sense and imagination, so Wolff's implicit conclusion in the *Psychologia Empirica* goes, our fundamental ontological concepts can fare no better.[24] This latter point emerges more clearly in Wolff's discussion of concept acquisition in the *Deutsche Logik* and *Philosophia rationalis, sive Logica*, where he lists "reflection, abstraction and arbitrary determination" as the three ways in which concepts are formed. Thus, although it might be thought to invalidate his Leibnizian credentials, Wolff endorses a form of concept empiricism, albeit only with respect to the origin of the content of our ideas, not their causal origin.[25]

While space prevents me from tracing these views among Wolff's many followers, they generally agree with him on these issues. In his 1755 *Erste Gründe der gesamten Weltweisheit*, the most successful textbook of Wolffian philosophy ever printed in Germany, Gottsched writes, "God alone has an understanding that is completely pure."[26] Baumgarten's 1739 *Metaphysica*, the fourth edition of which served as the basis for Kant's own metaphysics

---

[23] Wolff, *Psychologia Empirica*, §313.

[24] For further discussion, see Kuehn 1997:229–50 and Dyck 2011. I thus find myself in disagreement with Dyck (2011:478f.), who finds in Wolff's *Ontologia* an alternative account of the acquisition that applies exclusively to ontological concepts. While a complete examination of this point is beyond the scope of this chapter, it does not appear to me that Wolff's discussion of the linguistic origin of these concepts is incompatible with the threefold account in the *Deutsche Logik* and *Philosophia rationalis, sive Logica*. Moreover, even if it were to be, it does not seem to me that Wolff is presenting an alternative account of concept acquisition in the passages Dyck cites.

[25] Wolff's commitment to preestablished harmony as the most likely account of the mind-body relation precludes his being an empiricist with respect to the causal origin of our ideas but not with respect to the content of those ideas themselves. On the question of Leibniz's innatism as it was understood throughout most of the eighteenth century, see Tonelli 1974. For our purposes, the most important part of Tonelli's analysis is that the more sophisticated psychological account of the origin of ideas found in the *Nouveaux Essais* did not gain much traction after its first publication in Raspe's 1765 edition of Leibniz's works and that the accounts of the origin of ideas in the works known to Wolff and his followers emphasized the *causal* origin of our ideas rather than the origin of their content. From Wolff's early eighteenth-century perspective, then, and even well into the second half of the century, there would have been no obvious conflict between being an Leibnizian and endorsing the form of concept empiricism I attribute to Wolff. That Wolff frequently decried the suggestion that he was a mere follower of Leibniz is only further reason to conclude that his relation to Leibniz provides no evidence against the view I attribute to him here.

[26] Gottsched, *Erste Gründe der gesamten Weltweisheit*, §918. Gottsched's book went through seven separate editions before his death in 1766, far more than either Baumgarten's or Meier's.

Pure Understanding, the Categories, & Critique of Wolff   37

lectures, adopts the language of purity to describe the degree to which our understanding is distinct.[27] And in the 1757 volume of Meier's *Metaphysik* on empirical psychology, he refers to the "famous question" of whether the "human understanding can be a pure understanding," which he answers in the negative, and argues that all of our distinct cognition is "in part sensible."[28]

2 Kant's Rejection of the Wolffian Account

It is against these background assumptions about the human understanding and the terminology used to describe it that Kant writes the *Inaugural Dissertation*. Now that these assumptions have been made explicit, we are in a position to appreciate a point that to my knowledge has been entirely overlooked by previous commentators, namely that Kant's account of the "real use" of the understanding in the *Inaugural Dissertation* is an overt and fundamental rejection of the Wolffian denial of a pure understanding. Moreover, as I will suggest at the close of this section, it is Kant's affirmation of the spontaneity of the understanding, its ability to be a source of purely intellectual concepts, that forces him to address the array of questions that lead ultimately to the main problematic of the Transcendental Analytic: the task of explaining that and how the pure concepts of the understanding apply to objects given in intuition.

Since Kant's discussion of the real use of the understanding itself occurs against the background of an earlier phase of his break with Wolff, however, it will be helpful to begin our discussion with a brief account of this earlier phase. In his 1762 essay *On the False Subtlety of the Four Syllogistic Figures*, Kant tacitly endorses some aspects of the Wolffian account of the understanding while rejecting others. In particular, he agrees with Wolff and his followers that the understanding alone imparts distinctness to representations, but he also attempts to ground this capacity in the more general capacity to judge. The view Kant endorses in the *False Subtlety* is thus that the understanding is fundamentally a capacity to judge and that the Wolffian tradition errs in holding that the understanding is fundamentally a capacity to render concepts distinct since this latter capacity is, unbeknownst to them, simply derivative of the former.

Kant's justification for this view is compelling. My concept is distinct just in case I am conscious of the marks in virtue of which it represents its object. Thus, my concept of body is distinct if it includes a clear

---

[27] Baumgarten, *Metaphysica*, §§634–7.   [28] Meier, *Metaphysik*, §631 and §526.

representation – i.e., one that I recognize as a representation of its object – of impenetrability, which is one of the characteristics in virtue of which something is a body. But this concept, Kant insists, is made possible through the thought "bodies are impenetrable," which is simply a judgment about body. So, the act of making a distinct concept is just the act of judging. As Kant is careful to emphasize, however, this does not mean that concept and judgment are identical; rather, the judgment is the "action by means of which the distinct concept is made real, because the representation that arises from this action is distinct" (*DfS* 2:58, translation modified).

Kant gives a similar argument for complete concepts, which he, following the tradition, understands as concepts with a particularly high degree of distinctness, in particular ones in which I have a distinct (not merely a clear) representation of the marks in virtue of which a given distinct concept is distinct.[29] The possibility of such concepts, according to Kant, depends on the syllogism (*Vernunftschluß*). If my concept of body is distinct and my concept of impenetrability, which is a part of the former concept, is also distinct, then my concept of body is not only distinct but also complete. Yet, if my concept of impenetrability is distinct, I must also have a clear idea of one of its constitutive marks, i.e., of one of the properties in virtue of which something is impenetrable, say, that it has a repulsive force. If this is all true, however, then the complete concept of body – a distinct concept of body that includes as part of its content distinct concepts of the concepts in virtue of which the concept of body is distinct – arises from something like the following syllogism:

1. All bodies are impenetrable.
2. All impenetrable things have a repulsive force.
3. Therefore, all bodies have a repulsive force.

In other words, the judgment "all bodies are impenetrable" gives rise to a distinct concept of body, while the judgment "all impenetrable things have a repulsive force" gives rise to a distinct concept of impenetrability, and the inference made possible by these judgments gives rise to a *complete* concept of body. More importantly, this inference is the same action of judgment that operated at the level of the premises, operating now at a higher level.[30]

---

[29] See Wolff, *Deutsche Logik*, 1.16.

[30] As Kant puts it, "one and the same capacity [*Fähigkeit*] is used to immediately cognize something as a characteristic mark of a thing, represent in this characteristic mark a further characteristic mark, and thus to think of the thing by means of a more remote characteristic mark" (*DfS* 2:59, translation modified).

Pure Understanding, the Categories, & Critique of Wolff 39

Thus, the action of judgment makes possible not only distinct and complete concepts but also judgments and inferences, and each of these products (distinct concepts, complete concepts, and inferences) can be traced back to the understanding's capacity to judge.

The claim that the understanding is the capacity to judge is, of course, central to Kant's mature view in the *Critique*, and it is noteworthy that this aspect of Kant's mature view dates back at least to the publication of the *False Subtlety*.[31] For our immediate purposes, however, it is more important to note that this view is also found in the *Inaugural Dissertation*, where Kant discusses it under the heading of the "logical use" of the understanding. Initially, Kant merely describes this use as the subordination and comparison of concepts in accordance with the principle of contradiction (*MSI* 2:393). It quickly becomes clear, however, that this subordination and comparison are the same two expressions of the understanding's capacity to judge that Kant previously discussed in the *False Subtlety*. For, in explanation of the claim that the logical use of the understanding is "common to all the sciences," Kant writes, that "when a cognition has been given, no matter how, it is regarded as contained under or as opposed to a characteristic mark common to several cognitions, and that either immediately and directly, as in the case in *judgments*, which lead to a distinct cognition, or mediately, as in the case in *ratiocinations*, which lead to a complete cognition" (*MSI* 2:396).

To this extent, Kant's view in the *Inaugural Dissertation* is continuous with his view in the *False Subtlety*. In the *Inaugural Dissertation*, however, Kant also expands his conception of the understanding and, consequently, his break with the Wolffian tradition beyond anything found in the *False Subtlety* by asserting that there is also a "real use" of the understanding. More interesting still, in his discussion of this use, Kant ascribes to the understanding precisely what the Wolffian tradition denies of it when it denies that a pure understanding is possible. For in its real use, the understanding does not merely compare and subordinate concepts to others but is itself a *source* of concepts; and in contrast to his seeming ambivalence in the *Critique*, Kant is absolutely clear in the *Inaugural Dissertation* that these concepts arise solely from the understanding and have no relationship whatsoever to sensibility. For these concepts, Kant writes, are "given by the very nature of the understanding," "contain no form of sensitive cognition," and "have been abstracted from no use of the

---

[31] Cf. *KrV* A69/B94. Indeed, both Longuenesse (1998) and Allison (2004) have argued persuasively that this is Kant's fundamental characterization of the understanding.

senses" (*MSI* 2:394). Despite their purely intellectual origin, however, Kant is also clear that these concepts are not "innate" but are rather "abstracted from the laws inherent in the mind" and that we abstract them by "attending to its [i.e., the mind's] actions on occasion of an experience" (*MSI* 2:395). Finally, the examples of these concepts Kant introduces ("possibility, existence, necessity, substance, [and] cause") make clear that they are precisely the kind of ontological concepts that the mature Kant will introduce in the *Critique* as pure categories of the understanding (*MSI* 2:395).

The similarities between the concepts of the real use of the understanding whose existence Kant asserts in the *Inaugural Dissertation* and the pure concepts of the understanding whose existence he asserts in the *Critique* are thus striking. There are also, however, important questions left unanswered by the *Inaugural Dissertation*. For one, it is not clear whether the characterization of the understanding as the capacity to judge that Kant introduced in the *False Subtlety* and relies on in the *Inaugural Dissertation* can be extended to explain the possibility of the real use of the understanding. If Kant wants to maintain that both capacities are equally aspects of the understanding, he owes us an explanation of how this is possible. For another, Kant's insistence that the understanding has a real use, especially when viewed as a denial of the Wolffian claim that the understanding is never pure, means that he must explain how the concepts of the real use of the understanding ("possibility, existence, necessity, substance, cause, etc.") relate to objects that are given in sense.

This latter problem is, of course, the one Kant himself raises in his 1772 letter to Herz and that he does not resolve to his satisfaction until the Metaphysical and Transcendental Deductions of the *Critique*. And while it is sometimes thought that this problem arises for Kant as a result of the influence of skepticism, it is equally (and perhaps even primarily) one that arises as a result of his rejection of the Wolffian view.[32] For if the content of all concepts derives from what is given in sense, and no concept is ever completely divorced from sense and imagination, there is no reason to suspect that our concepts would not correspond in some way to objects. It would, of course, be possible for the imagination to create concepts of fantastical objects, but even in this case, the elements of such concepts would correspond to something real. Once Kant commits himself to the existence of pure concepts, however, it is incumbent on him to explain how they relate to objects given in sense.

---

[32] See, for example, Mensch 2007.

3 Wolffian Understanding and the *Critique*

While the foregoing has, I hope, made a compelling case for both an intellectualist reading of the concepts of the real use of the understanding in the *Inaugural Dissertation* and the importance of these concepts to Kant's critique of Wolff, it has only made an indirect case for an intellectualist reading of the categories in the *Critique* and their importance to Kant's critique of Wolff. This latter case can be summarized as follows:

(1) The concepts of the real use of the understanding are the forerunners of the categories, so what is true of the former is *caterus paribus* true of the latter.

(2) The former are clearly intellectual in origin and clearly a rejection of the Wolffian denial of the pure understanding.

(3) Therefore, the latter are intellectual in origin and a rejection of the Wolffian denial of the pure understanding, too.

Clearly, this argument would be weakened considerably if there were evidence from the *Reflexionen* of the silent decade that Kant began to rethink the intellectual origin of the categories. Yet, while Kant's views about the number and division of the categories clearly undergo development during this period, I have found no *Reflexionen* that suggest he ever wavered about their intellectual origin. Consequently, the next step in my defense of the intellectualist reading of the categories is to consider the evidence in favor of it from the *Critique* itself and to show that the putative evidence against it can be made consistent with that reading. The latter is, perhaps, less than the defender of a sensibilist reading of the categories would hope to hear, but in conjunction with the indirect case I have now made and the evidence from the *Critique* in support of an intellectualist reading I will shortly introduce, I believe it is sufficient to carry my burden.

First, as I suggested in the introduction, many of Kant's terminological choices in the *Critique* are most naturally read as attempts to position himself against the Wolffian denial of the pure understanding that he targets in the *Inaugural Dissertation*. Thus, when Kant describes the understanding in the introduction to the Transcendental Logic as the "ability to bring forth representations itself" and then glosses this ability as the "**spontaneity** of cognition," he is implicitly contrasting this account of the understanding with the Wolffian one according to which the understanding is *not* an independent source of representations (*KrV* A51/B75). Similarly, when Kant asserts in the introduction to the Transcendental Analytic that the subject matter of this portion of the *Critique*

BRIAN A. CHANCE

will be the "pure understanding" and that such an understanding "separates itself completely *not only from everything empirical,* but *even from all sensibility,*" it would have only been natural for his readers to interpret these statements as a rejection of the Wolffian doctrines we have been discussing (*KrV* A64–5/B89, my emphasis). The same is also true of Kant's comment in the introduction to the Analytic of Concepts (the first book of the Transcendental Analytic) that the subject matter of this portion of the *Critique* is as analysis of the "pure use" of the understanding (*KrV* A66/B91). Finally, in light of the claims of the previous two sections, it is difficult to see how Kant's readers would have interpreted his discussion of "pure concepts of the understandings" as anything but an overt rejection of the Wolffian view.

Second, there is no shortage of passages in the *Critique* in which Kant discusses the categories that mirror those passages in the *Inaugural Dissertation* touting the purely intellectual origin of the concepts of the real use of the understanding. In the Introduction to the Transcendental Analytic, for example, Kant claims that his "analysis of the entirety of our a priori cognition into the elements of the pure cognition of the understanding" will show that the concepts of the understanding "belong not to intuition and to sensibility, but rather to thinking and understanding" (*KrV* A64/B89). Similarly, in the introduction to the Analytic of Concepts, Kant writes that he will analyze the understanding itself "in order to research the possibility of a priori concepts by seeking them only in the understanding" (*KrV* A66/B91). In the first section of the portion of the Analytic called "On the Deduction of the Pure Concepts of the Understanding," Kant motivates the project of the Transcendental Deduction in large part by noting that the categories "speak of objects not through predicates of intuition and sensibility but those of pure a priori thinking" (*KrV* A88/B120). And in the crucial transition between the first and second parts of the B-Deduction, Kant emphasizes that the categories "arise **independently from sensibility**" and "merely in the understanding" (*KrV* B144). Moving to the second book of the Analytic, Kant writes that the categories retain a "significance" even "after abstraction from every sensible condition" (*KrV* A147/B186). Finally, in his summary of the main conclusions of the Transcendental Analytic, Kant again asserts that the "pure categories" have a "transcendental significance" even "without formal conditions of sensibility" (*KrV* B305).

Yet, as I noted in the introduction, not all of Kant's comments about the categories in the *Critique* appear consistent with this reading, and it is these comments that have led scholars such as Henry Allison to remark

Pure Understanding, the Categories, & Critique of Wolff 43

that "a reference to sensible intuition … is an essential component of the very concept of a category for Kant."[33] Thus, in the first chapter of the Analytic of Concepts, Kant writes both that the "a priori manifold of sensibility" whose existence has been established by the Transcendental Aesthetic "provide[s] the pure concepts of the understanding with a matter" and that absent this manifold these concepts would be "without any content" and "completely empty" (*KrV* A77/B102). Prior to this, at least in the B-edition, Kant also claims that we have "no concepts of the understanding … except insofar as an intuition can be given corresponding to these concepts" (*KrV* Bxxvi). Similarly, in the continuation of the A77/B102, Kant defines synthesis as "the action of putting different representations together with each other and comprehending their manifoldness in one cognition" and pure synthesis as the synthesis of a manifold that is "given not empirically but a priori," explicitly including the *a priori* intuitions of space and time as examples of such manifolds, before asserting that pure synthesis "provides the pure concepts of the understanding" (*KrV* A78/B104, translation modified). In the section of the B-Deduction that immediately precedes the one cited in the previous paragraph, Kant then writes that the categories are "nothing other" than the logical functions of judgment "insofar as the manifold of a given intuition is determined with regard to them" (*KrV* B143).[34] Finally, this claim is also echoed in Kant's comment in the B Paralogisms that the categories simply "are" the logical functions of judgment "applied to our sensible intuition" (*KrV* B429).[35] How can we reconcile these passages with those from the previous paragraph?

We can reconcile the passage from A77/B102 by appealing to a peculiarity in Kant's use of the word "content" (*Inhalt*). For as several commentators have observed, Kant sometimes uses the term to mean the intensional content of a concept, which is how I have tended to use it here, and sometimes to mean its ability to refer to an object.[36] Kant uses

---

[33] Allison 2004:156. This view appears to be in tension with some of Allison's other comments in the chapter, but it is also the view he chooses to emphasize at the close of his discussion of the Metaphysical Deduction.

[34] See also *Prol* 4:324; *MAN* 4:474; *KrV* B128; *HN* 20:272, 363.

[35] In addition to a number of these passages, Waxman (2005: 27f.) also cites *KrV* A348–9, *KrV* A401–2, *KrV* A321/B378 and *KrV* A79/B105 in support of the kind of reading I am criticizing. I omit discussion of the first two of these passages because they are not in the B-edition, and I omit discussion of the remaining because they do not strike me as evidence for the view Waxman develops.

[36] See Rosenkoetter 2009 and Watkins 2002. For a criticism of this approach, albeit one that focuses on the distinction between *Sinn* and *Bedeutung*, see Roche 2010.

44   BRIAN A. CHANCE

Inhalt in the first way in the *Prolegomena* when he writes that analytic judgments "add nothing to the content [*Inhalt*] of cognition" (*Prol* 4:266).[37] But this is certainly not the way Kant uses it at the beginning of the Transcendental Logic in his well-known comment that "thoughts without content [*Inhalt*] are empty [*leer*]," since as Rosenkoetter has remarked, it is unlikely that Kant means to inform us of the obvious fact that a thought with no intensional content is empty (*KrV* A51/B75).[38] Since this comment glosses Kant's previous comment that "no object would be given to us" without sensibility, it thus seems reasonable to interpret *Inhalt* in this particular context as something like reference or potential reference to an object (*KrV* A51/B75). And in the third section of this portion of the *Critique*, Kant explicitly glosses the "content of cognition" as its "relation to its object" (*KrV* A58/B83). Since these are, moreover, Kant's last discussions of content before the passage from *KrV* A77/B102, it is reasonable to suppose that it is the referential sense of *Inhalt* that he has in mind, which would allow us to read his claim that the categories would be empty and without *Inhalt* if pure intuition did not provide them with a matter in a way that is consistent with Kant's various claims about their origin in the understanding alone since we may say that the categories have an intensional content that derives from the understanding alone while denying that it is sufficient for them to refer to objects.

The passage from the B Preface is more challenging. To begin, however, note its ambiguity. For Kant writes both that we have "no concepts of the understanding" except "insofar as an intuition can be given" and that this intuition must be one "corresponding to these concepts" (*KrV* Bxxvi). Since Kant cannot mean that there are no categories without intuition *and* that an intuition corresponding to *the very same categories* is what allows them to come into being, it is perhaps better to interpret him as implicitly relying on the distinction between the categories and the schematized categories.[39] Moreover, it is clear that Kant does not intend this passage to be inconsistent with a contentful, transcendental use of the categories since he follows it by emphasizing that his view is consistent with our ability to have thoughts of objects as things in themselves and that this ability requires only that our concepts of things not be self-contradictory (*KrV* Bxxxvi). If there were truly no categories without intuition, it is hard

---

[37] Cf. *Jäsche*, 9:95.   [38] Rosenkoetter 2009: 215.

[39] See Paton 1936 (vol. 1):260–1,304 and (vol. 2): 41f., 67f. I also note *en passant* that the distinction between the categories and their schemata would seem difficult if not impossible to draw on the sensibilist reading since *a priori* intuition is precisely what is added on Kant's account to yield the latter from the former.

Pure Understanding, the Categories, & Critique of Wolff   45

to see what content these thoughts about things in themselves would have. Yet, if the categories have an intensional content derived solely from the understanding, the door is open for contentful, albeit non-cognitive thinking about things in themselves, including and especially the objects of traditional metaphysics that in Kant's view are the proper objects of rational belief.

There is also good reason to interpret the passage from B429 as relying implicitly on the distinction between the categories and the schematized categories. In this passage, which is drawn from the end of the B Paralogisms, Kant contrasts representing oneself as a "**subject** of a thought" and a "**ground** of thinking" with representing oneself as a substance or a cause of thinking, and when he writes that "these categories are those functions of thinking (of judging) applied to our sensible intuition," it is clear that he means "substance and cause" by "these categories" and "subject and ground" by "those functions." This would appear to support the view that what distinguishes the categories as such from the functions of thinking is the relation of the former to intuition, and this in turn suggests that the categories as such have an essential relation to intuition. When Kant discusses the categories of substance and cause in the phenomena/noumena chapter, however, he suggests, first, that there *are* categories as such absent any relation to intuition and, second, that what the categories of substance and cause are absent such a relation are precisely the concepts of subject and ground. Moreover, what Kant there suggests must be added to these concepts to yield the concepts of substance and cause is precisely what he in the schematism chapter suggests must be added to the pure concepts of substance and cause to yield the corresponding schematized concepts.[40]

Consider now the passage from the B-Deduction. Here Kant appears to assert what Allison has called the "quasi-identification" of the functions of judgments and the categories (Allison 2004:155). The former are identified with the latter "insofar as the manifold of a given intuition is determined with regard to them" (*KrV* B143). On Allison's reading, the categories are quasi-identified with the functions of judgment because the categories are nothing other than the functions of judgment when *those functions* determine a manifold given in intuition. Note, however, that Kant does not say the categories are the functions of judgments *only* insofar as they determine a manifold of intuition. So, the passage itself does not suggest, as Allison appears to believe it does, that "reference to sensible

---

[40] See *KrV* A242–3/B300–1 and *KrV* A143–4/B182–3.

46 BRIAN A. CHANCE

intuition" is an "essential component of the very concept of a category" (Allison 2004: 156). Further, when we turn to section 13 of the Deduction, to which the passage from B143 parenthetically refers, we find Kant emphasizing the *intellectual* nature of the categories.[41] So this passage, too, can be rendered consistent with the first set of passages.

We are left then with the passages from A78/B105. Here the problem seemed to be that pure synthesis "yields the categories" but that such a synthesis is by definition a synthesis *of* a pure manifold. Notice, however, that while a pure synthesis may require a pure manifold, it does not follow that *all* the products of that synthesis are constituted by that manifold. Rather, it may be that the presence of a manifold is an occasion, but not a necessary condition, for the actualization of our capacity to judge and that this actualization yields the categories. Since Kant in this passage is looking forward to the arguments of the Transcendental Deduction and Analytic of Principles, it of course makes sense for him to emphasize that pure synthesis "yields" the categories, but everything Kant says in this passage is compatible with the view that *any* exercise of the understanding yields the categories, which is, of course, also the position suggested by the first set of passages.

4 Conclusion

In this chapter, I have tried to illuminate the nature of Kant's categories by bringing three of his texts into dialogue with the Wolffian tradition. In so doing, my goal has been not only to defend an intellectualist reading of the categories – according to which their content arises from the understanding alone and, in particular, does not include any admixture from sensibility, *a priori* or otherwise – but also to firmly establish the anti-Wolffian roots of this reading and, by extension, of the categories themselves. I have argued that Kant's assertion in the *Inaugural Dissertation* of a real use of the understanding is a fundamental rejection of the Wolffian account of the understanding and that the first phase of this rejection had already begun in the *False Subtlety*. In the latter work, Kant rejects the Wolffian view that the understanding is fundamentally the capacity for distinct cognition by arguing that the understanding is fundamentally the capacity to judge and

---

[41] In his first statement of the problem of the Deduction, for example, Kant writes that a transcendental deduction of the categories is necessary because "they speak of objects *not through predicates of intuition and sensibility but through those of pure a priori thinking*" and hence "relate to objects generally and *without any conditions of sensibility*" (*KrV* A88/B120, my emphasis).

that this capacity grounds not only our ability to form distinct concepts but also our ability to make judgments and draw inferences. In the former, he extends his critique of Wolff even further by rejecting the Wolffian denial of the pure understanding and asserting the existence of purely intellectual concepts.

Moreover, I have argued that it was in part the process of working out the consequences of this rejection that led Kant to see the inadequacy of the view he articulated in the *Inaugural Dissertation* and begin the long process of writing the *Critique*. For when one accepts the existence of pure concepts, as opposed to the irreducibly empirical concepts of the Wolffian tradition, it is natural to ask whether these concepts are ever instantiated in experience; and this is precisely the question Kant asks in his letter to Herz and that he does not fully resolve to his satisfaction until the Transcendental Deduction of the *Critique*. Thus, Kant's rejection of the Wolffian denial of the pure understanding is of crucial importance not only to a proper understanding of the categories themselves but also of the entire problematic of the Transcendental Analytic.

Finally, bringing Kant into dialogue with the Wolffian tradition has also allowed us to see that Kant implicitly identifies the purity of the understanding as I have discussed it here with its spontaneity. For Kant believes this spontaneity consists in the understanding's ability to bring forth representations itself, and this is simply another way of asserting that our understanding is pure (Cf. *KrV* A51/B75). In this respect, Kant's critique of the Wolffian tradition's account of the understandings mirrors his critique of that tradition's account of reason. For at least on one recent version of this account, the latter consists in Kant's assertion that reason does not merely provide insight into an already existing order, as the Wolffian tradition suggests, but in both its theoretical and practical capacity is able to impose an order on the world (Guyer 2007:301). And while the implications of this claim cannot be explored here, it is clear that Kant's conception of the spontaneity of the understanding and, hence, its purity is central not only to his broader critique of Wolff but also to the aims of the critical philosophy as a whole.[42]

---

[42] I am grateful to Collin McQuillan, Andrew Roche, Timothy Rosenkoetter, and Reed Winegar for helpful written comments on previous versions of this chapter; to Corey Dyck, Michelle Grier, Paul Guyer, Sally Sedgwick, and Clinton Tolley for discussion; to Gerhard Keiser for assistance with the translations from the *Psychologia empirica*; and to the audiences at the 2013 Nature and Freedom in Kant conference at Brown and the 2015 meeting of the Midwest Study Group of the North American Kant Society at Northwestern for helpful comments and criticism.

CHAPTER 3

Transcendental Idealism in the B-Deduction

Michael Rohlf

1 Kant's Method of Argument

"*Philosophical* cognition," according to Kant, "is *rational cognition* from *concepts*" (*KrV* A713/B741). This passage occurs near the end of the first *Critique* in its Doctrine of Method, where Kant distinguishes the method appropriate to philosophy from that of mathematics. Both mathematics and philosophy deal with concepts, Kant explains, but only mathematics constructs concepts in *a priori* intuition, "and thus only mathematics has definitions" (*KrV* A729/B757). Because philosophical cognition, on the other hand, "confines itself solely to general concepts" without constructing them in *a priori* intuition, philosophy cannot, strictly speaking, give definitions (*KrV* A715/B743). In the strict sense, "*to define* properly means just to exhibit originally the exhaustive concept of a thing within its boundaries" (*KrV* A727/B755). What philosophy does instead of defining concepts, Kant says, is to explicate empirical concepts and to give expositions of *a priori* concepts. Kant's reservations about philosophical definitions of empirical concepts concern the uncertain relationship between them and words (*KrV* A731/B759). But he articulates his reservations about defining *a priori* concepts differently:

> For I can never be certain that the distinct representation of a (still confused) given concept has been exhaustively developed unless I know that it is adequate to its object. But since the concept of the latter, as it is given, can contain many obscure representations, which we pass by in our analysis though we always use them in application, the exhaustiveness of the analysis of my concept is always doubtful, and by many appropriate examples can only be made *problematically* but never *apodictically* certain. Instead of the expression "definition" I would rather use that of *exposition*, which is always cautious, and which the critic can accept as valid to a certain degree while yet retaining reservations about its exhaustiveness. (*KrV* A728–9/B756–7)

48

Immediately after saying this, however, Kant backtracks and allows that philosophy may, after all, arrive at definitions in the strict sense, but only via exposition: "philosophical definitions," he now says, "come about only as expositions of given concepts" (*KrV* A730/B758) but he adds that "in philosophy the definition, as distinctness made precise, must conclude rather than begin the work" (*KrV* A731/B759).

These remarks from the Doctrine of Method seem to accord well with Kant's procedure in the Transcendental Aesthetic, which is divided into sections providing what he calls expositions of the concepts of space and time, followed by sections presenting conclusions from these concepts, then an elucidation and general remarks. In the second edition, Kant distinguishes metaphysical and transcendental expositions of each concept,[1] which he explains as follows:

> I understand by *exposition* (*exposition*) the distinct (even if not complete) representation of that which belongs to a concept; but the exposition is *metaphysical* when it contains that which exhibits the concept *as given a priori*. (*KrV* B38)

> I understand by a *transcendental exposition* the explanation of a concept as a principle from which insight into the possibility of other synthetic *a priori* cognitions can be gained. For this aim it is required 1) that such cognitions actually flow from the given concept, and 2) that these cognitions are only possible under the presupposition of a given way of explaining this concept. (*KrV* B40)

Here, too, Kant is careful not to claim that his expositions are exhaustive, which seems to rule out interpreting the conclusions that immediately follow these sections as offering definitions in the strict sense specified in the Doctrine of Method. These conclusions are the claims that together go by the name "transcendental idealism" and arguably amount to the key philosophical position defended by Kant in the first *Critique*: Namely, that space and time are merely the subjective forms of human intuition; and that they are not properties, relations, or objective determinations of things in themselves that would remain if one abstracted from all subjective conditions of our intuition.[2]

Normally Kant is interpreted as drawing these transcendental idealist conclusions on the basis of arguments contained in the Aesthetic – either

---

[1] The first edition also calls them "expositions" (*KrV* A27) even though it does not draw this distinction.
[2] *KrV* A26/B42, *KrV* A32–4/B49–50. These conclusions are restated and discussed throughout the rest of the Aesthetic.

in the expositions immediately preceding them or in the elucidation and remarks immediately after them. This interpretation is supported by a passage in the Antinomy chapter, where Kant writes:

> We have sufficiently proved in the Transcendental Aesthetic that everything intuited in space or in time, hence all objects of an experience possible for us, are nothing but appearances, i.e., mere representations, which, as they are represented, as extended beings or series of alterations, have outside our thoughts no existence grounded in itself. This doctrine I call *transcendental idealism*.[3]

This passage likely refers specifically to the argument from geometry in the "general remarks" section that concludes the Aesthetic, because only in that argument does Kant use such strong language as to claim that transcendental idealism is not merely "a plausible hypothesis" but is "certain and indubitable."[4] The argument from geometry claims essentially that we know transcendental idealism is true on the grounds that we have certain knowledge of geometry, and that we could have certain knowledge of geometry only if we also knew that transcendental idealism is true.[5] But setting aside whatever philosophical merits or demerits the argument from geometry may have, this argument does not fit the method Kant ascribes to the first *Critique*, both in the *Prolegomena* and in the first *Critique* itself.

In the *Prolegomena*, Kant ascribes to the first *Critique* a synthetic or progressive method that "tries to develop cognition out of its original seeds without relying on any fact whatever" and that treats such facts as "having to be derived wholly *in abstracto* from concepts."[6] He contrasts this with the analytic or regressive method of the *Prolegomena*, which assumes that "some pure synthetic cognition *a priori* is actual and given, namely, *pure mathematics* and *pure natural science*," and derives the conditions of its possibility from the fact that we have such *a priori* cognition (*Prol* 4:75). Since the argument from geometry assumes that synthetic *a priori* cognition of geometry is given as a fact, it fits the method Kant ascribes to the *Prolegomena* but not the method he ascribes here to the first *Critique*. In the first *Critique's* Doctrine of Method, on the other hand, Kant does

---

[3] *KrV* A490–1/B518–19. Kant goes on to develop a separate, indirect proof of transcendental idealism (*KrV* A506/B534).

[4] *KrV* A46/B63. In the second edition, Kant suggests that the argument from geometry simply elaborates on the material in the Transcendental Exposition, which was also present in the first edition but not under that heading (*KrV* B64). The second edition also adds three new considerations "[f]or the confirmation of this theory" (*KrV* B66ff.), but the Antinomy passage quoted cannot refer to these since it was present in the first edition and they were not.

[5] See *KrV* A48–9/B66.   [6] *Prol* 4:274, 4:279. See *Prol* 4:263, 4:274–6, and *Prol* 4:279.

Transcendental Idealism in the B-Deduction

characterize the method of argument in the first *Critique* as relying on some given fact, but he describes that fact as "*possible experience*" and contrasts it with the "*mathemata*" or propositions demonstrated through the construction of concepts in mathematics (*KrV* A734–7/B762–5). What is distinctive to the method of argument appropriate to philosophy in contrast with mathematics, Kant says, is the following:

> it certainly erects secure principles, but not directly from concepts, but rather always only indirectly through the relation of these concepts to something entirely contingent, namely *possible experience*; since if this (something as object of possible experience) is presupposed, then they are of course apodictically certain, but in themselves they cannot even be cognized *a priori* (directly) at all. (*KrV* A737/B765)

If this passage applies to Kant's argument for transcendental idealism, which again is arguably the key philosophical position defended by Kant in the first *Critique*, then that argument cannot be contained entirely in the Aesthetic but must also go through Kant's arguments concerning the conditions of possible experience in the Analytic, the chief of which is the Transcendental Deduction. While the first *Critique* does contain arguments for transcendental idealism that Kant consistently distinguishes from the type of argument that is distinctive to the first *Critique*, such as the argument from geometry, these arguments must be supplementary to Kant's main argument for transcendental idealism.

Together, the remarks from the first *Critique's* Doctrine of Method that I have assembled here suggest that Kant's main argument for transcendental idealism has the following general form. The Metaphysical Expositions in the Aesthetic exhibit the concepts of space and time as given *a priori*, but the transcendental idealist conclusions that Kant states later in the Aesthetic follow only on the basis of arguments about the conditions of possible experience that are developed in the Analytic. Elsewhere, I have characterized the Metaphysical Expositions as issuing two promissory notes to be cashed in by arguments developed by Kant in the Analytic: Its first two numbered paragraphs claim that our representations of space and time are necessary conditions for determinate consciousness of appearances, while the last two numbered paragraphs claim that our representations of space and time are singular in the sense that we represent only one space-time (Rohlf 2013). In the same place, I claimed that in the Aesthetic Kant just asserts these promissory notes rather than arguing for them, but now I would rather say that the Metaphysical Expositions are one part phenomenology and one part promise of later arguments. Still, the phenomenological considerations adduced in the Metaphysical Expositions are not sufficient to establish transcendental idealism independently of Kant's arguments about the conditions of possible experience in the Analytic that finally cash in promissory notes issued in the Aesthetic.

The remainder of this chapter focuses on what I take to be Kant's argument for the second of these promissory notes issued in the Aesthetic – namely, that our representations of space and time are singular – which I claim is located in section 26 of the B-Deduction. To be clear, I am not claiming that section 26 is supposed to prove transcendental idealism on its own, but rather that it is one piece of an extended argument for transcendental idealism that begins in the Aesthetic and extends through the Analytic. Showing this will first require some discussion of the structure of the B-Deduction in the next section. I hope that what follows sheds light on both Kant's main argument for transcendental idealism and the importance of the B-Deduction to that argument.

2 The Structure of the B-Deduction

Paul Guyer has identified an argument in the B-Deduction that seems intended to provide independent support for transcendental idealism. According to Guyer, Kant argues in section 26 of the B-Deduction that "the unity of apperception or 'original consciousness' and with it the use of the categories are ... the condition of the possibility of the unity of space and time themselves" (Guyer 2010: 146). But Guyer does not find this line of argument promising and concludes that, "[a]t the very least, some additional explanation of the relation between the unity of individual consciousness and the unity of space and time is needed here to convince us that apperception, as the former, has anything to do with the latter."[7] My intention in the next section is to provide some additional explanation for this relationship between apperception and the unity of space and time. But this explanation will depend on how one interprets what the Deduction is supposed to prove, and what is left to prove in its second part once the first part is completed.

Guyer holds (and I agree) that "the goal of the Deduction is to prove that the categories necessarily apply to *all* our intuitions" (Guyer 2010: 121–2). But Guyer interprets Kant's transition from the first to the second parts of the B-Deduction as a move from an *abstract* to a *concrete* characterization of the categories as necessary conditions of apperception (Guyer

---

[7] Guyer 2010:147. See also Guyer 1987:153 and 371–83.

Transcendental Idealism in the B-Deduction 53

2010: 142–4). In doing so, Guyer rejects Dieter Henrich's view that the first part shows the categories to be necessary for *some* or one intuition, while the second part argues that they apply to *all* intuitions (Henrich 1982). There are indeed problems with Henrich's view, as Guyer and others have noted.[8] But in its place, Guyer develops an interpretation that seems to leave too little for the second part of the Deduction to do. The first part of the Deduction, as Guyer interprets it, appears to provide an abstract account that achieves the goal of the entire Deduction, while the second part is left simply to draw certain implications from the first part along with the concrete point that our intuition is spatio-temporal. For my purposes here, the important point is that the line of argument in section 26 that Guyer finds incoherent or insufficiently explained tries to do more than this, and taking it seriously requires giving a different account of the relation between the first and second parts of the Deduction.

I do not have room to go into details about Henrich's account here, but I think he must be more or less right that the transition from the first to the second part of the B-Deduction is not only a move from abstract to concrete (although it is that too), but also moves from arguing that the categories are necessary for some intuition(s) to arguing that they are necessary for all intuitions, as Kant's language in section 20 suggests. If the goal of the entire Deduction is (as Guyer also holds) to prove that the categories are necessary for all intuitions, then on such a reading only the second part of the Deduction will finally achieve this goal. The difficulty, however, in maintaining such a view is, of course, to explain *which* intuitions the first part of the Deduction has not yet shown the categories to be necessary for, and why not.

To explain this, I would like to invoke a well-known article by Lewis White Beck, which suggests that Kant's way of artificially isolating sensibility and understanding from one another prior to this point in the text created some ambiguities and misleading impressions that must be removed when Kant finally sets out in the second part of the Deduction to address the way these faculties function together to generate experience. For Beck, this led Kant to write specifically about experience and intuition in two different senses. What Beck calls "L-experience" refers to the raw material of sensible impressions without the conceptual and interpretive activities of the mind, while "K-experience" refers to knowledge or cognition of objects. And what Beck calls the "inspectional conception of intuition" refers to the raw material of sensible impressions, while the

---

[8] See Guyer 2010:142 and his references there.

"functional conception of intuition" refers to the unified presentation of an object as phenomenologically present (Beck 2002: 86–7). We can simplify Beck's point by mapping these two distinctions onto one another, since there is really one main ambiguity infecting Kant's language here: namely, between (1) sensible data that has *not* yet been processed by the understanding in any way, which I will call data$_1$ and (2) sensible data that *has* been processed in some way by the understanding, which I will call data$_2$.

Before unpacking this, let me assert that I think the B-Deduction is not finished after section 20 because Kant takes himself to have established by that point only that data$_2$ must conform to the categories, but he has not yet established this with respect to data$_1$. There might be data$_1$ that do not conform to the categories, for all the first part of the Deduction proves. Indeed, there might be sensory data (data$_1$) that our understanding *cannot* process into self-conscious experience. The aim of section 26 is then to rule this out and to show that even all data$_1$ must conform to the categories. So, to switch back to the language of intuition, only the second part of the Deduction establishes that *all* intuitions must conform to the categories. The first part establishes this with respect to some intuitions (namely, data$_2$), but not all of them (not data$_1$).

To begin unpacking this, let me follow Beck and many others in looking back to section 13 (which Kant himself does at the end of section 20) for insight into what remains to be achieved in the second part of the Deduction.[9] In section 13, Kant starts explaining what the entire Deduction is supposed to do, and he presents a counterfactual that the Deduction is charged with showing not to be a real possibility, even if it may be logically possible. The counterfactual, in Kant's words, is that

> appearances could after all be so constituted that the understanding would not find them in accord with the conditions of its unity, and everything would then lie in such confusion that, e.g., in the succession of appearances nothing would offer itself that would furnish a rule of synthesis and thus correspond to the concept of cause and effect, so that this concept would therefore be entirely empty, nugatory, and without significance. (*KrV* A90/B122–3)

Henry Allison calls this counterfactual scenario "the Kantian specter" (Allison 2004: 160). The worry expressed by Kant here, according to Allison, "is that the deliverances of sensibility might not correspond to the a priori rules of thought. Accordingly, the Kantian specter is one of

---

[9] Beck 2002:85. See also Ameriks 2003:65.

Transcendental Idealism in the B-Deduction

cognitive emptiness rather than of global skepticism" (Allison 2004: 160). So, for Allison, Kant is not worried simply that we might be self-conscious while some deliverances of sensibility escape our notice because they do not conform to the conditions of self-consciousness. Rather, Kant's aim in the Deduction is to rule out the possibility that we might not be able to generate self-consciousness at all.

While I concede that Allison's interpretation might fit this passage in section 13, I do not think it fits what Kant actually says and does in the second half of the Deduction. In section 21 and section 26, Kant repeatedly says that the goal of the second part of the Deduction is to show that the categories apply to *all* the deliverances of sensibility.[10] Allison may be right that Kant is not trying to refute global skepticism with this argument, since we already know from the first part of the Deduction that any sensible data of which we can become conscious – in my terminology, $data_2$ – must conform to the categories. But that's different from showing that we can become conscious of *all* sensible data, including all $data_1$, so that in principle none is left out of the unified whole of experience that our understanding makes possible. So, contrary to Allison, Kant is not trying to show that our experience is veridical. He's trying to show that it is, or at least in principle can be, *complete* – that there is nothing in nature of which we cannot in principle become aware. For a transcendental idealist, of course, this is not a claim about things in themselves. The claim is not that all of reality in itself can in principle appear to us, since such a claim would be obviously transcendent. Rather, the touchstone of nature for Kant is sensibility: that is, appearances, not things in themselves. So, on my view, the claim that Kant wants to establish in the second part of the Deduction is that our understanding makes out of all sensory data that we can ever encounter (all $data_1$ and $data_2$) a single, unified *whole* of experience, which Kant identifies with nature (considered formally, not in respect of its material content). The first part of the Deduction aims to show that the categories are conditions of self-consciousness; and the second part aims to show that they ground the fundamental laws of nature, which requires ruling out the possibility (articulated in section 13) that some sensible $data_1$ might not conform to the categories.

How, then, does Kant attempt to establish this claim in the second part of the Deduction? In section 21 Kant says that he intends to show "from the way in which the empirical intuition is given in sensibility that its unity

---

[10] See *KrV* B144–5, B159–61, and B163–5.

56 MICHAEL ROHLF

can be none other than the one the category prescribes."[11] Kant refers us to section 26 for his argument. Here is the key text:

> We have *forms* of outer as well as inner sensible intuition *a priori* in the representations of space and time, and the synthesis of the apprehension of the manifold of appearance must always be in agreement with the latter, since it can only occur in accordance with this form. But space and time are represented *a priori* not merely as *forms* of sensible intuition, but also as *intuitions* themselves (which contain a manifold), and thus with the determination of the *unity* of this manifold in them (see the Transcendental Aesthetic).[12] Thus even *unity of the synthesis* of the manifold, outside or within us, hence also a *combination* with which everything that is to be represented as determined in space or time must agree, is already given *a priori*, along with (not in) these intuitions, as condition of the synthesis of all *apprehension*. But this synthetic unity can be none other than that of the combination of the manifold of a given *intuition in general* in an original consciousness, in agreement with the categories, only applied to our *sensible intuition*. Consequently all synthesis, through which even perception itself becomes possible, stands under the categories, and since experience is cognition through connected perceptions, the categories are conditions of the possibility of experience, and are thus also valid *a priori* of all objects of experience.[13]

This passage is extremely dense. According to Béatrice Longuenesse, it amounts to:

> a revisiting, in light of the argument of part one, of "the manner in which things are given," namely the forms of intuition, space and time, that were expounded in the Transcendental Aesthetic. Kant's point is that space and time themselves, which have been described in the Transcendental Aesthetic as forms of intuition and pure intuitions, are now revealed to be the

---

[11] *KrV* B144–5. I take this use of "intuition" to be a reference to data₁, saying that the unity even of data that has not yet been processed by the understanding can be none other than what the category prescribes.

[12] Kant's note:

> Space, represented as *object* (as is really required in geometry), contains more than the mere form of intuition, namely *comprehension* of the manifold given in accordance with the form of sensibility in an *intuitive* representation, so that the *form of intuition* merely gives the manifold, but the *formal intuition* gives unity of the representation. In the Aesthetic I ascribed this unity merely to sensibility, only in order to note that it precedes all concepts, though to be sure it presupposes a synthesis, which does not belong to the senses but through which all concepts of space and time first become possible. For since through it (as the understanding determines the sensibility) space or time are first *given* as intuitions, the unity of this *a priori* intuition belongs to space and time, and not to the concept of the understanding. (section 24)

[13] *KrV* B160–1. Here I take "perception" to be used in the technical sense of data₁, while "experience" refers to data₂.

product of the "affection of sensibility by the understanding," namely by the unity of apperception as a capacity to judge. And so, by the mere fact of being given in space and time, all appearances are such that they are a priori in accordance with the categories, and thus eventually subsumable under them. (Longuenesse 2005:33)

In particular, Longuenesse reads Kant to be claiming here that "the unity, unicity (there is only one space and one time), and infinity of time and space" are "the product of *synthesis speciosa*, the transcendental synthesis of imagination," while "the qualitative features of spatiality and temporality depend on our sensibility, which thus provides 'first formal grounds' of the ordering of sensations that yields appearances" (Longuenesse 2005: 34–5). As I understand her interpretation, Longuenesse is not attributing to Kant the view that the transcendental synthesis of imagination produces conscious perception of the whole of space and time as actually infinite, but rather as limitless, because representing boundaries to space or time would undermine the conditions of self-consciousness. In other words, the result of the transcendental synthesis of imagination is that everything of which we ever can become conscious – in my terminology, all $data_1$ and $data_2$ – is represented *as* occurring in a single time, unlimited in both future and past; and as related in and to a single space that likewise is unlimited in all its dimensions. As Longuenesse puts it, the unity, unicity, and infinity of time and space "are features we imagine or anticipate and thus project as preconditions of the unity of experience."[14]

Now one could accept that the unity, unicity, and infinity of space and time are conditions of self-conscious experience without accepting Longuenesse's view that they are products of the transcendental synthesis of imagination. Again, for Longuenesse the transcendental synthesis of imagination produces the pure intuitions of time and space, and these features of them, which are conditions of experience. This transcendental synthesis in some sense precedes the empirical synthesis of apprehension, which is the ongoing process of generating specific unities of sensible data within the single space-time, and which occurs in accordance with or is a specification of the transcendental synthesis. In her words: "the unity of apperception, as a capacity to judge, generates the representation of the unity and unicity of space and time, as the condition for any specific act of judging at all, thus prior to any specific synthesis according to the

---

[14] Longuenesse 2005:34. This addresses Guyer's worry that if apperception were a condition of the unity of space and time themselves, then we would not represent the scope of space and time as extending beyond the scope of our own unified consciousness. See Guyer 2010:146–7.

58 MICHAEL ROHLF

categories, let alone any subsumption under the categories."[15] But Allison and Guyer both reject this view, while accepting that for Kant it is a condition of experience that space and time have the features that Longuenesse attributes to the transcendental synthesis of imagination. Allison denies not only that the transcendental synthesis of imagination plays this role, but also that it is distinct from the empirical synthesis of apprehension in the way Longuenesse claims it is. He writes the following about Kant's example later in section 26 of the perception of a house:

> Kant's point here is that the perception of a house, which tokens a three-dimensional object, is conditioned by the determination of the space it is perceived to occupy. It is not, however, a matter of two distinct syntheses: an *a priori* or transcendental synthesis that determines the space and an empirical one that determines the contours and extent of what is perceived in it. It is rather that these are related as the formal and material aspects of one synthesis. The transcendental synthesis of the imagination is the form of the empirical synthesis of apprehension in the sense that the apprehension or perception of a house is governed by the conditions of the determination of the space it is perceived to occupy. (Allison 2004:196–7)

Guyer, too, prefers to emphasize the second part of section 26 where this example of the perception of a house occurs (*KrV* B162), which he reads as suggesting an alternative to the account of the first part that I quoted earlier (*KrV* B160–1). According to this account, Guyer writes, "the categories are necessary not for the representation of the unity of space and time as such but rather for the representation, or judgment, of determinate objects of any kind *in* space and time" (Guyer 2010:147). To be fair, Longuenesse (whom Guyer is not addressing in his article) also does not believe *the categories* are necessary for representing the unity of space and time as such. She reads B160–1 as saying that *apperception* is necessary for representing the unity of space and time as such, and that apperception is distinct from and prior to any use of the categories.[16] But presumably, Guyer would agree with Allison that, at least according to the account Guyer favors at B162, both the transcendental and empirical syntheses proceed according to the categories, and that the empirical synthesis does not presuppose the completion of the transcendental synthesis in the way Longuenesse believes it does.

I think Longuenesse's account is closer to the truth. To see why, let us return once more to section 13 and to my earlier disagreements with

---

[15] Longuenesse 2005:36. See also Longuenesse 2005:35.
[16] Longuenesse 2005:36. See also Longuenesse 2005:35.

Guyer and Allison about what the second part of the Deduction is supposed to show. If it is supposed to show, as I claimed, that the categories ground the laws of nature, because our understanding makes a single, unified *whole* of experience out of all sensible data that we can ever encounter (all data$_1$ and data$_2$) – which had not yet been shown by the first part of the Deduction – then clearly the argument would fall well short of this goal on Guyer's and Allison's interpretation of section 26. Their interpretation might explain how (again to use Kant's example) we represent the unity of the space in which we perceive a house, or any other individual perceptions. But it does not even attempt to account for the *a priori* representation of the whole of space and time as unified, or (to use the language of the Aesthetic) that it is an infinite given magnitude. So Longuenesse is right to attribute such an account to Kant at B160–1 and to distinguish the transcendental synthesis of the imagination from the empirical synthesis that it conditions. Indeed, and here is my main point in this section, Kant's overall argument in the B-Deduction, interpreted as I have argued it should be, simply could not work and would not even make sense as an argument unless it involves the claim that apperception produces the unity and singularity of our representations of space and time. In other words, the B-Deduction could succeed only by cashing in the second promissory note from the Aesthetic that I identified in the previous section.

3 Formal Intuitions as a Condition of Time-Determination

Does the B-Deduction succeed or does it merely reassert the second promissory note from the Aesthetic, namely that our representations of space and time are unified and singular, and pass on to the Principles the task of finally proving this claim? I cannot hope to settle this question here. But in this final section let me defend an interpretation of how the claim I take Kant to be making in section 26 is different from and presupposed by some other claims he argues for in the Principles.

I propose that we interpret Kant as claiming at B160–1 that possessing formal intuitions of time and space is a condition of being able to assign specific time-determinations to our representations, which in turn is a condition of self-consciousness. Kant emphasizes from the first part of the Deduction through the Analogies that it is a condition of self-consciousness that we can assign specific time-determinations to our representations: for example, A represents something happening at T_1, B at T_2, and so on. But assigning specific time-determinations to our representations requires that we have a way of measuring time, a single standard by reference to which we can assign specific time-determinations to our representations. Even if our sensations, thoughts, and other representations originally occur in or are received in some temporal order, becoming conscious of that or indeed of any temporal order among representations requires that we use some sort of standard for measuring temporal relations. As Kant writes at the very beginning of the Deduction in section 15, "we can represent nothing as combined in the object without having previously combined it ourselves," and "all combination ... is an action of the understanding" (*KrV* B130). Representing temporal relations is a form of combination and requires some internal, subjective measure for assigning specific time-determinations to particular representations. I propose that the single, unified, and boundless intuition of time plays this role of acting as the abstract standard for measuring particular temporal relations. That is the sense in which, contrary to the interpretation of section 26 shared by Guyer and Allison, the empirical synthesis of apprehension is conditioned by a distinct and completed transcendental synthesis of the imagination. This transcendental synthesis produces the internal standard for measuring time in general (namely, the formal intuition of time), which is presupposed by all assigning of specific time-determinations to particular representations in the empirical synthesis of apprehension.

This argument can be applied to space as well, using Kant's point at B154 that we can represent time only by drawing a line in space. If we need a pure intuition for measuring time, and yet we can represent such a measure for time only by making reference to space, then it follows that we need a pure intuition of space, too, that is singular, unified, and boundless for all the same reasons. But I do not have room to develop the application of this argument to space here and will focus my remaining remarks on its application to time.

To be clear, I am not claiming that Kant regards the formal intuition of time as a specific metric for measuring temporal relations, such as a second or a centiday. At no point in Kant's argument – not in the Deduction, the Schematism, the Axioms of Intuition, etc. – does he descend to the level of specific metrics for measuring temporal relations, except by way of example.[17] Rather, I am claiming that Kant regards the formal intuition of time as a condition of assigning schemata to categories in the Schematism chapter, which in turn is a condition of deploying schematized

---

[17] See, for example, his reference to the decimal or base ten numeral system at *KrV* A78/B104.

categories to assign specific time-determinations to empirical representations, as discussed in the Principles section. What the formal intuition of time supplies that makes possible these more specific forms of time determination is the bare representation of unity as applied to time. This exquisitely abstract point is emphasized by Kant at *KrV* B160: "space and time are represented *a priori* not merely as *forms* of sensible intuition, but also as *intuitions* themselves (which contain a manifold), and thus with the determination of the *unity* of this manifold in them." In the footnote to this sentence he adds that "the *form of intuition* merely gives the manifold, but the *formal intuition* gives unity of the representation." Thus, all the work being done here is accomplished by adding unity to the form of time, which results not just in the representation of some unified time but of Time (that is, all of time) as a unity, or again it results in representing the singularity and unicity (as Longuenesse says) of time. The claim is that we need to represent time abstractly as a singular whole before (logically speaking) we can carve it up into aspects (schematism) or assign particular times to empirical representations. That is why, Kant says, that the representation of unity in the formal intuition of time is a "condition of the synthesis of all *apprehension*," in which specific time-determinations are assigned to our representations (*KrV* 161).

A critic of my interpretation might object that Kant assigns to the mathematical principles – namely, the Axioms of Intuition and Anticipations of Perception – something like the task I am imputing to the Deduction at B160–1. This critic may concede that Kant vaguely waves his hand in this direction in section 26 but maintain that B160–1 does no more than issue (or, if my interpretation of the Aesthetic from the first section of this chapter is granted, reassert) a promissory note that he finally argues for at length only in the Principles. The mathematical principles in particular, as Kant later summarizes, aim to show of appearances that "both their intuition and the real in their perception could be generated in accordance with rules of a mathematical synthesis, hence how in both cases numerical magnitudes and, with them, the determination of the appearance as magnitude, could be used" (*KrV* A178/B221). Focusing only on the Axioms of Intuition, Kant's task there is to argue that the categories of quantity guarantee both that the concept of number arises and that every intuition is measurable by numerical concepts. So, according to this objection, Kant must regard the standard for measuring time as fixed not by apperception in the Deduction but rather in the Axioms by the categories of quantity, whose schema, he says, "is *number*, which is a representation that summarizes the successive addition of one

62 MICHAEL ROHLF

(homogeneous) unit to another. Thus, number is nothing other than the unity of the synthesis of the manifold of a homogeneous intuition in general."[18]

To this objection I reply, first, by appealing to another passage from section 15:

> Combination is the representation of the *synthetic* unity of the manifold. The representation of this unity cannot, therefore, arise from the combination; rather, by being added to the representation of the manifold, it first makes the concept of combination possible. This unity, which precedes all concepts of combination *a priori*, is not the former category of unity (section 10); for all categories are grounded on logical functions in judgments, but in these combination, thus the unity of given concepts, is already thought. The category therefore already presupposes combination. We must therefore seek this unity (as qualitative, section 12) someplace higher, namely in that which itself contains the ground of the unity of different concepts in judgments, and hence of the possibility of the understanding, even in its logical use. (*KrV* B130–1)

This passage distinguishes the role of apperception from that of all categories and specifically the quantitative category of unity, which Kant says presupposes apperception. Second, in the Axioms, Kant invokes the categories of quantity to explain "empirical consciousness . . . of a determinate space or time," not the generation of pure, formal intuitions as standards for measuring space or time in general (*KrV* B202). Thus, the task of the Axioms aligns with the interpretation shared by Guyer and Allison of B162–3 but not with the claims of B160–1 as I have interpreted them. Third, it is consistent with my interpretation of the abstract claim of B160–1 that Kant would follow it up with examples (at B162–3) at a lower level of abstraction that track arguments about specific categories that he develops only later in the Principles. But the actual argument of the Axioms is an application of, and thus depends on, the abstract claim of B160–1. The Axioms argue that apprehending an intuition as a unified whole presupposes an act of synthesis, and now we learn that the categories of quantity are involved in composing a unified intuition out of the manifold of sensory data. Apparently, Kant means that we fix a unit by means of the category of unity, successively add units of data to one another by means of the category of plurality, and finally arrive at a whole intuition by means of the category of totality. As the quoted passage from

---

[18] *KrV* A142–3/B182. The passage continues: "because I generate time itself in the apprehension of the intuition." I understand this clause to mean that I generate empirical consciousness of time in the empirical synthesis of apprehension.

Transcendental Idealism in the B-Deduction 63

section 15 says, however, the first step of this argument in the Axioms presupposes a higher unity that obviously refers to apperception; and since the argument goes on to invoke successive synthesis, it also presupposes the application of apperception to the form of time. Thus, Kant's argument in the Axioms depends on and cannot replace his claim at B160–1 that we have a pure, formal intuition of time.

Moreover, we find further evidence in favor of my interpretation of B160–1, its importance in the Deduction, and the dependence of Kant's argument in the Principles on it, by considering the relationship between the mathematical principles and the Analogies of Experience, which Kant calls dynamical principles. He writes, "[i]n the application of the pure concepts of the understanding to possible experience the use of their synthesis is either *mathematical* or *dynamical*: for it pertains partly merely to the *intuition*, partly to the *existence* of an appearance in general" (*KrV* A160/B199). In other words, the mathematical principles describe how perception of intuitions is generated; and, on this basis, the dynamical principles describe how we relate these intuitions to existing objects understood as appearances. This distinction maps onto the one Kant draws in section 24 of the B-Deduction between two levels of cognitive processing: What he there calls the figurative synthesis (i.e., the empirical synthesis of apprehension)[19] turns out to involve using the categories of quantity and quality to generate perception of intuitions, as described by the Axioms and Anticipations; and the intellectual synthesis turns out to use categories of relation to generate self-conscious experience of objects (as appearances) distinct from these intuitions of them, as described by the Analogies.[20] Kant argues in the Axioms and Anticipations, in effect, that the output of the figurative synthesis is unified, empirical intuitions (and sensations) with both extensive and intensive magnitude, and that the way these are generated guarantees that they can be measured mathematically. But from the Deduction we remember that the figurative synthesis by itself is not sufficient for self-consciousness, which also requires the next level of cognitive processing. At this level, the intellectual synthesis, we interpret the output of the figurative synthesis as perceptions of existing objects that are distinct from our intuitions of them. This is Kant's concern in the first part of the B-Deduction, especially sections 16–19: Namely, to argue that

---

[19] The figurative synthesis seems to include both the transcendental synthesis of the imagination and the empirical synthesis of apprehension, or both are figurative syntheses. I have been arguing that these should be regarded as distinct syntheses and refer here only to the latter.

[20] *KrV* B151–2. See also *KrV* A158/B197.

64   MICHAEL ROHLF

becoming conscious of the identity of the self in all of our representations requires interpreting them as representations of objects distinct from us that interact in accordance with constant laws.

In the Deduction, Kant describes these laws generally as the categories, without naming particular (sets of) categories or distinguishing between categories that are operative at one level of processing and those that are operative at the other level. This distinction is made only later in the Principles. But Kant is often criticized for giving the misleading impression in the Deduction that all of the categories are operative at both levels of processing, as if his strategy for averting the counterfactual or specter articulated in section 13 was to argue that intuitions are generated in the figurative synthesis in accordance with the very same categories that we use to think them in the intellectual synthesis. Allison, for example, concludes that the Deduction is "at best only partly successful" because only its second part averts the specter of section 13 and this part turns out to apply only to the mathematical categories, as we learn later in the Principles; thus, since the first part of the Deduction turns out to concern the relational categories and does not avert the specter of section 13 as it applies to them, on Allison's view Kant fails to prove in the Deduction itself that all of the categories are objectively valid conditions of experience, and leaves it to the Analogies to prove this of the relational categories (Allison 2004:200).

But my interpretation of B160–1 explains why Kant thought the Deduction does prove the objective validity of all the categories. On my reading, the Axioms and Anticipations aim to show that our categories of relation can get a grip on all possible perception of intuitions *because* they are measurable magnitudes. In short, if I can measure the size of one intuition, then I can compare, correlate, *relate* it to other intuitions of the same or different size. If I can measure the intensity of a sensation, then I can compare it to the intensity of another sensation that I receive from the same object or different objects and draw inferences about the properties of objects through their *influence* on me.[21] Thus, in the Axioms and Anticipations, Kant is not only providing support for the science of applied mathematics but also explaining how he averts the specter from section 13: We know *a priori* that the categories of relation can get a grip on all possible perception of intuitions because they are generated by the categories of quantity and quality in such a way that they are mathematically

---

[21] See *KrV* A143/B182–3.

measurable. We ourselves must carry out such (perhaps implicit) measurements in order to make empirical judgments about existing objects that are related to but distinct from both our perceptions and one another. But for my purposes here, the key point is that this argument, linking the justification for the objective validity of the categories of relation to that of quantity and quality, depends on B160–1 having already established the unity and singularity of our representation(s) of time (and space), for two reasons. The first reason is again the abstract point that assigning time-determinations to representations presupposes a standard for measuring time. But, second, in order to draw inferences about the properties of objects from their influence on me, I must assume a single (space-)time in which all of my actual and possible representations can be related both to one another and to independently existing objects. It would not suffice to presuppose only the unity of the (space-)time in which I perceive the determinate object at hand, as Guyer and Allison would have it, because I am drawing inferences about objects whose locations in (space-)time may be different from those of my representations of them and which I do not know prior to drawing these inferences. For example, the feeling of warmth on my skin now was caused by light emitted from the surface of the sun more than eight minutes ago at a distance of around 150 million kilometers from the earth. Before inferring from this feeling of warmth to its cause, I do not know at what location in (space-)time to place it, and drawing such an inference requires me to assume that all objects that can influence me exist in a single (space-)time together with all of my representations of them.

So, I conclude that Kant's argument in the Principles cannot establish, but rather depends on his claim in section 26 of the B-Deduction, that our representations of time and space are unified and singular. Earlier I argued that the success of the B-Deduction depends on this claim, which also cashes in a promissory note in Kant's extended argument for transcendental idealism. Although I have not argued that the B-Deduction succeeds or defended transcendental idealism, I have tried to show that these arguments are linked in a deeper way than is typically noticed and to develop a plausible interpretation of the crucial claim on which both depend.

CHAPTER 4

Kant's A priori *Principle of Judgments of Taste*

Jennifer Dobe

There is still wide-ranging disagreement about a basic feature of Kant's *Critique of the Power of Judgment*, namely, what the *a priori* principle of judgments of taste *is*. This is not true of the *Critique of Pure Reason*: We know what the categories are, even if there are disagreements about whether Kant successfully proves that they are *a priori* and universally valid. And in the *Groundwork of the Metaphysics of Morals*, while there may be disagreements about whether one formulation of the moral law has priority over the others and is that from which the others are derived, there is no disagreement when identifying those formulations. We might fault Kant for not being clearer about such a fundamental issue in the *Critique of the Power of Judgment*. What I shall argue in this chapter, however, is that commentators have overlooked or dismissed out of hand what Kant explicitly identifies as the principle because it does not seem to be something that could be a principle at all: namely, our shared cognitive nature insofar as our imaginations are *predisposed* to be attuned to our understandings' need for unity.[1] On my reading, we judge on the basis of this *a priori* yet subjective and universally valid principle only when we judge on the basis of the harmonious play of our cognitive faculties.[2]

---

[1] In what follows, I clarify the relationship between the principle so identified and the feeling of pleasure, as well as explain how judgments of taste are nonetheless distinguished from all other sorts of judgments (cognition, judgments of the agreeable and judgments of the good [morally good, useful, perfect]).

[2] According to Paul Guyer's metacognitive approach, when the cognitive faculties harmonize with one another,

> The understanding's underlying objective or interest in unity is being satisfied in a way that goes beyond anything required for or dictated by satisfaction of the determinate concept or concepts on which mere identification of the object depends. A beautiful object can always be recognized to be an object of some determinate kind, but our experience of it always has even more unity and coherence than is required for it to be a member of that kind, or has a kind of unity and coherence that is not merely a necessary condition for our classification of it." (Guyer 2006a: 183)

Kant's A priori *Principle of Judgments of Taste* 67

In an effort to support my view I shall spend the bulk of this chapter carving out conceptual space for it within the terrain of dominant alternative accounts. Setting my candidate in relation to those offered by Henry Allison, Rachel Zuckert, and Paul Guyer will enable me to highlight weaknesses in the alternatives that mine can overcome. It will become clear the degree to which I am indebted to Guyer's account even as I depart from his in a few significant ways. In closing, I point to the promising implications of my view. I suggest that this way of understanding Kant's *a priori* principle helps us to deal with interpretive challenges in the Dialectic of Taste and to clarify the Resolution of the Antinomy. In addition, by recognizing the centrality of Kant's conception of human nature to his theory of taste, we are better positioned to grasp the third *Critique*'s political significance.[3]

1   A New Candidate Hidden in Plain Sight

Before turning to competing alternatives to the principle I propose, I should clarify a few issues and provide textual evidence so as to dispel some initial worries about this unusual candidate. On the view I am defending, it is a merely empirical, psychological fact that *my* imagination is predisposed to be attuned to *my* understanding's need for unity. In other words, if it were the case that no other individual shared this cognitive nature, then the predisposed attunement of these two faculties could only

---

Guyer's view allows us to acknowledge concepts at work in the perception of art and natural beauty, but recognizes that thanks in part to the imagination, the unification that is "felt" goes *beyond* the unification provided by any of those concepts. He distinguishes his metacognitive approach from what he calls "the precognitive approach" of Dieter Henrich, Donald Crawford, Ralf Meerbote, Rudolf Makkreel, Hannah Ginsborg, and his own earlier view, as well as from "the multi-cognitive approach" of Gerhard Seel, Fred Rush, and Henry Allison.

[3] As is well known, Hannah Arendt maintains that Kant's theory of taste reflects a new political insight and that the third *Critique* "should have become the book that otherwise is missing in Kant's great work," namely, his political philosophy (Arendt 1992:9). According to Arendt's reading of Kant's theory of taste, "sociability is the very origin, not the goal, of man's humanity" and thus "sociability is the very essence of men insofar as they are of this world only" (Arendt 1992:74). Arendt argues that his account is to be distinguished "from all those theories that stress human interdependence as dependence on our fellow men for our *needs* and *wants*. Kant stresses that at least one of our *mental faculties*, the faculty of judgment, presupposes the presence of others. And this mental faculty is not just what we terminologically call judgment; bound up with it is the notion that 'feelings and emotions [*Empfindungen*] are regarded as of worth only insofar as they can be generally communicated'; that is, bound up with judgment is our whole soul apparatus, so to speak" (Arendt 1992:74). My account, which identifies our shared cognitive nature as the *a priori* principle of judgments of taste, is not only consonant with Arendt's reading but also lends it support by illuminating the basis for the political insight Arendt ascribes to Kant.

68   JENNIFER DOBE

be a merely subjective basis of my judgment, and any experience of a harmonious play of the faculties could only serve as the basis for a judgment of the agreeable. Only if the imagination and understanding are attuned to one another – not only in me, but also in everyone else – are we able to experience a harmonious play of the faculties in response to the same representations and thus to judge aesthetically on the basis of an *a priori* principle. In that case, my own cognitive nature (the predisposition of the imagination to be attuned to the understanding) serves as a universal standard or principle precisely because this nature is shared by all judges. Thus, what makes the attunement of my cognitive faculties a principle is also what accounts for its correctness, or validity: the fact that this nature is universally shared. As a subjective yet universally valid principle it has no objective validity. Now, if we could know prior to the experience of universal agreement in judgment that it is universally shared by all subjects, then this principle (our shared cognitive nature) would be *a priori*. Though I cannot adequately defend my reading of Kant's Deduction of judgments of taste here, I take this important argument to be drawing the following conclusions: We can know *a priori* that everyone's imagination is predisposed to be attuned to the understanding, and, for this reason, our shared cognitive nature can be conceived of as an *a priori* and universally valid subjective principle of judgment.[4]

Admittedly, it is an odd candidate for a principle, for our shared cognitive nature (the imagination's predisposition to meet the understanding's requirement of unity) is not a discursive basis for judgments. But Kant unabashedly acknowledges that the basis of our judgments of beauty is not a concept, insisting instead that it is inaccessible to cognition.[5] While this attunement is not accessible to cognition, it *is* accessible to consciousness, at least indirectly. The predisposition of these faculties to be attuned to one another is manifested in aesthetic experience; in response to

---

[4] I defend my reading of the Deduction in Dobe 2010. The argument endorses Guyer's appeal to Kant's informative footnote to the Deduction that helps to clarify an implicit move in the Deduction: Being able to *communicate* our cognitions with one another entails that we possess all that is required for making correct (universally valid) judgments of taste (because taste simply requires the cognitive faculties we already possess and not some separate faculty of taste). This point supports my conclusion that the *sensus communis* conceived of as a "faculty" of taste is simply the power of judgment in its reflective use. Based on the argument I will be providing here, the *sensus communis* conceived of as a "feeling" may be identified as the universally communicable feeling of pleasure in judgments of taste.

[5] In the *First Introduction,* Kant insists that "since a merely subjective condition of a judgment does not permit a determinate concept of that judgment's determining ground, this can only be given in the feeling of pleasure, so that the aesthetic judgment is always a judgment of reflection" (*HN* 20:225).

Kant's A priori *Principle of Judgments of Taste*   69

certain forms, these faculties achieve a harmonious play, or heightened agreement in the absence of a unifying concept. In other words, they become active in accordance with their nature – their natural, predisposed attunement to one another.[6] When they are active in accordance with their natural attunement to one another, we experience pleasure. The only way we can have access to the attuned nature of these faculties is by "sensing" it when they harmonize and we feel pleasure for that reason.

At this point it should become clear that my view commits me to an account of pleasure more akin to Zuckert's than Guyer's. If I were to accept Guyer's account, according to which pleasures distinguish themselves only by way of their causal history, then I could not claim that my cognitive nature is in fact serving as the basis of my judgment of taste. For on his view, there is nothing a feeling of pleasure possesses that distinguishes it from any other feeling of pleasure; because of this, any judgment made solely on the basis of a feeling of pleasure (no matter what its causal history may be) could only ever be a judgment of the agreeable. My view depends upon an account of pleasure that allows the very identity of the feeling to include the harmonious play that brings it about. I believe this is precisely what Kant attempts to make room for when he describes pleasure in the *First Introduction*: "Pleasure is a state of the mind in which a representation is in agreement with itself, as a ground, either merely for preserving this state itself (for the state of the powers of the mind reciprocally promoting each other in a representation preserves itself), or for producing its object" (*HN* 20:231–2). That we "linger" with an object – rather than consume it or use it for some purpose, for instance – is an indication to us as judges that harmonious play is taking place. Kant seems to be at pains to point out that this feeling of pleasure can feel different to us; it can apparently feel communicable insofar as it feels active rather than passive and feels like it serves as its own ground: "Only where the imagination in its freedom arouses the understanding, and the latter, without concepts, sets the imagination into a regular play is the representation communicated, not as a thought, but as the inner feeling of a

---

[6] The important point for my argument is that the attunement of these faculties is evidence of a *natural* attunement or predisposition; so even if Kant characterizes the predisposition in slightly different terms (such as the cognitive faculties being naturally attuned *to each other* or some other variation), what is crucial for my account is that this attunement is conceived of as *natural*. This means that my proposal for a principle of judgments of taste is potentially consistent not only with Guyer's metacognitive approach to the harmonious play but also Melissa Zinkin's view that the harmonious play involves the judging of intensive as opposed to extensive magnitudes (see Zinkin 2006).

70   JENNIFER DOBE

purposive state of mind" (*KU* 5:276).[7] At the same time, because we can also be mistaken about whether the feeling *is* in fact communicable, I commit myself to the view that the identity of a feeling of pleasure can include the harmonious play even if it does not feel communicable. In doing so, I simply align myself with recent Kantian scholarship on pleasure that recognizes the pleasure felt through the harmonious play of the faculties as a complex state of mind rather than a "brute" sensation.[8] The fact that, as Kant says, it "strengthens and reproduces itself" (*KU* 5:222) suggests that the very identity of this state of mind could include both the pleasure and the ground of that pleasure (its own activity), whether or not we *feel* it to be different from consumptive or other sorts of pleasures. Thus, such an understanding of the complex identity of a feeling of pleasure makes room for the possibility of mistaken judgments: It is possible to feel pleasure that we think is universally communicable without it being so, and to feel a pleasure that we do not think is universally communicable even though it is in fact universally communicable. We will return to this issue subsequently.

Finally, let me offer some textual evidence for the candidate I am proposing. After providing his Deduction of judgments of taste, Kant remarks that "in the aesthetic power of judgment one subsumes [the representation of the object] under a relation that is merely a matter of sensation, that of the imagination and the understanding reciprocally attuned to each other in the represented form of the object" (*KU* 5:291). In Remark I after the Resolution of the Antinomy, he argues,

> since the beautiful must not be judged in accordance with concepts, but rather in accordance with the purposive disposition of the imagination for its correspondence with the faculty of concepts in general, it is not a rule or precept but only that which is merely nature in the subject ... which is to serve as the subjective standard of that aesthetic but unconditioned purposiveness in beautiful art, which is supposed to make a rightful claim to please everyone. (*KU* 5:344)

Section 58 of the Dialectic notes that "nature has the property of containing an occasion for us to perceive the inner purposiveness in the relationship of our mental powers in the judging of certain of its products" (*KU* 5:350). And in section 59, he observes that "taste ... represent[s] the imagination even in its freedom as purposively determinable for the

---

[7] Kant characterizes taste as "the faculty for judging that which makes our feeling in a given representation *universally communicable* without the mediation of a concept" (*KU* 5:295).

[8] See, for instance, Ginsborg 1997; Allison 2001; Zuckert 2002; and Zinkin 2006.

understanding" (*KU* 5:354). Earlier, in preparation for the Deduction, he explains that "the judgment of taste must rest on a mere sensation of the reciprocally animating imagination in its freedom and the understanding with its lawfulness" (*KU* 5:287); and that "taste ... contains a principle of subsumption ... of the faculty of intuitions or presentations (i.e., of the imagination) under the faculty of concepts (i.e., the understanding), insofar as the former in its freedom is in harmony with the latter in its lawfulness" (*KU* 5:287). He argues that the same principle grounds the production of art: "Yet since without a preceding rule a product can never be called art, nature in the subject (and by means of the disposition of its faculties) must give the rule to art" (*KU* 5:307); "in products of genius nature (that of the subject), not a deliberate end, gives the rule to art" (*KU* 5:344).

If we take Kant at his word, we judge beauty on the basis of the natural, predisposed attunement of the imagination and understanding to one another. When we pronounce something beautiful (and thereby demand agreement) because, in reflecting on a representation, we have a feeling of pleasure that feels universally communicable and is in fact brought about through the harmonious play of the faculties, we are in fact judging on the basis of this universally shared basis. It is the Deduction's task to justify our demand of agreement by arguing that we can know (prior to any experience of agreement among judges) that that natural, predisposed attunement is universally shared. Let me now consider three prominent alternatives.

2 Henry Allison

Allison's view identifies the *a priori* principle of judgments of taste as the power of judgment's *requirement* or norm that we proceed from intuitions to concepts. He maintains, "in a judgment of taste, representations are subsumed under the condition[s] of subsumption..."; "this condition turns out to be nothing other than the harmonious interplay of the imagination and the understanding" (Allison 2001:170). The power of judgment's norm is identified as *a priori* because, in the Deduction, it is shown to be an *a priori* principle of *cognition*. Both cognitive judgments and pure judgments of taste fulfill this basic requirement; what distinguishes judgments of taste is that they are reflective judgments in which concepts do not constrain the imagination's activity of unification. Our feeling of pleasure is our sensing of the fulfillment of the power of judgment's requirement or norm. For Allison, then, the *a priori* principle

JENNIFER DOBE

of judgments of taste is a necessary, but not a sufficient basis of these judgments. What is needed, in addition to fulfilling the power of judgment's requirement, is that these judgments fulfill this requirement "in a certain way," namely, in the absence of a concept and thus as reflective as opposed to determining judgments.

With the distinctions between these conditions in mind, we can see more clearly what Allison takes the aim of Kant's Deduction to be. According to Allison, the Deduction is only meant to "establish the normativity of the norm" (Allison 2001:172): in other words, to remind us that the power of judgment's requirement (that we move from intuitions to concepts) is a necessary condition of cognition.[9] That is, the Deduction shows that the norm of judgment, whose fulfillment is sensed (through pleasure) in pure judgments of taste, is a necessary condition of cognition. Successfully grounding the normativity of the norm does not justify particular judgments of taste, for it is always possible that we are not making a *pure* judgment of taste. The Deduction on Allison's reading only defends the possibility of pure judgments of taste by showing that the norm, which they fulfill in their own peculiar way, is a necessary requirement of cognition. Additionally, the aesthetic judgment's demand that others agree is qualified: I am only justified in demanding the agreement of others if I am actually making a pure judgment of taste.

Allison admits that his reading limits the aim and weakens the force of a successful Deduction considerably (Allison 2001:179). Indeed, we might think that the Deduction, so conceived, really sidesteps the question at the heart of aesthetic judgment: how to justify the demand that others agree with us, a demand whose justification seems to require that we ground both the normativity of this norm *and* the universality of the peculiar way in which that norm is supposed to be fulfilled in judgments of taste (namely, through harmonious play of the faculties in reflective judging in the absence of a concept). In other words, as Guyer has argued, wouldn't the successful justification of our judgments of taste require that we also demonstrate that everyone is capable of the harmonious play of the faculties and of responding to the same representations in this peculiar way?[10] On Allison's reading, the most the Deduction can do is to identify an *a priori* principle that reflective judging must meet in order to be a pure

---

[9] Allison states, "[T]he 'deduction' of §38 then affirms the universal validity of this *principle* of taste on the grounds that it is also a condition of cognition. Thus, . . . taste is grounded indirectly in the conditions of cognition by showing that its governing principle has that status" (Allison 2001: 177).

[10] In "Dialogue," Allison believes Guyer confuses the *quid facti* and *quid juris* by including justification in his characterization of the principle of taste. But for Guyer, what it means to

Kant's A priori *Principle of Judgments of Taste*

judgment, but a Deduction cannot assure us that everyone's cognitive faculties are even capable of reaching that standard reflectively and in response to the same objects. If even a successful Deduction on Allison's reading cannot preclude the possibility that some individuals are unable to meet the standard of judgment reflectively or even preclude the possibility that *pure* judgments could conflict with one another, then we have enough reason to look elsewhere for the *a priori* principle of taste. Allison attempts to answer this objection but does not ultimately succeed.

He begins with the insistence that the question we have raised about the possibility of a conflict in pure judgments of taste can be reduced to the question of whether a pure judgment of taste could be "erroneous" (Allison 2001:189). (As I indicated, this is only part of our concern, since we are also worried that some people may not even be capable of achieving the standard of judgment reflectively.) Allison points out that if one is "speaking with a universal voice," as the Fourth Moment purports, then "one's judgment ... cannot err"; so "since speaking with a universal voice is equivalent to making a pure judgment of taste, it likewise follows that a pure judgment of taste cannot err" (Allison 2001:189–90). The argument begs the question. That a person making a pure judgment of taste "speaks with a universal voice" (by definition) does not entail that she is justified in doing so. Being justified in doing so seems to require the Deduction to show that every person's cognitive faculties are capable of reflectively reaching agreement (through harmonious play) in response to the same objects. Allison admits that "this hardly resolves the problem, since it concerns merely a conceptual claim made with respect to the idea of a universal voice postulated in a judgment of taste purporting to be pure," but he believes we can resolve this issue by considering this point in connection to two further points. First, the Deduction on his reading shows that these judgments are *possible* since there is an *a priori* standard of

---

make a judgment of taste is to ground one's judgment on several jointly sufficient conditions: a feeling of pleasure, requisite information about the causal history of that feeling, and the assumption of common conditions. The *a priori* principle is then the judge's *assumption* of a common nature (which the Deductions shows is known *a priori*). So Guyer does not confuse the *quid juris* and *quid facti*: He believes the Deduction's aim is *to justify the justification* offered in a judgment of taste, or to justify the basis or principle of any judgment of taste. Guyer is perplexed as to why Allison does not think that the Deduction's aim is to justify the basis of particular judgments of taste. In fact, Allison sidesteps this crucial issue because he believes that a Deduction simply identifies the standard that the cognitive faculties would be fulfilling if they achieve harmony in reflection. I discuss both views in more detail shortly. Importantly, Allison follows Guyer in viewing the harmonious play and the feeling of pleasure as simply "facts of the matter" that cannot in themselves contain anything "normative"; for both Allison and Guyer, the pleasure and harmonious play are not identical with the principle of judgments of taste (see Guyer and Allison 2011).

74   JENNIFER DOBE

judgment that the harmonious attunement would be achieving; second, the success of the Deduction so conceived "is not undermined" by the "difficulty of subsuming a particular instance under it" (Allison 2001: 190). But these three points in combination hardly dispel our worry that different judges may disagree in their judgments of taste or even that some judges may be unable to judge reflectively. Even if we grant (1) that the judgment of taste (by definition) speaks with a universal voice, (2) that Kant has demonstrated that judgments of taste are possible because there is a norm of judgment that the activity of reflectively judging could meet, and (3) that the standard is not undermined by the difficulty of meeting it, we are still in no way assured that a conflict in judgments of taste is impossible (let alone that everyone's cognitive faculties are capable of this mental activity and in response to the same representations).

The point is not to question the very possibility of harmonious play, however, as if the activity itself possesses some problematic characteristic, but rather to question whether it can be expected to arise in all of us in response to the same representations. But turning to Zuckert's view, we see that she misidentifies the *a priori* principle because she focuses unnecessarily on the very possibility of harmonious play.

3   Rachel Zuckert

Zuckert's provocative and well-received account identifies Kant's principle of aesthetic judgment as a future-directed structure that is internal to the cognitive faculties' harmonious activity. In her words, the principle of aesthetic judgment is "a purposive temporal structure of anticipating the future within the present" (Zuckert 2007:313). For Zuckert, the cognitive faculties attempt to integrate the heterogeneity of the object into a coherent whole, thereby anticipating the unity of the object. This activity of engaging with the form of the object – of anticipating its unity while attending to different elements, one after the other – brings the faculties themselves into an internally harmonious play. This harmonious play perpetuates itself, thereby anticipating its own state and projecting it into the future. Thus, the harmonious play possesses the temporal structure of anticipating the future in the present. This structure is the principle of aesthetic judging (Zuckert 2007:179).

Zuckert maintains that, because the principle of aesthetic judgment is a temporal *structure*, it can govern more than the aesthetic state of mind, and indeed, she believes this is a virtue of her view. As we have seen, this

Kant's A priori *Principle of Judgments of Taste* 75

temporal structure can be internal to (constitutive of) our state of mind, as it is when it structures the harmonious play (Zuckert 2007:21). But it can also simply serve as a regulative principle for other sorts of judgments. For example, when we project systematic unity in our attempts to form empirical concepts from our experience of the heterogeneity of nature, our judging is, she claims, governed by this future-directed unifying structure (Zuckert 2007:179, 356). That is, in empirical concept forma-tion we anticipate the whole ("as a structure of reciprocal means-end relations that obtain among parts as heterogeneous or contingent") in which particulars are to be organized (Zuckert 2007:179). These two kinds of judging (empirical concept formation and aesthetic judgment) differ in an important respect. In the case of the former, the temporal structure is a merely regulative, though subjectively necessary, principle guiding our judgment, whereas in aesthetic judging, while this principle is used regulatively at first, it eventually becomes constitutive when the faculties themselves are brought into a future-directed activity and are themselves "governed by the principle of purposiveness without a purpose" (Zuckert 2007:337).

As I have already indicated, Zuckert's view illuminates nicely the rela-tionship between the harmonious play of the faculties and the feeling of pleasure. She provides strong textual evidence that the harmonious state of mind is formally identical to a feeling of pleasure. The harmonious play of the faculties is a pleasurable state of mind because it endorses itself by serving as the ground of its own perpetuation. But even though we may endorse this part of her account, we do not need to accept her candidate for the principle of aesthetic judgment. Indeed, her conception of the principle of aesthetic judgment as a future-directed structure is open to at least two serious criticisms. First, her account of Kant's justification of judgments of taste is, like Allison's view, too weak to ground the demand of agreement in judgments of taste. This is the result of the fact that, as in Allison's account, her version of the Deduction is aimed at showing that the basis of judgments of taste is a necessary principle for cognitive activities external to aesthetic judgment. In Zuckert's case, the principle is necessary for empirical concept formation (whereas for Allison, it is a principle necessary for cognition in general). For this reason, her account, like Allison's, will be unable to dispel the worries about whether we are all able to "internalize" this principle and whether we are able to do so in response to the same objects. Second, her account lacks textual evidence. I will develop each objection in turn.

76 JENNIFER DOBE

As already indicated, for Zuckert aesthetic judgment is based upon the same principle that grounds the acquisition of empirical concepts. Zuckert maintains that future-directed unification is so peculiar an activity that Kant has to show that it is subjectively required for creating empirical concepts.[11] Showing that the principle *must* be used to acquire empirical concepts is, according to Zuckert, enough to show that it is an *a priori* principle.[12] Moving on to aesthetic judgment, she claims that all a Deduction of judgments of taste needs to do is to identify that very same principle at work in the judge's own mental activity: Instead of being a merely regulative principle for the unification of objects, it is experienced as the internalized, future-directed structure of the activity of one's own cognitive faculties. She concludes that "All human subjects not only can, but ought to, engage in this cognitive activity because it is necessary for the possibility of aesthetic experience, and of empirical knowledge – and thus of experience in general. (Thus we may claim that all others ought to judge aesthetically as we do)" (Zuckert 2007:22).

But even if the Deduction so conceived successfully shows that the harmonious play is possible since it fulfills (is governed by, is structured by) a necessary principle of empirical concept formation, we are still left with the same worries about whether our cognitive faculties are able to achieve the harmonious play (the particular state of mind that is governed by the principle), and whether, if they are, they all respond in the same way to the same representations. The problem is that Zuckert follows Allison's lead in conceiving of the *a priori* principle as a *norm* of judgment in general that the harmonious play of the faculties happens to succeed in meeting in aesthetic judgment. But surely the strongest result such a Deduction can produce is the claim that *if* one of us succeeds in experiencing the harmonious play, this person's state of mind in fact meets the standard of an *a priori* principle. It is not clear how either an expectation or a "demand" that others share one's judgment is thereby justified. In other words, even if it is the case that (1) all of us *must* judge in accordance with this principle as we form empirical concepts, and that (2) I experience a harmonious play that *is* structured by this same principle, this does not justify me in expecting or demanding that others experience the

---

[11] "[S]uch unifying synthesis without following a conceptual rule would seem not to be possible on Kant's view" (Zuckert 2007:71).

[12] "[I]n order to have coherent experience, to render empirical knowledge possible and justified, we require a principle in addition to the categorical principles to guide reflective judging, a principle in accord with which the subject may discern the unity of the diverse as such. . ." (Zuckert 2007:61).

Kant's A priori *Principle of Judgments of Taste* 77

harmonious play (structured by this principle) in response to the same objects. The point is that the standard achieved by harmonious play on Zuckert's view is a standard that none of us can avoid using in a different sort of judging (forming empirical concepts), but we can certainly avoid using it when judging aesthetically; and, even if I am capable of internalizing that principle, it is not clear why I should be entitled to demand or even expect others to do so. That my cognitive activity internalizes this principle in response to certain objects may simply be a novel empirical fact. Thus, even if Zuckert's version of the Deduction were successful (by succeeding in showing that the harmonious play is structured by the principle required for empirical concept formation), it would not ground the *a priori* expectation or demand of universal assent.

Zuckert's account is also open to criticism because there are no passages where Kant discusses the temporal structure of harmonious play as problematic and therefore in need of grounding. On her view, the reason why judgments of taste require a Deduction is because the harmonious play, like empirical concept formation, is so peculiar in its future-directed anticipation of unity that it has to be shown to be structured by a *necessary* principle. But Zuckert admits that Kant raises no concerns about the temporal structure of this activity of the faculties in judging beauty. She openly acknowledges, for instance, that

> my interpretation of the principle of purposiveness as a principle of judgment – viz., as an anticipatory, temporal, and formal structure of the subject's judging activity . . . – both is the pivotal move in my interpretation of the *CJ*, and is not explicitly presented in the text. The plausibility of this interpretation of Kant's principle of purposiveness can only be evaluated, I believe, by seeing whether it sheds helpful light on Kant's discussions in the *CJ*. (Zuckert 2007: 17)

Zuckert defends her substantial reconstruction of Kant's view for its ability to unify the two halves of the third *Critique* (Zuckert 2007:5). But the unification her view achieves (assuming such unification is even desirable) comes at too high a cost: substantial reconstruction of Kant's arguments and a weak Deduction of judgments of taste.[13]

---

[13] If my candidate is in fact the principle of judgments of taste, then we have reason to maintain a clear distinction between the two halves of the third *Critique* (and thus to resist readings that provide deep unification of the work): The first half of the text arguably concerns human nature and its amenability to our cognitive, moral, social and political ends, whereas the second concerns external nature (and its amenability to these ends). See Section 6.

78 JENNIFER DOBE

4 Paul Guyer

Setting the issue of the possibility of harmonious play aside, we are able to clear a path to the main issue in Kant's Deduction. The judgment of taste is in need of a Deduction because, in Kant's own words, "we require that satisfaction of everyone as necessary" (*KU* 5:289). Guyer makes this point quite decisively: "[T]he only thing that is claimed to be known a priori in a judgment of taste is the universal validity of the pleasure that the judge has felt (*KU* 5:289)" (Guyer 2009a:204). Guyer's insight is that the *a priori* claim made in the judgment of taste can only be made in relation to others. If only one human being ever existed she would not judge anything to be beautiful. This may sound rather counter-intuitive, but Kant suggests as much when he claims that, "For himself alone a human being abandoned on a desert island would not adorn either his hut or himself, nor seek out or still less plant flowers in order to decorate himself; rather, only in society does it occur to him to be not merely a human being but also, in his own way, a refined human being" (*KU* 5:297). Having a universally communicable feeling of pleasure, a feeling that I "should" feel, is only possible if it is sharable with all other human beings. Thus, even if the sole human being in this thought experiment were to experience a harmonious play of the faculties in response to, say, a flower, the feeling of pleasure that arises could at most serve as the basis of an empirical judgment that the flower is purposive for, or agreeable to, her.

From this point on I will take for granted that the *a priori* claim made by the judgment of taste is the universal validity of my pleasure. Guyer then identifies the *a priori* principle by drawing what I believe to be an unwarranted conclusion from this insight: "Kant himself makes it clear that the only candidate for an *a priori* principle in the case of aesthetic judgment is the principle that is necessary in order to justify the only claim that is made *a priori* by an aesthetic judgment. . ." (Guyer 2009a:204). Guyer maintains that the *a priori* principle is therefore ". . . the *assumption* of the commonality of 'that subjective element one can presuppose in all human beings (as requisite for possible cognitions in general)' (*KU* 5:290), that is, the commonality of the necessary condition for cognition in general that is also supposed to be a sufficient condition for the commonality of aesthetic judgment" (Guyer 2009a:204, my emphasis). Guyer's view is that when we judge something is beautiful, we expect *a priori* that others will feel pleasure in response to the object we have experienced ourselves; that expectation rests on the justifiable assumption that the condition of my own pleasure is shared by everyone else.

Before I explain my concern, it is important to do better justice to Guyer's account. These quotations may seem to suggest that for Guyer the judgment of taste is not based on a feeling of pleasure, but this is because he makes a logical distinction between two moments within our aesthetic experience: first, the judging (*Beurteilung*), in which we feel pleasure that is caused by the harmony of the faculties, and then, second, the judgment itself (*Urteil*), which is an expectation of agreement, whose basis is the assumption of common conditions.[14] These moments are not always experienced as distinct; thus, he is proposing a logical rather than phenomenological distinction. At the same time, they could be experienced as distinct: The second could follow the first or the first could occur without the second. Importantly, Guyer's view allows for the possibility that we could feel the pleasure caused by the harmonious play *without* judging on the basis of the *a priori* principle.[15] As indicated already, to Guyer's mind the feeling of pleasure cannot, on its own, ground the judgment of taste because there are no clear marks that distinguish pleasure in beauty (caused by the harmonious play) from, for instance, pleasure in the agreeable. In order for a judgment to be grounded on the *a priori* principle of aesthetic judgment, the judge must ground her expectation of agreement on a conscious assumption of shared conditions. Only then, according to Guyer, is the judgment of taste grounded on an *a priori* principle.

My objection to Guyer's candidate may now be considered. Kant may say that the judgment is based or grounded upon an *a priori* principle of aesthetic judgment, but this is not equivalent to saying that the judgment *justifies* itself with an *a priori* principle. Consider first the *a priori* concepts: When we say that cognition is "grounded" upon these *a priori* concepts, we do not mean that when we cognize we justify our cognition by appeal to these *a priori* concepts. This is why Kant characterizes these principles as constitutive and leaves justification to a deduction.[16] Kant characterizes the principle of aesthetic judgments in the same way: "The power of judgment's concept of a purposiveness of nature still belongs among the concepts of nature, but only as a regulative principle of the faculty of

---

[14] According to Guyer, the judgment of taste "rests upon two conceptually distinct acts": "one, the 'unintentional' reflection which produces the pleasure of aesthetic response; the other, that further and quite possibly intentional exercise of reflective judgment which leads to an actual judgment of taste, or determines that the feeling of pleasure occasioned by a given object *is* such a pleasure, and thus is validly attributed to anyone perceiving that object" (Guyer 1979:97). The first reflective act can occur without the second, but the second cannot occur without the first.

[15] As I make clear toward the end of this section, my view also allows for this possibility.

[16] See note 10.

80 JENNIFER DOBE

cognition, *although the aesthetic judgment on certain objects (of nature or of art) that occasions it is a constitutive principle with regard to the feeling of pleasure or displeasure*" (*KU* 5:197, my emphasis). Second, consider judgments of the agreeable. In the case of the agreeable, pleasure grounds these judgments directly; this is what makes the judgment aesthetic and subjective. Kant insists in the First Moment that "even if the given representations were to be rational but related in a judgment solely to the subject (its feeling), then they are to that extent always aesthetic" (section 1, 5:205). In order to understand what it means for the aesthetic judgment to be "grounded on" or based upon an *a priori* principle, we should look to the way in which the constitutive principles of cognition "ground" cognition and the way in which the feeling of pleasure in the subject "grounds" judgments of the agreeable. We should take Kant at his word and consider the possibility that judgments of taste are grounded directly on a feeling, but a feeling that is universally communicable because it is (quite literally) constituted by an *a priori* principle (namely, our shared cognitive nature, according to which the imagination is predisposed to be attuned to the understanding).

Moreover, the earlier passage, in which Guyer provides textual evidence in support of his candidate, in fact provides evidence for my proposal and counter-evidence for his. The text he cites appears to support his proposal because of his own addition: The *a priori* principle is ". . . the *assumption* of the commonality of 'that subjective element one can presuppose in all human beings (as requisite for possible cognitions in general)' (*KU* 5:290)" (Guyer 2009:204, my emphasis). This addition should strike us now as significant, given that Kant has actually identified the candidate I propose rather than Guyer's. Guyer must supplement the text because of his view of pleasure. But if we take pleasure to be a complex state of mind that could bear more than a merely causal relation to the harmonious play of the faculties and to the universally shared nature of these faculties, then we are in a position to be able to embrace Kant's text as it stands.

These reflections lead me to the following conclusion: that a judgment of taste is based upon a single ground that unifies three elements: (1) the universally communicable feeling of pleasure that is *felt* to be universally communicable, (2) the harmonious play of the faculties, and (3) the common predisposition of our cognitive faculties to agree with one another. If we are feeling a universally communicable pleasure that we perceive *as* universally communicable and that is in fact generated through a harmonious play of the faculties (rather than the agreement of the concept of perfection with an intuition), we are judging on the basis of

Kant's A priori *Principle of Judgments of Taste* 81

an *a priori* principle, namely, our common cognitive nature according to which our imaginations are predisposed to be attuned to the needs of the understanding. If these conditions are met and we demand agreement by claiming the representation of the object in question to be beautiful, then we are making a full-fledged judgment of taste. We may possess (3) without experiencing both (2) and (1) (as we do whenever we are not judging aesthetically). But if we are experiencing (1), then it is possible that (2) is taking place as a manifestation of (3); and it is also possible to experience pleasure that we do not feel is universally communicable even if (2) is taking place as a manifestation of (3). In other words, if (2) is taking place, then it is a manifestation of (3) and we are likely to experience (1), though this experience is not necessary.[17] Of course, if (1) does not occur then we will not demand agreement and will therefore not make a full-fledged judgment of taste.

5 Possible Objections

Let me consider two possible objections from Allison and Guyer. I have argued that Allison sidelines the crucial issue of the agreement of particular judgments. He neglects to address the gravity of this worry because he believes the Deduction's task is more limited and the claim that "the harmonious play of the faculties occurs in different persons under the same conditions" concerns merely a "matter of fact." On Allison's view, it is "a causal claim about the conditions under which a certain mental state occurs," and for this reason, "might warrant an *expectation* of agreement (or, under ideal conditions, a prediction); but, as has often been noted, this is quite different from licensing a demand that others acknowledge the appropriateness of one's aesthetic response."[18] Allison may object to my reading for precisely the same reason: that the relationship among the three elements I have enumerated is merely causal and cannot serve a "normative" function. But if he makes this objection he will be following Guyer in reducing the relation among these three elements to a causal relation.[19]

---

[17] Of course, the "sole human being" thought experiment entails that if she experiences (2) she experiences it in the absence of (3) and (1).

[18] Guyer and Allison 2006:132; see Guyer 1979:129–30.

[19] In other words, Allison follows Guyer in overlooking the possibility that the way aesthetic judgments are grounded on an *a priori* principle is similar to the ways in which cognition is grounded on the *a priori* concepts and the judgment of the agreeable is based upon a feeling of pleasure in the subject.

JENNIFER DOBE

Indeed, the reason that Allison looks elsewhere for an *a priori* principle is because he accepts Guyer's view that the relationship among them could only be causal and presumes that a fact such as this could never "ground" aesthetic judgment because it cannot serve a "normative" function. First, why do we have to consider this relation to be merely causal, when (2) and (3) are conceivably nested within the very identity of (1)? When we judge beauty, we are basing this judgment on the very nature of these faculties to agree with one another; put another way, the judgment is based directly on a feeling that is universally communicable because it is a feeling of the harmonious play of the faculties that is itself the manifestation of the universally shared nature or predisposition of the imagination to be attuned to the understanding. Kant is at pains to make precisely this point after he resolves the Antinomy; and though I provided the quotation earlier, it is worth presenting it again:

> [F]or since the beautiful must not be judged in accordance with concepts, but rather in accordance with the purposive disposition of the imagination for its correspondence with the faculty of concepts in general, it is not a rule or precept but only that which is merely nature in the subject ... which is to serve as the subjective standard of that aesthetic but unconditioned purposiveness in beautiful art, which is supposed to make a rightful claim to please everyone. (*KU* 5:344)

I discuss the implications of my view for the Antinomy in the next section. At this point, however, it is important to emphasize that a shared cognitive nature can be considered and can serve as a *subjective a priori* principle, insofar as it is universally shared, and, thanks to a successful Deduction, we can know *a priori* that we do share it. So, while Allison might be right that a fact cannot serve as necessary norm (e.g., the moral law) or as an objective principle, it is simply incorrect to say that a fact cannot serve as an *inter-subjective* principle (insofar as it is universally shared). We can only consider this fact to be a principle of aesthetic judgment, however, once we can know *a priori* that it is universal (that for all of us the imagination is attuned to the requirements of the understanding). Once we do (thanks to a successful deduction),[20] we can consider this fact, which is known *a priori*, to be an *a priori* principle of aesthetic judgment.

The possible objection from Guyer takes a different approach. As already indicated, I support Zuckert's challenge to Guyer's reading of Kant's view of pleasure and the logical distinction he proposes. She argues

[20] In Dobe 2010, I argue that the Deduction shows that this "fact" is the necessary condition of some given (namely, our ability to communicate with one another).

Kant's A priori *Principle of Judgments of Taste*   83

(along the lines of Hannah Ginsborg and Allison) that pleasure is no brute sensation but a complex, intentional state of mind: Pleasure involves consciousness of itself and is therefore a more complex basis for our judgments of taste than Guyer allows. Guyer insists, however, that because she rejects his conception of pleasure and the logical distinction he proposes, she is unable to make room for two scenarios: first, our being able to take pleasure in judging aesthetically without expecting others to feel it, and second, our being able to make a mistaken judgment, in which we think we have felt a pleasure caused by the harmony of the faculties, but have not. These two scenarios are excluded, he thinks, if the basis of our judgment of taste is, as Zuckert believes, constitutive of the pleasurable harmonious play (by serving as its presumably odd temporal structure). Why? Guyer thinks that Zuckert's view entails that in feeling this pleasure we, by definition, judge *in accordance with* the principle. We cannot experience the pleasurable harmonious play without making a full-fledged judgment of taste. Guyer thinks the second scenario is also excluded by Zuckert's view because this intentional feeling of pleasure in beauty distinguishes itself clearly from other sorts of pleasure, so mistaking one's pleasure in the agreeable for pleasure in beauty, for instance, seems to be impossible.

Guyer may object to my view for the same reasons, so it is important to provide an adequate response. By making the distinction between *Beurteilung* and *Urteil* but modifying Guyer's account of this distinction somewhat, my view is able to allow for these two scenarios. The full-fledged judgment of taste is *das Urteil*; it is the conscious demand of agreement ("X is beautiful") that is consciously based upon one's own pleasure that one feels to be universally communicable and is in fact universally communicable because it is a feeling of the harmonious play of the faculties (and not a feeling in response to the agreement of a concept with an object). In other words, a full-fledged judgment of taste is a valid, or correct, judgment. Mistaken judgments are not judgments of taste but rather judgments of the agreeable or of the good. Mistakes occur (such that we think we are making a judgment of taste when we are not) because the feeling of pleasure generated through harmonious play does not, on its own, always provide clear marks that distinguish it from pleasure in the agreeable or in the good. Though our pleasure may *feel* universally communicable, we can be mistaken about whether it is in fact universally communicable by way of harmonious play. It is also possible to be conscious of the pleasure that arises through harmonious play but without the pleasure feeling universally communicable and therefore without demanding that others should

84 JENNIFER DOBE

also feel it. In this case, we may be in some sense judging "on the basis" of the principle (*Beurteilung*) but not conscious of this; we are thus judging "on its basis" in a much different sense than when we make a full-fledged judgment of taste. So, we may have a feeling of pleasure, which is in fact "constituted" by the *a priori* principle, without making a judgment (*Urteil*) of taste in accordance with it.

I may now address the worry that my view might render everything beautiful, even objects we merely cognize. In cognition we do not judge *on the basis* of the principle of aesthetic judgment (our shared cognitive nature that is characterized by imagination's predisposition to adhere to the understanding's need for unity). We cannot judge in accordance with it unless (among other things) the agreement of the two cognitive faculties is achieved *without* the use of a concept. Thus, when we judge in accordance with concepts or in accordance with a pleasure not brought about through the harmonious activity, it is not possible for us to be judging *on the basis of* this shared cognitive nature.

6 Implications

Having made the case that my interpretation of the principle of judgments of taste is plausible, textually supported, and internally consistent, I turn now to consider its implications. The first has to do with the notoriously perplexing argument set forth in the "Resolution of the Antinomy of Taste" (section 57). Even if a full defense of an interpretation of this argument cannot be offered here, my interpretation of the principle of judgments of taste (as our shared cognitive nature) introduces the possibility that Kant resolves the antinomy in the idea of a supersensible substratum *of humanity* rather than in a supersensible substratum *in general*.[21] If we narrow the conclusion in this way we can then raise the question of why Kant thinks he needs to make a transcendental distinction between the empirical facticity of humanity (as a group of discreet individuals that are determined by natural law) and the supersensible basis of this group of individuals.[22]

---

[21] Hegel interprets the resolution as a general substratum of appearances in *Faith and Knowledge*, 91 (see Longuenesse 2007:179). See also, among others, Caygill 1995:77; Dunham 1933:50–1; Guyer 1987:308; Matthews 1997:108; and Wenzel 2005:123.

[22] For Kant, conceiving of the possibility of judgments of taste seems to require us to think of our empirical nature not only as, in fact, shared, but as determinable through the collective use of freedom. Richard Dean has recently argued that the "idea" of humanity is a rational idea of virtue and thereby "serves as a practical 'model of virtue'" (Dean 2013:173). Thus, Kant's resolution may

Kant's A priori *Principle of Judgments of Taste*   85

A full consideration of this question would, it seems to me, call attention to the political significance of the third *Critique,* as well as provide yet another reason to reject the view that Kant is a "moral 'individualist'" (Wood 2003:41). My reading suggests that the first half of the third *Critique* directs our attention almost exclusively to human nature rather than to external nature and its apparently beautiful forms. According to Kant's lectures on anthropology, human nature is not determinate but is determinable only through freedom. Moreover, as Allen Wood points out, "determining" human nature is not an individualistic endeavor but rather a "social process"; the moral progress and, indeed, the very identity of an individual human being (as *Weltbürger*) are bound up with the progress of the human community (Wood 2003:41). If the principle of judgments of taste is our shared cognitive nature, then we should expect Kant to discuss the political significance of taste through its relation to human nature, given that his conception of human nature is tightly connected to his moral and political philosophy. This is precisely what he does in the final section of the Critique of the Aesthetic Power of Judgment. These investigations into taste lead him to emphasize the "sociability" of humanity that distinguishes us from animals and that is also in the process of becoming "lawful": "humanity means on the one hand the universal *feeling of participation* and on the other hand the capacity for being able to *communicate* one's inmost self universally" (*KU* 5:355).

Agreement in taste is politically significant for Kant because it concerns not merely "correctness" and the individual's moral progress, but also human connection, communication, and our collective progress. Indeed, agreement in taste concerns our relation *to* our own shared cognitive human nature, leaving open the possibility of estrangement that is reflected through a *lack* of feeling of unity within a cosmopolis. Melissa Zinkin makes a similar point, arguing that for Kant "if I do make such a claim and others disagree with me, I don't merely feel a difference between us, but alienated from an important aspect of humanity..." (Zinkin 2006: 160). At the same time, since human nature is indeterminate, Kant may be suggesting that the unification of human beings is not simply *given* through our empirical nature but must be achieved by making use of,

---

point to this idea of humanity as the ultimate standard of taste: That is, the ultimate standard of taste is not simply the similarity in the functioning of our cognitive faculties (their attunement to one another) but also the idea of humanity, which we use in order to make collective moral and political progress. It is, after all, for the sake of this idea that we are to make *use* of our shared cognitive nature and our ability to share one another's pleasures.

among other things, our common cognitive nature and the shareable pleasures it makes possible as we work toward ethical and political ideals. By recognizing the *a priori* principle of aesthetic judgment as our shared cognitive human nature, we are able to do better justice to the link Kant is attempting to forge between taste and politics in the Dialectic of Taste. Given these implications and the defense I have provided, I hope to have offered sufficient reason to take this unusual candidate seriously.

PART II

The Inner Value of the World: Freedom as the Keystone of Kant's Moral Philosophy

CHAPTER 5

Guyer on the Value of Freedom

Patricia Kitcher

1   Guyer's View

Over a number of years, Paul Guyer has argued that the ultimate value for Kant is not mere adherence to the moral law, but freedom and the morally deserved happiness that only a free creature can enjoy. By highlighting what he takes to be the essential roles of freedom and (warranted) happiness, Guyer aims to correct the common picture of Kant's moral thinking as excessively focused on duty and laws. On his account, the parade case of a deontologist turns out to have his gaze firmly directed to the final end of the creation (and of morality) and the notorious happiness-denier fully to understand that humans need happiness. I agree with the broad outlines of Guyer's kinder, gentler Kant, but I have some questions about the arguments he uses to support his interpretation; I also offer some friendly amendments to his account to make it (I hope) more distinctively Kantian.

Although I am sympathetic to Guyer's broad aims I argue against two claims that he makes in *Kant on Freedom, Law and Happiness*. The first concerns the relation between freedom and the moral law:

> Kant sees that moral reasoning must begin with a morally necessary end, his candidate for which is the fundamental value of freedom itself, and then argues that conformity to law is the means to the preservation and promotion of freedom. (Guyer 2000c:10)

I think it takes us too far from Kant's basic moral position to suggest that following the moral law should be understood as a means to *anything* else, except perhaps a world where everyone follows the moral law. The second claim lays out the relations among freedom, happiness, and end-setting:

> [Kant] can and must allow the idea of a rational and systematic conception of happiness, as the inevitable object of the free and systematic choices of human beings, to return into morality as the ultimate object of human

action that is defined for it by the fundamental value of freedom – as the capacity, after all, to set ends – itself. (Guyer 2000c:11)

Despite the distinguished adherents of this view, I doubt that Kant equated "freedom" with the "capacity to set ends." Thus, I question whether he would welcome the "return" of the idea of a system of happiness as the goal or object of free action.

Guyer makes his case for the ultimate value of freedom and (warranted) happiness by appealing to two issues: the implications of the role of the formula of humanity in the system of categorical imperatives, and the long-standing importance of the idea of the *summum bonum* (in which happiness is proportional to desert) to Kant's philosophical project. I have concerns about these two lines of argument, singly and collectively. Although the formula of humanity (FH) is based on the fundamental metaphysical "fact" of human freedom or autonomy, the fact on which all values depend, and although FH enjoins humans to further the ends of others, I doubt that any of this implies that Kant thinks that

> the ultimate locus of value seems to be universal happiness itself, as the maximal realization of a natural human end, and the law of reason, together with the freedom from which it arises, seems to be valuable primarily as the necessary condition of this universal happiness. (Guyer 2000c:107)

Despite the fact that the *summum bonum* appears in all three critiques and in other important writings, including *Religion within the Bounds of Mere Reason* and the essay on Theory and Practice, it seems to have a particular – and conflicted – role to play in Kant's system. It is part of what seems to be a circular argument for the necessity in believing in a moral Creator of the universe – an argument that he tries to keep in the practical sphere, while all the time noting that the belief is theoretical. In the present context, I will argue that the reasoning behind the *summum bonum* argument for maximizing happiness is so different from the argument for FH that it is probably a mistake to think of them as having a common aim. After raising concerns about some of the specifics of Guyer's proposals, I present what I hope is a defensible version of his basic interpretive strategy of rejecting the "deontological versus teleological" and the "he fails to realize the importance of human happiness" dogmas that have shaped generations of Kant interpretation.

2 Humanity as the Source of Value

FH has been enjoying great popularity among Kantian ethicists in recent years, but Guyer argues persuasively that a common view of the move from the formula of universal law (FUL) to FH in section 2 of the *Groundwork* is mistaken. There are at least two versions of this view. On one, the starting assumption is that according to ordinary moral understanding, some things have at least conditional value. The argument is that if anything has conditional value, then something must have unconditional or intrinsic value, and of the possible candidates: objects of inclination, inclinations themselves, non-human animals, and rational animals, only the latter is plausible (see, e.g., Timmermann 2007:94–5). A second avenue to the same conclusion starts with the assumption that since all human action must have an end, and since all humans are bound by the moral law, then the end of acting on that law must be a common, universal, or objective end, and, again, the only plausible candidate for the end is humanity itself (Guyer 2000c:144). Guyer rejects the latter reasoning as both fallacious – why must there be just one objective or intrinsic end? – and as missing what is at issue at this point in Kant's argument. Kant pivots to FH not (just) to find an end for moral action, but also to shore up the argument that humans are bound by FUL; he does not assume that the validity of FUL has already been shown.

Kant's explanation for why he is taking up the issue of humanity (and the formula connected to it) supports Guyer's reading. Kant writes:

> But we have not yet advanced so far as to prove *a priori* that there really is such an imperative, that there is a practical law, that commands absolutely of itself and without any incentives and that the observance of this law is a duty. (*GMS* 4:425)[1]

A further passage in the transition from the discussion of FUL to that of FH seems to seal the case for Guyer's reading. To answer the question of whether FUL is a necessary law for all rational beings, then

> [that law] must already be connected (completely *a priori*) with the concept of the will of a rational being as subject. But in order to discover this connection we must, however reluctantly, step forth, namely into … metaphysics of morals. (*GMS* 4:426–7)

When we take the step, we find something that has absolute or intrinsic value, *viz.*, rational nature. As Guyer notes, this answer is not the last word, since it raises the question of what it is about rational beings that gives them intrinsic worth. He thinks that Kant's answer to the question is that it is their capacity to set ends (Guyer 2000c:148–9).

---

[1] Translations of the *Groundwork* are from Gregor and Timmermann (2011). Translations from the *Critique of Practical Reason* are from Pluhar (1996).

PATRICIA KITCHER

This answer has also been offered by Christine Korsgaard (Korsgaard 1996b:124–32) and Allen Wood (Wood 1999:124–7), but Guyer disagrees with the reasoning that leads them to their shared interpretation. As he notes, even if the ability to set ends stops the regress of ends as means to further ends, it must be modified by something like "an ability to set ends by a creature who adheres to the categorical imperative." Otherwise, Korsgaard and Wood would be implausibly suggesting that Kant believed that the capacity to set arbitrary or bad ends was intrinsically valuable (Guyer 2000c:151).

Although Guyer's objection that Korsgaard's argument rests on an ambiguity between the capacity to set ends as value-conferring for any end, and value-conferring in the case of moral ends, his proposal seems to suffer from a similar ambiguity. He suggests that Kant's argument for the intrinsic value of end-setting is direct:

> [Kant] sees our capacity to set and pursue ends of our own choice as a fundamental manifestation of our freedom and freedom itself as possessing absolute value. (Guyer 2000c:151)

The ambiguity lies in the phrase "ends of our own choice." Does that mean simply ends that are chosen "as one pleases" rather than being determined by immediate inclination (*KrV* A802/B830), or does it refer to ends that are chosen independently of any inclination? Alternatively, are we dealing with merely psychological freedom or with transcendental freedom (*KrV* A534/B562)? Since there is little reason to suppose that Kant thought that psychological freedom was intrinsically valuable, the answer must be that what is intrinsically valuable is the ability to set and pursue ends independently of any inclination. But that capacity is not a manifestation of freedom but freedom itself (see, e.g., *GMS* 4:446).

Guyer's central thesis is that the fundamental, intrinsic value of freedom is the centerpiece of Kant's ethical theory. He defends the interpretation by invoking the capacity to set ends, which is what permits him to argue that the goal of ethical action is the maximal realization of human ends. I have argued that this defense introduces unwarranted elements into Kant's position and I will now try to show that these elements are also unnecessary for establishing Guyer's larger interpretive claim about the essential role of FH in the proof of the validity of FUL.

The thesis that freedom is the key to the intrinsic value of rational agency is strongly supported by the result of Kant's quest for an *a priori* connection between the concept of the will of a rational being and that creature's

Guyer on the Value of Freedom

being subject to the moral law, a result presented in *Groundwork* III. In that section, he argues that freedom of the will can be nothing other than

> autonomy, that is, the will's property of being a law to itself and [that] proposition indicates only the principle, to act on no other maxim than that which can also have as object itself as a universal law, [i.e., FUL]. (*GMS* 4:446–7)

That is, the *a priori* connection between the concept of the will of a rational being and the concept of a being who is bound by FUL is found in the concept of a free will. "Freedom" is thus the unique metaphysical answer to questions about both the bindingness of the moral law and the source of non-instrumental value.

Most Kant interpreters would agree with that claim, but few are content to rest with it. The problems are obvious. The alleged analytic connection between a free will and acting on the moral law seems dubious (although, see Schönecker 2013 for an influential defense of the analyticity thesis). Further, even if that point is granted, by the time of the *Critique of Practical Reason*, Kant had abandoned the argument that humans are bound by the moral law because they are, in fact, free. So there is an interpretive imperative to try to find a more solid argument for his conclusion. I, too, find this imperative compelling, but, for reasons already mentioned, I doubt that it helps to fasten on the capacity to set ends.

Kant's sketches his argument for FH in section II. After noting that material ends, inclinations, and things are merely subjective ends – have worth only because someone values them – he highlights a special feature of human beings. Each human being necessarily represents his own existence as intrinsically valuable (*GMS* 4:429). He continues that "every other rational being also represents his existence in this way consequent on just the same rational ground that also holds for me" (*GMS* 4:429). He appends a note explaining that he is only postulating the principle here, but will supply adequate supporting grounds for it in section 3. Thus, what the final section is supposed to show is that each person regards himself as having intrinsic worth on the same ground that every other person regards himself as having intrinsic worth. To justify FH, however, he needs to show more, namely that each person must regard every *other* person as having intrinsic worth on the same ground that he regards himself as having intrinsic worth.

If Guyer is right that the fundamental value for Kant is freedom, then the proposition to be established in *Groundwork* III would be: Each person

94 PATRICIA KITCHER

must regard himself as free on the same ground that he does or must regard every person as free. When we turn to what I take to be the key text in that section, that is just the proposition to be proved. Interestingly, the proof is presented as something that will establish the validity of FUL, not FH. That textual fact is strong support for Guyer's claim that FH plays a critical role in proving the validity of FUL – because the argument that completes the proof for FH is also the argument that establishes the bindingness of FUL for all humans.

Groundwork III is to eliminate the possibility that morality is chimerical by showing that the moral law is objectively valid for all rational beings, because they are free. Since the argument is based on freedom, freedom must be shown to be a property of all rational beings (*GMS* 4:447). Kant lays out how the proof works and its first steps, as follows:[2]

> 1. One must prove it [freedom] as belonging universally to the activity of rational beings endowed with a will as such. 2. Now I say: every being that cannot act otherwise than under the idea of freedom is actually free, in a practical respect... 3. Now I assert: that we must necessarily <u>lend</u> to every rational being that has a will also the idea of freedom, under which alone it acts. For in such a being we think [*denken*] a reason that is practical, i.e., has causality with regard to its objects. 4. <u>Now one cannot possibly think of a reason that would self-consciously receive guidance from any other quarter with regard to its judgments, since the subject would not then attribute the determination of judgment to his reason, but to an impulse.</u> (*GMS* 4:448, my numbering and underscoring)

The lynchpin of the argument for the universality of freedom and so for the objective validity of the moral law is premise (3), the claim that we must "lend" the idea of freedom to any being we think as having a reason that is practical, and so as having a will, as the only idea under which she can act. Why the peculiar expression "lend" in place of the more straightforward "attribute"?

I think the answer to this puzzle can be found in a little-noticed discussion at the beginning of the Paralogisms chapter of the first *Critique*. Kant is going to use the results of his exploration of the requirements of thinking from the Transcendental Deduction to illuminate the errors of Rational Psychology, and he pauses to consider a possible objection:

---

[2] The next seven pages draw on material that first appeared in my 2017a. See pages 224, 225, 228, 232, 234, 243.

Guyer on the Value of Freedom

It must, however, seem strange at the very outset that the condition under which I think at all, and which is therefore merely a characteristic of myself as subject, is to be valid also for everything that thinks; and <u>that upon a proposition that seems empirical</u> we can presume to base an apodeictic and universal judgment, *viz*: that everything that thinks is of such a character as the pronouncement of self-consciousness asserts of me. The cause of this, however, lies in the fact that we must necessarily ascribe to things a priori all of the properties that make up the conditions under which alone we think them. (*KrV* A346/B404–5, my underscoring; see also *KrV* A353–4)

That is, it is legitimate for Kant to use himself (or for any rational thinker to use herself) as a model for all rational thinkers, because that is the only way they have of understanding others as thinkers at all. Humans have no access to thinking through outer or inner sense. Rather, they come to understand thinking by engaging in it.

Consider making the judgment "nine" on the basis of counting or inferring that Socrates is mortal from the usual premises. Kant argues that these acts of rational cognition are possible only because the thinker is conscious in combining some representations in others. The reasoner must be conscious in concluding that Socrates is mortal from the premises, or her conclusion would not be an act of rational cognition, because she would not know the reasons for it (A303/B359–60); The counter must be conscious, in judging "nine," that she does so on the basis of counting "one," "two," etc. Otherwise, she would have no idea why she is saying "nine" (*KrV* A103–4). She would not be using a concept but parroting a phoneme. The act-consciousness that is essential to rational cognition is not sensory (*KrV* B153). Cognizers do not know the reasons for their judgments or inferences because they have observed themselves thinking through inner sense, but because they have consciously performed acts of judging and inferring – as they must for these to be the rational acts that they are. If Kant is right about the requirements of thinking – and I believe he is – then although it is inaccessible to the senses, it is known through the doing of it (see my 2017b:165–70 for further defense).

Under these circumstances, I can understand others as thinkers only through the one case I know, *viz.*, my own. Kant is not committing the infamous single-case induction to solve the problem of other minds. He is explicit that the self-as-model for others move is not an empirical general-ization, but merely *seems* to be one. It is, rather, a recognition from your own case that a special type of activity – thinking – exists, and that what it is, is actively, consciously combining some mental states in others. Alter-natively, the point at issue in these preliminaries to the arguments of the

96 PATRICIA KITCHER

Paralogisms chapter is not how humans know that other humans have minds, but how they must understand what it is for another to have a mind.

Given this background, we see why Kant says (in 4) that no rational agent could think of "judging" as receiving direction from the outside. Any such agent must understand that that would not be judging, and that any "actions" or bodily movements that flowed from such impulses would not be rational actions. We can also see why he might use the odd locution "lend." Kant cannot mean that we must think of others as temporarily or provisionally free, since the conclusion to be established is that they are free *simpliciter*. Rather he must mean that any rational agent will project on the action-producing judgments of others the same conscious activity or spontaneity that she enjoys when making action-producing judgments. On this reading, Kant would be providing just the argument he promised in section 2. Insofar as we take ourselves to have absolute or intrinsic worth because we recognize that we are free judgers – we would take any others we understand to be rational agents to have absolute worth on literally the same ground, *viz.*, our recognition of ourselves as free judgers. In this way, he would be demonstrating that rational agents really are bound by FUL (via the argument that a "free will" and "a will subject to FUL" mutually imply each other [*GMS* 4:447]) by completing his argument for FH, as the texts that transition from FUL to FH claim he will, and as Guyer argues, he must.

Unfortunately, Kant has not shown that the will is free from all incentives. He assumed that practical reasoning was syllogistic: The major premise contained the law or principle of action; the minor, subsumption under the law; and the conclusion laid down what to do in the present circumstances (*RL* 6:313). But the argument about lending the idea of freedom to any rational actor concerns only the reasoning from premises to conclusion and not the source of the principle. He extends the argument as follows:

> 5. Reason must view herself as the author of her principles, independently of alien influences, and must consequently, as practical reason, or as the will of a rational being, by herself be viewed as free; i.e., its will can be a will of his own only under the idea of freedom, and must thus for practical purposes be ascribed to all rational beings. (*GMS* 4:448, my numbering)

Then he raises a devastating objection to the argument:

> It seems as if in the idea of freedom we actually just presupposed the moral law, namely the principle of the autonomy of the will itself, and could not prove its reality and objective necessity. (*GMS* 4:449)

Given the alleged analytic connection between freedom and FUL, it would be inappropriate to try to prove one simply by assuming the other. In making the additional assumption (in step 5) of freedom or autonomy in the generation of the principle or maxim, he has thus begged the question (see Berger 2015 for a discussion of the apparently circular reasoning in *Groundwork* III). He was not, however, supposed to be assuming freedom, but arguing for it from the nature of rational willing. Since considerations about the necessary conditions for judging in general do not, however, imply (5), he has to simply assume it and thereby beg the question.

It is widely agreed that the failed argument of *Groundwork* III is recast in the fact of reason texts in the second *Critique* (i.e., in sections 6 and 7 and the Corollary to 7). As we have just seen, the argument failed, because Kant had no way to establish that reason must regard itself as the author of its principles of action (maxims) independently of alien influences. He returns to the issue of maxims in section 6 of the second *Critique*, after noting that knowledge of freedom and the moral law must begin with the latter:

> therefore, it is the moral law of which we become conscious directly (as soon as we frame or draft or pose maxims of the will for ourselves) which first offers itself to us, and which – inasmuch as reason displays it as a determining basis not to be outweighed by any sensible conditions and indeed entirely independently of them – leads straight to the idea of freedom. (*KpV* 5:29–30, my underscoring)

That is, when humans form a maxim or principle of action, they are immediately conscious of the moral law: "would they will a world where their intended action was universal law?" And they are not just conscious of the moral law, but conscious of it as determining their willing. That is the thesis to be established in the second *Critique* – not that pure reason has a hand in some action, which we know from the *Groundwork* could never be established with certainty (*GMS* 4:407) – but that pure reason is sufficient by itself alone to determine the willing (*das Wollen*) (*KpV* 5:15), i.e., to alter the subject's motivational structure. Kant's dramatic example of an individual who is threatened with immediate hanging if he refuses to give false testimony against an honest man provides a *Gedanken* experiment for his reader. In imagining being in that situation, the reader recognizes that, even when threatened with the extinction of all future pleasures, he still feels the pull of duty (*KpV* 5:30). Although not given a name until §7, that is the fact of reason doctrine – the fact that in deliberating about what to do, and so about what maxim to adopt, the subject is conscious of the moral law as producing a determinate willing, a rational desire to follow or abstain from a particular course of action.

Despite the very bad reputation of the "fact of reason" doctrine, it is not an alien presence in Kant's theory, something that arrived from Mars. It is implied by his account of moral motivation and by his theory of rational judging. By the argument of *Groundwork* I, ordinary moral agents take the moral character of an action to depend on its motive and they take an action to have moral worth only if it is motivated by duty (*GMS* 4:397–401). Ordinary rational agents also understand that a rational agent must be conscious of the grounds of her judgments and actions. It follows that, on the ordinary understanding, a subject can perform a morally worthy action only if she is conscious of its ground, and only if that ground includes her recognition that she can will a world that everyone does what she intends to do. The existence of the fact of reason is thus a consequence of his analysis of the ordinary human understanding of morality and of judging.

In section 7 the fact of reason is offered as a proof of the proposition that "you ought to act so that the maxim of your will could be a universal law." The proof invokes no premises and makes no inferences. It appeals only to the reader's consciousness in practical deliberation of the moral law as moving her willing. The Corollary to this section generalizes the efficacy of the moral law to all humans:

> Pure reason is practical by itself alone and gives (to the human being) a universal law, which we call the moral law. (*KpV* 5:31)

If this can be shown, then the promise of a proof for FH would finally be redeemed. Through its representation of the moral law, reason alone (i.e., without any incentives) would move the willing of rational beings, thereby showing them to be capable of free action and so have ultimate worth. Proving the Corollary would also finally establish the validity of FUL.

Kant opens the argument in support of the Corollary with the claim that the fact of reason is undeniable. Unfortunately, he then presents a step that we should reject and that he later rejects:

> Now, this principle of morality precisely on account of the universality of the lawgiving that makes it the formal supreme determining basis of the will regardless of all subjective differences of the will, <u>is declared by reason at the same time to be a law for all rational beings insofar as they have a will at all</u>, i.e., a power to determine their causality by the representation of rules. (*KpV* 5:32, my underscoring)

If reason declares that all rational creatures must have the moral law within, then it must be possible to *infer* the presence of an efficacious moral law from rationality. That view is, however, inconsistent with the claim he has just made, *viz.*, that the fact that reason moves the willing through the moral law cannot be derived from anything else (*KpV* 5:31).

Kant could, however, defend the Corollary without this false step. All he needs to do is redeploy the line of reasoning that he uses in the prefatory material of the Paralogisms. Through the *Gedanken* experiment, the reader is reminded of what she already implicitly knows. When she deliberates about what to do, she is aware of considerations about whether she could will that everyone does what she proposes to do as moving her willing. That is how she knows that she has an efficacious moral law within/is free and so has intrinsic moral worth. It is also how she understands what practical reasoning is. Since practical deliberation is a species of thinking, Kant must hold that it is inaccessible by the senses. Hence, insofar as one human can understand another as engaging in practical deliberation at all, she must use herself as a model for that person.

Although the Corollary has the form of a generalization, it is plainly not empirically based. Normal humans do not conduct experiments on other humans to determine whether they are rational or moral agents. They simply presume that their conspecifics are like themselves in their capacities for thinking and practical deliberating. This presumption can be defeated, but when it is not, then they must model other humans' practical deliberating on their own – because that is the only way that they can understand it at all. In that case, however, they would regard others as intrinsically valuable on exactly the same grounds that they regard themselves as valuable.

Kant did not extend the reasoning of *Groundwork* III in this way, but he could have, thereby finally filling in the argument for FH sketched in *Groundwork* II. Further, like the failed argument of *Groundwork* III, this argument for the validity of the moral law rests on a metaphysics of morals, on the non-empirical fact that humans have a will that can be moved by practical reason, and hence have absolute worth. Critics will protest that the fact of reason argument proves nothing more than that people are not aware of the forces directing their wills. A deliberator may believe that her consciousness of the moral law moves her willing against a proposed course of action, but how could she eliminate associative conditioning as the true source of the repulsion? Although this line of objection has problems – it seems to threaten the very possibility of rational action – I am not going to pursue them. Kant thought that the fact of reason demonstration worked, and I want to consider what FH would enjoin if it were proven along the lines that he originally sketched. In particular, would it require moral agents to promote maximal human happiness?

According to the fact of reason, humans automatically respect the moral law at the level of thinking. That is the fact of reason: When a person deliberates, she is conscious of the moral law *moving* her willing. Applying the considerations raised at the beginning of the Paralogisms, it would follow that when humans encounter conspecifics, they automatically regard them as moral deliberators, as rational beings whose reflections on what to do are affected by their consciousness of the moral law (because they model them on themselves). It would thus also follow that humans always and automatically respect other humans in thought. The idea that Kant takes humans automatically to respect the moral law and other moral agents at some level is consonant with his many remarks that, however depraved someone is, he can never turn off or even turn down the voice of reason (e.g., *KpV* 5:35, 5:69). This inevitable, inescapable respect in thought is the basis of the duty for respect in action.

Kant traces a complex psychological route from thought to action and employs surprisingly purple prose to explain the effect on people of realizing that they have the moral law within, that they and all (non-defective) humans are moral lawgivers (*GMS* 4:435–6, *KpV* 5:87). I am going to avoid most of the complications of his psychology of respect and focus on just two, seemingly incontestable, elements of his account. The first has already been discussed: Humans have exactly the same reasons for taking others to be (in part) pure, holy, etc., as they have for taking themselves to have these qualities. The second is also implied by the preceding discussion: What gives humans their exalted status is their moral law producing practical reason. In the second *Critique*, Kant argues from the lawgiver status of humans to FH. Precisely because every human is autonomous, no one can

> use [such a] subject merely as a means ... [by] subjecting him to any aim
> that is not possible in accordance with a law that could arise from the subject
> himself who undergoes [the action], thus never to use this subject merely as
> a means, but always at the same time as himself a purpose. (*KpV* 5:87)

To treat a person in a way that *he* could not will as a universal way of acting would be inconsistent with understanding him to be a moral lawgiver – as an arbiter of what is to be done.

Guyer on the Value of Freedom

I think that Kant is making the same point in his discussion of how FH rules out lying promises in *Groundwork* II:

> For, he whom I want to use for my purposes cannot possibly agree to my way of behaving toward him, and so himself contain the end of this action. (*GMS* 4:429–30)

This discussion may seem to support the idea that FH requires containing others' ends, and thus pursuing them and thereby enhancing their happiness. Telling the truth is, however, a strict duty, so the issue cannot be increasing happiness or even minimizing misery. A note clarifies the situation through a contrast with the negative version of the Golden Rule. The point is not about what people would hate having done to them. These matters can be subjective, whereas what is needed to ground duty is universal law. It is not that the victim would disagree on the subjective ground that he hates being lied to. It is that he cannot agree as a moral lawgiver and so could not contain the end of lying – in his own case or any other.

Kant discusses containing others' ends in the application of FH to the fourth example, but he presents it as a somewhat indirect duty. There would not be a positive agreement with humanity as an end in itself

> unless everyone also tries, as far as he can, to further the ends of others. For the ends of a subject who is an end in itself must as far as possible also be my ends, <u>if that representation is to have its full effect on me</u>. (*GMS* 4:430, my underscoring)

The last phrase suggests that what is good about promoting the ends of others is not the happiness thereby achieved, but the full recognition of others as ends in themselves.

Kant's explanation of the duty of beneficence in the *Metaphysics of Morals* takes a different approach:

> The reason that it is a duty to be beneficent is this: Since our self-love cannot be separated from our need to be loved (helped in the case of need) by others as well, we therefore make ourselves an end for others; and the only way this maxim can be binding is through its qualification as a universal law, hence through our will to make others our ends as well. The happiness of others is therefore an end that is a duty. (*TL* 6:393)

Here, the duty to promote the ends of others is not connected to their status as ends in themselves, and so to FH, but is defended via FUL. Further, the duty is based on a universal, but completely contingent fact about humans, namely, their desire for happiness. Further still, the only way to make one's contingent desire for happiness morally acceptable is to strive for the happiness of others. Hence, the duty to promote the happiness of others does not rest on the intrinsic value of happiness. Promoting happiness in general is an instrument for making one's contingent desire for happiness morally acceptable.

The *Metaphysics of Morals* is both late and meant to elaborate the fundamental principles uncovered in the *Groundwork* in relation to the human condition. But the *Groundwork* itself presents helping the needy as an exemplary case of a moral duty in the context of illustrating FUL, as well as FH, and this discussion should not rest on contingent facts about humans. The example has been widely discussed and I am mainly going to follow Barbara Herman's analysis (Herman 1984). If the needs in question are understood as "true needs" – that are virtually essential to the continuing capacity for autonomy – then the duty to help the needy stems not from the value of maximal human happiness, but from the value of preserving their status as moral beings. I say "mainly," because the discussion of this case in relation to FH seems to add a further dimension. There is also merit in promoting inessential wants of people, because it is a recognition of their special status. In sum, although Kant clearly holds that it is a duty to promote the happiness of others, it is not at all clear that he takes the basis of that duty to be the intrinsic value of happiness.

3 God's Justice

I will treat the issues surrounding happiness and the *summum bonum* much more briefly. Kant is inconsistent about whether the religious postulate arises from practical or theoretical reason. In the Canon of the first *Critique*, he famously asks three questions: What can I know? What ought I to do? What can I hope? (*KrV* A804–5/B832–3). The answer to the second question is that you should do that which makes you worthy of happiness, which is to try to bring into being a moral world – a world in complete accord with all moral laws. He then claims that the answer to the third question about hope is, like that to the second, practical. But he continues by explaining that

> just as moral principles are necessary according to reason in its practical use, so it is equally necessary also according to reason in its theoretical use to assume that everyone has cause to hope for happiness insofar as he has made himself worthy of it in his conduct. (*KrV* A809/B837)

Since this result cannot be guaranteed through the operation of nature, the connection between worthiness to be happy and happiness can only be secured through a supreme intelligence, i.e., God. Is this argument for God supposed to be practical or theoretical, or both?

Kant suggests the third answer in a passage that lends credence to Christian Garve's criticism that he maintains that the moral law cannot motivate without the promise of commensurate happiness (*TP* 8:279):

> Reason finds itself compelled either to assume such a being ... or to regard the moral laws as idle chimeras, because without this presupposition the necessary result that reason connects with these laws would have to vanish. (*KrV* A811/B839)

Here, he seems to say that without the theoretical presumption of a God, and so the distribution of proportional happiness, then reason would find it impossible to act on moral laws.

In the second *Critique*, Kant's considered argument for the religious postulate brings the issues into sharper focus. The argument for God is practical, and not at all theoretical (see *KpV* 5:125), and there is a clear difference between the driver of morality (the *Triebfeder* [*KpV* 5.72ff.]), which can only be the moral law itself and the respect that is inseparable from the consciousness of it, and the ultimate object of moral action, *viz.*, the highest good. Why must humans aim at the highest good and thus presume a moral Creator of the universe? Kant's answer is clear:

> Virtue is not yet ... the whole and complete good as the object of the power of desire of rational finite beings. For, in order to be that, happiness too is required in addition, and this not merely in the partial eyes of a person ... but even in the judgment of an impartial reason, which regards a person as such ... as a purpose in itself. For, to be in need of happiness, and also worthy of it, but nonetheless not to partake of it is not at all consistent with the perfect volition of a rational being that also had all power, even if we only think such a being by way of experiment. (*KpV* 5:110, my underscoring)

But why should an ordinary, rational agent engage in this thought experiment, since, as far as he *knows*, there are no rational beings who are all-powerful?

In a Reflection, Kant observes that if the moral law obligates humans only because they believe in God and an afterlife, then it would be absurd to argue that they must believe in God and an afterlife in order to meet their moral obligations (R6432, *AA* 18:714). The belief in God and an afterlife is what is creating the need for the belief in God and an afterlife! Why is it any less circular to argue that, since a world lacking in the highest good would be inconsistent with an all-powerful (and all-benevolent) Creator, then to avoid this inconsistency rational beings must believe in an all-powerful and all-benevolent Creator who would bring about a world in which the highest good is realized? The supposition of an all-powerful and all-benevolent Creator is the source of the inconsistency with a world where the morally worthy are unhappy, and so of the rational need to suppose the existence of an all-powerful Creator who ensures that they are justly rewarded. Without this supposition, unrewarded virtue is a matter of bad luck, not inconsistency.

If this argument were successful, then it would show that the goal of morality is maximal human happiness. Any moral agent must aim to produce a world in which everyone acts morally (*KrV* A808/B836; *TP* 8:280), and if happiness must be proportional to desert, then in a perfect world, everyone would receive his or her full measure of happiness, compatible with all others receiving their full measures. Further, even if unsuccessful, the argument can support Guyer's interpretive thesis that Kant *took* maximal happiness to be the ultimate aim of morality – since he presumably accepted considerations based on the *summum bonum.*

Still, I am not convinced, because the pieces of the argument from FH and from the *summum bonum* fit uneasily together. In the latter argument, maximal happiness enters the moral calculus very differently from the way in which the "happiness" of others becomes a duty in relation to FH. According to FH, I must help those in need, either to prevent the loss of their autonomy or to show my respect for them. By contrast, the maximal happiness that would be part of the complete good is a matter of distributional justice. The difference in the bases for promoting the happiness of others parallels Stephen Darwall's well-known distinction between two kinds of respect (Darwall 1977). The happiness I must promote on the basis of FH applies equally to all humans; the happiness deserved in a perfect world is a matter of the kind of person someone is.

Further, at least in the 1790's, Kant offers theses that are incompatible with the interpretive claims that he believed that what is valuable about humans is their rationality (their ability to set ends), and that he took FH to be the basis of the duty of promoting the ends of others. As noted, in his final attempt to explain the duty to help others, in the *Metaphysics of Morals*, he does not rely on FH, but on FUL. I have some obligation to give you a dollar so that you have enough to buy the hot fudge sundae you really want and would much enjoy, because I could not will a world in which no one helped those in want. This particular obligation has nothing to do with your rational capacity to set ends, however, and everything to do with your physical capacities to yearn for things and to enjoy them. The ability to set ends means that people have many projects for which they need the assistance of others, but for Kant, although the satisfaction of bringing such projects to fruition may be more intense or more permanent than that of eating ice cream, the pleasures are not different in kind (*KpV* 5:23). More importantly, at least late in his life, he was clear that the ability to sustain rational projects is not what gives humans their ultimate worth. In *Perpetual Peace* (1795), he explains that even a nation of devils could set up a state based on Hobbesian principles of rational self-interest (*ZeF* 8:366). Presumably such folks are seriously lacking in ultimate worth.

For these reasons, I do not think that Kant took maximal happiness to be the ultimate value on the basis of his advocacy of FH. Still, it seems to me that the prominent place of the *summum bonum* in his practical thinking does support Guyer's more limited claim that he took human happiness to be valuable. Happiness must be supplied to meet the demands of cosmic justice (under the supposition of a moral Creator), but that reward would be appropriate only if happiness were valuable, or at least valued. Kant clearly thinks that all humans value happiness, but he may also think that happiness is valuable, under the obvious restriction, *viz.*, that the desire for pleasure or success does not lead the person to contravene her duty. That condition is met when happiness is proportional to virtue, so in discussing the *summum bonum*, Kant can endorse the value of happiness without in any way suggesting that it is good without qualification, and so a suitable basis for morality. In this way, Kant can find a place for the constrained but real value of happiness alongside the ultimate value of humanity.

Although I think the argument works differently than he does, I have also offered reasons in favor of Guyer's view that the ultimate proof of FUL rests on the proof of the value of humanity. This result supports his broad interpretive claim that the deontological in Kant is inseparable from the teleological. I argued further that having the moral law within not only gives humans intrinsic worth, it also sets them the goal of creating a world where human behavior is governed by a system of common, objective laws. So the validity of FUL rests on a metaphysical fact about value – that humans have FUL within – and it creates the end of a morally harmonious world. Kant's theory is not about value-free procedures that make sense

106 PATRICIA KITCHER

separately from metaphysical assumptions. Since being free is the same as having an efficacious moral law within, Guyer is also right that freedom is the ultimate value for Kant.

Exploring the exact roles of value, teleology, and happiness in Kant's moral theory is crucial to adequately understanding it. Or this project certainly seems crucial now that Guyer has shown that, contrary to popular belief, these elements are not outcasts of his ethical thinking.

CHAPTER 6

Kant, Guyer, and Tomasello on the Capacity to Recognize the Humanity of Others

Lucas Thorpe

Much has been written in the last few decades on the content of Kant's moral law, but relatively little on its scope. That is, there has been much discussion on how we should treat morally relevant others, but far less discussion of who or what we should count as morally relevant others. Before jumping into my argument let me say a few words on my terminology.

A Few Remarks about Terminology

Firstly, by "human" in the morally relevant sense I mean those who are demanding of moral respect in the Kantian sense. Some Kantians today, often worried about the moral status of non-human animals, make a distinction between different types of morally relevant others. On the one hand there are organisms that are free and rational and are deserving of moral respect and are members of the sphere of justice. On other hand there are non-rational sentient beings that are capable of feeling pain and are deserving of compassion and concern. Kant himself clearly rejects this distinction, as he thinks our duties toward non-human nature are indirect, being rooted in duties toward ourselves. I am open to such a distinction and think that there are parts of nature that demand a certain type of concern even though they do not demand respect. However, in this chapter, when I talk of "morally relevant others" or being "human" in the morally relevant sense I will mean those beings that are demanding of respect in the first sense. Such organisms are members of the sphere of justice and our relations toward them involve considerations of fairness and mutual respect. Commonly those who draw a line between rational and non-rational nature implicitly assume that this boundary corresponds to the division between language-using and non-linguistic organisms. The assumption being that rationality presupposes linguistic capacities. In this chapter, however, I will argue that the boundary cannot be defined in terms of the distinction between the linguistic and non-linguistic, and the account I offer leaves space for the possibility that there are non-linguistic beings that are deserving of respect in the Kantian sense.

Secondly, I often talk of "moral status attribution." By this I mean the judgment (which I think normally doesn't involve any inference) that a bit of the world around us is deserving of respect in the Kantian sense. By talking about "attribution" rather than "recognition" I mean to remain neutral about whether such attribution is justified or correct. As such, moral status attribution is something that can be studied empirically as part of a naturalistic science. The question of whether such attribution is justified or correct is a separate issue. When I am assuming that such attribution is correct, I will talk of "recognition" of the moral status of others.

Thirdly, as we shall see, Kant himself does not identify being "human" in the morally relevant sense with being a member of a particular biological species. Thus, being "human" in the moral sense is not to be identified with being biologically human. In order to avoid ambiguity, when I intend to talk about humanity in the moral sense I will use the word "human" in quotation marks. When I want to talk about being human in the biological sense I will use the word without inverted commas.

Finally, I do not often explicitly talk about freedom in this chapter. However, Kant himself identifies being "human" in the morally relevant sense with being free, in the sense of either being autonomous or having the capacity for autonomy. So this chapter could have been titled "recognizing freedom." Elsewhere I have argued that the capacity for autonomy should be identified with the capacity to be a member of a realm of ends.[1] In this chapter I develop this idea, appealing to recent work in developmental psychology and primatology, and suggest that this capacity for autonomy (the capacity to be a member of a realm of ends) can be understood in terms of the capacity to engage in shared cooperative activity. Hopefully my reasons for this should become clearer through the chapter.

1 Introduction

On the surface Kant himself seems quite clear about who is deserving of respect: The morally relevant others are all "rational, free beings" or all "human beings." It is clear, however, that Kant does not want to identify

---

[1] Thorpe 2011, 2010, and 2013.

The Capacity to Recognize the Humanity of Others   109

"human beings" in this sense with members of a particular biological species, for he is explicitly open to the idea that there might be non-biologically human rational beings. Thus, for example he is explicitly open to the possibility of extraterrestrial rational beings, who would not be members of the same biological species as us, but who would, presumably, be worthy of respect.[2] And it would seem possible that there are members of our biological species who are not "human" in the morally relevant sense. For example, it is possible that Kant might think that some severely brain damaged biological human beings, and perhaps psychopaths, are not "human" in the morally relevant sense. Given these facts, a Kantian needs to give some account of how we are to recognize who or what counts as "human" in the morally relevant sense.

There are a number of distinct questions a Kantian faces when dealing with the question of what is involved in recognizing the "humanity" of others, and appealing to a concrete example may help clarify this issue. John is sitting on the chair in front of me. If I were to take the chair he was sitting on home and saw it in half, this might be a stupid thing to do; it might even be illegal, if I do not own the chair. There would, however, be nothing intrinsically wrong with the action. Sawing John in half, on the other hand, whatever I think of him, would not only be wrong, it would be reprehensible. Splitting the atom is fine, splitting John is not. But why? What's the difference? Kant's answer is that John is a different type of being from the chair, and a type of being that demands respect. Following Kant, I will name the type of being that John is "human" (in the morally relevant sense), a rational being, a moral subject or a person, and in this chapter I will treat these terms as co-extensional.[3] Now, for Kant there is no (logical) contradiction involved in judging that the chair is a person and John is not. To respect the chair but not the person sitting on it would not be a theoretical mistake but a moral, practical one. If I decided to saw John in half I would not be making a theoretical mistake about his true nature, but would be doing something morally reprehensible.

---

[2] Thus in his *Anthropology from a Pragmatic Point of View* he writes that, "The highest species concept may be that of a *terrestrial* rational being, however we will not be able to name its character because we have no knowledge of *non-terrestrial* rational beings that would enable us to indicate their characteristic property and so to characterize this terrestrial being among rational beings in general. It seems, therefore, that the problem of indicating the character of the human species is absolutely insoluble, because the solution would have to be made through experience by means of the comparison of two *species* of rational being, but experience does not offer us this" (*Anth* 7:322).

[3] Following Kant, I will use the term "human being" in a moral sense, allowing for the possibility that there are possibly some biological human beings who are not human in the moral sense and possibly some beings that are not biologically human that are human in the moral sense.

We attribute a certain moral status to John but not to the chair, and this raises at least three questions:

(1) What is the content of this judgment? In other words, what is it to be "human" in the morally relevant sense?
(2) How do we, in fact, go about ascribing moral status to others?
(3) What, if anything, justifies this ascription?

This chapter has three main sections. In the first two, I examine Kant's answers to these three questions. In the final section I discuss recent work in developmental psychology that supports what I take to be the Kantian thesis that we have a natural capacity to recognize the humanity of others, and I suggest a reformulation of Kant's position in contemporary terms.

In terms of the first question, I will argue that to be "human" in the morally relevant sense is to have the capacity for morality, and that this involves: (a) the capacity to recognize others as ends rather than merely as means and (b) the capacity to enter into relations of ethical community with us.

In terms of the second and third questions, we need to remember that whenever we ask a "how do we know that p?" question we should be careful about the fact that this question contains two distinct questions: (1) The "how question." The answer to this can be a naturalistic, mechanistic, causal story. This has to do with how we go about making certain attributions. (2) The "epistemic question." The answer to this is essentially normative. This has to do with whether our attributions are justified. Our answers to the "how question" and the "epistemic question" may or may not be related. For example, in contemporary reliabilist accounts in epistemology the "how" and the "epistemic" questions are related; for reliabilists argue that if how we make an attribution is the result of a reliable process (and the attribution is true), then we know. So our answer to the question: "How do I know that John, but not the chair he is sitting on, deserves moral respect?" has two aspects: (1) How do we, in fact, go about making such moral status attributions? This seems to be an empirical question. (2) What (if anything) justifies such moral status attributions?

In a recent paper, Paul Guyer has suggested that our recognition of morally relevant others is based upon an argument from analogy. It is not clear whether he is offering this as an account both of *how* we go about attributing moral status to others and an account of what *justifies* such attribution, or whether this is merely meant to be an account of what justifies such attribution. I will assume, however, that his account is

The Capacity to Recognize the Humanity of Others 111

supposed to be an answer both to the how question and the justification question. And I will offer criticisms of it as an answer to both questions.

I will defend, in contrast, a version of what I call *moral reliabilism*. It is not clear that this is the position Kant himself took, as he does not himself offer a detailed account of what is involved in the recognition of the humanity of others, but I will argue this is the most plausible position for a contemporary Kantian ethicist to take. Moral reliabilism consists of two claims.

Firstly, there is the empirical, naturalistic claim that (a) we have a quasi-perceptual capacity to directly ascribe moral status to various bits of the world around us. I will argue that this capacity is best thought of in Gibsonian terms as a capacity to pick up on certain types of social affordances; morally relevant others have the capacity to engage in ethical interaction with us, and recognizing the humanity of others involves picking up on this capacity. Those beings who are "human" in the morally relevant sense, then, afford interaction based on mutual respect. I will explain what I mean by this in more detail later in the chapter.

Secondly, there is the normative claim that, (b) we should assume as a postulate of practical reason that this capacity is reliable (although fallible). I suggest, then, that the most plausible story to tell here is that we have a natural (biological) capacity to recognize the humanity of others, and we must make a moral assumption that this capacity can reliably pick out the morally relevant bits of the phenomenal world around us. In Kantian terms we can think of the assumption that this natural capacity is normatively reliable as a postulate of practical reason. For our moral practice presupposes that we can reliably recognize morally relevant others, and so if morality is not to be an empty figment of our imagination we must assume (for moral, not theoretical reasons) that our capacity to identify which beings are deserving of respect is reliable.

At the heart of my position is a particular understanding of what it is to be "human" in the morally relevant sense. There has been much disagreement among Kant scholars as to what it is to be "human" in the morally relevant sense. Kant himself seems to identify being "human" with rational nature. But this has been interpreted in numerous ways. There are three main broad interpretations of what it is to be "human" in the morally relevant sense.

Firstly, some commentators, such as Christine Korsgaard and Allen Wood, identify "humanity" with the capacity for agency broadly understood. Thus, for example, Christine Korsgaard identifies "humanity" with the capacity to set ends arguing that, "[b]y 'humanity' Kant means the power of free rational choice, for 'the capacity to propose an end to oneself is the characteristic of humanity'" (*TL* 6:392) (Korsgaard 1996a:346). Similarly, Allen Wood identifies "humanity" with the capacity to set and to systematize ends. Thus Wood argues,

> The predisposition to humanity lies in between the predispositions to animality and personality. It encompasses all our rational capacities having no specific reference to morality. Put most generally, humanity is the capacity to set ends through reason... It enables us not only to set ends but to compare the ends we set and organize them into a system... Hence humanity also involves the capacity to form the idea of our happiness or well-being as a whole. (Wood 1999:118–19)

Secondly, many commentators stress that "humanity" essentially involves the capacity for morality. So, for example, John Rawls argues that,

> Kant means by humanity those of our powers and capacities that characterize us as reasonable and rational persons who belong to the natural world... These powers include, first, those of moral personality, which make it possible for us to have a good will and a good moral character; and second, those capacities and skills to be developed by culture: by the arts and sciences and so forth. (Rawls 2000:188)

A similar position, stressing that "humanity" in the morally relevant sense involves our capacity for morality, is defended by, among others, Thomas E. Hill, Barbara Herman, and Onora O'Neill.[4]

Finally, Richard Dean has argued that "humanity" should be identified not merely with the capacity for morality, but with the possession of a good will. Thus he has argued that,

> Humanity, in the sense of the humanity formulation, is indeed equivalent to some feature possessed by rational beings, but not by all minimally rational beings. Instead, "humanity" is Kant's name for the more fully rational nature that is only possessed by a being who actually accepts moral principles as providing sufficient reasons for action. The humanity that should be treated as an end in itself is a properly ordered will, which gives priority to moral considerations over self-interest. To employ Kant's terminology, the end in itself is a good will.[5]

---

[4] Thus, Thomas E. Hill (2002:77) argues that "Our humanity includes our capacity and disposition to follow the allegedly unconditional rational supreme principle of morality." And Onora O'Neill (1989:138) argues that "Rational beings presumably must be non-conditional values because they alone can will anything, hence they alone can have a good will." See also Herman 1993:238.

[5] Dean 2006:6. See also Dean 2009:83–101.

The Capacity to Recognize the Humanity of Others   113

Although I have some sympathy for Richard Dean's account, in this chapter I will assume a version of the second position, namely that "humanity" in the morally relevant sense involves our capacity for morality.[6] This capacity for morality can be understood as the capacity to interact with others on the basis of mutual respect, or as the capacity to become a member of a certain type of moral community (a realm of ends). I take these two characterizations to be extensionally equivalent. According to such a reading, it is only those bits of the phenomenal world that are capable of morality that demand moral respect. Now, many of those who defend such a reading take the first formulation of the categorical imperative as primary, and so suggest that it is only those beings that are capable of moral reasoning that are deserving of respect. Such a position, I believe, is overly intellectualist. One might think that only language-using creatures are capable of moral reasoning and so only such creatures are deserving of respect. In contrast, I defend a position that takes the second and third formulation of the categorical imperatives seriously and will argue that those beings which are deserving of respect are those who are (a) capable of recognizing others as ends and not merely as means and (b) capable of entering into relations of ethical community with us. On this approach it may turn out, as a contingent fact, that the only beings who are deserving of respect are those with linguistic capacities. But it is at least logically possible that there are creatures not capable of language which are capable of interaction based on mutual respect and of forming relations of ethical community with us. And in the final section of this chapter I will argue that there is evidence that pre-linguistic babies are such organisms, and that it is an open question whether there are non-human animals which have such capacities.

According to this position, there is no theoretical criterion we can apply to determine which individuals we are capable of forming such relations with, and so the only way to try and determine which individuals are deserving of respect is to try and form such relations with them. Recognizing the humanity of others is a matter of knowing *how* rather than knowing *that*.

Drawing on recent research in developmental psychology and primatology, especially the work of Tomasello and his associates, I will defend a

---

[6] Epistemically the "capacity for morality" reading and the "good will" reading could be reconciled if we were to assume that every being that has a capacity for morality will ultimately realize this capacity, and so having the capacity for morality and being moral are equivalent. I think Kant sometimes flirts with such a position.

114   LUCAS THORPE

modified version of what I take to be Kant's account. This research suggests that, unlike non-human animals, healthy human beings develop a capacity, between the ages of six months and two years, to engage in joint or shared cooperative activities.[7] My suggestion is that what it is to be "human" (in a morally relevant sense) is to be a being we can engage in shared cooperative activities with.[8] Tomasello and associates have suggested that it is this capacity that differentiates humans from non-human animals.[9] Drawing on the work of Bratman (1989), they argue that joint cooperative activities have three essential characteristics:

> (1) the interactants are mutually responsive to one another, (2) there is a shared goal in the sense that each participant has the goal the we (in mutual knowledge) do X together, and (3) the participants coordinate their plans of action and intentions some way down the hierarchy... the cognitive representation of the [joint] goal contains both self and other; that is, it contains not only the self's goal that the box be open, but also the self's goal that this be accomplished with the partner. (Tomasello, et al. 2005: 680)

And they provide evidence to show how this capacity slowly develops (and has its basis in simpler capacities) between the age of six months and two years. One thing Tomasello and his associates stress is that the capacity to engage in joint cooperative activities presupposes a capacity for joint attention, which they believe is not to be found in non-human animals.[10] And I will argue later in the chapter that joint attention itself should be

---

[7] I will use "joint cooperative activity" and "shared cooperative activity" interchangeably. A joint cooperative activity is a shared cooperative activity involving only two individuals.

[8] Elsewhere I argue that Kant's ethics should be understood as an "ethics of interaction," for the idea of a realm of ends is the idea of a community in which there is real interaction, and so, for Kant, to be moral is to really interact with others. I am suggesting here that we should understand interaction in terms of engaging in joint cooperative activities.

[9] Thus Moll and Tomasello, reporting on their own research, claim that although chimpanzees are "mutually responsive," "In none of the tasks did a chimpanzee ever make a communicative attempt to re-engage the partner... The absence of any efforts by the chimpanzees to re-engage their human partner is crucial: it shows that the chimpanzees did not cooperate in the true sense, since they had not formed a joint goal with the human. If they had been committed to a joint goal, then we would expect them, at least in some instances, to persist in trying to bring it about and in trying to keep the cooperation going. For humans the situation is different from very early on in ontogeny. [within 18 months] when the adult stopped participating at a certain point during the activity, every child at least once produced a communicative attempt in order to re-engage him... [H]uman infants by the age of 18 months, in contrast to apes, are able to jointly commit to a shared goal" (Moll and Tomasello 2007:641).

[10] Thus, Moll and Tomasello (2007:643) claim that although "apes do sometimes point for humans ... it seems that what the apes have learned from their experience with humans is that the human will help them, and that they can use the pointing gesture instrumentally in order to make him help them... However, no ape has ever been observed to point for another ape or for a human declaratively – that is, just for the sake of sharing attention to some outside entity, or to inform others of things cooperatively, as humans often do... [E]ven when they first begin to point

The Capacity to Recognize the Humanity of Others 115

thought of as a basic type of joint cooperative activity. They reach the (provisional) conclusion that it is this capacity that distinguishes human beings from non-human animals.[11] This suggestion that only biologically human beings are capable of joint cooperative activity, however, has been controversial and many primatologists, especially those using more of an ethnographic methodology, believe that some non-human primates are capable of some forms of joint cooperative activity.

The capacity to engage in such shared cooperative activities involves both a motivational element and a cognitive element. In order to engage in shared cooperative activities, organisms must have the motivation to cooperate, and must also have various cognitive capacities, for example the capacities to represent shared goals, the capacity for role reversal, and the capacity for joint attention. Although Tomasello is engaged in a naturalistic project of explanation, I suggest that this account of what it is to be human corresponds to the Kantian understanding of what it is to be "human" in a morally relevant sense, and that the morally relevant others are those we can engage in joint cooperative activities with.[12] It is interesting that Moll and Tomasello also suggest that the capacity to engage in joint cooperative activities lies at the heart of our moral capacities. Thus they claim that,

> [p]erspectival cognitive representations and the understanding of beliefs also pave the way for what may be called, very generally, collective intentionality... That is, the essentially social nature of perspectival cognitive

---

at around 1 year of age, human infants do this with a full range of different motives, including the motive to share attention."

[11] "Although non-human animals may engage with one another in complex social interactions in which they know the goals of one another and exploit this, they are not motivated to create shared goals to which they are jointly committed in the same ways as humans" Moll and Tomasello (2007:682).

[12] I am not suggesting that we have no moral duties to those beings which we can't engage in joint cooperative activities with. Kant himself believes that we have no direct duties toward non-human animals, but rather that our duties to non-human animals are indirect, being based on a duty toward ourselves. His basic argument is that cruelty toward animals can cause us to become callous and that we have a duty toward ourselves not to be callous. Thus, Kant explains in the *Metaphysics of Morals*, that, "with regard to the animate but non-rational part of creation, violent and cruel treatment of animals is far more intimately opposed to a human being's duty to himself, and he has a duty to refrain from this; for it dulls his shared feeling of their suffering and so weakens and gradually uproots a natural predisposition that is very serviceable to morality in one's relationship with other people" (*MS* 6:443). I suggest a more plausible account would be to argue that there are two types of morally relevant others: those to whom we have duties of respect (which I have suggested consists of all those beings with which we can engage in joint cooperative activities with) and those toward which we have a duty of care (which would include at least most living beings, and perhaps all beings). In this chapter I have only concerned myself with morally relevant others understood in terms of those to whom we have duties of respect.

representations enables children, later in the preschool period, to construct the generalized social norms that make possible the creation of social-institutional facts, such as money, marriage and government, whose reality is grounded totally in the collective practices and beliefs of a social group conceived generally... Importantly, when children internalize generalized collective conventions and norms and use them to regulate their own behaviour, this provides for a new kind of social rationality (morality) involving what Searle calls "desire-independent reasons for action." At this point, children have become norm following participants in institutional reality, that is to say, fully functioning members of their cultural group. (Moll and Tomasello 2007:646)

I have argued that Kant's ethics can be understood as an ethics of interaction, and my suggestion at the end of this chapter is that the best way of interpreting this in contemporary terms is to claim that the morally relevant others are those we are capable of engaging in joint cooperative activity with. If this is the case, then we have no criterion or principle to pick out which bits of the world are human in the morally relevant sense, for the only way we have of establishing whether a being is the sort we can engage in a joint cooperative activity with is to try and do so.

One way of thinking about this capacity to engage in shared cooperative activity is in terms of possessing certain types of social "affordances." The notion of an affordance was introduced by the ecological psychologist J. J. Gibson. Gibson argues that affordances are to be understood in terms of the possibilities of action that the environment offers an organism, and he argues that in perception organisms are able to directly pick up on such affordances. On the account I am proposing, being "human" in the morally relevant sense is to be understood in terms of the possession of certain types of social affordance. Such social affordances are not to be understood in terms of the possibility of *action* offered by an object or environmental feature, but in terms of the possibility of *interaction* offered by another organism. Morally relevant others have the capacity to interact with us in a cooperative way, such that we are able to engage in shared cooperative activities with them. To recognize the "humanity" of others is to pick up on this possibility of interaction. Gibson explains the notion of an affordance in the following terms:

> The affordances of the environment are what it offers the animal, what it provides or furnishes, either for good or ill. The verb to afford is found in the dictionary, but the noun affordance is not. I have made it up. I mean by it something that refers to both the environment and the animal in a way that no existing term does... If a terrestrial surface is nearly horizontal

The Capacity to Recognize the Humanity of Others   117

(instead of slanted), nearly flat (instead of convex or concave), and sufficiently extended (relative to the size of the animal) and if its substance is
rigid (relative to the weight of the animal), then the surface affords support.
It is a surface of support, and we call it a substratum, ground, or floor. It is
stand-on-able, permitting an upright posture for quadrupeds and bipeds. It
is therefore walk-on-able and run-over-able. It is not sink-into-able like a
surface of water or a swamp, that is, not for heavy terrestrial animals.
Support for water bugs is different... Note that the four properties listed –
horizontal, flat, extended, and rigid – would be physical properties of a
surface if they were measured with the scales and standard units used in
physics. As an affordance of support for a species of animal, however, they
have to be measured relative to the animal. (Gibson 2015: 119)

Affordances, then, are the possibilities of action an environment offers
an organism. Thus, for example, a pathway through a cluttered environment is an affordance as it allows for locomotion between two points. An
opening in a horizontal surface, such as a doorway, is also an affordance in
that it offers the possibility of passing-through. Now, I suggest that there
are social affordances. These should be understood not in terms of the
possibility of *action*, but in terms of the possibility of *interaction*.

Now, even non-human primates are able to pick up on some social
affordances. For example, chimpanzees are able to recognize a hand-raise
signal as an invitation to play.[13] In so doing, chimpanzees are able to
recognize certain possibilities of interaction. Now, I suggest that organisms
that are "human" in the morally relevant sense possess the capacity to
engage in certain types of interaction with us: namely, interaction that
involves mutual respect and allows for shared cooperative activity. Thus,
our capacity to recognize the "humanity" of others involves the capacity to
pick up on the possibility of such interaction. To be "human" is to invite
others to interact on the basis of mutual respect, and to recognize the
"humanity" is to pick up on such an invitation.

The account I am offering has an essentially first person plural starting
point: To pick up on the humanity of others is to implicitly recognize the

---

[13] Tomasello (2008:23) explains how chimpanzees develop this capacity to pick up on a hand-raise as
an invitation to play in the following terms:

   (i)   initially one youngster approaches another with rough-and-tumble play in mind, raises his
        arm in preparation to play-hit the other, and then actually hits, jumps on, and begins playing;

  (ii) over repeated instances, the recipient learns to anticipate this sequence on the basis of the
        initial arm-raise alone, and so begins to play upon perceiving this initial step; and

 (iii) the communicator eventually learns to anticipate this anticipation, and so raises his arm,
        monitors the recipient, and waits for her to react – expecting this arm-raise to initiate
        the play.

possibility of becoming a "we." In contrast, Guyer's account, which will be examined later in the chapter, has an essentially first person singular starting point. According to Guyer, I start by recognizing my own moral status, and then judge that others are demanding of moral respect because they are relevantly similar to me.[14]

The reason I think that this implies that there is no theoretical criterion to decide whether another bit of the world is "human" in the morally relevant sense is because, following Gibson, I think there is a clear difference between picking up on an affordance, on the one hand, and classifying or labeling an object on the other. To pick up on an affordance involves a type of know-how, rather than classifying an object theoretically; it involves knowing how an object can be used or interacted with. As Gibson explains,

> The theory of affordances rescues us from the philosophical muddle of assuming fixed classes of objects, each defined by its common features and then given a name. As Ludwig Wittgenstein knew, you cannot specify the necessary and sufficient features of the class of things to which a name is given. They have only a "family resemblance." But this does not mean you cannot learn how to use things and perceive their uses. You do not have to classify and label things in order to perceive what they afford. (Gibson 2015:126)

Learning how we can interact with various bits of the world involves trying to interact and learning which bits of the world allow for what types of interaction. This involves a practical rather than a theoretical capacity. It involves *knowing-how* rather than *knowing-that*. Those bits of

---

[14] It is interesting to note that although many followers of John Rawls also seem to have an essentially first person singular starting point, there is a way in which Rawls himself also starts with the "we." For Rawls himself is clear that the question of justice has to do with the distribution of the social product and his starting point is the idea that "society is a cooperative venture for mutual advantage." Thus, Rawls's theory takes as its starting point the fact that those in the sphere of justice are engaged in some sort of shared collective cooperative activity. Rawls's theory of justice has to do with how to share the benefits and burdens of social cooperation, and so the sphere of justice presupposes a background of shared cooperative activity. Thus, he argues that the principles of social justice "provide a way of assigning rights and duties in the basic institutions of society and they define the appropriate distribution of the benefits and burdens of social cooperation" (Rawls 1999:4). This stress on the sharing of the collective social product is central to Rawls's account, thus he points out that, "In a well-ordered society individuals acquire claims to a share of the social product by doing certain things encouraged by the existing arrangements. The legitimate expectations that arise are the other side, so to speak, of the principle of fairness and the natural duty of justice. For in the way that one has a duty to uphold just arrangements, and an obligation to do one's part when one has accepted a position in them, so a person who has complied with the scheme and done his share has a right to be treated accordingly by others. They are bound to meet his legitimate expectations" (275).

The Capacity to Recognize the Humanity of Others 119

the phenomenal world that are "human" in the morally relevant sense are those bits of the world that we can interact with on the basis of mutual respect. And learning how to recognize which bits of the world are "human" in the morally relevant sense involves picking up on *how* we are able to interact with various bits of the world; we can only learn which parts of the world we can interact with morally by trying to so interact, and being open to the possibility of such interaction.

The account I am suggesting has two implications that Kant himself may not have accepted. Firstly, it suggests that it is an open question as to whether there are non-biologically-human animals that are "human" in the moral sense. Secondly, it suggests that being "human" in the morally relevant sense may be something that comes in degrees rather than being an either-or matter. The reason for this is because there are many different types of collaborative activity differing in complexity, and there are individuals that are capable of engaging in certain types of collaborative activities but not in others. For example, some severely autistic adults are not able to engage in those cooperative activates that involve language. But they may have the capacity to engage in other types of cooperative activities. Although Kant himself may not have accepted these claims, I believe that contemporary Kantian ethicists should welcome these positions.

2 Recognizing Humanity

In the previous section of this chapter I argued that, for Kant, the morally relevant others are those capable of morality, and I have suggested that this should be understood in terms of the capacity to engage in shared cooperative activity. In this section I will examine what, if anything, justifies our judgment that a bit of the world has the capacity to be moral. There would seem to be at least four possible options here. The first three would provide me with some theoretical justification for my belief that John is a human being in a morally relevant sense, the fourth denies such a theoretical justification is possible. In this chapter I will defend this final option. The four options are:

(a) That there is some theoretical criterion we can use to distinguish between what falls under the concept "moral subject" and what does not. In Kantian terminology this would imply that the concept "moral subject" could be schematized (and that some sort of theoretical deduction of the objective reality of this concept could be given).

120   LUCAS THORPE

However, it seems clear that for Kant such an account is a non-starter, and so I will not discuss this option any further in this chapter.

(b) Inference to the best/only explanation.[15]

(c) An argument from Analogy. I am justified in believing that I am a moral subject and John is relevantly like me whereas the chair is not. This is the argument suggested by Paul Guyer in a recent paper (Guyer 2013).

(d) There is no theoretical justification of my judgment that John is a moral subject, so we must assume, as a postulate of practical reason, that we have a non-theoretical but reliable capacity to recognize other morally relevant subjects (and certain things, such as language, works of art, etc., as the product of such subjects).

In this section I will focus on the final two possibilities. I will argue that the final option is more plausible, both as an interpretation of Kant and as an ethical position, than Guyer's position. If I am right, then my judgment that John is an end in himself has no theoretical justification, not even a probable one. Although I will focus on arguing against Guyer's position, I believe that most of my arguments against the argument from analogy will also be telling against justifications that appeal to inference to the best explanation.

Guyer begins his paper by examining Kant's argument that I am (practically) justified in judging myself to be free from the first-person perspective, and rightly notes that such an argument cannot be used from the third-person perspective to judge that another person is a free moral subject.[16] This seems to be a problem for Kant for, as Guyer asks, "if I can prove *myself* to be free and subject to the moral law, but if *others* are due moral treatment from me only because *they* are free and rational beings who are ends in themselves, how can I prove to myself that others *are* indeed ends in themselves who must always be treated as such and never merely as means?" (Guyer 2016: 158) Guyer's solution is to suggest that

---

[15] Kant suggests such an account at the end of the *Critique of Judgment*. Here he writes, "If I determine the causality of the human being with regard to certain products that are explicable only by means of intentional purposiveness by thinking of it as an understanding, I do not have to stop there, but can attribute this predicate to him as a well-known property, and I have cognition of him by this means" (5:484). This is the only place I know of where Kant makes such a suggestion.

[16] "What Kant now offers are arguments by means of which each of us may prove him- or herself free, but not arguments by means of which any of us can prove that any or all *others* are free. Kant's arguments address the first-person question of how I should choose to behave, not the third-person question of whether I can hold others responsible for their actions" (Guyer 2016:153).

The Capacity to Recognize the Humanity of Others 121

our belief that others are free moral subjects can be justified by an argument from analogy. Thus he argues that,

> Kant never explicitly asks whether one can know that other human beings actually possess free wills or attempts to prove it, presumably taking it to be obvious to each of us that other human beings[17] (and nothing else) are actually rational beings. Yet it is clear that on Kant's premises we can be directly acquainted only with the outward appearances of other persons, and cannot have any immediate knowledge of their inner states, let alone of the noumenal reality behind that. So *the attribution of any inner states at all to others must presumably be based on analogy with our experience of our own inner states, mediated by our assumptions about the connections between our own states of inner sense and our own outwardly observable bodily states.* (Guyer 2016:156, my emphasis)

Now, as Guyer notes, Kant is committed to the view that analogical arguments can only provide us with probability and never certainty, and so he suggests that our belief in the existence of other subjects can at most be "highly probable but not certain" and perhaps must ultimately be based on "some sort of moral Pascalian wager."[18] Now, rather than thinking of this as posing a problem Guyer suggests that, "uncertainty about the real freedom of others could lead us to temper our retributive instincts with humility and mercy... leaving us to be rigorous in our moral demands on ourselves but merciful in our judgments about others" (Guyer 2016: 160).

Now, there is some textual evidence that Kant appeals to some form of the argument from analogy in his empirical psychology. Thus, he suggests in his *Anthropology from a Pragmatic Point of View* that a proper knowledge of human nature needs to start from a first person singular point of view, namely with introspection (inner experience). Thus Kant argues that,

> [k]nowledge of the human being through inner experience, because to a large extent one also judges others according to it, is more important than correct judgment of others, but nevertheless at the same time perhaps more difficult... So it is advisable and even necessary to begin with observed appearances in oneself, and then to progress above all to the assertion of certain propositions that concern human nature; that is to inner experience. (*Anth* 7:143)

---

[17] And here Guyer seems to mean "human beings" in the first sense of being a member of the biological species.

[18] "[T]he value of treating others morally if they really are free and rational beings is so high, and the error of failing to treat them morally if they really are the kinds of beings who should be morally treated would be so grave, that even just a probability – or indeed just the possibility – that the other human bodies I observe and interact with are really also bearers of moral personality is enough to make it rational to treat them as if they are" (Guyer 2016:159).

122 LUCAS THORPE

And in his lectures he explicitly appeals to the argument from analogy, arguing that,

> I consider thinking beings ... through experience, which happens in part internally in myself, or externally, where I perceive other natures, and cognize according to the analogy that they have with me; and that is empirical psychology, where I consider thinking natures through experience. (*V-Anth* 28:224)

These passages, however, are about the proper method of empirical psychology and do not obviously concern moral status attribution. There is no good reason to think that the proper methodology for predicting and explaining the behavior of others should also provide an account or justification of how we recognize which bits of the world around us are deserving of moral respect. So, the fact that Kant suggests a first person singular starting point and appeals to the argument for analogy in his empirical psychology should not be taken as evidence that his account of moral status attribution should also be thought of as appealing to an argument from analogy. In addition, there has been some debate, even with regard to his empirical psychology, of whether Kant really is committed to taking introspection as his starting point.[19]

As we have seen, Guyer suggests that Kant thinks that my belief that John is a moral subject can only be justified by an argument from analogy. I believe, however, that there is an alternative explanation that is both morally more plausible and Kantian in spirit, namely that such beliefs cannot and do not need to be justified theoretically. Instead I assume that I have a reliable but non-theoretical capacity to immediately ascribe moral status to others and although we cannot know theoretically that this capacity is reliable we must assume for moral reasons (as a postulate of practical reason) that this capacity is reliable, in that it is capable of reliably picking out those parts of the phenomenal world that are demanding of respect. Kant himself seems committed to the view that certain capacities

---

[19] Thus, for example, Thomas Sturm has argued that for Kant the proper starting point of empirical psychology is not introspection but the observation of the external actions of ourselves and others. Thus, he argues that from "at least the 1780s on, [Kant] advances a methodological claim against introspection as the primary method of knowing the human mind. He claims that one can experience "the state of one's own mind ... through attention to one's own actions just as well" (Sturm 2001:174), and he continues to claim that, "[o]ur vocabulary of representations, thoughts, feelings, passions, traits of personal character, and so on, is intimately connected to a careful observation of human action and human life as it occurs and as it can be observed, especially in society (7:119–20). 'Psychological phenomena' are open to public observation in Kant's view, contrary to what Nayak and Sotnak and others have claimed" (175). Sturm's Interpretation has been forcefully criticized by Patrick R. Frierson (2014:4–9).

The Capacity to Recognize the Humanity of Others   123

are necessary (albeit subjective) conditions of morality. He makes this clear in the *Metaphysics of Morals* where he argues that, "[t]here are certain moral endowments such that anyone lacking them could have no duty to acquire them. – they are *moral feeling, conscience, love* of one's neighbor and *respect* for oneself (*self-esteem*). There is no obligation to have these because they lie at the basis of morality, as subjective conditions of receptiveness to the concept of duty... All of them are natural predispositions of the mind..." (*TL* 6:399). I suggest that our capacity to recognize the humanity of others should be thought of as one of the aesthetic presuppositions of morality. Indeed, the natural predisposition to love one's neighbor presumably involves a capacity to recognize one's neighbor.

This capacity is manifested in our capacity to immediately recognize noise as meaningful speech, to hear a scream as a cry for help. I think that thinking of this moral capacity to recognize others in terms of hearing is very Kantian in spirit, as much of the vocabulary Kant uses when talking of reason and understanding has to do with hearing. For example, the main activity of understanding is *bestimmen* (to determine) which, of course, has the root *stimme* (voice). And as Allen Wood points out, "Kant's German word for 'reason' (*Vernunft*) is derived from the verb *vernehmen*, which means to hear, and more specifically to understand what you hear."[20] I suggest then that ultimately, for Kant, a rational being or moral subject is something that has a voice (and so can make moral demands) and can listen (*vernehmen*) to the moral demands of others.[21] It can make demands and understand the demands of others. And I believe that this capacity to understand (*vernehmen*) the voice of the other is immediate. To argue that there is some sort of (unconscious?) argument from analogy going on here does not fit in with our moral phenomenology. I don't think that I hear the baby scream and quickly and unconsciously think that the baby is like me and so its crying must be a call for help, but instead I believe that I just immediately hear the screams of the child *as* a cry for help, *as* a moral demand. And Kant believes that such demands are irresistible.[22] If I do not

---

[20] Wood 2008:18.

[21] I believe that this is what Kant is getting at in the *Opus Postumum*, where he repeatedly defines the human being as a being with both rights and duties. (Here he opposes the human being to God who is a being with only rights).

[22] Although his moral ear may have been closed to the cries of babies (and the singing of prisoners): "A child that comes into the world apart from marriage is born outside the law (for the law is marriage) and therefore outside the protection of the law. It has, as it were, stolen into the commonwealth (like contraband merchandise), so that the commonwealth can ignore its existence (since it was not right that it should have come to exist this way), and can therefore also ignore its annihilation" (MM 6:336). No one is perfect.

block my moral ear and If do not drown out the cry for help with other voices I cannot but help to react to it.[23] This capacity to make and recognize demands of others, is at the heart of what it is to be "human" in the morally relevant sense. Now, I suggested that this capacity can be thought of in terms of having a "voice," but I think that having such a voice does not necessarily require natural language. For, as we shall see, pre-linguistic young babies are capable of making and recognizing such demands. And perhaps some members of other species are too.

I believe such an account is more plausible ethically than Guyer's account. Explaining our belief in the existence of other moral subjects as resting on probabilistic reasoning also does a bad job of explaining evil acts.[24] I think that the Nazi who refuses to see the Jew in front of him as a human being is not making a bad analogical inference, but is refusing to recognize the humanity of the person suffering in front of him. He is refusing to hear the scream as a cry for help. Doing bad things to other people is often very difficult.[25] Thus, John Doris points out that "The *Einsatzgruppen* shot thousands of jews in the back of the neck, one by one, so there was very close contact with the victims. They were apparently expected to work for only an hour at a time, despite the fact that this task was not physically demanding, and they were liberally provided with alcohol" (Doris 2002: 56). Christopher Browning makes clear in his book based upon the reports of members of a German police unit that was given the order to massacre Jews in Poland, shutting out the voices and demands

[23] For a fuller account of the irresistibility of the voice of conscience, see my paper "The Point of Studying Ethics According to Kant" (Thorpe: 2006). See also Sticker 2017.

[24] And I believe that for Kant, evil acts can be done by good people. I think this is true even in the case for Nazis. This belief is, in part, based upon my experience as a tour guide in Europe. I sometimes gave "Holocaust Tours" and we sometimes organized meetings with ex-members of the Hitler youth who were fervent Nazis in their youth and now met with groups of mainly Jewish visitors at the Wansee Conference house, where the decision on the "final solution" was made. These ex-members of the Hitler youth were rabidly anti-Semitic (and evil?) in their teens, but the judgment of most of the participants at the meeting were that they were good people (now).

[25] Thus, for example, in his discussion of the Milgram experiments, where subjects were showed a remarkable willingness to administer seemingly painful shocks to a confederate of the experimenter, John Doris argues that, "the most striking feature of the demonstration is not blind obedience but *conflicted* obedience. Horribly conflicted obedience: Subjects were often observed to 'sweat, tremble, stutter, bite their lips, groan and dig their fingernails into their flesh' (Milgram)." And he suggests that historical studies, especially of the Holocaust, suggest that such conflict was not merely a result of the experimental circumstances (Doris 2002:42–3). The quote from Milgram is from 1963:375.

The Capacity to Recognize the Humanity of Others 125

of the victims was very difficult indeed, at least for most of the perpetrators.[26] Now, the Nazis made numerous films that were made for the purpose of convincing viewers that certain groups, such as Jews and the physically and mentally disabled, were not really human and their lives were "not worth living." Some of these films were made specifically to "help" the perpetrators deal with their "difficult work."[27] But even for most of those committed to the ideology, killing was not easy. Surely an argument from analogy is not that hard to shut off?

Finally, I disagree with Guyer's suggestion that our uncertainty about the moral status of other human bodies around us as free moral subjects could be the basis for us "to temper our retributive instincts with humility and mercy" (Guyer 2016:160). If a person does something morally wrong, surely to doubt their status as a moral subject will not lead us to humility and mercy but may instead lead us to think of them as rabid dogs. Yes, it may remove our retributive instincts, for one does not punish a rabid dog, but I am not sure that such doubt will lead to moral compassion. As an alternative I suggest that, for Kant our attitude of humility and mercy, the need to treat ourselves harshly and others gently for our and their moral failings, is not based on a skepticism about whether or not the person in front of us is a free moral subject but on a skepticism about whether the evil acts of others are really an indication that they do not actually have good wills.[28] When confronted by evil or bad acts we may be tempted to believe that the individual that committed these acts has an evil will. The skepticism that leads to compassion and humility is one that doubts whether such acts are an indication of a bad will. A skepticism that does not doubt the voice of our moral ear that tells us that the body in front of us is a human being and demanding of respect, but doubts that their evil actions are really a manifestation of an evil will. The fact that a virtuous agent can do appalling things is, I believe, central to Kantian ethics. For a virtuous person is not, for Kant, someone who has a perfect or holy will, but is instead someone who is striving for such moral perfection. As such, a

---

[26] Browning 1992. It is based on the same documentary evidence that Daniel Goldhagen used for his later and unfortunately better known book *Hitler's Willing Executioners* (1996), and reaches a very different, and in my eyes, a far more plausible conclusion.

[27] One of these films is called "A life not worth living" and was made to be shown to doctors involved in the "Euthanasia" program against the physically and mentally disabled.

[28] Thus Kant explains that, "Now through experience we can indeed notice unlawful actions, and also notice (at least within ourselves) that they are consciously contrary to law. But we cannot observe maxims, we cannot do so unproblematically even within ourselves; hence the judgment that an agent is an evil human being cannot reliably be based on experience" (*RGV* 6:20). Similar passages are not hard to find.

virtuous person is someone who slowly converges on holiness over time, who over their life slowly gives in to the temptation of listening to their conscience and the moral demands of others. Now, such a process may involve a long series of two steps forward and one step back. But if we think that having a good will does not consist in always doing the right things, but in terms of having a phenomenal character that slowly converges on doing the right thing (gladly), then we can always be skeptical about whether a particular bad act, or any finite series of bad acts, is necessarily the manifestation of a vicious character. We can always be forgiving, merciful, and humble because we can always tell ourselves that we do not know where in their life the seemingly vicious person in front of us is. For all we know they may be in the middle of a step back rather than two steps forward. At least for me, this fits with my moral intuitions. If, for example, I catch a student plagiarizing and decide to be merciful, this is not because I think "maybe she is not free, maybe she is just a machine that has been programmed by the society around her," but because I think "she is young, she will grow older and hopefully better."

3 The Capacity to Recognize Humanity and Recent Research in Developmental Psychology

Up until this point in the chapter I have been primarily interested in defending an interpretation of Kant's position. I have argued that Kant believes that we have no criterion of principle for judging which bits of the world around us are human in the morally relevant sense, but that a Kantian should assume as a postulate of practical reason that we possess a reliable capacity to recognize the humanity of others. In this final section, drawing on recent research in developmental psychology, I will briefly suggest a more sophisticated naturalistic version of this thesis. This research suggests that we are born with an innate capacity to recognize other human beings, and in particular to distinguish between human faces and other images and between human voices and other sounds,[29] and that at a very early age humans, unlike non-human animals, begin to develop a capacity to engage in joint cooperative activity.[30] And I have argued that

---

[29] As Janet Wayne Astington argues, "Looking at faces, listening to voices, babies seem tuned into people right from the start. They are born that way... It is not that all their understanding is innate but that they have innate predispositions and these help them to distinguish one person from another and from other things in the world" (Astington 1993:38).

[30] And this research suggests that the capacity to engage in joint cooperative activities presupposes a capacity for sophisticated joint attention (which also seems to be a capacity lacking in all other

The Capacity to Recognize the Humanity of Others 127

what it is to be human (in a morally relevant sense) is to be a being we can engage in shared cooperative activities with.[31] If this is the case, then we have no criterion or principle to pick out which bits of the world are human in the morally relevant sense, for the only way we have of establishing whether a being is the sort we can engage in a joint cooperative activity with is to try and do so. If the conclusions of this research are correct then the more sophisticated version of my thesis is, the capacity to recognize other human beings is either innate or develops over the first two years after birth and that, as a postulate of practical reason, we must assume that this natural capacity is able to reliably pick out human beings in a morally relevant sense.

Although the seemingly innate capacity to recognize faces and distinguish between voices and other sounds is obviously not a capacity to recognize human beings in a morally relevant sense, it seems likely that such capacities are at the basis of the more complex capacity to engage in joint cooperative activity that seems to develop slowly between the ages of six months and two years – the capacity to engage in joint cooperative activities. I believe that this capacity does lie at the heart of our capacity to recognize morally relevant others, as, for a Kantian, the morally relevant others are those we can engage in joint cooperative activities with. In the previous section of this chapter I criticized Guyer's reading of Kant. Guyer suggested that Kant's position that our judgment that someone or something is a morally relevant other is based on an argument from analogy. I criticized this as a reading of Kant. In this section I will argue that even if this were a correct reading of Kant, contemporary research would suggest that it is false, for our capacity to engage in joint cooperative activities clearly seems to develop before we develop (and hence does not depend on) the capacity to engage in complex analogical reasoning.

Starting in the 1920s Jean Piaget, basing his research on the verbal responses of young children, reached the conclusion that young children cannot distinguish between people and things nor between thoughts and things. This remained the orthodoxy for many decades. More recent research, however, using different techniques, primarily the habituation/

---

non-human animals) and that in healthy infants this capacity for joint attention uses the innate capacities to recognize faces and to distinguish between voices and other sounds.

[31] Elsewhere I argue that Kant's ethics should be understood as an "ethics of interaction," for the idea of a realm of ends is the idea of a community in which there is real interaction, and so, for Kant, to be moral is to strive to really interact with others. I am suggesting here that we should understand interaction in terms of engaging in joint cooperative activities.

dishabituation methodology, has suggested that Piaget's findings were false.[32] Recent studies suggest that even in the first months, and probably even hours, young babies seem to have the capacity to distinguish between people and things. In particular, these studies seem to show a discriminating response between human faces and voices on the one hand, and non-human patterns and noises on the other.

Facial recognition in young infants. Astington, writing in 1993, explains that, "although some researchers have found that two-month-olds prefer a face over other patterns of equal complexity, generally this work has shown that babies don't reliably show this preference until four or five months of age. However, research using real faces, which are moving and three-dimensional as well as having contrast and complexity, has shown that much younger infants, even those two or three days old, can discriminate between their mothers face and that of a stranger" (Astington 1993: 38).

More recent research seems to suggest that the capacity to distinguish faces from other patterns is present from birth. Thus Bushnell, in a 2001 study, writes that "There is no doubt that the human infant is capable of face discrimination and face recognition within a surprisingly short time after birth" (Bushnell 2001:67) and provides evidence from an experiment on 29 newborns that within 72 hours of birth young infants are able to remember their mothers' faces.[33] Mondloch et al. (1999) provide evidence that six-week-old infants have a marked visual preference for the human face. In addition, young infants are able to distinguish between human faces and faces of other species (De Haan et al. 2002). There is even evidence to suggest that babies as young as four months discriminate between attractive and unattractive faces (Samuels et al. 1994). One interesting result suggested by Pascalis, Haan, and Nelson is that the human capacity to recognize faces is generic but begins to narrow after about three months, "becoming more human face specific" (Pascalis et al. 2002). This study suggests that young infants (six months) are actually better at distinguishing between the faces of individual monkeys than

---

[32] Astington quite clearly explains this methodology in the following terms: "We keep showing her the same things time and time again until she is bored with it and doesn't look at it for very long; she is habituated to it. Then we show her something different. Does she spend longer looking at the new thing or does she seem bored with it as the one she has seen repeatedly? If she spends longer, that is, if she dishabituates, we know it seems different to her from what she was looking at before" (Astington 1993:39).

[33] The evidence of this experiment suggests that even within the first three days of birth "an increased opportunity to view the mother's face is associated with stronger visual preference levels" (Bushnell 2001:70).

The Capacity to Recognize the Humanity of Others   129

slightly older infants (nine months). In this study, six-month-old infants, nine-month-old infants, and adults were shown pictures of both monkey and human faces, and only the youngest group showed signs of discrimination between individuals of both species. That is, six-month-olds showed signs of discriminating between monkey Bob and monkey Bill. Nine-month-olds and adults did not.

The capacity to distinguish between voices and other sounds in very young infants. Astington writes that, "(n)ewborns can also distinguish their mother's voice from that of someone else. They are startled by sudden noises and soothed by rhythmic music, but it is human voices they really seem to listen to. A crying baby may stop crying when he hears his mother's voice; another baby, lying quietly, may start to kick excitedly when her father starts to talk to her" (Astington 1993:38).

Once again, Ashington's claims seem to be confirmed by recent experimental evidence. For example, in a classic study of four-day-old French infants, Mahler et al. have shown that four-day-old infants "distinguish utterance in their native language from those of another language" (Mehler et al. 2002:25). And in a recent study, Vouloumanos and Werker argue that "humans are born with a preference for listening to speech" and cite recent studies that seem to show that newborn infants are "sensitive to word boundaries, distinguish between rhythmically dissimilar languages, distinguish between stress patterns of multisyllabic words, categorically discriminate lexical versus grammatical words and differentiate between good and poor syllable forms."[34] There is a great amount of additional research that suggests that the capacity to distinguish between the human and the non-human, in very sophisticated ways, is found at a very early age.[35]

Now, of course, these seemingly innate capacities to recognize faces and distinguish between speech and other sounds are not themselves capacities to recognize the humanity of others in any moral sense. However, I suggest

---

[34] Vouloumanos et al. 2007:159. Worried that past studies may have only showed a preference for speech over white noise, in their study Vouloumanos and Werker show that newborns discriminate between speech and "complex non-speech analogues" that "were modeled on sine-wave analogues of speech" (160).

[35] For example, Tomasello claims that "Infants recognize self-produced, biological motion within a few months after birth, and they soon turn to look in the same direction as other persons as well. By around six months of age, infants have developed sufficient expectations about human animate actions to be able to predict what others will do in familiar situations. Thus, for example, using habituation methodology, Woodward found that infants of this age expect people (specifically, human hands) to do such things as reach for objects they were just reaching for previously. Infants do not expect inanimate objects that resemble human hands (e.g., a garden-tool claw) to 'reach' toward the familiar object in similar circumstances" (2005:678).

that, in healthy infants, these basic innate capacities play a role in the more complex capacity to engage in joint cooperative activity, and I argue that this capacity lies at the heart of our capacity to recognize the humanity of others in a moral sense.[36]

The capacity to engage in shared cooperative activity and declarative pointing. The previous two capacities do not, in themselves, seem to be moral capacities, although they probably play a role in the genesis and development of the fully moral capacities. I have suggested that a central role in the development of moral capacities is played by the capacity to engage in joint cooperative activity. One aspect of our capacity to recognize the humanity of others has to do with declarative pointing, and our capacity to recognize such pointing as an invitation to look. Declarative pointing, which seems to be uniquely human, is pointing "for the sake of sharing attention to some outside entity, or to inform others of things cooperatively, as humans often do" (Moll and Tomasello 2007: 643). Such pointing can be understood as an invitation to look, and I have argued that recognizing such activity is best thought of as picking up on a social affordance, that is picking up on the possibility of a certain type of interaction. One reason why I feel it is important to discuss the capacity of declarative pointing is because this is a capacity to initiate a certain type of collaborative activity that seems to develop before human infants develop linguistic capacities. Given the fact that I have suggested "humanity" in the morally relevant sense should be identified with the capacity to engage in joint or shared cooperative activities, the facts I will discuss subsequently suggest that being "human" should not be identified with the possession of linguistic capacities. I will follow the account of the development of the capacity to point and engage in shared cooperative activity as offered by Michael Tomasello and his team. And it should be pointed out that his account is quite conservative in that it suggests a quite late development of these capacities in the normally developing human infant. Other researchers, such as Vasudevi Reddy have suggested that the capacity to engage in shared cooperative activity emerges much earlier in infant development and is, for example, manifested in the dyadic sharing

---

[36] Now, of course, such capacities will not be singularly necessary for the development of the capacity to recognize humanity (in a moral sense), for obviously blind and deaf individuals are capable of morality, but taken together a child who was born without any innate capacity to distinguish sensitively between the human and non-human might not be able to develop such a capacity. In addition, sociopaths, if there are any, are presumably born with these capacities, and so these capacities will not be sufficient. But my suggestion is that such innate capacities probably play a role in the development of our moral capacity.

The Capacity to Recognize the Humanity of Others   131

of emotions between mothers and their babies (see Reddy 2010). I am sympathetic to Reddy's account, but for my purposes, the important point to establish is that this capacity develops before the development of linguistic abilities. And even on a conservative account of the developmental sequence, such as Tomasello's, the capacity to initiate joint cooperative activities through pointing develops prior to the development of linguistic capacities. Indeed, Tomasello himself believes that these pre-linguistic capacities are what make the development of linguistic capacities possible as the semantic character of language essentially involves reference, and our capacity to refer is rooted in our capacity for joint attention and pointing. And so the possession of these capacities is a necessary condition for the development of language.

Declarative pointing is a complex activity and presupposes a number of other capacities. Pointing in normally developing human infants begins in the months around the first birthday, prior to the emergence of linguistic abilities (Tomasello 2008:113). Evidence suggests that young infants start to point communicatively for two motives: to request things and to share emotions (Tomasello 2008:113). Tomasello distinguishes between two types of declaratives: (a) "declaratives as expressives" are those which the infant uses to share an attitude with an adult about a common referent and (b) "declaratives as informatives" which are used by the infant to provide the adult with information. And he cites experimental evidence that suggests that the first manifestation of cooperative pointing in infants starts with expressive pointing, which begins at about 12 months. Thus, Liszkowski et al. conducted a series of experiments to test the motivation for pointing in 12-month-old infants (Liszkowski et al. 2004). They introduced novel objects that would appear at some distance, and experimentally manipulated the adult's reaction, to test whether the infant's intention was to share their attitude (surprise, or interest in the novel object). The adults could react in one of four ways: (1) looking at the event without looking at the infant (Event Condition), (2) emoting positively toward the infant without looking at the event (Face Condition), (3) doing nothing (Ignore Condition) or, (4) alternating their gaze between the infant and the event while emoting positively (Joint Attention/Share Condition). The results showed that,

> when the adult simply looked to the indicated referent while ignoring the infant (Event condition), or when the adult simply expressed positive emotions to the infant while ignoring the indicated referent (Face condition), infants were not satisfied. In comparison with the Joint Attention condition, in which infants typically gave one long point, infants in these

conditions (as well as in the Ignore condition) tended to repeat their pointing gesture more often within trials – apparently as persistent attempts to establish shared attention and interest. Moreover, infants in these conditions (as well as in the Ignore condition) pointed less often across trials than in the Joint Attention condition – apparently indicating growing dissatisfaction with this adult as a communicative partner since she did not respond by sharing infants' attitude to the referent. (Tomasello 2008: 119)

This and other experiments that show the pre-linguistic infants engaging in pointing in order to share their emotional attitudes with others are significant, as they show a capacity and motivation to engage in some sort of joint activity (in this case joint attention) prior to the development of linguistic development. Now one may ask why we should consider the sharing of emotions in joint attention as a form of joint cooperative activity. Now, Tomasello argues, rightly in my opinion, that "The *sine qua non* of collaborative action is a joint goal and a joint commitment among participants to pursue it together, with a mutual understanding among all that they share this joint goal and commitment" (Tomasello 2008: 181). And I take it that in the sharing of excitement with an infant about an object, the evidence suggests that there is a joint goal (namely to share the excitement) and a joint commitment, evidenced by the infants attempts to re-engage if the adult disengages. And it seems plausible to assume that the infant recognizes that the adult shares the goal. So, I think there is good reason to think that even the sharing of excitement about a new object with an infant counts as a simple form of joint collaborative activity.

There is also experimental evidence that 12-month-old infants also point declaratively to help adults by providing them with information they may need. These experiments involve adults searching for a misplaced object. And the results show that 12-month-old infants often point to the object to help the adult with their search (Tomasello 2008:121). Tomasello argues that such behavior presupposes an understanding that others can have or lack information, plus an altruistic motive. I would add that such behavior shows the beginning of a capacity to recognize others as ends in themselves, who one can help in the pursuit of their own ends.

A further, morally relevant capacity is the capacity for role reversal. Young human infants are able to play games that involve distinct roles: such as a giver and a receiver. Once they have learnt the game having played one of the roles they are able to play the same game taking the other role. Such an ability involves the capacity to take a "birds eye" view of the activity and to recognize that there are different roles that different individuals can take. This capacity to understand that roles in an activity are fungible and can be played by different individuals is important for being able to see things from the perspective of others and is probably necessary for the capacity to decide whether a certain type of activity is universalizable. Once again there is some evidence to suggest that this capacity is unique to biological human beings.[37]

In terms of how this empirical research is related to Kant's ethics, I would suggest that the capacity to engage in helpful informative declaratives is related to the second formulation of the categorical imperative (the formulation of respect for humanity), for it shows the beginning of the capacity to recognize and incorporate the ends of others into one's own ends. The capacity to engage in expressive declaratives, with the intention to share attention, is related to the third formulation of the categorical imperative as it shows the capacity and desire for creating a "we." What is important to the infant is that we are looking at the object of interest together and sharing our emotions. And there is a normative element to this shared attention as the infant demands that we look and share the emotion, and is concerned to re-engage us if we do not share the moment. Although a 12-month-old baby is clearly not capable of fully moral agency, I suggest that these two capacities show some form of moral agency. And organisms capable of such activities are demanding of some moral respect. I have suggested that rather than being a binary either-or matter, the capacity for moral agency comes in degrees, and if what is demanding of respect is the capacity for moral agency, then the sort of respect that is required is also something that comes in degrees depending on the type of moral agency of the organism concerned. If I am right, then someone who systematically refuses to engage with infants who are attempting, for example, to engage in sharing of emotions is failing to show respect for humanity.

---

[37] "But in a series of simple cooperative tasks in which a human played one role and the chimpanzee a complementary role – for example, the human held out a plate and the chimpanzee placed a toy on it – when the human forced a role reversal chimpanzees basically either did not reverse roles, or else they performed their action without reference to the human. In a similar series of tasks, human infants not only reversed roles, but when they did so they looked expectantly to the adult in anticipation of her playing her new role in their shared task... Our interpretation is that human infants understand joint activity from a 'bird's-eye view,' with the joint goal and complementary roles all in a single representational format – which enables them to reverse roles as needed. In contrast, chimpanzees understand their own action from a first-person perspective and that of the partner from a third-person perspective, but they do not have a bird's-eye view of the interaction – and so there really are no roles, and so no sense in which they can reverse roles, in 'the same' activity" (Tomasello 2008:178–9).

I have suggested that the work of Tomasello and his associates suggests that 12-month-old babies are deserving of some degree of moral respect. And the work of Reddy and others suggests that the capacities that Tomasello thinks develop at around 12 months develop earlier in infancy. This raises the question of whether there are non-human animals that are deserving of some degree of moral respect (rather than mere compassion). Here I think the empirical evidence is inconclusive.

Many animals are territorial. And one question concerning our moral relationship to non-human animals has to do with whether we should respect their territories. There is often conflict between humans and non-human animals regarding territory. And such conflict is often the result of humans encroaching on the territory of non-human animals.[38] There are many moral reasons to recognize and protect various animal species, and this may involve recognizing their territories. But there is a further question as to whether we should recolonize non-human animals as having some sort of property rights to their territories. Here, I believe the Kantian response would have to do with whether non-human animal species are capable of anything like mutual respect and have the capacity to recognize that they are sharing the land with us. And here the evidence is inconclusive. Many non-human animals are clearly able to recognize boundaries between, say, the forest and cultivated lands, and show behavior differences in terms of how they forage in cultivated land. So, for example, Sukumar points out that "Adult Asian elephant bulls are predominantly solitary during their daytime movements in the wild. I noticed, however, a distinct tendency among bulls to associate with each other while raiding crop fields at night" (Sukumar 2003:3017). This differential behavior clearly indicates that elephants recognize a difference between forest land and cultivated land. But such behavior may just be a result of learning about different risks involved in foraging in cultivated land. From the evidence I have examined it is unclear whether any non-human animals living in proximity to humans are able to mutually respect the territory of one another, and I think a Kantian should take this capacity as the basis for whether we should regard non-human animals as being subjects of property rights.

Also relevant is whether non-human animals are capable of altruistic behavior and whether they are able to treat others as ends rather than merely as means. Comparative research by Tomasello and his associates on the pointing capacities of human infants and chimpanzees suggests that

[38] See, for example, Chatterjee 2016, Leblan 2016, Sukumar 2003, chapter 2 and chapter 8.

The Capacity to Recognize the Humanity of Others   135

chimpanzees are able to interact with others, but only see others as social tools to be used, rather than ends in themselves. If this research is reliable, it would suggest that chimpanzees are not capable of relationships based on mutual respect. Thus, they claim that although chimpanzees do not point in the wild, chimpanzees who have had experience of contact with humans do learn to point imperatively. They point out, however, that,

> Importantly though, they use this manual gesture imperatively only. That is, they point for humans either in order to obtain a desirable object from them directly . . . or indirectly by requesting from the human to provide the necessary conditions for them to get the object themselves. . . It thus seems that what the apes have learned from their experience with humans is that the human will help them, and that they can use the pointing gesture instrumentally in order to make him help them. They thus "use" the human as a "social tool" in order to get things they otherwise could not get, and they have learned that pointing gets this tool to work. . . However, no ape has ever been observed to point for another ape or for a human declaratively – that is, just for the sake of sharing attention to some outside entity, or to inform others of things cooperatively, as humans often do. (Moll and Tomasello 2007:643)

Tomasello also argues that chimpanzees have very limited motivations for altruistic behavior. Indeed, he thinks that chimpanzees are fundamentally competitive and lack the motivation and the skills to engage in collaborative activity (Tomasello 2008:177). And he suggests that the development of altruistic, cooperative motivation was the first major development in the evolution of humanity away from the other apes. And other apes show very limited motivation to help others, especially in situations involving food.[39]

If Tomasello is right, this would suggest that although chimpanzees may be subjects of compassion, they are not objects of respect in the Kantian sense. However, Tomasello's research has been questioned by a number of prominent primatologists. One major criticism is methodological. Tomasello's research is primarily in the form of laboratory experiments, and some primatologists believe that in such unnatural settings the capacities they are interested in are less likely to manifest themselves, and that a more ethological approach is required. So, for example, de Waal has shown that chimpanzees in the wild show a pattern to share food in exchange for

---

[39] Thus Tomasello argues that "chimpanzees sometimes help humans and one another. . . they do not help others in situations in which they themselves have a chance to obtain food – even when it would be easy for them to do so at no cost" (p.184). For empirical support for these claims see: Silk et al. 2005; Jensen et al. 2006; and Warneken and Tomasello 2006 and 2007.

136 LUCAS THORPE

grooming, which suggests some capacity for reciprocity, which De Waal labels reciprocal altruism (de Waal 1997). Such food sharing is, he argues, governed by turn-taking conventions and he even suggests that such sharing leads to some form of mutual obligation (de Waal 1989). And Sarah F. Brosnan and de Waal have even presented some evidence that capuchin monkeys have some sense of fairness (Brosnan and de Waal 2003). The interpretation of the experiments that claim to show a concern for fairness among monkeys has, however, been questioned by Tomasello and his research group.[40]

The empirical research, then, on whether or not there are non-human animals that have some sort of moral capacities is inconclusive. And there is, on the account I have offered, no criterion or principle we can apply to determine who we are capable of engaging in joint cooperative activities with; the only way of finding this out is by trying, and for us to have an openness to the invitations being made to us by the world around us. To recognize that another bit of the phenomenal world is "human" in the morally relevant sense is not to categorize that part of the world by applying a concept that has necessary and sufficient conditions of application, but to pick up on the possibility of a certain type of interaction. The fact that we have not succeeded in engaging in joint cooperative activities with non-human nature does not mean that such activities are impossible. It might just mean that we have not tried hard enough. And the empirical research on this issue is inconclusive.

In terms of how we go about recognizing morally relevant others, I believe that the best answer to this question is most likely to be provided by psychologists like Tomasello who are trying to understand the psychological basis and development of our capacity to engage in joint cooperative activities.[41]

---

[40] Bräuer, Call, and Tomasello 2006 and 2009.
[41] Support for work on this chapter was provided by Boğaziçi -Southampton Newton-Katip Çelebi project AF140071, Bogazici University BAP project 9320 and Tubitak Project 114k348 "Concepts and Belief: From Perception to Action." I would like to thank the following people for comments on previous drafts: Paul Guyer, Ken Westphal, Zübeyde Karadağ, Martin Sticker, Gözde Yıldırım, Sasha Mudd, Merve Tapinc, Hakkı Kaan Arıkan, Taylan Susam and Bill Wringe.

CHAPTER 7

Does Kantian Constructivism Rest on a Mistake?

Julian Wuerth

As described by Kant, ethics provides us with the "laws of freedom," telling us what we *ought* to do, while physics provides us with the "laws of nature," merely describing what is. Far less obvious and far more controversial is the distinction that Kant draws within both ethics and physics: between the empirical, or sensible, and the pure, or rational. It is this distinction that is central to Kant's most important project in ethics: to determine once and for all the exact nature of the moral law.

Section 1 of this chapter argues that there is a single basic procedure employed by Kant, across his writings in ethics, for laying bare the moral law in any of its formulations. I term this Kant's "Elimination of Sensibility Procedure," or "ESP." It is by means of ESP that Kant separates the pure from the empirical in ethics and achieves clarity on the moral law. ESP begins on a reflective, even romantic note, with a moment of wonder. In a world otherwise advancing lock-step according to the laws of nature, we feel wonder at the sheer fact of the existence of morality – at the fact of the existence of moral imperatives and the implied fact of our ability to freely choose out of respect for these imperatives. As Kant most famously describes this wonder at the moral law within us (as well as at the starry heavens above) in his *Critique of Practical Reason*, it is an "ever new and increasing admiration and awe" (*KpV* 5:161). But this moment of wonder is just the beginning of Kant's inquiry concerning the principles of morals, an inquiry that will take him in a markedly different direction than Hume's before him. The general strategy of what remains of this inquiry is revealed two pages later in the *Critique of Practical Reason*, in the final paragraph of the book, when Kant explains that we ought to proceed in our study of ethics just as we do in the broader study of nature: We ought to use "a process similar to that of chemistry ... [whereby] we ... separate the empirical from the rational, exhibit each of them in a pure state, and show what each by itself can accomplish" (*KpV* 5:163). To achieve this separation, Kant's ESP highlights a single, crucial feature about the basic

137

fact of morality: its modality. The moral law is unique in commanding with necessity, telling us that we should do something not because it will promote our happiness, but simply because it is the right thing to do, *in itself*. Not only does the moral law command with necessity, but the will determined by this moral law, in turn, has necessary, unqualified worth. Having identified necessity as a defining characteristic of moral imperatives, Kant's ESP advances with an eye to Kant's distinction in kind between reason and sensibility, asking which of our faculties could ground such laws that command "absolutely (not merely hypothetically under the presupposition of other empirical ends), and are necessary in every respect" (*KrV* A807/B835). ESP, then, systematically rejects our sensibility in part and in whole as a possible source of such a moral law or of a good will determined by this moral law. Having systematically rejected sensibility, ESP turns to reason alone, now clearly distinguished from sensibility, and next specifies how it, in its purity, authors the moral law, and what this moral law is.

The second part of this chapter applies these positive findings regarding ESP to an assessment of recent "constructivist" interpretations of Kant. I point to some problems with a number of constructivist systems and then argue against Korsgaard's constructivist interpretation of Kant that it, like the other constructivist strategies, rests on precisely the mistake that Kant repeatedly says has haunted the history of moral philosophy, namely, that of conflating sensibility's pragmatic good and understanding's moral good. This is the mistake to which the title of the chapter refers. Of course, the title also alludes to H. A. Prichard's classic 1912 essay, "Does Moral Philosophy Rest on a Mistake?" The mistake to which Prichard drew attention was that of demanding a *reason* for something that is already self-evident. This mistake also in part defines Korsgaard's account, as Korsgaard interprets Kant to hold that our sensible incentives as well as our conviction that humanity has value in itself are both in need of further supporting reasons before they can serve as grounds for a choice.

1   A Distinction in Kind: The Morally Good vs. the Pragmatically Good

Across Kant's work in ethics – in his *Groundwork*, his *Critique of Practical Reason*, his lectures on ethics, and many other sources – Kant maintains that the single mistake that has most consistently plagued moral philosophers throughout history is a very fundamental one. This is the mistake of not distinguishing properly, i.e., of not distinguishing *in kind*, between the realm of sensibility and the realm of intellectuality. This is the same mistake that has plagued theoretical philosophy throughout history, with Kant famously observing that it has led some to "intellectualize" sensibility and others to "sensitivize" intellectuality. This failure is just as crucial within moral philosophy because it has brought with it the failure to draw the distinction in kind between two irreducible senses of "good."

The first kind of good is the pragmatic good, happiness. The kind of desires that aim at this good, according to Kant's theory of action, are what Kant refers to as our sensible incentives (*Triebfedern*). Sensible incentives are one of two fundamental kinds of desire, or "conative currency," as I call it, in Kant's theory of action.

The second kind of good is the morally good. The morally good has its value in itself, not, say, because of any happiness it may or may not give rise to. Our intellectual incentives, or motives, to choose morally are the second of the two fundamental kinds of desire, or conative currency.

In notes on Kant's lectures on ethics from 1774–8 as taken by Johann Friedrich Kaehler, which are reproduced in the better-known 1784–5 *Lectures on Ethics Collins*, Kant lays out the division between ethics as grounded in either of these two kinds of good, i.e., in either an empirical or intellectual good. He explains that "morality rests either on empirical or intellectual grounds, and must be derived from either empirical or intellectual principles. Empirical grounds are those that are derived from the senses, insofar as our *senses are satisfied thereby*. Intellectual grounds are those where all morality is derived from the conformity of our action with the *laws of reason*" (*Collins* 27:252–3).

Those grounding their ethics on empirical grounds can do so in a number of ways, Kant explains. First, they can ground them on empirical inner grounds. These grounds are inner in that they issue from within our psychological domain, in inner sense, and they are empirical in that they issue from our lower, sensible faculties, which are passive in the sense that they do not presuppose our self-conscious, reflective, active involvement. One type of inner empirical ground is what Kant here calls *physical feeling*, the feeling of "self love," which breaks down into vanity and self-interest. This anticipates Kant's "selfish purpose" of the prudent merchant in *Groundwork I* (*GMS* 4:397). Here Kant points us to Epicurus, Helvetius, and Mandeville as philosophers grounding their ethics in these sources. Another empirical inner ground, in addition to physical feeling, is moral feeling, and here Kant points us to Shaftesbury and Hutcheson. This anticipates Kant's "immediate inclination" of the "friend of mankind" in *Groundwork* I (*GMS* 4:398). Kant also identifies empirical external

140   JULIAN WUERTH

grounds, such as education and government, and here he cites Montaigne and Hobbes as philosophers who ground their moral principles in these external forces.

Time and again, Kant notes the shared modality of all of these empirical grounds for morality: the modality of contingency or conditionality. Each rests on something that is conditional or contingent to us in our status as rational agents, i.e., each rests on something that is not necessary to us simply as rational beings per se; for example, they rest on what happens to provoke a physical feeling or what happens to provoke a moral feeling in us, given our particular sensible nature, or they rest on the particular system of education or government that has shaped us: "However, if the principle of morality rests on self-love, it rests on a contingent ground, for the nature of actions, whereby they bring me pleasure or not, rests on contingent circumstances. If the principle rests on a moral feeling, where the action is judged by the satisfaction or dissatisfaction, by the sensation or in general the feeling of taste, it also rests on a contingent ground... And so it is also with the external grounds of education and government. Under the empirical system, the principle of morality rests on contingent grounds." (*Collins* 27:253–4)

But what is so bad about a conditional, contingent foundation for morality? Kant's response is simple: It is a self-evident fact that moral imperatives simply do command with necessity, unconditionally. And if this is the case, they can only come from a source that holds for all of us necessarily as rational agents, and this source is our purely intellectual faculty of reason. In Kant's words: "Those principles which are supposed to be everywhere, always and necessarily valid, cannot be derived from experience, but only from pure reason. Yes, the moral law expresses categorical necessity, and not a necessity fashioned from experience," and that because "all necessary rules must hold good a priori ... the principles are *intellectual*" (*Collins* 27:254).

So there are two kinds of good, moral and pragmatic. Moral imperatives command categorically; our sensibility cannot ground categorical commands while our reason can; and so the categorical imperative must issue from reason.

Any attempt to determine the morally good is also doomed from the start, Kant argues, insofar as it *combines* these two senses of good in one, with a single foundation. Here the culprit, as so often for Kant, is the tendency to take reason's demand for simplicity as constitutive rather than regulative: "Philosophy endeavors to bring about unity in our knowledge, and to reduce it to the fewest principles, [and so] the attempt was *made to see if *one* principle might not be put together out of these *two*" (*Collins* 27:249).

Kant believes that the murkiness, across the history of moral philosophy, surrounding the distinction between sensibility and intellectuality, and the failure to isolate the origin of the moral law in intellectuality and specifically pure reason alone, has naturally enough led to a great deal of confusion about the relationship between living morally and living happily. If it is a feeling – whether a moral or physical one – that determines our moral obligations, it begins to appear plausible that moral living has some causal connection with our own pragmatic goal, of (sensible) happiness. Thus throughout history, Kant argues, there have been countless misconstruals of the highest good, or *summum bonum*, which combines virtue and happiness. Thus some of the mentioned empiricists, Epicurus, Helvetius, and Mandeville, went astray in thinking that the highest good was happiness alone and that virtue would conveniently serve as a means to happiness, while others, the stoics, were equally misguided, reducing the highest good to virtue alone, also believing that virtue would conveniently serve as a means to happiness. Again, Kant's point is that the moral, intellectual good and the pragmatic, sensible good are distinct in kind, with neither the moral good nor the pragmatic good serving as the necessary or sufficient condition for the other.

Jumping ahead to 1793 for a moment, to Kant's "On the Common Saying: That May Be True in Theory, but It Is of No Use in Practice," we get a taste for how consistent Kant was, across his writings, in pinning failures in ethics on the problem of the conflation of the moral and the pragmatic in ethics. Here Kant summarizes Garve's complaint about Kant as follows: that all action must be directed to what we prefer, that what we prefer must be something we take to be "*good*," that what we take to be good is what is described by the word happiness, and that, accordingly, the motive for acting on the moral law, too, must be our pursuit of happiness (*TP* 8:281). In response, Kant predictably explains that "this argument is nothing but a play upon the *ambiguity of the word the good*; for this [can be taken to mean] either what is *good in itself and unconditionally* as opposed to what is evil in itself, or else what is only *conditionally good* as compared with what is a lesser or greater good. . ." and that what we have here is "*a difference in kind*" (*TP* 8:282).

Likewise, in his 1795 "Perpetual Peace" Kant considers the objection that morality demands of us things that are impossible in politics. His response is that morality never commands what we cannot do, and that what must really be meant here with the objection is that morality demands of us things that are impossible to do in a manner consistent with our happiness. But if *this* is the tension, then acting on the moral law is only impossible if we misconstrue the moral law itself as a "general doctrine of *prudence.*" And to misconstrue the moral law as a general doctrine of prudence is, of course, in effect, to "deny that there is a [doctrine of morals] at all" (*ZeF* 8:370). Indeed, as Kant would put it two years later, in his 1797 *Metaphysics of Morals*, these philosophers who conflate the pragmatic and moral good are guilty of "the euthanasia (easy death) of morals" (*MS* 6:378).

What is important to note about Kant's discussions about the persistent confusion around the roles of sensibility and intellectuality in morality – both for the purpose of understanding Kant's criticisms of rationalism and empiricism in ethics and, in turn, for recognizing constructivists' misunderstanding of Kant's criticism of rationalism in ethics, as we will see in our next section – is that they do not only implicate empiricists, but also rationalists. For while rationalists would seem to be on the same page as Kant in their reliance on reason for their findings in moral philosophy (and all else), Kant sees significant daylight between his and their positions. In Kant's view, they simply are not in a position to do a good job of relying on reason: Their failure is due not to their reliance on reason's insights per se but to their failure to distinguish in kind between reason and sensibility, as they accordingly fail to separate out reason's insights from sensibility's. Thus, just as Kant, in the *Critique's* chapter on the Amphiboly, sees both empiricists and rationalists guilty of the conflation of empirical and intellectual concepts, so, too, does he here see both empiricists and rationalists guilty of this conflation in the moral realm, with the result that neither is able to isolate reason and identify the moral law, including the rationalists.

Thus in his lectures on ethics, Kant attacks the perfectionism of Alexander Baumgarten, a Wolffian. Baumgarten's principle of morality, he argues, demands that we do good and abstain from evil. This principle, however, suffers the same fate for Kant as Garve's and others' conceptions of morality, insofar as it fails to distinguish the pragmatically good from the morally good. What Baumgarten offers is accordingly not merely a tautology, insofar as it tells us simply to do the good thing. It is also, and even worse, in Kant's view, a "*principium vagum*" (*Collins* 27:264), because it does not even manage to distinguish *as desiderata* definitions of a *sensible* and a *moral* good before failing to define the moral good.

In failing to distinguish between a moral and a pragmatic principle, Baumgarten has also failed to identify a principle of *obligation*, Kant argues, because only a *moral* principle *obligates*, while a *sensible* principle,

Does Kantian Constructivism Rest on a Mistake?   143

of skill or prudence, is a mere *problematic* imperative. To the extent that Baumgarten also enjoins us to seek *perfection*, he likewise is confused, Kant argues, because "perfection and moral goodness are different" (*Collins* 27:265): Perfection, Kant argues, concerns the generic "completeness of man in regard to his powers" (*Collins* 27:265), while goodness "consists in the perfection of the *will*, not the capacities," so that Baumgarten is again looking in the wrong place, in addition to never specifying what the moral law is that would perfect our will, and in the end gives us only a principle that is tautologous and vague in an amphibolous manner.

Our review of these sources from before and after the *Groundwork* positions us to consider Kant's rejection of rationalist perfectionism in the preface to his 1785 *Groundwork*. Here Kant rejects rationalist perfectionism again, this time as presented by Wolff himself. And again, his criticism homes in on the conflation of empirical and intellectual imperatives in this rationalist perfectionism. Thus, Kant strikes preemptively against those who might see him peddling stale goods already supplied by Wolff, by making clear how Wolff has fallen short of what Kant will attempt to do. How so? Again, Wolff has merely "considered volition *in general*" (*GMS* 4:390). Wolff has, that is, failed to isolate the rational, or moral volition, because he has failed to strip it of all that is empirical. In other words, Wolff has failed to recognize, as described in the *Critique's* Amphiboly, the distinction in kind between the two basic sources of determination of actions: rational ones, deriving from reason, and empirical ones, deriving from our inclinations. Here Kant summarizes these points about how Wolff and other rationalist perfectionists fail, saying that they

> do not distinguish motives that, as such, are represented completely a priori by reason alone and are properly moral from empirical motives, which the understanding raises to universal concepts merely by comparing experiences; instead they consider motives only in terms of the greater or smaller amount of them, without paying attention to the difference of their sources (since all of them are regarded as of the same kind); and this is how they form their conception of *obligation*, which is anything but moral, athough the way it is constituted is all that can be desired in a philosophy that does not judge at all about the *origin* of all possible practical concepts, whether they occur only a posteriori or a priori as well. (*GMS* 4:391)

By contrast, Kant explains that his own moral philosophy will present a foundation, or groundwork, of a metaphysics of morals, precisely by isolating our intellectual faculty of reason and its *a priori* insights. He tells us that "moral philosophy rests entirely on its pure part" (*GMS* 4:389) and that "a metaphysics of morals is thus indispensably necessary" (*GMS* 4:389) among other reasons because otherwise "morals themselves are liable to all kinds of corruption" (*GMS* 4:390).

We have now seen how Kant views his own moral philosophy departing most fundamentally from previous moral philosophies by virtue of its distinction in kind between sensibility and intellectuality. And we have seen how these previous accounts include even rationalist, perfectionist ones. Turning to *Groundwork* I and II we can also use this background regarding this fundamental distinction in kind to expose a common strategy in the first and second sections of the *Groundwork*, which are otherwise so different. This is the mentioned Elimination of Sensibility Procedure, or ESP. I will review this process only briefly before turning to the topic of constructivism.

Kant begins *Groundwork* I with a simple assertion: We all recognize, as a fact, that a good will is good without qualification. Even where such a good will is useless, he writes, it will nonetheless "like a jewel, still shine by its own light" (*GMS* 4:394). Likewise, *Groundwork* II properly gets started when Kant simply asserts the following: "Finally, there is one imperative which immediately commands a certain conduct without having as its condition any other purpose to be attained by it. This imperative is categorical... This imperative may be called that of morality" (*GMS* 4:416). As in his lectures on ethics, in *Groundwork* I Kant takes it for granted that we all recognize the unqualified and necessary value of a good will. Likewise, in *Groundwork* II Kant argues that we all recognize that there is a moral law and that it commands with necessity. These starting points are moral realist starting points, asserting the value in itself of a good will and the existence of a moral law that commands categorically.

And this is what gets the ball rolling for Kant. It is ESP that takes us to the categorical imperative, which, in turn, is what supplies us with a method for testing the moral status of particular maxims, a method referred to by Rawls as the "CI-procedure." These starting points are what constructivists neglect, not recognizing that they are what serve as the crucial foundation for Kant's eventual embrace of the categorical imperative, which supplies the constructive procedures that they so value, in the various formulations of the categorical imperative. In other words, Kant does not think that the categorical imperative and its procedures come from nowhere or are themselves constructed without an underlying moral realist foundation. Instead, it is because we first recognize that wills determined by the moral law are good without qualification and that there are moral imperatives that command with necessity (and that determine a good will), that we can subsequently recognize the various formulations of the categorical imperatives as formulations of the moral law. As Kant puts this point – about the need to begin our exploration into the nature of the moral from our recognition of the fact of its necessity – in the *Critique of Practical Reason*, "But how is the consciousness of the moral law possible? We can come to know pure practical laws in the same way we know pure theoretical principles, *by attending to the necessity with which reason prescribes them to us and to the elimination from them of all empirical conditions, which reason directs*" (KpV 5:30).

It is this "elimination . . . of all empirical conditions" to which we next turn. In *Groundwork* I, on the basis of the conclusion of the necessary worth of a good will, Kant is able to systematically eliminate all empirical, or sensible, determinations of the will, as such determinations will only always yield a will with conditional value. Having eliminated all the offerings of sensibility, Kant asks what else could possibly determine the will, and now, having eliminated sensibility, we arrive at the Formula of Universal Law (FUL), or at least an early version of it. In Groundwork II, the structure of the argument is the same, with Kant first arguing that moral laws are by their nature categorical, eliminating as possible moral laws all hypothetical imperatives of sensibility. The question is then what the moral law could be, given a lack of empirical grounds, and the answer is again FUL (and then, after switching to consideration not of the form but of the matter of such a necessary moral law, the Formula of Humanity as an End in Itself, etc.). Kant thus recognizes a distinction in kind between sensibility and intellectuality; sees other accounts failing to recognize this distinction and therefore arriving at confused accounts of morality; and then himself sets things right by carefully navigating the waters of this distinction, eliminating the offerings of sensibility, and isolating the teachings of pure reason.

2   Does Constructivism Rest on a Mistake?

I now turn to constructivism. As is well known, John Rawls revitalized normative ethics in the 1960s and 1970s, most famously with his 1971 *A Theory of Justice*. Rawls was writing not only at a time when normative ethics was out of favor, but also at a time when, in the area of metaethics, there was a great deal of hostility toward moral realism. There was, likewise, a great deal of hostility toward rational intuitionism, which claims that we can arrive at insights regarding objective moral truths by means of rational intuitions that are self-evident. That is, these self-evident truths do not have a binary justification structure, where the proposition demands a separate justification, but instead have a unary justification structure, where the proposition is self-evident. Rawls and the later Kantian constructivists do not challenge what had been (at the time of Rawls's writing) this dominant hostility toward moral realism and yet they hope to secure an objectivist ethics, not a mere relativism. They hope to square this circle by recourse to a new "constructivist" strategy, according to which they will offer an underlying procedure instead of some alleged insight of some alleged moral fact. This procedure will then be used to construct the content of the moral doctrine. But while this approach certainly has us investing a procedure with a great deal of responsibility for determining the content of the doctrine, this does not necessarily eliminate a place for moral realism or even a dependence on one. For the obvious question that still remains is Why should we defer to this procedure and not some other one, if any at all? In the words of Onora O'Neill, discussing the procedures of the various formulations of the Categorical Imperative in relation to Rawls, "The more demanding question is whether they [these procedures] can *themselves* be justified without reintroducing some form of moral realism by the back door" (O'Neill 2002:355).

In an attempt to answer this question about the justification of Rawls's "CI-Procedure" itself, and to do so without recourse to moral realism, Rawls, after asking the question "Is the CI-Procedure itself constructed?" answers "No, it is not. Rather, it is simply laid out. Kant believes that our everyday human understanding is implicitly aware of the requirements of practical reason, both pure and empirical" (Rawls 1989:99) – a characterization of the starting point for justification of the CI Procedure that sounds like rational intuitionism and in turn moral realism. Rawls also says that this procedure is justified on a coherentist basis, as it is a procedure that squares with our conception of free and equal persons as rational and reasonable. But, again, why defer to our conception of a person as reasonable, and how is this different from having a rational intuition of what it is to be reasonable, or moral? Moving to Rawls's political theory, we find a parallel in his account of the Original Position. How is this procedure justified? Rawls again offers a coherentist justification, whereby we look at the principles dictated by the Original Position and see whether they conform to *our* "considered judgments." Again, however, *whose* considered moral judgments is Rawls referring to, and *why* should they or we defer to them, if not because they or we think that these considered judgments grasp moral truths, and how would that avoid moral intuitionism and moral realism? As is well known, Rawls

Does Kantian Constructivism Rest on a Mistake? 147

eventually backs away from these views, or at least becomes more explicit about the limited scope of his claims. That is, finding his objectivist account vulnerable to the charge of moral realism, Rawls scales back his ambitions, limiting himself to more modest, political, relativist conclusions, that find their grounding in local, non-universalizable sources.

Before moving on to discussion of the next attempt at a Kantian constructivism, in the work of Onora O'Neill, it is worth pausing to ask why Rawls might take such pains to avoid ascribing to Kant a moral realism or (rationalist) intuitionism that could ground the constructive procedures spelled out by the categorical imperative. After all, we saw Rawls conceding that for Kant the categorical imperative itself "is simply *laid out*" by our "everyday human understanding" (Rawls 1989: 99), and he also acknowledges that "Kant says that the moral law can be given no deduction, that is, no justification of its objective and universal validity, but rests on the fact of reason. This fact (as I understand it) is the fact that in our common moral consciousness we recognize and acknowledge the moral law as supremely authoritative and immediately directive for us" (Rawls 1989: 102). Moreover, Kant consistently employs other examples of moral realist language, as when he asserts that rational nature is "something whose existence has in itself an absolute worth" and that "rational beings are called persons inasmuch as their nature already marks them out as ends in themselves" (*GMS* 4:428); that the moral law "rests on the inner nature of the action, so far as we apprehend it through the understanding" (*Collins* 27:254); and that "the moral imperative expresses the goodness of the action in and for itself, so that moral necessitation is categorical and not hypothetical" (Collins 27:255–6).

Did Rawls's own philosophical discomfort with intuitionism incline him in this direction? Did he feel pressure to exhaust alternatives to an intuitionist interpretation of Kant, given that, as J. L. Mackie put it about the intellectual climate in which Rawls was writing (in Mackie's 1977 *Ethics: Inventing Right and Wrong*), "Intuitionism has long been out of favor, and it is indeed easy to point out its implausibilities" (Mackie 1977: 38). Regardless, the main reason that Rawls cites for rejecting a moral realist interpretation of Kant's ethics, which reason is then echoed in the work of O'Neill (O'Neill: 355), is Kant's rejection of a Leibnizian/Wolffian/Baumgartian perfectionism (Rawls 1989: section 3). But as we have seen, while Kant does indeed reject these rationalists' views, the charge he levels against them is not one of moral realism. Far from it, Kant pinpoints their failure to adequately distinguish, i.e., to distinguish in-kind, between reason and sensibility; and as a result of this, and with a mere distinction-in-degree in place between reason and sensibility, they bungle the distinction between moral good and pragmatic good, in the end having only heteronomous goods to show for it. While Kant acknowledges that their error is an extremely difficult (and transcendental) one to identify, Kant believes that once he has done so (at no small cost in effort), reason can now be exercised to yield insights into facts about moral right and moral wrong. Ironically, having understood Kant's criticisms as, instead, targeting the rationalists' use of reason in a moral realist manner, the Kantian constructivists go on to not only reject a moral realist interpretation of Kant but also embrace an alternative interpretation of Kant that imputes to him a constructivism that itself falls prey to precisely the timeless problem that Kant identified in the rationalists' ethics, of conflating reason and sensibility.

Rejecting Rawls's particular version of a constructivist interpretation of Kant's ethics, Onora O'Neill incorporates into her own version an alternative move that we earlier saw Rawls quickly reject, namely, a constructivist justification of the constructivist principles *themselves*. To the question, Why *this* procedure? Or Why should *I* follow it? Onora O'Neill offers a constructivist response: Kant's morality "begins simply with the thought that a *plurality* of agents lacks antecedent principles of *coordination*, and aims to build an account of reason, of ethics, and specifically of justice on this basis. He thinks of human beings as doers *before* they become reasoners or citizens" (O'Neill 2002:362). O'Neill addresses the question of whether the mere need to coordinate a plurality of agents' actions is a sufficiently restrictive one to yield rich moral content, and she asserts that it is, albeit under the assumption that "coordination" rules out coercion and deception. But it seems that this assumption only pushes back the question, to why *this* sort of coordination should be chosen. Here O'Neill appeals to the notion of the "arbitrary," noting that some factors are arbitrary and should not be taken into account. Indeed, Kant does reject appeal to "arbitrary" considerations, when he rejects merely subjectively valid considerations. But this rejection is not dictated by a morally neutral concept. Instead, Kant rejects merely subjectively valid considerations insofar as they conflict with an independent moral criterion, of objectivity and universality. For subjectively valid considerations may well be far from arbitrary in another sense, according to Kant: They may be those considerations crucial to our attainment of our pragmatic good, happiness. If we adjust O'Neill's account to Kant's usage, we would accordingly have to disambiguate the term "arbitrary" and instead use the term "morally arbitrary" here, but in this case we would still need to explain the basis for this moral judgment.

Does Kantian Constructivism Rest on a Mistake?   149

We turn, finally, to the constructivist view of Christine Korsgaard. Korsgaard's account is the most ambitious of the constructivisms in an important sense, and in a sense that also makes it the most alluring of the constructivist options – if not the most successful. We saw that, without a moral realist foundation, Rawls's constructivism opts for a relativist anchoring, while O'Neill aims higher, hoping to achieve objectivity through an anchoring in the fact of our predicament as a plurality of agents without antecedent coordination, though in the end she is unable to wring such a rich morality from such a normatively spare set of facts. By contrast, Korsgaard wants to anchor morality in something even more basic to our human condition and even more universal, arguing that absolutely everyone, regardless of who they are or what they think or do, is, and must be, committed to the categorical imperative, simply by virtue of making self-conscious choices: "When you will a maxim you must take it to be universal. If you do not, you are not operating as a self-conscious cause, and then you are not willing. To put the point in familiar Kantian terms, we can only attach the 'I will' to our choices if we will our maxims as universal laws" (Korsgaard 1999:27). By arguing that morality is the condition for any self-conscious choice, or, elsewhere, any rational choice or any voluntary choice whatsoever,[1] and that there is no coherent alternative to moral choice, her account is the most ambitious in its claims of objectivity and universality.

Here Korsgaard's interpretation consistently centers on what is commonly referred to as her "regress argument interpretation" of a passage leading up to Kant's presentation of the Formula of Humanity formulation of the categorical imperative in the *Groundwork*. Here is the familiar passage:

> Now I say that man, and in general every rational being, exists as an end in himself and not merely as a means to be arbitrarily used by this or that will. He must in all his actions, whether directed to himself or to other rational beings, always be regarded at the same time as an end. [1] All the objects of inclinations have only a conditioned value; for if there were not these inclinations and the needs founded on them, then their object would be without value. [2] But the inclinations themselves, being sources of needs, are so far from having an absolute value such as to render them desirable for their own sake that the universal wish of every rational being must be, rather, to be wholly free from them. Accordingly, the value of any object obtainable by our action is always conditioned. [3] Beings whose existence depends not on our will but on nature have, nevertheless, if they are not rational beings, only a relative value as means and are therefore called

---

[1] See also Korsgaard 1996a:162, 120.

things. [4] On the other hand, rational beings are called persons inasmuch as their nature already marks them out as ends in themselves, i.e., as something which is not to be used merely as means and hence there is imposed thereby a limit on all arbitrary use of such beings, which are thus objects of respect. (*GMS* 4:428)

As Korsgaard characterizes it, Kant's search here for something with categorical value is *not* an attempt to find something that will render coherent a specifically moral choice by supplying this sort of choice with a grounding in something with unconditional value, even though Kant has said he is searching for "something whose existence has in itself an absolute worth, something which as an end in itself could be . . . the ground of a possible *categorical* imperative" (*GMS* 4:428). Instead, and in what should already give us pause, in Korsgaard's view Kant is searching for something with categorical value to serve as the ground for any rational, sufficient, or coherent choice whatsoever (Korsgaard 1996a:162, 120). So from the start Korsgaard takes what is actually Kant's specifically moral inquiry, into whether there is something with absolute worth that could render coherent our moral choices, for a mere generic inquiry, into whether there is something with absolute worth that could render coherent any rational choice whatsoever. Moreover, the search as she characterizes it is not in the form of Kant's rejection of so many candidates in a list of possible categorically valuable ends. The items are instead said by Korsgaard to be *connected* in a different way, as a *single* value *regress*, where Kant would have each item in the list grounded in the value of the next item (Korsgaard 1996a:120).

Korsgaard accordingly argues first, and in my view correctly, that [1] Kant rejects objects of inclinations as having absolute value, asserting that their value is conditional, not categorical (Korsgaard 1996a:121) and that he next [2] identifies inclinations as the source of the value of these objects but likewise rejects them (Korsgaard 1996a:122). She argues that Kant then looks for the source of value of these inclinations, that he then fails to find anything of value at all, *including rational nature*, and that he then concludes that we are therefore choosing even though we fail to locate anything of absolute value at all that could serve as the basis for our choice, and that we must therefore, in spite of ourselves . . . be implicitly valuing our own humanity. . . and that we must therefore, in spite of ourselves, be valuing the humanity of all.

Before moving on, I will now pause to address the title of this chapter, "Does Constructivism Rest on a Mistake?" and tie in some points covered in Section 1. The title is an allusion, of course, to H. A. Prichard's famous

1912 essay "Does Moral Philosophy Rest on a Mistake?" Prichard's main point was that we naturally know right and wrong, that it is self-evident (providing a unary justification procedure rather than a binary one resting on some further proposition), but that, in response to the challenge to morality posed by our inclinations (like Kant's "natural dialectic," at *GMS* 4:405), we mistakenly disregard this self-evident, foundational grasp of value, looking elsewhere for a proof of value.

Next, we saw in Section 1 of this chapter that Kant consistently charges others in the history of philosophy with a failure to recognize that sensibility and intellectuality are distinct *in kind*, a recognition at the heart of Kant's critical turn in philosophy, and that for lack of this distinction in kind, these philosophers committed the "euthanasia of morals" (*TL* 6:378) or, in Kant's words in the *Groundwork*, "substitute[ed] for morality some bastard patched up from limbs of varied ancestry" (GMS 4:426). Here Kant repeatedly judges these ethicists with having failed to recognize that there are two *basic* and *irreducible* conative currencies: our *sensible* inclinations and our *moral* motives. We also saw that Kant, in his attempt to *isolate* the moral law of our intellect, accordingly eliminates, time and again in his treatment of the topic, the offerings of sensibility before turning to intellectuality.

Returning now to Korsgaard's interpretation, we can see that what Korsgaard has in effect done, in shooting for the stars with a radical argument for why every self-conscious choice commits us to the moral law, is to commit precisely the error that Kant sees plaguing the history of moral philosophy, and most importantly his rationalist predecessors and contemporaries, who see all choice as directed toward what is best, where they draw no distinction in kind between what is best sensibly and intellectually. She has not recognized the distinction in kind between sensibility and understanding and between inclinations and moral motives. She has instead argued that *any* and *all* choices are ultimately grounded in *one kind of value*, namely a commitment to the moral law, or humanity. Moreover, this failure to recognize this distinction in kind manifests itself in the form, twice, of the sort of mistake to which Prichard drew our attention: the mistake of not recognizing when we have reached rock bottom in a self-evident fact. Kant does not think inclinations have *moral* value, but he also does not think that they need have moral value in order to be an irreducible kind of conative currency. Kant recognizes that the burden is not on us to provide a *reason* for why an inclination should *incline*; inclinations per se do already incline us, even when we are choosing from a reflective distance, which is why they are states of the faculty of desire, or the *Begehrungsvermögen* (it is accordingly worth noting that Korsgaard misidentifies Kant's incentives as pleasures rather than as desires, because that latter but not the former already have us desiring, inclining, or being motivated toward the object in question, whereas pleasure per se does not[2]). Korsgaard's lack of recognition of the fact that for Kant inclinations can provide grounds for action independent of their moral status is thus the moment at which she fails to recognize the irreducible distinction in kind between the sensible and intellectual realms, and so it is the amphibolous moment in her interpretation that I refer to as its "intellectualization moment."

Next, notice the subsequent item in the list, [3]: animals. The ESP reading of this part of Kant's argument for the Formula of Humanity formulation of the categorical imperative has Kant here eliminating, as a candidate for something with unconditioned value, not merely our inclinations in particular but our sensibility as a whole. And how might Kant represent our sensibility as a whole, independent of our reason? As an animal, because animals are just that: sensibility without an accompanying intellectuality. And so the question for Kant is whether animals could be an end with categorical value, and he of course, given his views on animals, answers No. But, turning back to Korsgaard's interpretation, though Korsgaard claims that a regress to value is ongoing, she never mentions the place of animals on this list, even though her regress interpretation would imply that animals are the basis of the value of our inclinations (Korsgaard 1996a: 122).

We next turn to our intellectual, or rational nature, in [4]. Here, Korsgaard does not have Kant recognizing that it is the *nature* of rational beings *as rational* that makes them ends in themselves, with *Würde*, or dignity. This is the second instance, in Korsgaard's interpretation of Kant's argument for the Formula of Humanity, of the sort of move that Prichard flags, and I refer to it as Korsgaard's "moral anti-realist moment." Rather than understanding Kant to be helping us to conceptually isolate rational nature from sensibility so that we can now recognize that it is what has value in itself, Korsgaard would have Kant turning to rational nature and *not* recognizing its value in itself, and thus have Kant coming up empty-handed in an attempt to identify *something, anything,* with unconditional, absolute value.

Where we saw Kant repeatedly recognizing that there are *two distinct kinds* of irreducible conative currency, moral and pragmatic, Korsgaard

[2] For more on this, Wuerth 2014: chapter 8, section 2.

Does Kantian Constructivism Rest on a Mistake? 153

thus has Kant recognizing *none*. Korsgaard instead has Kant leading us, by regress, to a place where there is no ground for any choice (Korsgaard 1996a:122). I accordingly refer to this as the "conative vacuum moment" of her interpretation.

As Korsgaard describes it, Kant believes we are confronted with a need to choose despite lacking any conative currencies that incline or impel us to make a choice. Faced with this conative vacuum, we make choices *anyway*, Korsgaard asserts, and this fact of choice in the face of a conative vacuum tells us that . . . we must *implicitly* be *committed* to the value of not only *our own* humanity but also the humanity of *everyone else* (Korsgaard 1996a:122).[3] Given the vast riches that emerge from this conative vacuum, I call this part of Korsgaard's argument her "moment of magic." And because this commitment supposedly grounds *every* choice, even immoral ones, it follows that *any* choice at odds with the value of humanity is at odds with *its own* motivational underpinning. Accordingly, choice at odds with the value of humanity is both unmotivated and also incoherent, given that is contradicts its real ground, commitment to the value of all humanity. As a result, on this interpretation there is no basis for immoral choices, and, what's more, any choice that we might commonly refer to as "immoral" is actually not only *unmotivated* but also *incoherent*. Having thus equated coherent choice with moral choice, Korsgaard merges the pragmatic and the moral, as throughout pre-Kantian history (Korsgaard 1996a:123).[4]

The first big problem with this constructivist attempt to shift the burden of normativity onto some implicit commitment is that normativity does not work that way for Kant. Kant would reject this as one version of the Euthyphro problem: The moral law is not the moral law because we are committed to it; instead we are committed to it because it is the moral law. And we must think for ourselves and use our reason to ascertain that it is the moral law, and only then will we respect it and be committed to it. That we would take pleasure in something or even be implicitly committed to it still leaves what both G. E. Moore and Kant would see as the wide open question, of why it is *morally* good. This is the open question that would still face Korsgaard's "implicit commitment" at the end of the day, just as it does O'Neill's plurality of uncoordinated agents. In Kant's view,

---

[3] See also Korsgaard 1996b:122.
[4] For more on Kant's moral realism, his ESP as employed in his argument for the various formulations of the categorical imperative, and Korsgaard's constructivist interpretation of his ethics, see Wuerth 2014, chapter 9.

morality is too important a thing to delegate to an implicit commitment. Moreover, if it were thus delegated, the result would not be an ethics of autonomy, as we would here not be submitting to the authority of our own reason, but instead to something outside it.

Moreover, Kant simply rejects the view that the moral choice is the only coherent choice. Unfortunately, given that we are embodied beings with a faculty of sensibility, *we* do have irreducibly sensible inclinations, and in Kant's view these inclinations are *not* grounded in an implicit commitment to all of humanity but instead in our sensible nature, and they can provide their own all-too-*coherent* basis for choice that is nonetheless all-too-human, and *immoral*. As Kant asserts against his predecessors and contemporaries alike, it is this recognition that allows us to not only clarify the true meaning of the moral law, but also properly gauge the nature of the challenge of moral living and respond in a clear-eyed manner. It is Kant's recognition of the fact that inclinations are *not* ultimately grounded in a commitment to moral law, that choices can indeed be coherent even if immoral, and that moral living and happiness can sadly go their own separate, coherent ways, that allows Kant to recognize that one of the most important tasks of moral living is to do our part to cultivate our inclinations and develop our character so that, at least to the extent possible, we can bring happiness and morality into harmony in this life.

CHAPTER 8

Moral Realism and the Inner Value of the World

Frederick Rauscher

Paul Guyer is rather fond of one particular passage from the Mrongovius and Collins Lectures on Ethics where Kant declares "if all creatures had a faculty of choice bound to sensuous desires, the world would have no value; the inner value of the world, the *summum bonum*, is the freedom to act in accordance with a faculty of choice that is not necessitated. Freedom is therefore the inner value of the world" (*Mrong* 27:1482). Guyer quotes this passage in at least eight different places.[1] I am not even counting in that total the related passage he is also fond of quoting from the Naturrecht Feyerabend course lectures to the effect that the value of the human being is due to freedom rather than rationality as such: "If only rational beings can be an end in themselves, that is not because they have reason, but because they have freedom" (*NF* 27:1321). Guyer takes Kant to have a "morality of freedom" in which the highest value is the freedom of human beings (and other beings like us). Guyer presents this emphasis on freedom in contrast to what others have seen as possessing absolute value for Kant, such as rational nature itself.[2]

In this chapter I want to argue that Guyer's use of the claim that "freedom is the inner value of the world" is misplaced. My concern is with the "inner value of the world" part of the claim, which raises the metaethical question regarding the meaning of the term "inner value." I am not concerned here about the claim that freedom rather than some other thing is of value. To say that a value is "inner" implies an ontology in

---

[1] He quotes the passage at different lengths, and using either the Mrongovious (*Mrong* 27:1482) or the Collins Lectures (*Collins* 27:344) versions, in Guyer 2000d; Guyer 2000a; Guyer 1996a; Guyer 1996c; Guyer 2005b; his survey book *Kant* (Guyer 2006b:178); at least one book review (Guyer 1996d); and at least one paper in Portuguese (Guyer 1995).

[2] Guyer particularly argues that freedom rather than reason must be of moral value in a review essay on Christine Korsgaard's book *Creating the Kingdom of Ends* (Guyer 1998), but lays out his argument for the unconditional value of freedom in the two papers just cited (Guyer 2000a and 2000d).

155

which value is understood as a property of objects independent of any perceiver or moral evaluator. I will argue that such a property conflicts with Kant's own epistemology and ontology.

1 Realism and Value

What kind of thing is "inner value"? Specifically, I want to determine where this absolute moral value lies in the debate over whether Kant is a moral realist or moral idealist (or anti-realist or constructivist, depending on whose terminology is in use). An *inner* value of the world identifies value as an intrinsic property of the world; in the case of freedom this value presumably lies in moral agents themselves as an intrinsic property. Properties are an ontological matter and so the question about value realism is properly viewed using a metaphysical conception of realism. The definition of moral realism that I favor is metaphysical:

> *Moral realism*: the moral principles, properties, or objects of the world are independent of the transcendental or empirical moral agent.[3]

Correspondingly, moral idealism (a better term than "antirealism" with its negative connotations) sees principles, properties, and objects as all dependent on the moral agent.[4] I understand dependence on the moral agent to mean dependence on the moral subject, the agent as active.[5]

---

[3] I offer this definition in Rauscher 2015:14.

[4] This kind of realism differs from one focused on the existence of moral facts or the objective validity of moral claims. A widely used definition from Geofrey Sayre-McCord centers on truth: He takes realism to consist of two theses: "(1) the claims in question, when literally construed, are literally true or false (cognitivism) and (2) some are literally true" (Sayre-McCord 1988:5). I take this kind of definition to be lacking when applied to Kant, for surely it is wrong to equate "true" and "real" when discussing transcendental idealism. Kant certainly claims that all *a priori* knowledge is true even when it is understood as ideal rather than real in a transcendental sense. To equate "true" and "real" is wrongly to place the dividing line between realists and non-realists, who make different kinds of metaphysical claims, precisely atop the dividing line between those who accept and those who reject morality, who make much broader claims about the validity of moral practice as a whole. Certainly in Kant interpretation the interesting question that divides realists and anti-realists is not whether the moral law is valid but what makes it valid. This kind of definition is particularly unhelpful with regard to moral value, since no one disputes that Kant thinks that there is absolute value. The disagreement centers on what kind of thing that value is.

[5] My emphasis on the agent as moral subject as opposed to the agent as moral object precludes any quick and trivial argument to idealism through a claim that freedom (or humanity or dignity) are properties of moral agents as objects (items of concern in morality) and so dependent on the very existence of rational agents. If it were to turn out that moral value were an intrinsic property of rational agents as objects independent of whether any moral agents as subjects considered them to be so, then moral value would be real, not ideal.

Moral Realism and the Inner Value of the World 157

For example, the value of particular ends that an agent chooses to pursue is uncontroversially dependent on that agent's valuing those ends and so would be ideal rather than real. My assessment here is targeted at the ontological claim that there is an intrinsic value to something in the world that is not dependent upon the moral agent in any kind of similar way.

In my definition I distinguish between the "transcendental" and "empirical" as two levels of possible realism in Kant. This novel approach has important implications for my argument. The transcendental level – and here I am using transcendental in its methodological sense in relation to transcendental arguments – consists of the very conditions for moral agency as such, parameters that would apply universally to all possible moral beings, or, in modified Kantian terminology, the transcendental conditions for the possibility of moral experience. The empirical level consists of the specific characteristics of actual moral agents that do not have such transcendental justification. There would be only one description of the transcendental moral agent, just as there is only one description of the subject of the transcendental unity of apperception in theoretical philosophy, but there are many different empirical moral agents with different characteristics. These two different conceptions of moral agents do not imply that there are two different moral agents in each human being; rather, human beings as empirical agents can be exemplars of transcendental moral agency if they possess these universal features. At the very least Kant argues that as empirical moral agents, human beings must also view themselves as transcendental moral agents. It is also possible conceptually that the transcendental moral agent would require some non-empirical property or ontology, which would then have to be attributed to specific moral agents as a non-natural property or ontology. Whether this is so or not is to be determined by an examination of the transcendental conditions for moral experience that Kant actually advocates.

Most of Kant's discussion of morality in the *Groundwork* and the *Critique of Practical Reason* are at the transcendental level, concerned with the practical nature of finite rational beings and with pure practical reason. There is some discussion of empirical moral agency, for example, in *Groundwork* III when Kant asks whether actual human moral agents may assume that they are transcendental moral agents, and in the second *Critique* when the fact of reason plays a similar role. Overall, I take the derivation and formulas of the categorical imperative, the distinction between autonomy and heteronomy, and the requirements for freedom to operate at the transcendental level.

Some of Guyer's statements indicate that he takes Kant to be a moral realist about value. Many others call Guyer a value realist[6] and he himself takes the critical Kant to base a claim of the absolute value of freedom on an argument that claims that we really are free, rational, noumenal selves.[7] The picture that one has is that Kant's critical moral theory requires the existence of moral agents as things in themselves independent of nature in space and time, freely able to determine their own actions, with that freedom possessing value of itself. Guyer accepts this as an interpretation of Kant but also argues that it is philosophically untenable because of the difficulties in, for example, explaining how this purely rational acting being should end up making some of the bad decisions it exhibits in nature in space and time. Guyer would prefer a more naturalistic Kant who avoids transcendental claims and instead understands the value of freedom as simply the fact that actual human beings really do desire freedom, a tendency that Guyer sees in the pre-critical Kant.

But there are other indications that Guyer rejects value realism as an interpretation of Kant.[8] He often notes that Kant steps back from the strong metaphysical claim that human beings are *really* free, rational, beings in themselves independent of nature in space and time to the less realist position that human beings merely *act under the idea* that they are free, rational, beings in themselves independent of nature in space and time. After presenting Kant's *Groundwork* III in strongly metaphysical terms, Guyer quickly notes that "Kant drops the argument we have just examined almost as soon as he has expounded it," that is, Kant retreats from the position that human beings *are* rational beings in themselves to the less demanding position that they can *think* of themselves that way because humans might be other than the way they appear.[9]

There is thus inconclusive evidence from Guyer's published writings to determine whether he interprets Kant as a value realist or not.[10] Either way the issue remains whether it would be a *correct interpretation* of Kant to say

[6] See Stern 2011:27; Johnson 2007:135; Formosa 2013:170; and Hills 2008.

[7] In Guyer 2007b:452, he argues that the pre-critical Kant possessed a naturalistic view of morality that the critical Kant superseded with his transcendental, *a priori* account.

[8] But for an argument that Guyer does not take value to be an independent property, see Sensen 2011:79–87. Sensen claims that "Guyer does not present the value of freedom as a distinct metaphysical property" and a footnote to this sentence claims that Guyer confirmed this fact in a personal conversation (Sensen 2011:84).

[9] Guyer notes this reversal in a few places: e.g., (Guyer 2007a:167) and (Guyer 2007b:461) but is more strongly metaphysical in Guyer 2009b.

[10] In conversations he has stepped back from the realist ontological implications of the term "inner value," including conversations stemming from the version of this chapter read at the "Nature and Freedom in Kant" conference in 2013.

Moral Realism and the Inner Value of the World 159

he is or is not a value realist, and to understand the term "inner value" to refer to an intrinsic property of the object. This is a complex issue, and in this chapter I will present only a few key points in support of my claim. I will examine, in turn, the lack of a place in Kant's ontology for any inner value property and the nature of value as a formal ordering of ends by reason.

2 Moral Value Cannot be an Intrinsic Property

In this section I argue that moral value cannot be understood as something existing as a property of objects independent of either transcendental or empirical moral agency. The textual evidence at first glance is itself ambiguous. There are places where Kant says that a rational being is something "the existence of which in itself has absolute value" (*Groundwork* 4:428) but also passages in which he just as emphatically states that "nothing has any value other than that which the law determines for it" (Groundwork 4:435).[11] Instead of trying to settle the issue by throwing textual passages at one another, a better method is to see which fits better with Kant's broader philosophy. I claim that there is no room in Kant's ontology for any such property.

1 The first reason to reject any independent value is that the very idea of independent normative properties does not square with Kant's division of philosophy into the theoretical – a study of what is, or ontology – and the practical – a study of what ought to be, or the normative. This division is not just a separation of one larger homogeneous topic into two sub-topics, as one might divide the study of life into various taxa such as bacteria, animals, or plants. The theoretical and practical have fundamentally different tasks covering fundamentally different domains (e.g., *KrV* A841/B869). The domain of theoretical philosophy is knowledge of what exists. The domain of practical philosophy is the determination of free acts, and practical reason provides the law for determining those acts (this is clearest at 27:243 in the Collins metaphysics lectures). The practical concerns behavior, not being. Prima facie the burden is on a value realist to show how the practical is supposed to provide an ontology.

One might object that surely this simple division does not prevent the practical from possessing an ontology of its own. Doesn't Kant, in fact,

---

[11] Two recent studies evaluate these and other passages in detail. Robert Stern argues that they support realism (Stern 2011:26–40); Oliver Sensen that they do not (Sensen 2011:21–3, 39–51).

discuss on ontology that practical reason apparently provides in the form of the postulates of practical reason: the immortality of the soul, the existence of God, and freedom of the will. But an appeal to the postulates does not help. One reason is that the postulates themselves have nothing to do with moral value. If the postulates do contain Kant's practical ontology, then the fact that no moral value property is mentioned as a postulate would count as evidence against any claim that practical reason requires that ontology. Further, if the way that practical reason were to offer an ontology would be through the postulates, then it would not help in defending an ontology of moral value unless moral value were also a subject of theoretical reason. In the *Critique of Pure Reason*, Kant explains the relation of ontology to the practical when in the Canon he discusses the famous three questions of philosophy: what can I know, what ought I to do, and what may I hope? (*KrV* A805/B833). He says that the first question is speculative, the second practical, and the third "simultaneously practical and theoretical." Kant raises the need for immortality and God only in answering the last question. The ontology related to the practical is not a product of the practical alone but of the practical in conjunction with the theoretical. The postulates are fully consistent with Kant's general division of philosophy into practical and theoretical, with only the latter concerning ontology.

2 The second reason that value cannot be an independent property of things is that there is no place for it in Kant's conception of nature, which is to say it could not be empirically real. Nature is constituted by concepts applied to intuitions and is extended past actual intuitions only through laws of nature.[12] Oliver Sensen makes this argument by specifying the manner in which intuitions would give human beings access to independent things or properties.[13] Any value property would have to come from sensation (outer intuition) or feeling (inner intuition). No value comes through sensation, and any value derived through feeling would be contingent and not the necessary value of humanity and would also reflect the agent and not merely be a property of the object. These considerations show that, absent any other way of determining the ontology of nature, there could be no empirically real intrinsic value properties in nature.

---

[12] Kant makes the point that ontology of the actual is a product of intuitions and laws of nature when discussing the possibility of magnetic matter at *KrV* A225–6/B272–4.

[13] Sensen 2011:19–20, where his main point is that even if there were an independent value property, it would be inaccessible to moral agents and could play no role in morality.

Moral Realism and the Inner Value of the World 161

3 For there to be an inner value to the world or to humanity at the transcendental level of moral agency, it would have to be a property of things in themselves that would be independent of the transcendental moral agent as subject (and thus also independent of the empirical moral agent). Presumably this would be a property of moral agents as objects as beings in themselves independent of their appearance in space and time. But there is a clear difficulty with this position: Transcendental moral agents as subjects would have no access to this property of the transcendental moral agent as object.

The obvious candidate for another mode of access to value properties is practical reason itself. And the third reason that Kant cannot be claiming that there are independent value properties is that reason could not know them directly. Practical reason cannot function in this way. Suppose that practical reason were to be the mode of access for an independent value property. It would have to access it either actively or passively. It is reason's nature to be active, but by hypothesis reason cannot create this value property because it is independent of the moral agent's pure practical reason. Reason would have to be able to intuit the independent value of humanity as an end in itself in other beings in themselves, in which case it would have to be passive relative to the value property and the latter would have to actively affect reason. But there is no mechanism by which one being in itself can affect another being in itself except through intuition as appearance, which brings back the point that there is no place in nature for any independent value property.

4 But perhaps reason has no direct *access* to the independent value property of moral agents in themselves, either actively or passively, but reason can *know* or *prove* that there must be such a thing. The fourth point against independent value is that such a claim would be restricted by the nature of reason itself. This option would require that there be some proof by reason that there must be such an independent value. The first *Critique*'s main goal is to show that *a priori* arguments by reason cannot be trusted. The best that reason can do is to provide us with *ideas* that we can use to enhance other claims regarding experience, as the idea of God can be used to see the world teleologically. Reason can make no ontological claim that objects or properties it requires for its own systematic purposes actually exist. One might object here that Kant's restriction applies to theoretical but not practical reason, since practical reason seems to make existence claims in the postulates. A few paragraphs earlier, I provided reason to think that any ontological claim in the postulates would have to

conform to theoretical reason. I also argue elsewhere that the status of the postulates is more like the theoretical ideas of reason than like an assertion of reality (Rauscher 2007). A defender of an *a priori* argument by practical reason would have to provide some argument to the effect that practical reason, despite as reason being generally untrustworthy in determining existence claims, and despite centering on normative and not ontological claims, is better positioned than theoretical reason to make *a priori* arguments with ontological conclusions.

5 Perhaps one would claim that the argument is not *a priori* but depends upon some a posteriori premise. The premise would have to be based on something in moral experience rather than nature. Given the lack of accessibility to any external normative properties as I have argued, the most plausible candidate is the fact of reason, which presents us with the categorical imperative. Assuming that we can take our awareness of the categorical imperative to be a solid enough experience to be the basis of a further argument with ontological conclusions, the issue now comes to precisely what Kant means when he talks about the categorical imperative's need for a necessary end, that is, humanity as an end in itself.

The specific argument that value realist interpretations use to claim that humanity is intrinsically valuable occurs in Kant's discussion of the formula of humanity. What Kant claims there is that there must be an end in itself, something the existence of which is an end, and he appears to equate this property of being an end in itself with absolute value (*GMS* 4:428). Now, what is an end? An end is not a property of anything considered in isolation, as an independent property would have to be, but is conceivable only in relation to some active means-ends reasoning by a moral agent. Even a rational being in isolation could be an end as moral object only in relation to herself as active moral subject. To say that a being is an end in itself is just shorthand for saying that it must be *treated* as an end at all times. So when Kant does employ reason in an argument that rational beings have absolute value, the conclusion is not that an independent value property exists in them but that they must be treated in a certain way.

6 But perhaps the reason that they must be treated that way is because they have an independent value property that is not "being an end in itself" but is something else. This brings up the sixth reason that value is not an intrinsic property. Kant's language does not seem to support any other *value* as being the basis for the status of end in itself; rather, the basis is the non-normative property of humanity. Kant says, "rational beings are called 'persons' because their nature already *marks them out* [*auszeichnet*] as ends

Moral Realism and the Inner Value of the World 163

in themselves" (*GMS* 4:428, my emphasis). The word *"auszeichnet"* has the connotation not of a revelation of something intrinsic but of the assignment of a value to something – one receiving an honor or a good receiving a price. The term then suggests that there is a property of rational beings, their humanity, whether that be their freedom or their rationality or their capacity to choose to follow the moral law, that makes them something that reason would elevate in the order of ends above all others. So, to say that rational beings in themselves have value is not to say that the value is *in* the rational beings, but that there is a non-normative property of the rational beings that pure practical reason recognizes. This is the same thing as saying that the moral agent, through the categorical imperative given by pure practical reason, is commanded to treat certain beings as ends in themselves because they possess some non-normative property that reason itself holds is deserving of that treatment. The *existence* of rational beings and even their humanity are intrinsic properties of the moral *object* independent of the moral *subject*, but the *value* of that humanity is dependent upon practical reason in the moral subject.

These reasons show that value cannot be an intrinsic property of objects independent of the transcendental or empirical moral agent. This is not to say that rational beings are not ends-in-themselves but only to say that what is meant by "end-in-itself" is not a property that rational beings have as objects independent of moral agency. There is no independent value property, there are only non-normative independent properties that reason uses as a basis for its value claims. This relation is best explained by relating value to the order of reason, the topic of my next section.

3 Moral Value Is Only a Formal Ordering by Reason

The value of humanity is not an "inner" or intrinsic property of rational beings. Rather it is merely a part of the formal order of practical reason.

Kant talks about the formal order of reason in several places, using terms such as "intelligible order" and "moral world." In the solution to the third antinomy, during a discussion of the causality of reason in moral decisions, Kant says that "reason does not give in to those grounds which are empirically given, and it does not follow the order of things as they are presented in intuition, but with complete spontaneity it makes its own order according to ideas to which it fits the empirical conditions" (*KrV* A548/B576). In the Canon he denies that the "moral world" has any ontological status except to the extent that rational beings, through their actions, impose that order on the world (A808/B837). In the second *Critique* he refers to an "intelligible order" in at least three places (5:42, 5:86–7, and 5:106). He is clear that the direct application of the moral order to the sensible world provides it with the form of an intelligible world.

> This law is to furnish the sensible world, as a *sensible nature* (in what concerns rational beings), with the form of an intelligible world, that is, of a *supersensible nature*, though without infringing upon the mechanism of the former... supersensible nature, in so far as we can make a concept of it, is nothing else than *a nature under the autonomy of practical reason*. (*KpV* 5:43)

The intelligible order of things is the formal ordering that practical reason provides to nature through the categorical imperative. The *intelligible order of things* is not an *order of intelligible things* but an order of things in our experience, particularly in relation to rational beings. Any value has to be understood in relation to this formal ordering by reason.

The best way to understand the formal ordering by reason is to compare it to ordinary empirical ordering of values. An empirical agent is faced with many possible ends, the pursuit of each contingent upon the choice of the empirical agent. No empirical agent can pursue all ends simultaneously and only a finite number successively. Pragmatic empirical agents select from among all possible ends those to pursue and by so doing place a value upon them. As Kant recognizes, this value is entirely dependent upon the subject's discretion (*GMS* 4:427) and is not an intrinsic property of the ends or objects related to those ends. Further, an empirical agent values some ends more than others and so creates a hierarchy of ends. For an empirical end to be valuable at all is for it to have a place in some empirical agent's set of chosen ends, for an end to be more valuable is for it to have a higher rank in such a hierarchy.

The intelligible order of reason is analogous to this empirical order of contingent ends. At the transcendental level, the moral agent is considered only abstractly and does not have access to particular ends. But the moral agent is aware that there are two possible *kinds* of ends: the contingent ends from which she will be able to select her particular ends as an empirical agent, and necessary ends that would not be optional at the empirical level. Pure practical reason, as a faculty of the transcendental moral agent, identifies humanity (understood by Guyer as freedom) as this necessary end. Pure practical reason's selection of humanity as an end is what gives humanity value, and the ranking it provides in setting this necessary end above all possible contingent ends is what gives humanity absolute value. Reason provides its own order at the transcendental level that parallels the empirical level in that in both levels the value of the ends, whether contingent or necessary, is dependent upon the moral agent. Rather than being an independent property of rational beings independent of reason's imposition of order through the categorical imperative, absolute value is only the place of some ends in the formal ordering of ends by pure practical reason.

The order of reason is a reflection of the formal character of the categorical imperative. Practical reason operates through form alone. Through the categorical imperative, pure practical reason imposes its own intelligible order on nature without adding any content to nature except the actions that reason itself causes. It does this by insisting on a certain order of ends in which humanity is given priority over all other ends. The demand of reason is for empirical moral agents to use humanity as a limiting condition when deliberating about subjectively chosen ends, and the means used to reach those ends. Those empirical moral agents are restricted in their choices by the demands of transcendental moral agency.

The specific formulas of the categorical imperative that impose this necessary order of reason in relation to ends are the formula of humanity and, derivatively, the formula of the kingdom of ends. Here is the place to show how I can account for Kant calling the value of humanity the "matter" of the categorical imperative even though the ordering of reason is merely formal. He also says, as I quoted already, that a rational being is something "the existence of which *in itself* has absolute value" (*GMS* 4:428, my emphasis).

Absolute value as ranking in the merely formal order of ends and not an intrinsic property of rational agents is still compatible with these claims. Consider the claim that the categorical imperative has the value of humanity as necessary ends as its "matter." This need not mean that the "matter" is an independent existent that reason recognizes; it can just as easily mean that reason determines *a priori* that certain ends are of value and will then constitute the "matter" at issue. There are two possible scopes for the necessity of the end: It can be a necessary end for *maxims* or a necessary end of *the moral law* itself. Kant's summary of the formulas of the categorical imperative identifies the necessary end to be an end for *maxims,* not for the categorical imperative as such.

> all *maxims* have, namely ... a *form*, which consists in universality, ... a *matter*, namely an end, and in this respect the formula says that a rational being, as an end by its nature and hence as an end in itself, must *in every maxim serve as the limiting condition* of all merely relative and arbitrary ends. (*GMS* 4:436, first and last emphases are mine)

The necessity is for maxims to conform to humanity as an end in itself, not for the categorical imperative to conform to humanity as an end in itself. When Kant presents the formula of humanity he says that rational being as an end in itself "is at the same time an objective principle from which, as a supreme practical ground, it must be possible to derive all *laws* of the will" (*GMS* 4:429, my emphasis). Kant here treats ends in themselves not as the ground of the categorical imperative but as the ground of laws that we would derive using the categorical imperative. The categorical imperative can, as the command of reason to order ends in a certain way, itself provide the necessity to the ends that maxims must take into account. The categorical imperative as the means by which pure practical reason imposes its formal order onto nature is still purely formal in the broad sense.

A typical realist objection to this claim is to ask for a basis on which reason would assign value. Is there a ground for reason's assignment of value to humanity and not something else? Surely, the objection goes, that ground would itself have to be a preexisting value, for otherwise it would appear that reason is creating value arbitrarily. This is a broad topic about which I will only make a suggestion. Many understand "humanity" in Kant as referring to the ability to rationally deliberate and decide upon courses of action. We have value in virtue of that practical rational capacity. If this is true, then there is a ground for practical reason to assign value to humanity because in doing so practical reason is assigning value to its own free exercise. Reason valuing itself should be no surprise. Reason's selecting of rational activity as an end is not arbitrary at all. Further, there is good reason to think that if humanity is understood this way but the value of humanity is understood in realist terms as an intrinsic property *not* stemming from reason, then it would appear that practical reason simply lucked out that it is able to command as a moral imperative the maximization of itself.

In this section I have argued that the best way to understand Kant's claims about the value of humanity is in terms of the ordering of ends imposed on moral agents by pure practical reason. No independent value property is needed to explain the role of absolute value in Kant.

4 Conclusion

The answer to the broad question of whether Kant is a value realist is "no." There is no property of objects "absolutely valuable" that is independent of either the transcendental moral agent or the empirical moral agent. Kant's ontology of nature does not allow for such a property, the nature of

Moral Realism and the Inner Value of the World 167

practical reason precludes ontological claims, and when examined closely the alleged independent value, that of "end in itself," is at best relational because of its dependence on active beings who pursue ends. Instead I have shown that Kant's theory of absolute value is both transcendentally and empirically idealist because it is constituted by the formal order imposed by reason.

So why would Kant say, as so frequently quoted by Guyer, "freedom is the inner value of the world"? Kant never received any awards for consistency, but I speculate that when Kant uses language about inner value, particularly to the young students in the lectures on ethics from which this quotation comes, he is simply trying to stress that we human beings are subject to dictates of reason that command absolutely and that, in this particular case, freedom is the focal point of reason's normative ordering of our experience. I have no problem with occasional imprecision for the sake of rhetorical flourish, but we must read his claims in their broader context.[14]

[14] I would like to thank my commentator Rob Hoffman at the Nature and Freedom in Kant conference, as well as that audience and the audience at Western Michigan University for comments on earlier versions of this chapter.

PART III

Freedom as Autonomous Willing: Kant's Sensible Agent

CHAPTER 9

On the Many Senses of "Self-Determination"

Karl Ameriks

1 Preliminary Overview

Many a Scylla and Charybdis threatens the navigations of the dutiful *Groundwork* reader. By focusing on a clarification of some of the very different meanings of "self-determination" in Kant's work, the following apologetic interpretation seeks to steer a middle path between two extreme but common ways of reacting to the *Groundwork*'s account of moral self-determination as autonomy. In this case, the Scylla objection claims, in view of the "auto" component of Kantian "autonomy," that to speak of the moral law as rooted in self-legislation is to be too ambitious, and overly subjective, and to do an injustice to the essentially receptive character of our reason. Here the contention is that Kant misunderstands how reason is a capacity that basically appreciates reasons to act given to the subject by what is outside of it. The contrasting Charybdis concern stems from a worry about what can appear to be an overly close connection drawn between morality and freedom as autonomy. Here the critic's contention is that the "nomos" component of self-determination in the *Groundwork* is too restrictive, and in a sense overly objective, insofar as it makes our action appear so thoroughly law-oriented that it seems to leave only the options of being forced either by our reason to follow the moral law or by the "natural necessity" of our sensibility to go against it, and thus – in contrast to Kant's own later works – it does injustice to our faculty of free choice, or at least our ability to act in ways more complex than these two narrow options.

2 Vindicating Kantian Self-Determination

2.1 *On "Determination" and* Bestimmung

Unlike "autonomy," the components of "self-determination," as well as those of its German correlate *Selbstbestimmung*, are everyday terms in their

171

native languages, and ones that have many similar meanings and ambiguities. The verb *bestimmen* ("determine") is used repeatedly in numerous contexts by Kant, and yet, like casual English speakers, he generally does not bother to make explicit the quite different senses that the term can have.

One basic ambiguity concerns two distinct philosophical senses of "determination," namely, an *epistemological* (E) and a *causal* (C) sense. We can say, in a first, or E sense, that we determine something when – even without having any relevant effect on it – we simply learn something informative about it, for example, when we cognitively determine the fact that a surface appears warm. We can also say, in a second, or C sense, that we determine it when we simply bring about that something beyond our immediate situation is the case, for example, when we causally determine that a surface is warm – even when, in the relevant sense, we may not at all know what we are doing. It can, of course, also happen that cognitive and causal kinds of determination combine in one complex event; we can come to learn that something is warm in the very act of making it warm. (In English, these meanings are combined in a further sense when we use knowledge in a decisive way to try to bring something about, as when we say, for example, that, "no matter what," we are "determined to" heat a surface.)

In addition to these basic E and C senses of "determine," there are, especially for the noun form of the term, what I will call its basic F and N senses, namely a *formal* or definitional sense,[1] as well as a *normative* sense, one that, for Kant, ultimately is to be understood as having a complex moral and teleological meaning. For example, in the course of determining the composition of a metal, in the E sense of merely finding out some things about it, we may eventually arrive at its determination in the more exact F sense of a formula defining its basic nature.[2] (Here the English term has roots in the French verb *determiner* and the process of fixing a thing's boundaries and gaining a relevantly complete notion of it.) In Kant's tradition, the nature of something can, furthermore, be something more than a mere physically defined arrangement, in a broadly mechanical sense, for this nature can need to be understood in terms of an ideal practical form such as, above all, the notion of a moral telos or destiny.

---

[1] See, e.g., *GMS* 4:461: "*autonomy* – as the formal condition under which it alone can be determined."
[2] See, e.g., *GMS* 4:436: "a complete *determination* (*Bestimmung*) of all maxims by that formula."

On the Many Senses of "Self-Determination" 173

It is this biblical and broadly Lutheran sense that is most relevant when, after J. J. Spalding's very popular 1748 volume *Die Bestimmung des Menschen*,[3] Kant and numerous other German philosophers, including especially Fichte, focus on *Bestimmung* in the N sense of our essential "vocation," or "calling," at a species as well as individual level. The term "determination" does not have this normative meaning in English, and thus its relation to the other terms can often get lost in translation, but this sense must always be kept in mind when reading Kant and his use of various forms of the term *bestimmen*, for it is this kind of determination that always is of greatest significance to him.[4]

Kant's very early works, such as his 1755 *Universal Natural History*, go along with the dominant broadly Leibnizian view of his era, which stresses that human beings have a significant normative determination but maintains a compatibilist doctrine of freedom, one that denies absolute free choice. This view distinguishes, as basically a matter of mere degree, our rational essence as human beings with this kind of (merely relative) freedom from the broadly mechanistic nature of lower kinds of beings, while still allowing that, according to a more inclusive meaning of the term "nature," human beings are thoroughly determined as parts of nature in the E, C, F, and N senses. Although Kant holds to this view throughout his earliest works, he then, after the fundamental revolution in his thinking upon reading Rousseau and achieving philosophical maturity at the age of forty in the early 1760s, adopts a very different conception of the relation of nature and human freedom.[5] From that time on, Kant believes that our own nature is unique in having a non-compatibilist *Bestimmung* in its pure moral vocation, a vocation that cannot be understood as being fulfilled, as Leibnizians and other compatibilists claim, simply by attaining higher degrees of clear representation and consequent power.

2.2 On the "Self" of Selbstbestimmung

Although the notion of "determination" will be my main focus, it is also necessary to add a few preliminary observations about the "self" component in the complex term "self-determination." In a Kantian context, it is of course crucial to keep in mind that his use of the word "self" is not limited

---

[3] On Spalding's significance, see, e.g., Brandt 2007 and Munzel 2012.

[4] See, e.g., *GMS* 4:396, "the true vocation (*Bestimmung*) of human beings must be to produce a will that is good."

[5] See Ameriks 2012: chapter 1.

to ordinary empirical particulars. When he speaks of "simple acts of reason," that is, our fundamental logical capacities, as being found "in my own self,"[6] he clearly has in mind, in part, a general and pure faculty that cannot be explained as the product of empirical actions or capacities. It is then, I believe, an additional – and of course still much disputed – feature of Kant's ultimate moral metaphysics that it favors affirming that the self (of each of us) has not only a range of pure general capacities (for pure intuiting, pure understanding, pure theoretical and practical reasoning, and even for generating feelings that in part have a pure origin) but also a kind of pure and particular independent form of existence, that is, an immortality conceived of as in itself lacking any sensory qualities, spatial or temporal.[7]

In addition to these basic *empirical* and *pure* senses of "self," which I take to include substantial as well as functional characterizations, there is a complex *reflexive* meaning to the term "self" that has a fundamental significance in the context of self-determination.[8] To begin with, this reflexive meaning needs to be understood as having at least a threefold structure with implications at both empirical and pure levels of determination (and concerning all E, C, F, and N senses). For Kant, to say that we are self-determined reflexively is to say, at the least, that, at both levels, the self is determined (1) *in* (or, one could also say, *of*) itself and (2) *by* itself as well as (3) *for* itself.

At the first level, this means that human beings, individually and as a group, are commonly understood to be acting with empirical effects that are in part within them, and that are caused by empirical sources in them, and that exist for the sake of empirical ideals concerning them. Thus we can speak, as Lincoln did at Gettysburg, of a government "of the people, by the people, and for the people." But Kant would go on to insist that we speak, in addition, in terms of three parallel forms of pure reflexivity, and thus affirm, at a second level, pure effects, pure causings, and pure ideals – all to be understood as part of our own self-determined existence and not merely a possibility for divine beings.

---

[6] *KrV* Axiv: "ich demütig gestehe . . . ich es lediglich mit der Vernunft selbst und ihrem reinen Denken zu tun habe . . . weil ich sie [deren ausführlichen Kenntnis] *in mir selbst* antreffe . . . alle *ihre einfache Handlungen.*"

[7] See especially Kant's criticism cf the notion of resurrection in *Religion within the Boundaries of Mere Reason* (*RGV* 6:128–9 n.).

[8] See Prauss 1989:253–63 and O'Neill 2013:282–7. I take the general picture of autonomy that I am developing here to be consistent as well with most of the other essays in this helpful recent collection.

The mere general or structural feature of reflexivity thus does not by itself capture what Kant takes to be most important about us. That is, the three kinds of Gettysburg empirical reflexivity just listed are by themselves merely empirical, and they could exhaust the capacities of the kind of agents that Kant memorably stigmatizes in terms of the image of a mere "turnspit" (*Bratenwender*) (*KpV* 5:97). In saying this, he realizes, of course, that even at the empirical level human beings are not literally mechanical turnspits, for, as rational animals, their reflexive acts have a conscious intentionality aimed at complex ideals. But if Kant had lived long enough to hear Lincoln's threefold reflexive remark about government, and understood all that it was directly saying as a merely empirical statement, presumably he still would have maintained what he says in his 1783 review of Pastor J. H. Schulz's "well-intentioned" quasi-Leibnizian tract on penal reform, namely, that by itself it still misses our essential (for our *Bestimmung*) and absolutely pure (in E, C, F, and N senses) freedom to act and to think (*RezSchulz* 8:13),[9] which is denied in all compatibilist systems, no matter how sophisticated their picture of us as conscious, rational, and power-enhancing agents.

Once the full context and multiple meanings of Kant's *Groundwork* Section II discussion of autonomy as reflexive self-determination by reason has been spelled out, and once the pure normative sense of autonomy is understood as its essential meaning there – in contrast to merely political and psychological senses of "thinking for oneself," or being "self-governing" according to just any rational principles that contrast with merely reacting to "threats and rewards"[10] – it becomes possible to deflect common objections to Kantian autonomy as overly subjective. Explaining this sense can also help clarify aspects of the *Groundwork*'s difficult transition from Section II to Section III, and this can set the stage for responding to objections that Kant has an overly objective or law-obsessed understanding of action in general.

---

[9] Here Kant at first calls this a freedom to "always act *as if one were free* [and such that] this idea also actually produces the deed," and then he adds that "the understanding is able to determine (*bestimmen*) one's judgment in accordance with objective grounds that are always valid," and hence we must "always admit freedom to think, without which there is no reason" (*RezSchulz* 8:13). These ways of characterizing the absolute freedom to act and to think are not clearly in line with the best formulations of Kant's position, but they vividly disclose, in an initial way, the topic that he is most concerned with writing about right at this time. See the end of his essay "An Answer to the Question: What is Enlightenment?" (1784) and his reviews of Herder (1785) as well as the *Groundwork* (1785). His "Idea for a Universal History with a Cosmopolitan Intent" (1784) also has a basic, although indirectly expressed, concern with absolute freedom. See Ameriks 2012: chapters 9 and 10.

[10] See Larmore 2011:11.

3 *Groundwork*, Section III, *de capo*

3.1 *Preconditions*

The title of the first subsection of Section III is "The concept of freedom is the key to the explanation of the autonomy of the will (*Wille*)" (*GMS* 4:440). This title might suggest to some readers that we already have a distinct concept of freedom at hand, and now we can directly apply this concept to explain a mysterious feature called "autonomy of the will." This kind of approach is problematic, however, because the previous Section culminates in an argument that already elucidates a principle of autonomy, whereas it is the nature and existence of freedom, especially in its fundamental philosophical sense, that is, a transcendental causal one, that has not yet been addressed in a direct way. In other words, at the outset of Section III, there is an at least partially well understood notion of autonomy that Kant is taking as given at this point – one involving self-determination basically in the E, F, and N senses – and it is now his goal to introduce a direct discussion of freedom that may begin to shed light on further features of autonomy – features that abruptly shift the discussion of determination largely from its previously mentioned senses to its C sense.[11]

Prior to this new causal discussion, autonomy is treated in strict normative terms, as in the title of Section II's subsection: "The autonomy of the will as the supreme principle of morality" (*GMS* 4:440). That title expresses an initial and relatively non-mysterious idea of what Kant means by autonomy, namely, a way of characterizing the normative principle of morality as necessarily supreme. Here the most basic feature of the norm that Kant is concerned with is that it not only meet the condition of definitely concerning a principle that is "supreme" within morality, but also that it not endanger the claim of morality's principle to be practically supreme overall. Kant is looking for a principle that is not threatened by even the possibility of being normatively derivative, and hence is necessarily supreme in the sense of being wholly unconditioned in its value, even if it may in other respects depend on general non-moral features. For this principle to be able to concern, as Kant has already argued that it must, an imperative that is categorical, it has to be such that it does not get its

---

[11] Hence the title of the *Groundwork* itself, and of Section III, which introduces the notion of a "Critique [i.e., explanation] of Pure Practical Reason."

On the Many Senses of "Self-Determination"   177

distinctive normative status from outside, from "something else" (*GMS* 4:433).[12] The supreme principle is therefore a kind of essentially reflexive principle in a new and axiological sense. At this point the idea of a will with autonomy is basically the idea of the *faculty* of the will as something that does not take the *value* of its supreme norm from outside, that is, merely through faculties external to *Wille*. In this way the principle can be said to have a value that holds true *of* the will not merely in some kind of psychological sense but in a reflexively normative sense, that is, in terms of its own basic resources, and thus purely *by* or through it, as opposed to on account of some other source of standards (such as mere sensation).

Given this context, it is understandable that the end of Section II treats what is outside primarily in negative terms, as when it argues that traditional factors external to the will, such as empirical conditions – whether turned psychologically inward or not (i.e., involving feelings for others and not just oneself) – or dogmatic theological or teleological considerations, whatever significance they may have otherwise, have a kind of externality and contingency[13] that conflicts with the pure standard of necessary value that other parts of the *Groundwork* already connect in categorical moral terms with the notion of the will. Hence, when we then turn to what appears to be the only option left, namely, to what is inside the will, it turns out that it cannot, after all, be internality in any ordinary sense that carries the weight of Kant's argument. This is because, if we were to try to focus on features that seem in an ordinary sense internal to the will but contingent, we would immediately have to concede that, as conditional, these features are still inappropriate for determining, in an E, F, or N sense, what Kant requires of a "supreme principle" of morality.[14]

Therefore, instead of loading Kant's idea of autonomy with the weight of some kind of extra and mysterious boot-strapping "willful"

---

[12] See also *GMS* 4:458 and 4:427, where *Wille* is described as "the capacity to determine itself to action *in conformity with certain laws* ... the objective ground of its self-determination is the *end*." The term "end" makes clear that the point of speaking of the will's ("objective") self-determination is to stress a matter of normative determination.

[13] See *GMS* 4:425, which says the ground of value cannot be in any "special natural predisposition of humanity."

[14] See *GMS* 4:432–3: "[When] one thought of [oneself] as subject to [*unterworfen*, i.e., merely passively subject in contrast to "legislating"] a law ... it had to carry with it some interest or constraint ... necessitated (*genötigt*) by something else [because not arising from the will's own law] in conformity with a law ... a certain interest, be it one's own interest or another... But then the imperative also had to be conditional." Later Kant also speaks of "interests" generated by reason itself, in which case they have an intrinsically necessary status.

process – which readers are understandably still tempted to do[15] – it is essential to see that the underlying claim of Section II depends not on an appeal to internality or even reflexivity in a traditional, general sense but simply on the specific need for finding a basic faculty that is normatively relevant because of an at least possibly appropriate connection to an unconditionally necessary principle of value. On this interpretation, Kant's basic thought is that we have no adequate access to such necessity from some faculty altogether outside reason (hence also his constant attacks on mystical intuition), whereas reason, the faculty that concerns the unconditioned in general, also belongs, in particular, to *Wille*, that is, the pure practical side of the self.[16]

For Kant, *Wille* essentially has such a special feature simply because it is defined as a faculty of practical *reason*, and by this he means *pure* practical reason, in contrast to mere instrumental rationality, let alone mere *arbitrium brutum* (*GMS* 4:412).[17] Although this feature, the appreciation of absolute necessity, is in one sense internal because, on Kant's view, it is intrinsically needed for us to be what we most fundamentally are, and thus it reflects what one always is in one's "ownmost" self,[18] this is not a matter of internality in any kind of ordinary psychological, subjectivistic, or humanistic sense. Hence, insofar as it rests on a previously affirmed respect (in principle, in the second formula of the categorical imperative) for the absolute value of rational agency in this pure sense,[19] the normative self-determination of Kantian morality, as explained in the *Groundwork*'s discussion of the supreme practical principle of autonomy, can be read as the very opposite of what it has appeared to be to many unsympathetic readers – and even to many others who have been trying to be sympathetic. Because Kant argues for the principle from the basis of a respect for absolute necessity, the burden is on others to show that his notion of self-determination has the ultimately subjectivist and limited character that is

---

[15] A similar common and understandable, but also self-defeating, approach is often taken to the metaphysics of Kant's idealism, as if somehow a special process of human "making" could provide a consistent Kantian explanation of the necessary conditions of our grasp of spatio-temporality itself.

[16] Kant therefore stresses later in Section III that reasons still need to be given for the synthetic claim that *we* do have will in a strong sense, or at least in some persuasive sense must regard ourselves in this way.

[17] See also *KrV* B562 and Deligiorgi 2012: 90.

[18] See, e. g., *GMS* 4:455, "das moralische Sollen ist also unser eigenes notwendiges Wollen als Glied einer intelligiblen Welt," and 4:457 and 4:458, "das eigentliche Selbst."

[19] I take this absolute value of being an end in itself to reside for Kant neither in actually acting with a perfectly good will, nor in simply setting whatever ends, but in having the *capacity* always to set ends that meet the conditions of pure morality.

On the Many Senses of "Self-Determination" 179

attached to it in most contemporary uses of the notion of autonomy,[20] and even in many otherwise perceptive discussions of Kant himself.[21]

3.2   How to Undercut What Can Seem to be Kant's Self-Undercutting

There are, of course, passages that can understandably lead readers astray and make it appear as if Kant himself goes on to undercut the fundamentally objective position just discussed. The most frequently cited text of this sort is a passage from *Groundwork* II that expresses a principle of autonomy as *normatively reflexive pure self-determination*, which I will call NRSPD: "Hence the will (*Wille*) is not merely subject to the law [as it would still seem to be on moral theories rooted in contingent factors such as fear or good feeling] but subject to it in such a way that it must be viewed as also *giving the law to itself* (*als selbstgesetzgebend*) and just because of this as first subject to the law" (*GMS* 4:431).[22] Taken out of context, NRSPD might appear to be stressing, after all, an act of arbitrary imposition. The context of NRSPD, however, as indicated by the word "hence," shows that it is meant to *follow* from preceding considerations, and thus, methodologically considered, it does not invoke mere imposition (or, to be precise, what the rest of the sentence calls the will's "regarding itself as the author") — in the loose popular sense of autonomy — as an Archimedean point. The immediately preceding sentence, and the logical precondition for NRSPD, is that "all maxims are repudiated" that are inconsistent with "the will's own universal-law-giving" (*GMS* 4:431).[23] In addition to the special significance of the qualification "universal" (discussed further subsequently) in the essentially unified term "universal-law-giving," there are two other basic points here that must be reiterated whenever trying to understand sentences like this in Kant.

The first point is that the term Kant uses throughout for "will" here is *Wille* and not *Willkür* (choice),[24] which means that it does not at all have

---

[20] On the need to sharply distinguish Kantian autonomy from less demanding uses of the term, which concern contingent political or psychological matters, see again the helpful essays in Sensen 2012. This point about the absolutely necessary character of Kantian autonomy is compatible, I believe, with the argument there by Paul Guyer (2012:71–86), that Kant also develops an empirical account of how humanity gets better over time at *committing* itself to autonomous principles.

[21] See Ameriks 2012: chapter 6.   [22] Cited at Larmore 2011:9.

[23] "der eigenen allgemeinen Gesetzgebung des Willens." My translation substitutes for the Cambridge, "the will's own giving of universal law," because the latter translation (see also note 31) might suggest a contingent relation between the terms, as many Anglophone interpretations tend to assume. For criticism of this tendency, see Ameriks 2012: chapter 6.

[24] This term has a common connotation of arbitrariness in German, e.g., at *GMS* 4:428.

the common casual and contingent English meaning of a derivative capacity or arbitrary act – or, for that matter, of anything characterized independently of the rigorous conditions of what Kant calls pure "practical reason." The second point is that by such reason, in this context, Kant precisely also does not mean any kind of casual and contingent reasoning about merely accidental ends[25] – in contrast to almost all English uses of this phrase. What he means is not just any form of practical rationality but instead the strictly universal "legislation" of pure practical reason, which intends a law that applies by unconditional necessity and not as a matter of mere general empirical fact, as in Lincoln's political phrase. What pure reason alone allows for is a determination of not just any kind of maxims but ones appropriate for what Kant calls "lawfulness" – that is to say, law as such, which, in the pure context of morality, signifies its having the "form" of absolute necessity – unlike the accidentally posited laws that characterize our merely empirical existence and "counsels of prudence" (*GMS* 4:416).

Unfortunately, Kant tends to signal this condition of strictness by simply calling the relevant kind of law "universal," and this has led to considerable confusion about what most concerns him. Kant's frequent use of the term "universal" is understandable in a sense, as a reminder that laws that are merely posited do not in fact tend to be universally valid, nor are they generally even meant to apply universally (and, even if they have a general intention, as with the principles of a rational egoist or an advocate of mere prudence, this is not an unrestricted universality, but conditional, Kant would say, on limited interests not shared by all). But this is just an accidental truth, although it can function as a convenient touchstone, for if something can be shown to be in no way universal, then it cannot be necessary. Kant's fundamental concern, however, as he makes explicit at least on some occasions, is with not just any kind of universality but rather a condition of "strict universality"[26] tantamount to necessity. Moreover, in this case, it is a practical necessity that is absolute, involving a law that holds even for divine nature, and hence it goes beyond even the transcendental schematized Kantian necessities of the Analytic of the first *Critique*, which apply merely at the sensory and ultimately contingent levels of our existence.

---

[25] These are ends that one could be "subject to," so as to meet the first, but only the first, part of the key phrase, just cited, characterizing autonomy at *GMS* 4:431. I bracket here the vexed external issue of whether happiness or universal well-being in general, rather than either accidental particular ends or the Kantian notion of pure duty, may by itself be an absolutely necessary value.

[26] Cf. *GMS* 4:430–1: "because of its universality it applies to all rational beings as such." This phrase surely must be understood as expressing a necessary essence, and not a universality reflecting mere contingent applicability. See also: *GMS* 4:426, "it is a necessary law *for all rational beings*. . ."

On the Many Senses of "Self-Determination" 181

Only once all these qualifications are appreciated can one properly begin to understand what Kant intends by repeatedly speaking here of the "universal law" as a matter of *Wille's* "own giving." This reflexive claim is made in both sentences of the short paragraph that contains NRSPD, as well as in the concluding sentence of the long immediately preceding paragraph. The reason why Kant insists on calling the law a matter of *Wille's* "own giving" is basically that he is trying to find a way to express, as he says in this sentence, that a proper normative principle of *Wille* must not be rooted in something that would not allow it to serve "as supreme condition of its [i.e., the will's] harmony with universal practical reason" (*GMS* 4:431). In other words, the "own giving" by *Wille* here is not a free-floating feature but is one directly tied to Kant's attempt to characterize its principle in such a way that it makes possible a "harmony" with practical reason insofar as such reason is *strictly* universal, that is, "fit to be a law" (*GMS* 4:431).

Kant's concern here with "harmony" is tied to his thought that the principle of morality, in accord with the general organizational principle of reason, must have a consistent threefold specification in "form," "matter," and "complete determination" (*GMS* 4:436). This harmony has a transcendental faculty assignment aspect[27] as well as, derivatively, a concrete intersubjective aspect. First, practical reason as *Wille*, unlike the other basic faculties of mere sensibility and mere understanding, just is the only faculty that is, as Kant goes on to say, harmonious in the sense of "well suited" (4:432; see the contrast of reason and understanding at 4:452) for such universal norms simply because reason is defined as the faculty alone appropriate for expressing and systematizing unconditional necessity. In this regard, it alone is not possibly dependent in its authority on contingent factors, what Kant here calls the "interests" of the other faculties.[28]

This is why, secondly, he goes on to note that its norms can *always* be intended to apply harmoniously in a "complete determination" or structural specification of an *entire* ethical commonwealth (*Reich der Zwecke*).[29] As he stresses in the universal-law-giving passage right before the NRSPD passage, its norms equally concern "*every rational being*" (*GMS* 4:431) as

---

[27] This is part of Kant's general project of demarcating the transcendental "location" of the diversity of our faculties, in opposition to empiricist and rationalist "single root" tendencies that eliminate any non-derivative conception of will.

[28] 4:432: "the principle of ... *universally legislating* ... is *founded on no interest*, and thus can alone, among all possible imperatives, be unconditional."

[29] The presumption of this harmony is overly swift. As later work in logic has revealed, even seemingly necessary formal principles of theoretical reason can lead to paradoxes and a multiplicity of incompatible options, and so one should keep in mind that even Kantian practical norms based on pure reason may be vulnerable to similar problems.

182   KARL AMERIKS

an agent and thus, as a Kantian Lincoln might say, they can be understood as having validity in a pure sense, and are necessarily not only "of" and "by" but also "for" each rational being as *Wille*. It is this interpersonal but *a priori* sense of normativity, and not any empirical process, that is crucial to Kant's understanding of moral authority. Because it is the precondition driving Kant's overall argument toward NRSPD and is sufficient for his distinctive purposes, the idea of a strict moral necessity and independence of *Wille* as a faculty, as expressed in NRSPD itself, should not be read as characterizing some kind of extra process of literal "giving," in either a humanist or supernaturalist sense, for this would replace the supreme principle of moral law with what would have to appear to be a mere quasi-necessity of arbitrary acts of authorship that could claim no more than ultimately subjective validity. In other words, Kant's autonomy formula builds on, rather than undercuts, the thought that the moral law, and a person's being an "end itself," is something that has a value "in itself," with an unrestricted validity for all agents as such.[30] Kant's third basic formula for morality can be understood as simply meant to express the point that this value must not only concern (i.e., be "of" and "for") beings with reason but also cannot be explained independently of being rooted in the faculty of will, which alone can be at once pure – unlike mere feeling – and practical – unlike mere understanding.

The full final clause of the sentence immediately prior to the paragraph of NRSPD is: "from this there follows now the third practical principle of the will, as supreme condition of its harmony with universal practical reason, the idea *of the will of every rational being as a universal-lawgiving-will*" (*GMS* 4:431).[31] Note that in this sentence, which is the crucial step

---

[30] This worry is raised by Larmore (2011:8–9, and 19), who raises the common, and self-defeating, worry that Kant is literally turning reason into an "agent." I take my reading of the *Groundwork*, as basically just trying to give moral principles their proper faculty location, to entail all that Larmore wants from his own (allegedly more realistic) normative theory, especially insofar as Larmore goes on to state that what is valuable is not to be thought of existing in a totally isolated way but as in correspondence with our reason. Larmore himself says, "reasons have a relational character," that is, involve relations to "possibilities of thought and action" that need to be "discovered" (Larmore (2011:20) – presumably by agents with the faculty of reason. Anti-Kantians tend to believe this kind of response is ruled out by Kant's characterization of heteronomy as a matter of allowing the "object" to determine the (moral) law (*GMS* 4:441), but this is to overlook that what Kant is rejecting is simply the thought that a normatively contingent or indeterminate "object" could be law-determining; in other contexts he is willing to speak of the law itself as the proper "object" of practical reason.

[31] This again is my modification of the Cambridge translation, which reads, "will giving universal law," and thus does not as exactly reflect the German "allgemein gesetzgebenden Willens," a phrase that is found on the next page and elsewhere without a break between the terms characteriz-ing will: "allgemeingesetzgebenden Willens." The combining of the terms without a break best

On the Many Senses of "Self-Determination"

supplementing the first two basic formulations of the Categorical Imperative, Kant is taking NRSPD itself as something that "follows." I propose
that this means that, for Kant, to fill out normative reflexive self-
determination in transcendentally reflective, intersubjectively "universal,"
and "complete determination" terms,[32] is simply to reiterate, in the new
language of the third formulation, our need to resist any reliance on any
contingent use of faculties that would undermine a kind of already
assumed necessary practical "harmony." Rather than imposing on Kant
an odd and invalid extra meaning to the notion of self-determination, one
can read him as basically just repeating a point that is made throughout
his work and that is systematically elaborated, in an explicitly negative
manner, in the concluding subsections of *Groundwork* II, "Heteronomy
of the Will as the Source of all Spurious Principles of Morality," namely,
that if one were to try normatively to account for the necessary authority of
morality in terms of exercises of faculties that are manifestly contingent,
such as our sensitivity to either external or internal empirical pressures,
or even theological concepts characterized in a merely arbitrary fashion
(concerning a desire to please the whims of a tyrannical superpower), then
this would be tantamount to sacrificing the normative necessity of the
moral law and its chance for harmony with universal reason.[33]

Note that although it is true that there is a contingent causal relation
between our awareness of such mere pressures and the existence of particular stimuli for them, it is not the relational *causal* contingency of the
pressures that is the key to Kant's objection to them; what matters is the

---

expresses the crucial point that Kant is making an essential and not an accidental characterization
of what he calls *Wille*.

[32] This three-step structure dominates the *Groundwork* from the beginning, although sometimes in a
partially inverted order. The three principles of Section I are introduced heuristically in the order of,
first, "subjective" (that is, existing in the subject) content, that is, the good will and its necessary
value (the notion of necessary value is also placed first in the Preface, *GMS* 4:389), then "objective"
form, that is, having a right (universalizable) maxim, and, third, "determination" through "*pure
respect* for practical law," which "outweighs" all mere inclination (*GMS* 4:400) and is expressed later
in terms of the formula of autonomy. In the initial presentation of the three basic formulae of the
categorical imperative in Section II, and then also in the summary at 4:431, the order becomes
(1) the "objective" form of universality, (2) the "subjective" content of the necessary value of being
an agent with reason, and (3) the unity of these in the notion of a "legislating" rather than simply
passive *Wille* – a third point that "follows" on reflection because the preceding two points about the
universality and necessity of the supreme principle of morality cannot be understood in terms of a
merely contingently determined will. See also Allison 2011:124, and note 42.

[33] Here Kant has a special problem insofar as he must concede that, of the four basic options, the
perfectionist theory of value need not be vulnerable to the objection of relying on contingent values
at its base. This may be part of the reason why Kant is especially interested in the feature of the
universalizability of maxims, which he thinks gives his theory a special advantage, given what he
takes to be the inescapable indeterminacy of the notion of "perfection" alone.

184   KARL AMERIKS

immediately evident contingency of their *value* relevance.[34] There is, for example, no reason to think that the prestige often associated with social rank is necessarily a moral good. But if contingent sources of normativity do not as such harmonize with the strict modal and universal nature of the moral demands of practical reason, some kind of fitting and necessary location for the possibility of this harmony needs to be sought. From a Kantian perspective, there is one and only one obvious alternative here, namely, to look toward practical reason itself. Reason in general is characterized throughout Kant's philosophy as precisely that faculty which determines (in E, F, C, and N senses)[35] all strictly necessary truths, and hence it only makes sense to say that the practical necessities of morality must be sought within the faculty of practical reason, what Kant also calls *Wille*.

Given that these necessities are unavoidably valid, it may be disconcerting at first that Kant uses an active voice here and speaks of "the will" as "giving" the law[36] rather than simply seeing, understanding, or appreciating it. But there are understandable reasons for his use of the active voice here. The most obvious one is that he wants to mark a strong contrast with what he takes to be the manifestly passive and inadequate putative sources of unconditional value that others tend to rely on: mere sensation, tradition, threats and such. Moreover, even when, in a moral context, Kant does use, and even emphasizes, a term that is translated as "impose" (*auferlegen*), he also uses it in part in a passive voice, as something imposed "upon the will." That is, he states that for actions (e.g., not lying to someone about a truth that they have a right to know) out of "immediate respect," "nothing but reason is required to *impose* them upon the will," since "these actions need no recommendation from any subjective

---

[34] Hence I assume there is concern about a judgment (ultimately involving freedom) of value, and not a mere causal relation, at work in passages such as this (*GMS* 4:460): "it is not because the law interests us that it has validity for us (for that is *heteronomy* and dependence [normative!] of practical reason [this is a point about reason, not mere psychology]. . .)."

[35] This statement about "reason in general" is compatible with allowing that reason "in particular," that is, as it is actually taken up on a particular occasion by a person reasoning in action, is part of what allows that person to be causally effective. The causality of practical reason has been emphasized in recent work by Stephen Engstrom.

[36] One should also keep in mind that what look like German uses of the term "give," that is, *geben*, are often translated more properly in non-activist terms. *Es gibt* does not mean "it gives," but simply "there is," just as in English, when we say "it rains," we really are not speaking of a separate "it" but just mean that "rain is falling." I suspect that Kant is most attracted to the word "give" here simply because he wants to use a verb that contrasts with "take," which in this context signifies merely taking over from an external source in a normatively lazy way. Another complication is that here "give" and "take" have connotations that contrast with how they are generally used in relation to the English philosophical notion of the "myth of the (merely passively) given."

On the Many Senses of "Self-Determination" 185

proclivity ... to *coax* [*erschmeicheln*, that is, lure by mere flattery] them" (*GMS* 4:435).[37] Here again it is clear that the cash value of the term "impose" is simply to sharply oppose the idea of accepting only manifestly contingent sources of value. As *Wille*, we "give ourselves" the law most basically insofar as we cannot, as beings of reason, let a "supreme principle," no matter how flattering, be contingently imposed upon us as normatively decisive. We understand that mere efficient causal determination, as a contingent fact about events, cannot be the same thing as the normative determination of a necessary standard of value – and this is true even if the causation is a matter of our own active imagination.

Throughout his philosophy, Kant makes use of a basic distinction between *Tun* and *Lassen* (*GMS* 4:396), that is, between being active in a paradigmatic initiating sense, in contrast to allowing something to happen. But even "allowing" is understood in this context as also a kind of action, and it is clearly Kant's general view that, in the context of our relation to the status of norms, for us even to merely allow any of these to hold sway is to engage in a kind of act and to determine oneself in a "self-incurred" way.[38] Hence, intentions in which one chooses to ignore the claim of morality and to accept as basic what Kant calls the merely heteronomous standards of sensibility and self-love must also involve a kind of act on our part, even if not in an explicit phenomenological sense.[39]

A common objection at this point is to say that even if the value of a law is not something to be merely "taken" in the sense of a natural process that is undergone totally passively, this does not mean that we should say it is self-given either, for one might want to characterize it as simply recognized as authoritatively present.[40] Against this gambit, a Kantian might at first argue that we should speak of the faculty of reason in active terms simply because of considerations that go back to a long-standing Scholastic and rationalist tradition of understanding intentionality in general as active because at least it is implicitly propositional (and thus involving synthesis, in contrast to mere sensation and primitive feeling), although by no means in a necessarily arbitrary way. Here, however, one must distinguish between reason's *general* normative (N and F) determination of the standing of a practical law, and the cognitive and appreciative acts in which a *particular* reasoning subject determines itself, through reason in a concrete

---

[37] I have inserted the phrase "these actions ... proclivity" from an earlier part of the paragraph, for grammatical and explanatory reasons. Without the insertion, the translation of Kant's phrase reads, "to *impose* them upon the will, not to *coax*. . .," and here one sees perhaps even more directly how Kant's main aim is simply to make a contrast with contingent sources such as mere "coaxing."
[38] See Section 4.   [39] See Pippin 2013.   [40] See again Larmore 2011.

186   KARL AMERIKS

E and C sense, to be committed to a maxim in a way that takes an actual stance on the law. Even though the latter kind of determination, on each occasion, is understandably always a matter of activity rather than mere passivity, this may leave it unclear why the general formal and normative determination of the law's status as supreme should be said to be self-given. Nonetheless, there remain the reasons already given for speaking of even the mere formal determination of the law's standing as something that is self-determined, in a non-subjectivist, pure, and distinctively internal sense, rather than other-determined. Kant's view is that, even before trying to ground the synthetic claim that the moral law is in fact binding on us, the philosophical analysis of what the acceptance of such law would entail[41] does point directly to a non-subjectivist understanding of NRSPD. The key point here, once again, is simply that it must be within practical reason itself, and neither of the two other faculties distinct from it, namely, mere feeling and mere theoretical understanding, that such a strict standard for practical life would have to reside.

It is, to be sure, a bit of provocative language to speak of this necessary harmony between pure reason, as a basic faculty, and pure morality, as a practical standard with content, in terms of reason's "authoring" and "legislating" morality's pure law (cf. *GMS* 4:448), for this might suggest to some readers the existence of something like an independent being, such as a person or a government, engaged with a totally independent other item, that is, an entity that need not be. Reason, however, is not a separate individual but is just Kant's term for a pure general faculty, and as such it has a necessary relation to content that has lawful form, and hence it can be said to be "legislating." Kant sees that in the case of practical reason, the "legislator" and its work are not only in close harmony but are in a necessary and reciprocal relation, for without any work, without some content in necessary laws, the faculty of reason would be an *Unding*, far emptier than any mere thought of a thing in itself. All the same, pure reason itself is responsible simply for the lawful aspect of value, the universal conditions required to respect the absolute value of being an agent with reason. Kant recognizes that the manifold empirical contents of the particular and conditioned values and reasons that arise in everyday life, prior to regulation, are not themselves rooted in pure reason, let alone the bare notion of its universal legislation. His speaking of reason's authorship can thus be understood as a technical move, limited to a very specific meaning concerning faculties, and as having only partial, metaphorical overlaps with familiar notions of empirical authorship and legislation.

---

[41] Note Kant's cautious language in this section: "if there is a categorical imperative" (*GMS* 4:432).

On the Many Senses of "Self-Determination" 187

The point of the *Groundwork*, as a "groundwork," is basically just to express general formulae for a necessary practical principle, and to ask the question of which faculty can be consistently understood as correlated with such a principle, and so in this context it is not mysterious to propose that reason is crucial, for it is the only faculty that can be consistently regarded as the relevant authority.[42] In a textual sense, this means that the formula of autonomy need not be regarded as itself independent or *methodologically* autonomous, insofar as it depends thoroughly on a prior acceptance of the first two formulae. Moreover, the independence, or strict lawgiving capacity, of reason by itself is only a crucial necessary, but not a sufficient, condition for moral guidance in the complexities of human life.

4 Section III and Freedom

4.1 A New Ambiguity: Heteronomous Principles and "Heteronomy" in Causes

The fundamental normative meaning of "heteronomy," as the opposite of the purely normative conception of autonomy, must be kept in mind when turning back to the text at the very beginning of Section III, which is the prime exhibit of Kant's mixing, without a detailed warning, two quite different notions of determination. In Section II, Kant makes frequent normative references to *Wille* but does not begin to provide a formal ontological exposition. The first sentence of Section III abruptly starts such an exposition by saying, "*Will* (*Wille*) is a kind of causality of living beings insofar as they are rational" (*GMS* 4:446). The mystery of why this quite different sense of determination is being brought in is clarified by the remainder of the sentence, which introduces the topic of freedom, the

---

[42] A fundamental and very different objection to Kant is to insist that it is not clear that reason itself can have practical content, for it can seem that it is at most a faculty for testing consistency or, as in its theoretical use, for illegitimately positing unconditioned conditions for items given to it by other faculties. This kind of objection is not clearly relevant at this point in the text, however, for Kant introduces the notion of reason's practical self-determination only after he has *already* characterized morality in terms of what he calls its "formal" and "material," or "objective" and "subjective" aspects, the two aspects that need to be understood as being in "harmony" through a relation to a common third factor, our faculty of reason's "complete determination" (*GMS* 4:431). By these two aspects he means, first, the *formal* "objectivity in the rule" that is given with the first formulation of the moral law and the determination of the categorical imperative in terms of a condition of (necessary) universalizability (*GMS* 4:431); and, second, the "matter" or *content* that is there, as he says, "subjectively," meaning (using the pre-modern sense of the term) that is present with subjects that can and (normatively) must have the "end" of rational agency, which is the need to observe the second formulation of the categorical imperative and the demand to respect "rational being . . . as an end in itself" (*GMS* 4:431). The content of the theory is thus provided by the basic conditions for preserving and enhancing rational being in this sense.

188   KARL AMERIKS

concept that the heading of the first subsection indicates will be a "key" to the "explanation"[43] of "the autonomy of will." The notion of causality has to be brought in because, given Kant's general categorial theory, freedom is basically a kind of causality, a causality at first described here as one that "can be efficient independently of alien causes *determining* it" (*GMS* 4:446).

Kant realizes full well that this is not the only way a philosopher might try to characterize freedom. As noted earlier, Schulz's characterization, as well as Kant's own earliest work, adheres to a compatibilist doctrine of human freedom that allows for the presence of "alien causes" (at least of certain types). Here in Section III, Kant goes on immediately to indicate that his first remark about freedom does not amount to a proper definition but simply provides what he calls a partial and "negative" "explication." He moves toward a positive characterization by making a connection between freedom and lawfulness. Freedom is a kind of causality, but, contrary to what others have held, and what is assumed in Kant's own earliest works (an assumption that is later criticized, in the dialectic of the first *Critique*, e.g., A447/B475), as the dogmatic presumption that freedom would have to be "lawless"), it should not be thought of as possibly a matter of "lawlessness." Causality as such, he now contends (not uncontroversially, to say the least), requires lawfulness,[44] that is, a kind of necessity, for, given a cause, "something else, namely an effect, *must* be posited" (*GMS* 4:446). The alternative he calls an "absurdity" (*Unding*), although presumably not because it is meant to be impossible on trivial analytic grounds.

Up to this point, the subsection has been discussing determination only in an "efficient" sense. It continues along this line in the next sentence but takes a surprising turn by introducing a new phrase and saying "natural necessity was a kind of heteronomy of efficient causes" (*GMS* 4:447).[45]

---

[43] *Erklärung*, a term that on this topic Kant tends to use in the sense of providing a *detailed causal* explanation. The subtle structure of section III is that it introduces the notion of freedom as if it might be used to provide such an explanation, but the section concludes by stressing that we can only defend but not employ, in any particular explanation, the Idea of freedom as an efficient determining cause ("wirkende ... bestimmende Ursache," *GMS* 4:462). Freedom can, however, help to "explain," in a formal, or purely conceptual sense, what is central to the *notion* of moral autonomy. Similarly, what we find out, after the worry is raised at the end of section II that the moral law, and the freedom that is its condition, might itself be a mere "phantom of the brain" (*Hirngespenst*), is that what is really a *Hirngespenst* is rather the thought that we need to and can obtain an *Erklärung* of *how* freedom "works" (*GMS* 4:462).

[44] See, e.g., *Vigil* 28:212, "every nature has laws." Cf. Ameriks 2012: chapter 12.

[45] A similar phrase, "heteronomy of nature," is used again at *GMS* 4:452 (cf. 4:458), but it is important to see that at this point Kant is speaking explicitly of regarding our actions as being "appropriate to" (*gemäß*) a specific value "principle" (either "pure will" or "happiness") of action (*Handlung*). Here Kant is pointing to N and not mere C determination, and this can be lost in a translation that simply says "conform entirely with the natural law of desires. . ." See earlier note 12, regarding *GMS* 4:427.

The use of "heteronomy" in this way is surprising because one might have assumed, from the extensive discussion at the end of Section II, that it is simply a normative notion. "Heteronomy" is treated earlier not in causal terms but as a matter of the approval of a kind of ultimate "principle" (*GMS* 4:443) of value, one that comes from "something else," that is, from a contingent value rather than one that is necessarily authoritative because it is essential to (respect for) one's own self as an agent with reason.

Although heteronomy is introduced in this way as a normative concept, a linking complication here is the fact that any principles and choices that are heteronomous in the normative sense also have implications at a causal level. To approve a heteronomous standard as supreme is to be ready, above all, to move one's will, as an efficient cause, to generate intentions and external events with an aim to satisfying this standard and attaining what Kant calls merely subjective ends. Furthermore, the typical way that Kant appears to be assuming that people adopt heteronomous standards is by a process of incorrectly allowing factors that they merely passively experience through efficient causation (such as appealing sensory temptations) to count by themselves as providing sufficient grounds for moral decisions. Nonetheless, in this paragraph Kant surprisingly does not use the term "heteronomy" with reference to a situation of normative decision and choice about what counts, for he refers simply to instances of "natural necessity."

4.2 Section III in Context

Perhaps because of unusual texts like this, it is sometimes thought that, at least in this period of his work, Kant does not have a robust view of agency, one according to which actions not in line with morality are free choices rather than merely reactions in line with natural necessity.[46] The problem here may rest in part on the mistake of thinking that when Kant speaks of a "heteronomy of efficient causes" as a kind of "natural necessity," one can infer that he is committed to thinking that heteronomy in genuine human action must be a matter of mere necessity. I do not subscribe to this interpretation. This is not only because of features of the *Groundwork* itself, but also because of the often neglected fact that if one looks at Kant's other main works immediately prior to the *Groundwork*, one finds that they are distinguished by a new and noteworthy explicit concern with the issue of free choice *in general*, and, in particular, a concern with not allowing *immoral* actions to be regarded as matters of natural necessity,

---

[46] This criticism is often identified with Henry Sedgwick, but others, from Kant's time to our own, have shared this worry.

190   KARL AMERIKS

such as ignorance, innate pressure, or mere external force. In taking time out then, in the most intense period of his career, to publish a critical review of the relatively unknown figure, J. H. Schulz, Kant's obvious preoccupation is with insisting on a general rejection of compatibilism, and in particular of the idea that "vice" and "moral good or evil" can be explained as a mere matter of "degree" (*RezSchulz* 8:12), of nature keeping us relatively ignorant and weak, so that there would be "*no free will*" and "all *remorse* is idle and absurd" (*RezSchulz* 8:11). Even though Kant's arguments in the review of Schulz are too brief to be persuasive and are formulated in some ways that contrast with his other writings,[47] the review's clear insistence at this time on absolute and general human causal freedom, absolute moral value, and an absolute notion of reason is consistent with what is already indicated in the first *Critique* (1781), and it defines a position that has to be taken as at least implicitly present in each of the succeeding writings of the mid-1780s.

If the Critical Kant had the belief that our practical errors were simply a matter of failing naturally to try to do the good, solely because of the natural necessity of a lack of sufficient knowledge or power, then there would be no reason for him to be upset, as he manifestly is, by a theory that appears to have no room for "remorse" with respect to the relevant "frame of mind" (*RezSchulz* 8:11). Precisely because Schulz's book is primarily about punishment, that is, the negative side of human action, Kant wants to draw attention to the fact that a compatibilist account here conflicts with what he takes to be the obvious proper belief that vice is evil in a sense that calls for "just" (*RezSchulz* 8:12) retribution, rather than being regarded as simply bad, that is, illegal or weak in its perceptual underpinning. The review mocks Schulz's view for turning "all [NB] human conduct into a mere puppet show" (*RezSchultz* 8:13), a mockery that would be out of place if Kant's own view were that when we act immorally we are simply *by nature* failing to follow the moral law of reason, rather than freely rejecting it by adopting a maxim contrary to its supremacy.

In the *Groundwork* itself, "transgression of a duty" is similarly described not as a mere failure to do the right thing, or the result of an inevitable force that makes us do less than the best for ourselves. Kant's account is that, in not being moral, we "really will . . . that the opposite of our maxim should instead remain a universal one, [and] we take the liberty (*Freiheit*) of making an exception to it for ourselves" (*GMS* 4:424). This "real

---

[47] Here I have in mind especially Kant's linking of arguments for freedom from conditions of mere thinking, to those for action, and his speaking of "reason" in general terms without distinguishing the demands of pure reason, and its "Idea," from ordinary rational considerations.

On the Many Senses of "Self-Determination" 191

willing," "taking freedom," and "making" an exception is introduced precisely as relevant for moral blame rather than excuse or mere regret, because insisting on "blame" makes sense for Kant only on the assumption that agents are exerting freedom of choice even when doing evil rather than good. All this is only to be expected, given Kant's crucial reference to blame already within the 1781 edition of the first *Critique*'s third Antinomy discussion of absolute free choice (*KrV* A555/B583).

Furthermore, Kant's 1784 essay on enlightenment has a similar underlying preoccupation with free evil, even though it is expressed in diplomatic terms that have led many readers to suppose that Kant's topic here is merely political and concerned with choice in a relative and empirical sense. The essay's initial, fundamental, and most striking claim is that our lack of enlightenment is *"self-incurred"* (*WA* 8:35), hence a matter of our own activity and presumably something to be blamed in a non-Schulzian way. This claim is meant to directly counter the excuse that mere natural stupidity, internal "laziness," or "cowardice" (*WA* 8:36), which would be the last word in other theories, are the ultimate causes of our problem. In saying, twice and with emphasis in the first paragraph, that our general attitude is "self-incurred," Kant is stressing that it us up to each of us to determine the kind of concerns we in fact give absolute and not merely relative priority, namely, either the understandable but merely local and contingent "private" demands to obey only local figures such as "the officer," "the tax official," and "the [state-appointed] clergyman," or, instead, the cosmopolitan call to follow, as supreme, the norm of the free "public use of one's reason in all matters" (*WA* 8:36).

This public use is normatively determined by principles of justice valid for the world as a whole, that is, the proper kind of law that Kant says a people as such "could impose upon itself" (*WA* 8:39). The "could" is crucial, for it implies that Kant is not asking about the mere empirical question of what a group of citizens might happen to do. He is asking about a form of "law" that they could properly formulate and accept just as "a people,"[48] that is, a community of human beings regulating their actions by a common faculty of reason for discerning rules that can be

---

[48] I say "just as a people" because of the noteworthy fact that here Kant asserts that even the "legislative authority" of a monarch derives from the "collective will" of the people (*WA* 8:40; see also *TP* 8:304; *ZeF* 8:381; *RL* 6:313, 329, 342). This broadly democratic sentiment contrasts only superficially with the pragmatic advice concerning obeying the king that Kant gives at this time, which has tended to mislead critics into supposing that his position is inherently conservative. Here my reading of Kant is somewhat to the left of the helpful analysis by Katrin Flikschuh (2012). Because I take absolute moral autonomy, involving the universal necessary values of public reason and not mere "modest" self-governance (i.e., mere independence of pressures from other people), to be the concern already of the Enlightenment essay, my reading also differs from Larmore 2011: 8.

universally and necessary valid and that respect persons as rational beings.[49] This is also why Kant's injunction to dare to "think for oneself" ("*Sapere aude!*" WA 8:39) is not redundant – on the ground that, as some have objected, on his own theory human beings are in fact always in some way (empirically) thinking for themselves[50] – nor is it absurdly anarchic, as some have objected, as if Kant is proposing that persons should never listen to or learn from others. Rather, the essay's point is an appeal to free agents to listen, above all, to the voice of pure reason in them, which, as noted before, is characterized already in the first *Critique* as that which reflects "one's own self." Admittedly, Kant does not *explicitly* say here that any individual giving priority to maxims that transgress the rules of reason is to be blamed for an evil use of free will,[51] but the stressed and unrestricted scope of his use of the term "self-incurred," especially at this anti-Schulzian time in his career, leaves this conclusion as an obvious inference. Moreover, this line of interpretation is substantively supported by the fact that the very same concern is evident in Kant's other work immediately prior to the *Groundwork*, namely, the caustic reviews of his former student Herder, in which Kant repeatedly goes out of his way to mock a theory of human nature that relies merely on a hierarchy of natural forces rather than any reference to absolute individual freedom of choice.[52]

This is not to deny that it is only later, in his book on religion and numerous related essays (such as his 1786 essay, "What is Orientation in Thinking?"), that Kant goes into full detail about a theory of will and free

[49] An especially good indication that Kant has this kind of pure normative notion in mind can be found in sentences immediately prior to this remark, in which Kant discusses the possibility (quite relevant to his own situation with regard to the state church in Prussia) of a presumably mature and uncoerced "ecclesiastical synod" getting together and agreeing that its doctrines would henceforth never be allowed to be subject to revision by critical reasoners. Although one might think that such a group is a paradigm of trying to bind and "give oneself a law" in an *empirical* sense, Kant declares the idea of such a contract philosophically "absolutely null and void, even if it is ratified by the supreme power," for it is directly contrary to "public" practical reason's necessary respect for our "original vocation" (*des Berufs jeden Menschen*) (WA 8:39).

[50] See Bittner 1996:345–58. Bittner's further worry, about how Kant could consistently think that people were "mature" before they fell into this state of "immaturity," can be answered by looking at the details of his reaction to Rousseau, where Kant gives a complex account of how what he mostly has in mind is the special tendency of modern agents to get so caught up in the "luxury" of intellectual and scientific pursuits that they have begun to undermine the healthy common sense that they were born with. At a deeper level, of course, the problem is the old theological issue of how human beings can start by being created with a "good seed" and yet, in any context, tend toward radical evil, until their self-incurred inversion of priorities is reversed.

[51] In passages that directly invoke the key terms of the Schulz essay, the end of the Enlightenment essay speaks of our having, above all in our nature, "the calling to think freely" (WA 8:41) and to engage "*freedom* in action" (WA 8:42). In their context, these phrases have a significant empirical and political sense, but Kant also expresses, in a final phrase, his absolute moral claim, the need to treat human beings above all in accord with their "dignity" (WA 8:42).

[52] On Herder and Kant, see Ameriks 2012: chapter 9.

On the Many Senses of "Self-Determination" 193

choice by characterizing as "radical evil" humanity's self-determined rejection of morality. An appreciation of his earlier commitment to the underlying idea here can be – and has been – complicated by the fact that, already in the beginning of Section III of the *Groundwork*, Kant supplements the negative component of his account of freedom, the independence from "alien causes," with a positive component, defined as respect for the moral law, and he goes so far as to say "a free will (*freier Wille*) and will (*Wille*) under moral laws, are one and the same" (*GMS* 4:447, similar formulations occur in the second *Critique*). Readers can fall into a trap here by skipping over the key term "under" – which can apply to a potentially free and evil as well as a good will – and then thinking that Kant is *identifying* freedom of choice only with action that is positively moral. He is not doing that, for he is not using the term for choice (*Willkür*) but is basically just reiterating that his concept of *Wille* is a normative concept, and it has within it positive standards of pure practical reason, rather than being a mere neutral or indifferent "rational" source of effects. A merely prudent maxim, such as that of the shopkeeper at the beginning of the *Groundwork*, is clearly rational in an ordinary sense, but Kant's main point in introducing such a maxim is precisely to claim that, when it is given priority over the moral law by an agent, we should not say this leads merely naturally to a life with a lower degree of goodness, power, and intelligence. Instead, we should presume that this agent, like all rational agents, has *Wille* and therefore should know better, and so is to be condemned for a blamable and therefore freely chosen maxim that is not a matter of natural necessity's "heteronomy of efficient causes." The merely prudent shopkeeper's decision is a "self-incurred" determination in an absolute sense, one that the rest of the *Groundwork* aims at length to show is to be regarded as a self-determination that is an uncaused causing, and not like the effect of a mere turnspit.

5 Conclusion

In sum, I have been arguing that proper reflexive self-determination by the basic faculty of practical reason, which is neither a matter of overly subjective arbitrariness nor of overly objective mere subjection to law, is the essence of the *Groundwork*'s doctrine of autonomy, and – contrary to the implications of numerous common interpretations – is simply meant to follow immediately from reflection on what is needed to maintain the earlier formulations of the principle of morality. This is, of course, not to say that Kant is demonstrably correct in holding to this principle, or that the principle also demands the kind of absolute metaphysical freedom in

194 KARL AMERIKS

the making of good or evil choices that he insists upon, but that is another topic, and, in Fontane's phrase, *ein weites Feld.*[53]

[53] For the purpose of textual orientation and a very brief review of the main issues under discussion, I provide a bare bones outline of what I take to be the main arguments relevant here, which concern Kant's *Groundwork of the Metaphysics of Morals*, 4:431–48, that is, the end of its Section II and the beginning of its Section III. The argument sketches are listed under the headings: IIb, IIIa, IIIb, and IIIc. The last step of IIIc, namely 4*, is very important in its own right, but it has been much discussed elsewhere and is bracketed on this occasion. The main concern of my discussion is indicated under heading IIIb, which simply notes the ambiguity of "self-determination" and the underappreciated difficulty of directly connecting Kant's reasoning toward the end of Section II with his remarks right at the beginning of Section III:

IIb. An Argument at the End of Section II (4:430–40)
1 Suppose there is a "supreme principle of morality."
2 This principle requires a normative rule that is absolutely necessary.
3 An absolutely necessary rule cannot be normatively determined (i.e., "N-determined") by what we access through faculties other than reason.
4 So, the supreme principle of morality must be N-determined through reason.
5 The will, as *Wille*, is the faculty of practical reason.
6 As such, it N-determines principles that are normatively necessary.
7 In N-determining such principles it cannot be N-determined by what is outside it, and so its N-determination must be internal, by its "own universal-law-giving."
8 Hence the "supreme principle of morality" is an internal N-determination of "the will," a matter of its "autonomy" in the sense of *normative self-determination*.

IIIa An Argument at the Beginning of Section III (4:446–8)
1 *Wille* is a faculty of being an efficient determining cause (i.e., "C-determining").
2 Causality is always C-determination in accord with some law.
3 Free *Wille* is a freely acting efficient cause.
4 Free *Wille* is therefore efficient C-determination in accord with some law.
5 As a free causality in a negative sense, *Wille* cannot be efficiently C-determined from outside by "natural necessity," that is, the "alien causes" covered by the laws of nature.
6 As free causality in a positive sense, *Wille* needs some "non-alien" causal law, so (given 5) the law in accord with which it is C-determined must be internal.
7 Free *Wille* as a cause is therefore internally C-determining in a non-alien causal sense, that is, it has autonomy in the sense of *causal self-determination*.

IIIb Transition
Even if arguments IIb and IIIa are accepted, it is not clear yet how they, and their various senses of "self-determination," relate to each other and to the overall strategy at the end of the *Groundwork*. A natural interpretive hypothesis is that Kant has an encompassing argument of the following form:

IIIc Overview
1 There is a supreme principle of morality valid for us only if we have *Wille* in the sense of being autonomous as *fully self-determined*.
2 To be fully self-determined is to have *Wille* that is at once normatively self-determined and causally self-determined in an absolute sense, that is, with uncaused efficient causing.
3 We can now understand what it is to be normatively self-determined, as well as what it is to be causally self-determining in an absolute sense, but we cannot understand how to reflectively affirm autonomous morality as valid for us until it is shown that we should in fact regard ourselves as in fact having *Wille* that is self-determining not only normatively but also in the absolute causal sense.
4* It can be shown that we should in fact regard ourselves as causally self-determining in an absolute sense (argued for only in the remainder of Section III – and in a controversial way that Kant appears to have retreated from soon after), and so, as fully self-determined, we should affirm that we are autonomous.

CHAPTER 10

Inclination, Need, and Moral Misery

Kate Moran

1 Introduction

Most people who have even a passing acquaintance with Kant's moral theory will acknowledge that inclination has a dubious reputation.[1] Perhaps it is not the villain of the story: Villains seem altogether more crafty and cunning than this passive feature of our sensible nature. But inclination is, at the very least, an antagonist in the story, since it prompts us to formulate maxims that find themselves restricted or rejected by the moral law. What is more, it seems to be an utterly unexceptional antagonist. Autonomy – the hero of our story – is singular, and the defining feature of our will. Inclinations are more like the rabble of our empirical selves. Perhaps it is no wonder, then, that Kant says that "to be entirely free from [inclination] must ... be the wish of every rational being" (*GMS* 4:428).

But perhaps this wish is a step too far. Might not the wish to be rid of inclination concede too much to this passive and unremarkable antagonist? And in renouncing inclination, might we not also lose something of value, even if only contingent value? The question is, of course, purely theoretical – it is impossible for sensible agents ever to be rid of inclination. Nevertheless, the answer to these questions may be philosophically informative. In the first instance, the answer may help to shed light on the Kantian conception of virtue and character. Is virtuous struggle a continuous, vigilant suppression or diffusing of inclination – a lifelong game of "whack-a-mole"? Or, is virtue better described in some other way – perhaps as a matter of shaping, conditioning, and controlling inclination? The answer to these questions, in turn, might give us a more complete and nuanced picture of Kantian happiness and well-being.

---

[1] I would like to thank Wiebke Deimling for her comments on an earlier version of this chapter at the "Nature and Freedom in Kant" conference at Brown University in 2013. A later version was presented at Leipzig University in 2016. I am grateful to audience members at both events for their comments and questions. Thanks also to Jens Timmermann for comments on the chapter.

195

In particular, it may seem as though merely having inclinations – *a fortiori* having inclinations that we cannot fulfill – leads to a kind of discontent or misery. Surely there is some truth to this account, but perhaps there is a more detailed tale to be told about the way that inclination and desire contribute to discontent. Perhaps there is even a way to live happily – or at least contentedly – alongside our inclinations.

The discussion that follows proceeds as follows: In Section 2, I examine what is perhaps Kant's most famous indictment of inclination – his claim in the *Groundwork* that "every rational being" would wish or hope to be rid of inclination entirely. I will argue that what may initially strike the reader as an offhand remark actually contains an important argumentative clue about what, precisely, is so dangerous about inclination. In particular, it is inclination's association with need and contingency that makes it problematic. In Section 3, I proceed to examine notions of need and neediness in Kant's texts. Though a single, unified account of need is difficult to pin down, themes emerge that help to shed more light on Kant's ultimate concern with desire and inclination. With this analysis in place, Section 4 considers Kant's discussion of the ideal stance toward inclination – something he refers to as independence or beatitude (*Seligkeit*). Far from consisting of *renunciation* of inclination, however, independence requires autocracy and an awareness or certainty of one's autocracy. Complete independence is an ideal, but agents can fall short of this ideal to varying degrees. Section 5 offers a sketch of the moral and psychological consequences of failing in one's attempts to attain independence, in particular, the "misery" that Kant associates with awareness of moral failure, and the futile strategies that agents pursue in order to avoid such misery. The chapter concludes with a few optimistic observations about the role of inclination in the life of a sensible moral agent.

2 Inclination and Neediness

Let us begin our search for the ideal Kantian stance toward inclination with one of Kant's strongest statements on the matter: his assertion in the *Groundwork* that every rational being must wish to be free from inclination.[2]

---

[2] I follow Frierson's (2014:68–70) account of Kantian inclination. Inclinations are parts of the faculty of desire, but not predispositions or instincts. Rather, they "are the result of experiences of objects for which someone has a propensity" (Frierson 2014:70). However, as Frierson observes, Kant sometimes uses "inclination" to refer to the entire lower faculty of desire. This discussion assumes the narrower definition. For further discussion of inclination, see Schapiro 2009.

> But the inclinations themselves, as sources of need, are so far from having absolute worth – so as to make one wish for them as such – that to be entirely free from them must rather be the universal wish of every rational being. (*GMS* 4:428)

On its face, we appear to have an open and shut case: Inclinations are burdensome and have no absolute worth. Ideally, a rational agent would be rid of them entirely. There is an element of truth to this reading, but as is so often the case, context is important when it comes to appreciating the subtlety of Kant's remarks. The assertion appears immediately after Kant first introduces humanity as the source of absolute worth in the *Groundwork*. The assertion of this absolute worth – "Now I say: a human being and generally every rational being *exists* as an end in itself" (*GMS* 4:428) – may seem frustratingly short on justification. Indeed, the reader is at this stage only promised a normative justification (i.e., a deduction) for the formula of humanity in the last section of the *Groundwork* (*GMS* 4:429n). Nevertheless, Kant gestures toward an argument by elimination for the absolute worth of humanity in the sentences that follow this initial assertion.[3] First, Kant argues that objects of inclination are excluded from having absolute worth. These have only "conditional worth; for if the inclinations, and the needs founded on them, did not exist, their object would be without worth" (*GMS* 4:428). Objects of inclination, in other words, are only valuable insofar as our inclinations and needs make them objects of worth. They cannot, therefore, have absolute worth.

Crucially, the next sentence – the sentence at issue here – is a response to a silent interlocutor who asks the next obvious question: *If objects of inclination are valuable only contingently and depending on inclination, why not suppose that inclinations themselves are of absolute value?* Kant's answer to this unstated question is that "the inclinations themselves, as sources of need, are so far from having absolute worth – so as to make one wish for them as such – that to be entirely free from them must rather be the universal wish of every rational being." Kant's assertion that any rational agent would wish to be rid of inclination is thus not an off-the-cuff remark about the moral or psychological burden associated with inclination, but rather an argument that inclination itself cannot be a serious contender for the source of absolute worth in the moral theory he is presenting. But as an argument for that claim, the sentence seems, on its face, to offer little of substance. On a cursory reading, Kant seems merely to assert that

---

[3] For a discussion of the argument by elimination, see Timmermann 2007. For an influential alternate interpretation that Kant is offering a regress argument, see Korsgaard 1996a, chapter 4.

inclinations themselves cannot have absolute worth because no rational being would wish for them as such.

Read in this way, the argument is unsatisfying on at least two counts. First, it is awkward, in Kantian terms, to describe something of absolute value as something to be wished for. Even humanity itself is not the sort of end that one ought produce or maximize. Rather, it is the sort of thing one protects and promotes where it already exists. This, of course, is just to say that humanity is a self-existent end, and not an end to be effected.

Perhaps, then, we can charitably assume that Kant means something like, "inclination is so far from being a necessary end for a rational being that any such being would actually wish to be rid of it." But here we encounter a second problem: that assertion is either question begging or overly psychological. If the argument is that inclination cannot have absolute worth because it is not a necessary end for a rational being, then Kant is simply repeating what it means for something to have absolute worth. Assuming that something's having absolute worth and its being a necessary end for a rational being are close bedfellows, if not exactly the same thing, then Kant has not offered an *argument* for why inclinations cannot have absolute worth, but rather scoffed at the apparent absurdity of the idea. If, on the other hand, the force of the argument is meant to rest on what rational beings tend to wish for, then it also falls short. There are, it would seem, plenty of rational beings who do not seem to wish to be rid of inclination, even when it causes suffering on a regular basis. And if Kant means that a truly rational being – a sage, perhaps – would wish to be rid of inclination, then he would seem to owe us some justification for this claim. If the implicit argument is simply that a truly rational being would recognize that inclination cannot be a necessary end, then it would seem to reduce to the earlier question-begging sort of claim. Nor does it seem sufficient to suggest that a sage would recognize how burdensome inclinations can be, and so wish to be rid of them.[4] After all, the obligations suggested by the absolute worth of humanity can be burdensome, too.[5] To understand why one type of burden is consistent with autonomy, and the other type opposed or detrimental to it, we would need precisely the argument for which we are searching here – an argument establishing the source of absolute worth for rational creatures.

Fortunately, there is more to Kant's assertion than initially meets the eye. Crucially, the passage states that inclinations – as sources of need

[4] Compare *KpV* 5:118.
[5] Of course, the source of that burden is the continued resistance of inclination.

Inclination, Need, and Moral Misery 199

(*Quellen der Bedürfniß*) – are so far from having absolute worth that no rational being would wish for them. The force of Kant's argument would appear to rest upon the observation that *inclinations are the sources of need*. We might rephrase Kant's argument by elimination for the absolute worth of humanity – such as it is – as follows: Objects of inclination cannot have absolute worth because their worth is contingent upon inclination, and inclination itself cannot have absolute worth because it is the *source* of neediness and contingency. The implicit claim, then, would be that something has absolute worth if and only if it is neither contingent upon something else for its existence, nor itself the sort of thing that generates contingency. Humanity, as a self-existent end, fits both descriptions.[6] This reading also helps make sense of the assertion that rational beings would wish to be rid of inclinations in a non-psychological and non-question-begging way. A rational being would not consider something that generates need and contingency to be a plausible candidate for a necessary end.

The preceding analysis of the *Groundwork's* indictment of inclination demonstrates that it is inclination's association with neediness – specifically, that inclination generates neediness and contingency – that makes it both psychologically burdensome and morally threatening. But this claim raises a host of new interpretative questions. What, precisely, does Kant mean by "need"? Do some forms of neediness exist that are more acceptable than others, either from a moral or from a psychological perspective? Does inclination necessarily generate neediness? Or might inclination sometimes exist absent need, such that the dangers described earlier can be avoided?

3 Kant's Conception of Neediness

The preceding analysis of Kant's apparent renunciation of inclination in the *Groundwork* leaves us with a new set of questions about his conception of need. Locating a precise understanding of the term is not a straightforward task, however, since Kant's use of it is not always consistent or determinate. Further, one should be cautious to differentiate philosophical use of this term from what is perhaps more colloquial usage – especially in the transcribed lectures. Despite these challenges, however, certain themes emerge amongst the references to need and neediness in Kant's texts and lectures.

---

[6] Though Kant's argument for a duty of beneficence certainly relies upon claims about the contingent, finite nature of human beings, this is a feature of our sensible nature, and not of humanity as such.

First, need is associated with satisfaction and dissatisfaction. Kant often describes need as striving for or demanding satisfaction. Satisfaction is a "problem thrust upon the being by its finite nature" (*KpV* 5:25). Finite beings are "needy, and this need pertains to the matter of its power of desire, i.e., to something that renders to a subjectively underlying feeling of pleasure or displeasure which determines what the being needs in order to be satisfied with its [own] state" (*KpV* 5:25). Unfortunately, "reason is not sufficiently fit to guide the will reliably with regard to . . . the satisfaction of all our needs" (*GMS* 4:396). Indeed, reason often multiplies these needs unnecessarily – an important point discussed later in this chapter. In its demand for satisfaction, need operates as a counterweight to morality. Kant concedes, for example, that securing one's own happiness is indirectly a duty, since "unsatisfied needs" can become "a great temptation to transgress one's duties" (*GMS* 4:399). And if a rational subject is not also a "legislating member of the kingdom of ends," then that person can only be represented as "subject to the natural law of his needs" (*GMS* 4:439).

These observations regarding need and satisfaction may prompt the reader to wonder whether need isn't the same thing as inclination, or at least a subspecies of inclination. After all, Kant also describes inclination as a temptation or counterweight to morality – sometimes in the same breath as a reference to need. In the *Groundwork*, he describes need *and* inclination as counterweights to morality, adding that maxims based on need and inclination stand in contrast to a correct determination of the will (*GMS* 4:405). And in the *Critique of Practical Reason*, Kant defines beatitude – a term discussed in the next section – as "complete independence from need and inclination."[7] And in at least one passage, Kant describes happiness as "the entire satisfaction of need and inclination" (*GMS* 4:405).

Still other passages suggest that Kant thinks of need and inclination as conceptually distinct. In a footnote to his introduction of the notion of an imperative in the *Groundwork*, Kant remarks that "[t]he dependence of the desiderative faculty on sensations is called inclination, and this therefore always proves (*beweißt*) a need."[8] The assertion appears to draw a clear conceptual distinction between inclination and need, since it would be peculiar – or at the very least uninteresting – to say that one always proves the other if the two terms were mere synonyms. Still, nothing in that

---

[7] *KpV* 5:118. See also *RGV* 6:61, where Kant describes sensible beings as "being[s] pertaining to this world and dependent on needs and inclinations."
[8] *GMS* 4:413n. See Timmermann 2009 for a discussion of this footnote.

passage or its context (a discussion of the distinction between practical interest and pathological interest) makes the details of this conceptual distinction clear. Does inclination necessarily generate need? Or does inclination necessarily appeal to or rely upon need? Perhaps the relationship between inclination and need is not a causal one at all: Need might be an aspect or component of inclination, for example.

Looking elsewhere in Kant's texts, one finds several passages in which Kant indicates that inclination at least sometimes generates need. One of these, of course, is the passage from the *Groundwork* analyzed in Section 2 in which Kant describes inclination as the source of need. Similarly, in a lecture given around the same time as the publication of the *Groundwork*, Kant notes that the "thing toward which we are inclined pleases us, but not the inclination itself, since without inclination we would not have so many needs" (*Mrong* II 29:610). Again, one ought to be cautious about making too much out of a few words in a transcribed lecture, but this assertion does seem to echo two of the conclusions drawn in the preceding section: first, that inclination at least sometimes generates need, and second, that *this* fact makes inclination burdensome or unpleasant. Another suggestion that inclination generates need appears in the *Critique of Practical Reason*'s discussion of the need of reason, where Kant responds in a footnote to Thomas Wizenmann's objection that a hope or a wish cannot provide proof of its object. Kant responds in part by pointing out that the need of reason is different from needs that are based on inclination. Inclination generates needs than can often lead to frustration and disappointment, but the need of reason is, according to Kant, a reliable indicator of at least the possibility of the postulates of pure practical reason (*KpV* 143n).

The preceding passages suggest that inclination at least sometimes generates need, but readers familiar with the *Critique of Judgment* may at this point wonder if Kant doesn't make just the opposite assertion in that text, when he observes that "all interest assumes a need or creates one" (*KU* 5:210). The claim makes a distinction between moral interest and pathological interest: moral interest creates a need (i.e., the need of reason), while pathological interest relies upon or assumes a preceding need. But here, it is important to recall that interest is not the same as inclination. As Kant explains in the *Groundwork* footnote cited earlier, interest is "the dependence ... of a contingently determinable will on principles of reason" (*GMS* 4:413n). Crucially, then, interest involves principles of reason, whereas inclination need not.[9] So it does not necessarily suggest

---

[9] Compare *RL* 6:212–13.

a contradiction in Kant's thought for him to claim that pathological *interest* depends on need, since pathological interest is cognitively a step more advanced, so to speak, than inclination. Inclination might, for example, generate need, and both might be assumed, together with reason, in the formation of pathological interest.[10]

Further complicating matters is the fact that Kant points, in at least one passage, to the possibility of need existing absent inclination. In the *Religion*, he defines instinct as "a felt need to do or enjoy something of which we still do not have a concept" (*RGV* 6:28n). As such, instinct lies between propensity and inclination. Inclination, Kant argues "presupposes acquaintance with the object of desire," whereas the felt need of instinct does not. Of course, it is impossible to say whether the felt need that characterizes instinct is the same sort of need that concerns Kant in other passages. Still, Kant's remarks regarding need and instinct may help explain the phenomenon of finding something pleasant in the absence of any inclination for that thing, or, conversely, the phenomenon of having the sense that there's something that would be pleasant, but not being sure what it is.

There is also a clear suggestion in the texts and lectures that inclination does not always have to generate need. This notion comes across most forcefully in passages in which Kant cautions against allowing certain inclinations – for example, inclinations toward luxury and amenity – to become needs. Kant warns in the Vigilantius lecture that we should "[n]ever seize upon the amenities (*Annehmlichkeiten*) of life with such inclination that they can become needful to us," since, when we do this, these inclinations become "a burden, and restrict our freedom in the fulfillment of duty" (*Vigil* 27:652). And Kant regularly draws a contrast between "true" or "natural" needs, and other sorts of needs, suggesting that it is the latter sort of need that reason itself has a tendency to multiply unnecessarily (e.g., *GMS* 4:396). According to the early Kaehler/Collins lectures on moral philosophy, for example, Kant admits of a kind of gradation of neediness, distinguishing among distress (*Nothdurft*); other kinds of needs (*Bedürfnisse*); and mere amenity (*Annehmlichkeit*) (*Collins* 27:441). And in the Doctrine of Method of the *Critique of Practical Reason*, Kant notes that the right kind of moral example "withdraws the learner from the constraint of even *true needs*," thus allowing for a "liberation from the manifold of dissatisfaction in which *all needs* entangle him" (*KpV* 5:160, author's emphasis). A similar distinction appears in the *Doctrine of Virtue*, when Kant defines prodigal avarice as

---

[10] On this discussion, see also Achim Vesper's entry on "*Bedürfniß*" in Willaschek et al. 2015.

Inclination, Need, and Moral Misery 203

acquisition of the "means to good in excess of true needs" (*TL* 6:432). Like Rousseau, Kant recognizes that the proliferation of need beyond "true" or "natural" needs is fueled by anxious comparison and competition in society. As Kant describes him in the *Religion*, the human being's "needs are but limited, and his state of mind in providing for them moderate and tranquil. He is poor (or considers himself so) only to the extent that he is anxious that others will consider him poor and will despise him for it" (*RGV* 6:93). Kant cites this anxiety as the source of greed, envy, and the desire for domination.

Based on the preceding observations, we can draw a few conclusions. First, Kant appears to be operating with at least two senses of need. "True" or "natural" needs may describe something like instinct – or at least the set of desires that begin as instincts. But Kant also uses the term in an almost adverbial sense, to denote the strength of a desire, or the intensity of the demand that it be satisfied. Of course, the two senses of the term are not unrelated. Though few, natural or true needs are precisely those instincts or desires that would seem to demand satisfaction most strenuously. But we make a moral error and generate unnecessary psychological burdens for ourselves when we allow other inclinations to take on the urgency of need. It is, I suspect, this kind of burden – including the effort that it takes to keep it at bay – that Kant has in mind when he observes that inclinations are so burdensome that any rational agent would wish to be rid of them. Importantly, however, inclination and need do not appear to be synonymous. Many inclinations probably depend to some degree on natural need or instinct. And inclination can often generate need, when we allow it to, but it must not do so in every case. In principle, it seems possible to have an inclination toward something – a small luxury perhaps – without allowing that inclination to take on the force or demandingness of need. This would certainly require a good deal of moral strength and vigilance, since danger exists wherever inclinations are allowed to flourish. Still, conceptual space between inclination and neediness exists. Most importantly, perhaps, the slide from inclination to need is, in these cases, a moral failure, albeit a subtle one that occurs over time.

4 Independence and Beatitude

We are left with a question about how to respond to or manage inclination and neediness. Kant asserts that the appropriate stance or goal with respect to inclination is "independence" (*Unabhängigkeit*), and he sometimes associates this notion with beatitude (*Seligkeit*), which he defines as "complete independence from inclinations and needs" (*KpV* 5:118). Further, his discussion of independence in the *Critique of Practical Reason* repeats the earlier observation that any rational being would wish to be rid of inclination, so the reader may be tempted to conclude that independence and beatitude are ideals that involve renunciation or suppression of inclination. However, renunciation and suppression of inclination are neither sufficient nor, in many cases, necessary for independence or beatitude. Instead, independence requires something more difficult of the agent: a kind of mastery of inclination – or autocracy – *and* a second-order awareness or certainty of this autocracy.[11] Of course, like renunciation, these are ultimately unattainable ideals for embodied agents. Precisely because agents are unavoidably subject to need and inclination, certainty of autocracy is impossible. Agents are aware of their *capacity* for autonomy, but they cannot be certain that they will always properly subordinate inclination to the moral law, or indeed that they have done so in the past. Kant notes that this uncertainty about future moral conduct, and a related uncertainty about how to interpret past action, leads to a kind of moral anxiety (*TL* 6:440).

Before examining the ideal of beatitude, or *Seligkeit*, in more detail, it is worth pausing to take note of the use of the term "*selig*" (or "*sälig*") in Kant's time. The Grimm dictionary notes that *selig* can have active and passive senses. In its active sense, *selig* describes a property of something that makes it good, or grants some sort of advantage. Weather, for example, can be *selig* if it brings much needed rain or sunshine. In its passive sense, *selig* or *Seligkeit* describes the condition of being protected or safeguarded against something – a threat or temptation, for example. But even when the term describes protection or safeguarding, it comes along with connotations of contributing to a person's advantage or happiness, for example, in the saying "*Sälig ist der Mann der sich für Weiberlist hüten kann*" (Blessed is the man who can protect himself from the cunning of women).

Kant himself seems to pun on this dual sense of "*Seligkeit*" in the Vigilantius lecture, where he remarks that:

> [A] state whose comfort has its source merely in things of nature, or in good fortune, and of which I am not the author through my freedom, would not be called "blessed" (*selig*), and would have to be called "fortunate" (*sälig*), in that here the word "*Saal*" is at the bottom of it – as with every state of

---

[11] On autocracy, see Baxley 2015 and Denis 2011a.

things – just as it has this meaning in the words *Schicksaal* (fortune) and *Trübsaal* (misfortune). (*Vigil* 27:644)

So even if blessedness can describe a state of being contented, such contentment cannot come about through mere fortune or gifts of nature for it to count as Kantian *Seligkeit*. Instead, a Kantian understanding of *Seligkeit* will have to have an agent's free power of choice at its foundation.

But just what sort of choice does Kant have in mind? In particular, is it necessarily a choice to strive to renounce inclination and neediness? A useful discussion of independence and beatitude appears early in the *Critique of Practical Reason*, in the context of a discussion about happiness:

> To be happy is necessarily the demand of every rational but finite being and therefore an unavoidable determining ground of its faculty of desire. For satisfaction with one's whole existence is not, as it were, an original possession and a beatitude, which would presuppose a consciousness of one's independent self-sufficiency (*unabhängige Selbstgenugsamkeit*), but is instead a problem imposed upon him by his finite nature itself, because he is needy and this need is directed to the matter of his faculty of desire. (*KpV* 5:25)

Two observations should be made about this passage. First, Kant calls beatitude a possession (*Besitz*), and associates it with self-sufficiency (*Selbstgenugsamkeit*). Again, it is clearly more than having the good luck not to be affected by inclination – free power of choice is central to beatitude. And in calling beatitude a possession, the passage brings to mind prominent themes in the discussion of virtue in the *Metaphysics of Morals*, in particular the observation that virtue is to be regarded as a strength. Second, Kant's definition of beatitude in this passage is, at least in part, a second-order definition: It includes a consciousness (*Bewußtsein*) of independence and self-sufficiency. Beatitude is thus a kind of strength or possession, and an awareness or consciousness of this strength.

Later, in the Dialectic, Kant returns to these themes (*KpV* 5:117–18). On its face, the discussion looks again like an indictment of the inclinations, leading the reader to perhaps conclude that Kant is recommending renunciation. Kant observes that the inclinations always "change and grow with the indulgence that one allows them" and are for this reason "always burdensome to a rational being who wishes to be rid of them" (*KpV* 5:118). But if we pay attention to the beginning of the next paragraph ("from this it follows"), it becomes clear that Kant's observations are psychological and prudential. They are meant to show why consciousness of virtue can only ever provide negative satisfaction: Precisely because inclinations are always shifting and changing, we can never achieve certainty and positive satisfaction that we have mastered them completely.

In what follows, Kant goes on to define beatitude as a "complete independence (*Unabhängigkeit*) from inclinations and needs" (*KpV* 5:118). Again, one might be tempted to think of this as the elimination or renunciation of inclination, or at least a striving toward that aim. But in the previous paragraph, Kant has given us a definition of independence that warns against such an interpretation. He tells us that "[f]reedom, and the consciousness of freedom as an *ability to follow the moral law with an unyielding disposition*, is independence (*Unabhängigkeit*) from the inclinations" (*KpV* 5:117, author's emphasis). The definition of "independence" offered here should thus not be understood as freedom from inclinations, but rather as a type of self-mastery and strength to follow the moral law. Independence from inclination is thus not the renunciation of inclination but virtuous strength and consciousness of this strength as the proper use of freedom. *Complete* independence (or beatitude) would then presumably be to have this consciousness or certainty about all of one's inclinations – past, present, and future.

Complete independence, thus described, is an impossible ideal. First, since independence describes a state of affairs in which one is certain of having acted from duty, agents quickly run into trouble because of the obscurity of moral motivation. We can never know whether we have acted from duty, and conscience continually brings our actions before "an internal court" where our "thoughts accuse or excuse one another" (*TL* 6:438). Second, even when conscience acquits us, we can never be certain of similar future success. When it comes to knowledge of our own autocracy, we find ourselves in a state of anxiety and uncertainty – never in a state of complete independence. As Kant remarks in the *Doctrine of Virtue*, "the blessedness found in the comforting encouragement of one's conscience is not positive (joy) but merely negative (relief from preceding anxiety); and this alone is what can be ascribed to virtue, as a struggle against the influence of the evil principle in a human being" (*TL* 6:440).

5 Living with Inclination

Independence is thus an ideal that is impossible to achieve or secure with lasting certainty. Nevertheless, it is an informative ideal: Just as independence includes consciousness of moral strength, so too does a deficit of independence include a consciousness of relative weakness. Crucial to the Kantian account of moral failure is the observation that agents are also

Inclination, Need, and Moral Misery 207

aware of falling short of independence, even if only dimly. To a large extent, it is this awareness of moral failure and the futile attempt to disguise or compensate for it that accounts for the psychological burden that Kant associates with inclination and need – a burden that he calls "moral misery." This chapter concludes with a few remarks about the contours of moral misery, in the hopes that this will shed light on how finite agents might strive to live peaceably alongside their inclinations, even if complete independence is impossible.

As is often observed, Kant parts ways with the Stoics in asserting that happiness does not simply consist of virtue, or consciousness of one's virtue. Still, he concedes that there is a kind of satisfaction that accompanies consciousness of virtue. In the *Critique of Practical Reason*, he calls this kind of satisfaction "contentment" (*Zufriedenheit*), describing it as "an analogue of happiness that must necessarily accompany consciousness of virtue" (*KpV* 5:117). As we have already noted, complete certainty about one's virtue is impossible: The most an agent can ever hope for is relief from the anxiety that pangs of conscience generate. As such, Kant observes, contentment can only be "a negative satisfaction with one's existence, in which one is conscious of *needing nothing* (my emphasis)." Notably, the absence of need – and not of inclination – lies at the core of Kant's definition.

Kant is eager to distinguish contentment from happiness, but we should be careful not to assume that contentment is merely a placeholder concept, or that contentment is not itself a large part of what constitutes a person's well-being. Usefully, a later discussion of contentment in the Vigilantius lecture on moral philosophy offers a more detailed account of its centrality, and of the misery associated with unchecked neediness and falling short of independence. There, Kant reportedly describes the condition in which one judges oneself "unworthy of [one's] own contentment, because he has made himself unworthy of his own existence" as a kind of misery (*Elend*). In particular, he elaborates, misery signifies a want with respect to "conditions of our contentment":

> Conditions of our contentment in general are called *needs* (*Bedürfnisse*); but that need whose non-fulfillment must make us discontented with our whole existence is called a necessity; in the physical sense, for example, hunger, when we want for food. In the moral sense, the outcome is *misery (Elend)*, just as, in the physical sense, it is ill-fortune. Both are based on the fact that no substitute means are available, to remedy the means to contentment that are wanting, and to make the want superfluous. (*Vigil* section 102)

Again, Kant associates need with satisfaction and dissatisfaction: The satisfaction of a need yields contentment, while the failure to satisfy a need yields discontentment. Indeed, some needs – so-called necessities – yield a thoroughgoing "discontentment with our whole existence" when they are left unfulfilled. Necessities can be physical or moral, but either way the discontent associated with them stems from the fact that "no substitute means are available" for their fulfillment. Proper nourishment is thus a necessity in the physical sense, since nothing can take its place and its lack constitutes a state of being discontented (to say the least) with one's whole physical existence. We can also make two further observations about physical necessity. First, the conditions of its fulfillment are often a matter of luck or circumstance, and no finite being is immune to the vagaries of fortune that put fulfillment of physical necessity in danger. This, in no small part, is an observation at the heart of Kant's argument for the duty of beneficence. Second, it is only reasonable to expect that even the threat of deprivation when it comes to physical necessity will be the source of great and understandable anxiety.

But Kant also asserts that rational, sensible agents are susceptible to a kind of moral necessity, namely, the contentment that Kant describes in the *Critique of Practical Reason*. Instead of proper nourishment, it is *awareness of one's virtue* that is the irreplaceable means to the fulfillment of this necessity. Again, this awareness of one's virtue can at best be backward looking and pertain only to having a mastery over one's needs (having done one's duty) thus far. Unlike physical necessity, in the case of moral necessity, the means to fulfillment are not a matter of fortune; they are entirely up to the agent. In this light, Kant's remarks about the difference between *Säligkeit* (good fortune) and *Seligkeit* (blessedness) become all the more trenchant. In the case of physical necessity, it is good fortune on which the fulfillment of necessity is based. In the moral case, it is virtue, and this involves striving for the kind of blessedness – *Seligkeit* – associated with independence from one's inclinations.

Still, there are similarities between physical necessity and moral necessity. As with physical necessity and proper nourishment, there is no substitute for awareness of one's virtue. As we have already seen, even the prospect of losing the means to moral contentment – whether via the introspection of conscience or the thought of future moral challenge – is the source of a kind of moral anxiety. But there is an important difference between the misery associated with physical necessity and the misery associated with moral necessity. In the case of moral necessity, though substitute means are unavailable, agents nevertheless attempt to find

Inclination, Need, and Moral Misery 209

alternate means of contentment when virtue and awareness of virtue are lacking. This pursuit of alternate means typically follows one of two strategies.

The first of these is to seek the certainty of moral contentment through external means. An example of this tendency appears in Kant's discussion of miserliness in various texts and lectures. Kant classifies miserliness as a species of avarice: The miser's maxim "is to acquire as well as maintain all the means to good living, but with no intention of enjoyment (i.e., in such a way that one's end is only possession, not enjoyment)" (*TL* 6:432). In essence, the miser allows a principle of savings to overwhelm his power of free choice. Individuals prone to miserliness often belong to groups whose livelihood or subsistence is insecure – Kant mentions women, the elderly, and scholars in this context. Kant repeatedly describes miserliness as a passion, and this gives the reader an important clue about the etiology of miserliness. Specifically, it is the sort of inclination that becomes entrenched slowly over time. In the case of miserliness, the otherwise reasonable maxim to set aside some money in case of emergency turns eventually into the principle of miserliness, spurred on in large part by a ceaseless anxiety about the future. Indeed, Kant thinks that miserliness cannot come about any other way, since to devise a maxim of miserliness out of whole cloth and then adopt such a maxim would be patently irrational.

The miser is an instructive case study of a fruitless attempt to find alternate means to moral contentment. Recall that Kant defines contentment (*Zufriedenheit*) as *consciousness of needing nothing*. Of course, the only way to approach having such a consciousness is to cultivate one's strength of will. But this is not the strategy that the miser pursues: Instead of pursuing independence from inclination and need, the miser essentially doubles down on inclination and need. Instead of cultivating the moral strength to overcome the neediness associated with the desire to acquire things, the miser pursues an avaricious principle of savings, grounded in fear and anxiety about the future. But in so doing the miser has not overcome inclination and need. Rather, he has simply replaced the need of acquisition or accumulation with the need of fretful penny-pinching. This observation brings us to another important point: There is a sense in which the miser and others like him have given up on themselves morally. Instead of trusting in his own ability to cultivate moral strength in the face of need, the miser instead surrenders to need and anxiously piles one inclination on top of another. The miser thus evinces despondency – a "mistrust of one's powers" and a forgetting of "self-possession" that Kant counts among the violations of one's duty to oneself in the Vigilantius lectures (*Vigil* 27:606). A moral agent, he elaborates, must locate his existence "in his own person," and not in things outside him. But this is precisely how the miser goes wrong: Rather than responding to the awareness of his own lack of independence and autocracy by asserting self-possession and moral strength, the miser looks to external sources in a fruitless attempt to buttress his neediness. Moral misery and despondency thus seem to go hand-in-hand. As Kant observes in the Vigilantius passage cited earlier, misery is "coupled at the same time with such depression of spirits, that it no longer permits any consciousness of the superiority of one's strength of mind."[12]

The miser and others like him seek to assuage their moral misery through external means. But there is a second, more or less internal, method that agents often pursue in order to escape moral misery – this is self-deception. As Kant describes it in the *Groundwork*, self-deception is rooted in a tendency to question the "strictness and the purity" of the moral law, or the extent of the requirements of duty and the demand that morally worthy action be motivated by the moral law (*GMS* 4:398–9). Of course, this is only a very general description of the tendency: Self-deception can be remarkably subtle and clever, as Kant describes it – indeed, it is perhaps most insidious and intractable when it appeals to apparent virtue in its own defense. So, for example, a main source of the vice of ingratitude is a tendency to "misunderstand" (or, presumably, deceive oneself about) the duty of self-sufficiency, such that gratitude is understood as an admission of dependence on others and ingratitude is recast as an assertion of one's own rugged individualism and self-sufficiency (*TL* 6:459). As a strategy to attempt to avoid misery, self-deception is primarily effective retrospectively, that is with respect to concerns about past moral failure. But in rationalizing, the agent also allows himself to be less concerned about his ability to rise to moral challenges in the future. After all, if being "perfect" has been so straight-forward thus far, why presume it should be any different in the future?

The despondent agent essentially gives up on herself as a moral agent, hoping instead to achieve some analogue of contentment via external means. Meanwhile, the agent who pursues the route of self-deception

---

[12] *Vigil* 27:644. Compare Kant's remark in the *Doctrine of Virtue* that "moral cognition of oneself will ... dispel fanatical contempt for oneself as a human being" (*TL* 6:441). One gloss of this claim is that the person who engages in the difficult work of self-scrutiny will at the very least exercise enough self-possession to dispel complete despondency, since only a being with some moral strength is capable of self-examination.

Inclination, Need, and Moral Misery

insists on her virtue and her status as a moral agent, but re-describes the demands of morality in order to fool herself into thinking that she can achieve them effortlessly. Crucially, however, neither strategy is effective. It is easiest to see how the first strategy is doomed from the beginning. Responding to need by acquiring ever more need is something like the moral version of going into more debt to pay an existing debt. Prudentially, the strategy only produces more misery. The miser, it would seem, is *doubly* tortured since he is beset by the penny-pinching anxieties of his own making, but nevertheless still concerned with the original objects of his inclinations. As Kant describes him, the miser peevishly begrudges others their small luxuries, since he is unable to enjoy any of his own.

It is, admittedly, less obvious that the strategy of self-deception is bound to fail, since Kant evinces a decided pessimism about how skilled agents are at deceiving themselves. Still, his remarks about conscience would seem to suggest that self-deception can never be "complete" in the sense that an agent can never cease to hear the voice of conscience altogether.[13] Note, too, that even if self-deception could be complete, or close to complete, it would only be complete with respect to retrospective moral questions. The self-deceiver, in order to maintain the illusion of virtue, must constantly be weaving new tales of apparent virtue. Both the "external" and the "internal" strategies are thus accompanied by the restless anxiety of needing constantly to keep up these endeavors in order to avoid moral misery.

6   Conclusion

In light of the preceding discussion, we can make some concluding observations about inclination, need, and moral misery. First, when Kant asserts that inclinations are burdensome and that a rational agent would wish to be rid of them, I suspect he has in mind inclinations *qua* needs, or inclinations that have taken on the urgency and unruliness of need. When inclinations become needs, the pursuit of independence – understood as autocracy – becomes nearly impossible. Crucially, Kant's account of beatitude and independence demonstrates that this moral struggle is also accompanied by a painful *awareness of moral failure*, a discontent and misery that agents will go to great lengths to avoid. Neediness thus ushers in the further burdens of misery, despondency, and self-deception

---

[13] For more comprehensive discussions of conscience in Kant's ethics, see Esser 2013 and Ware 2009. For an argument that self-deception can be "complete," see Sticker 2017.

described in the preceding section. So it is not inclination as such that any rational agent should wish to be rid of, but rather the moral hazards and psychological burdens of neediness. But this brings us to a second, altogether more optimistic point: Inclination itself does not imply subjection to these burdens necessarily.[14] Indeed, Kant's moral philosophy reserves at least a theoretical space for an autonomous agent who is able to enjoy the pleasure that accompanies satisfied inclination. The ideal of independence suggests that the appropriate approach to inclination is not one of vigilant suppression and constant checking, but rather conscientious cultivation. Such cultivation may indeed involve avoiding certain inclinations to the best of one's ability (especially those that cannot be managed or fulfilled). But it may also involve *encouraging* other kinds of inclinations or ends, specifically, those that do not always "change and grow with the indulgence that one allows" it (*KpV* 5:118). To see what shape such a policy might take, let us return to the passage in which Kant discusses the relief from anxiety that comes along with the "comforting encouragement of one's conscience":

> [T]he blessedness (*Seligkeit*) found in the comforting encouragement of one's conscience is not *positive* (joy), but merely negative (relief from preceding anxiety); and this alone is what can be ascribed to virtue, as a struggle against the influence of the evil principle in a human being. (*TL* 6:440)

Kant suggests that there is something *beyond* independence and the "relief from preceding anxiety" that embodied agents can enjoy. This "positive" blessedness is "joy" (*Freude*). A question naturally presents itself: *What would Kantian joy look like?* The account sketched here may provide a template: Kantian joy would involve having inclinations, having control over these inclinations (and knowing that one has such control), and yet still taking some pleasure in those inclinations and their satisfaction.

What would such joy be like? There is perhaps a hint in the *Anthropology* and fragments on anthropology, where Kant sometimes associates joy with friendship and society (e.g., *Anth* 7:171 and *HN* 15:263). The link is speculative, but fruitful. If we *were* to take pleasure in inclination, even while being *completely independent* of inclination, the best candidates for such inclinations would seem to be unselfish or other-directed ones. We could easily take pleasure in their fulfillment (when this is consistent with the moral law, of course) but not suffer (at least for selfish reasons) when

---

[14] Grenberg (2011:153–4) makes a similar observation.

Inclination, Need, and Moral Misery 213

these go unfulfilled. Note, too, that the pleasure of friendship does not tend to generate ever-increasing and unsatisfiable inclination: When we develop a new friendship, we do not begin to seek out more of the same. And when we lose a friend, we do not simply acquire a replacement. Indeed, if this link between joy and society with others is apt, the account of independence offered here may tell us something about our relationships with others. Far from being an inevitable locus of dependence, they may in fact be a source of Kantian joy.

CHAPTER 11

Religion and the Highest Good: Speaking to the Heart of Even the Best of Us

Barbara Herman

This chapter is about the idea of the highest good in Kant: the unity of virtue and happiness as the whole object of pure practical reason. About the highest good, I start out as a skeptic. Its content and its place in Kant's moral thought have always made me uneasy; I am perplexed by many of the arguments that led Kant to embrace it.[1] However, my current interest in the highest good is primarily *practical*: I want to understand how engaging with the idea would play out in the moral life of the good person. My worry is less about system and argument and more about whether embrace of the idea of the highest good would corrupt the heart of even the best of us. I have found the question hard to frame and the answer hard to find. The text that I have found most intriguing on these matters is Kant's *Religion Within the Boundaries of Mere Reason*. In what follows, I will try to explain why.

1 Like many, my unease about the highest good centers on the idea of securing proportionality between virtue and happiness. One can agree that when happiness comes by way of wrongdoing, it can seem as if something is won or gained by cheating. But the "as if" matters, since happiness is not a prize or a reward (*KrV* 5:118). It is also true that we feel distress when the good suffer. But why is this a *moral* matter? Why should morality or practical reason or nature or God have the job of securing happiness for the virtuous, now or in the hereafter, for the individual or for the race? If the fix for this feeling of cosmic disorder is the highest good, it comes with the high cost of imagining a micromanaged eternity. Even if one can see how the postulates of practical reason could allow such a story to be told, it's hard to come to terms with the need for it. I'm going to argue on Kant's behalf that we don't have to go that way.

[1] I have for a long time shared John Rawls' sense of disappointment that the marvelous edifice of Kant's moral philosophy was judged, by Kant, to require religion for support. This chapter attempts to ease some of that.

214

Religion and the Highest Good

In the *Critique of Practical Reason*, the highest good enters as the central topic of the Dialectic – that part of a critique that deals with tendencies of human reason to go beyond the cognitions warranted by the terms of its Analytic. When reason's ideas outstrip our cognitive powers, we become vulnerable to illusions and contradictions. The danger posed by the highest good is the necessary connection it supposes between virtue and happiness: It is not conceptual; it can't be causal. If we must have the highest good, and if it cannot be managed with critical reason's resources, the moral law will be shown to be fantastic and therefore false (*KrV* 5:114). Faced with an antinomy, Kant resolves it through an appeal to the noumenal will and the postulates of God and the immortality of the soul; they render secure the necessary connection between virtue and happiness. For our purposes here, we don't need to know the details.

What we do need to know is why practical reason has to venture into this dangerous space. I think there are two roads taken to the highest good. The first is internal to Kant's system. The object of *pure* practical reason does not require the highest good – its object is the will willing well (*KrV* 5:57ff). But the *faculty* of practical reason has more in its portfolio than the good will; it also manages the pursuit of happiness, a necessary end for us finite and sensible rational beings, and, Kant insists, it is a happiness that involves feeling, inclinations, and needs.[2] As the faculty charged with the good, practical reason must create unity out of this heterogeneity. This opens the door to the highest good. Call this the *objective* road to the idea of the highest good. We will not be taking that road.

There is also a *subjective* road. It looks something like this. While the human being's pursuit of happiness can bend and accept morality as a condition, the concern with happiness cannot be set aside. It is then unbearable that virtue might leave happiness hostage to luck, or, if virtue is a condition of worthiness to be happy, that virtue might be out of reach, despite our best efforts. In response to this distress, the highest good might provide assurance: God will provide.

But is it clear that we must go down this road? After all, although we cannot have an end whose pursuit is or is seen to be impossible, the fact that intervening events, external or internal, prevent success in reaching an end is not practical incoherence, it's just the way things go. Why should it be different with happiness and virtue? Thinking of the highest good in terms of deferred gratification writ large might be a source of (infinite?)

---

[2] Kant sets aside both the so-called happiness of Stoic contentment that jettisons desire-satisfaction and the beatitude of the holy will (*KrV* 5:118).

patience, but if the prospect of failure to gain happiness affects our will to be good, then we are not good.

Further, the highest good can't mitigate the sacrifice a person makes when faced with a hard choice. There is no conceptual failure in the very idea of absorbing a moral cost; it is what virtue requires. Perhaps it's this: It is one thing to find that your integrity as a moral person can require a sacrifice of happiness, it is quite another to accept a view of one's life, the life of a human being, as hostage to morality. Such a view devalues our nature. From the human point of view, the moral order that reason would bring forth has to be friendly to human happiness. But even if the highest good could deliver this, it would not speak to the struggling individual's subjective need. That might make us worry that the subjective road is a dead end.

2 We get a somewhat different account of what might be at stake subjectively with the highest good in the *Religion*. Unlike the *Critique of Practical Reason*, where the main focus is connecting the highest good to the formal conditions for the unity of the rational faculty, the *Religion*'s focus on the highest good is as a final end for us as morally striving agents. In the Preface to the first edition of the *Religion*, Kant argues that morality as such needs no end, no higher being, nothing beyond itself or its law as a determining ground of the will. The idea of a highest good – bringing virtue and happiness together – arises out of the practice of morality as something that "meets our natural need, which would otherwise be a hindrance, to think for all our doings and nondoings taken as a whole some sort of ultimate end which reason can justify" (*RGV* 6:5). The highest good is that end: It is an end the human being can love *and* an end proposed by reason alone (*RGV* 6:7n). One *will not* as a result of accepting the highest good as a final end do anything other than what one is morally required to do; one *will* be able to regard one's already completely determined actions as having an *additional* purpose. Because the highest good is an end the realization of which requires the contribution of an omnipotent moral being as ruler of the world, "morality leads inevitably to religion" (*RGV* 6:8n).

The second Preface tells us that the primary task of the *Religion* is to show that and how a liberal *Christian* theology both articulates and secures for us the needed object of rational faith and love. That makes the subject of the *Religion* **religion**: not the formal concepts that make rational space for religion – that's the province of the *Critique of Practical Reason* – but religion as an historical phenomenon, embedded in sacred texts and practices and institutions.[3] Kant's view is that it is religion in this full sense that positions the highest good to answer the moral subject's need. Its being able to play this role is in turn part of a religion's rational defense.[4] For the modern secular Kantian, this is surely a startling and uncomfortable claim – possibly part of the reason the *Religion* is a somewhat marginalized text.

Some moral philosophers coming to the *Religion* restrict themselves to the sections of Part One that amplify and greatly enrich Kant's moral psychology (the account of the three predispositions to good in human nature [*RGV* 6:26–8], and [parts of] the discussion of the propensity to evil [*RGV* 6:28–32]). There is strain in doing even this, since the compelling parts are joined to the theology of original sin and radical evil and the philosophically difficult notion of a fundamental or supreme maxim (the *Gesinnung*), a disposition arising from an intelligible deed, an act not cognizable in time. Others are drawn to the idea of an ethical community introduced in Part Three which is thought to offer some insight into how Kant thinks concretely about a kingdom of ends. Of less interest is Kant's view that the ethical community needs to be a *church*. The focus on Christology, church structure and priestcraft has no doubt kept moral philosophers away from Parts Two and Four. It's always a delicate thing to abstract out bits of argument one finds useful from a text that does not overall appeal. The salvaged bits are easily mistaken for things they are not when the context that explains them is lost. It's surely worth trying for a more complete view.

The main text of the *Religion* begins with the threat posed to morality by the Christian idea of radical evil in human nature. Were human nature at its root resistant to morality, were we determined to evil, then autonomy is not the defining principle of the will, or at least not the principle of the human power of choice, and morality is without a rational ground. Yet the doctrine of radical evil is a defining element of Christian theology. Kant takes the conflict seriously: Something has to give and it cannot be morality. If the doctrine of radical evil cannot be jettisoned, it can be interpreted: that is, a place for it found in morality's agenda. Kant

---

[3] The General Remark that closes each part of the *Religion* details the aspects of the historical religions that cannot survive philosophical and moral scrutiny. Sometimes because the piece of a religion is metaphysically preposterous; sometimes because it would undermine morality. The relation between philosophy and religion is not unlike that between philosophy and natural science. In both cases the philosophical subject-matter is a human practice, found, not given *a priori*, yet making claims that stand only if they can be explicated in terms that connect them to an *a priori* principle or foundation.

[4] It will turn out to be an open question whether only religion can play this role.

introduces the three "predispositions to the good" (animality, humanity, personality) and the three "propensities to evil" (frailty, impurity, depravity[5]) to relocate the religious idea of radical evil as part of an account of moral failure, thereby protecting human autonomy and freedom. As we shall see, it also opens the door to the highest good (*RGV* 6:26ff).

In the way that the three predispositions combine to generate moral character, there is enough turbulence in our good-oriented development to establish the potential, the propensity, for evil. Morality may be the telos of human nature, but *moral character* is the completion and resolution of a dynamic process that involves elements of our animal nature and the ordering of ends in the pursuit of happiness. Inevitably, empirically, we come to morality with confusion about ultimate ends and our status as persons. The condition is *objectively* resolved in the relations of equality and respect that come with acknowledgment of the moral law. But *subjectively*, a person's moral character is the fragile terminus of a developmental path – rational telos combined with dramatic contingency. "Radical evil" is then identified as the permanent subjective instability of moral character that mars even the best of us: Despite being formed under the aegis of the good, we remain drawn to wrongful principles and choices supported by residual elements of moral character formation. So interpreted, radical evil is a threat to our moral goodness, not to morality itself.

To be clear: All three predispositions to the good are present in potential from the beginning of a human life; however, their expression is teleologically staged, and in any actual moral biography, partial and contingent. To get to morality each of us must negotiate instincts difficult to control, engage emergent rationality, and be challenged by a natural and comparative idea of happiness that introduces envy and jealousy (necessary for the acquisition of self-discipline and attention to others as separate selves). Teleology does not imply a straight path.[6] One may, as it happens, have unusually strong passions; they may, as it happens, influence growth

---

[5] Frailty is a kind of weakness of heart in the face of contra-moral impulse; impurity marks a tendency to mix moral and nonmoral motives; depravity or corruption is the willful subordination of the moral principle to the principle of self-love.

[6] This pattern of telic development is not unique to morality. Consider, to take a very different example, the emergence of sexual or gender identity. It too is the end-result of multiple tendencies present from the start of life that are triggered and realized sequentially. A child moves from primitive bond to object-sensitive love in a way that organizes sexuality and gender identity. The process is uneven, occurring in stages, never quite complete. Many think it requires a dynamic crisis – like the oedipal complex – to regiment emergent sexuality. New kinds of attachment are made possible: mature love and friendship regulable by choice. Alongside new powers there are also new vulnerabilities. While the overall structure is teleologically organized, an individual's trajectory through it may be subject to contingencies.

toward moral weakness or moral strength. It can matter to developmental success when and how the strictures of moral duties are introduced. Too early and they might yield a tendency to rigidity; too late might make it harder to freely accept moral discipline. And so on.

So while the objective telic aim of human nature is a character moved by the moral law as an incentive, taking conformity of the will to the moral law as its supreme object, the human being in real time falls short. Residues of earlier stages subsist in the mature adult, nourishing three propensities to evil. We are prone to weakness and frailty concerning action, too easily overcome by contrary feeling (the engine of animal self-love is not turned off as moral character is formed). Two more grave sources of failure – impurity and depravity – compromise moral character (*RGV* 6:29–30). With impurity, compliance with morality in action partly depends on incentives other than respect for the moral law (we can't resist the comparative and competitive demands of happiness – a kind of moral immaturity). In depravity, the incentives of the moral law are subordinated to nonmoral ones (often a vain or usurpatory self-conceit). As a product of our coming to morality, the *propensity* to evil belongs to each human being, even the best of us ("it is woven into human nature" [*RGV* 6:30]).

However, since a propensity is not a cause, it is consistent with free acts of the human power of choice, even if it is also an inescapable siren call. We are free, so can and should be moral; we are also, by our nature, drawn to invert the order of incentives. This fact produces a crisis in even the best of us. For if there is even the hint that we question the order of incentives we have already failed. And since happiness cannot (and should not) be ignored or absorbed into or guaranteed by morality, the question will arise. Given our nature, this is as far as we can go on our own. This is stage-setting for the highest good: It arrives to help resolve the question for even the best of us in a way that neutralizes the propensity to evil (permitting us to disown the enemy within, as it were).

The problem is that if what the doctrine of the highest good offers us is warranted belief in the soul's immortality and the eventual balance of virtue and happiness in a divinely ordered nature, it won't help us get the order of incentives right. We are at risk because we rightly fear that we cannot maintain the correct inner alignment between virtue and happiness. Shifting that responsibility to a higher being removes the problem in one sense, but in a manner that confirms rather than resolves our doubts about our character. Autonomy would require dependency to maintain itself. I think this cannot be the role of the highest good in our moral economy.

220   BARBARA HERMAN

Now, when Kant describes the human propensity to evil, he locates it in the *heart*, not the will. Why he does this is important. Recall that the predispositions are "elements of the determination of a human being": structural attributes that dispose the person to self-organize around the good. They are not the root of any vices, though they generate elements of character onto which vices can be grafted. Their job is to prompt the developmental stages for the emerging human will as a rational power. The propensities to evil, on the other hand, are systematic vulnerabilities of the human as a practical being. They are not of the will, for the will cannot be or incline to evil and still be free (the will also does not *incline* to the good: the good is the object of its principle). Evil is rooted in the heart.

Metaphorically, the heart is the seat of our loves. We can know the good but not love it, or not love it enough, or love something else as well. That is why what is true *for* us objectively may not also be true *of* us subjectively. Even the best of us. The way(s) the human being comes to care about the good leave her vulnerable to contingencies of the heart. Passions, attractions, false ideals, loves – catch at the heart, taxing one's attachment to the will's principle.[7] The resulting failure need not involve acting badly, for we can, even when the heart is weak or impure or depraved, comply with the law. The failure is about the alignment of our subjectivity, our heart, with the law's authority – whether we are one with ourselves. Since the alignment is not necessary, and the heart is both hidden and burdened, there is always reason to worry about the integrity of our attachment to the good.

This suggests a different spin on the subjective path to the highest good arising from the propensity to evil. The problem that even the best of us faces is not about undeserved suffering or failures in the permissible pursuit of happiness – conditions that might be compensated for in the hereafter. It is not about bringing the external world into conformity with moral effort. The real worry is *internal*, about one's heart, about what one loves. What the best of us wants is to be virtuous – to succeed in strength and purity and in the well-orderedness of her ends. Wanting this, she can do various things. She will resolve to make the moral law her highest principle; she can recognize past failure and embark on programs of self-improvement; she can discipline her body, avoid dangerous or corrupting relationships; and so on. What she cannot do is insure that her heart is in the right place (*RGV* 6:48–51). Neither her good actions nor her discipline

---

[7] Objectively, the human being's relation to the will's principle is not a matter of attachment but of realization.

Religion and the Highest Good 221

stand guarantee for this. What the best of us must want is to be rid of the anxiety that, despite all her efforts, there resides in her heart a worm of corruption that compromises her moral commitment, her most fundamental maxim (*Gesinnung*). The best of us can't be sure that she is who she thinks she is and aims to be; she can't fully rely on herself or earn the satisfaction that comes with acting well. Because this anxiety is well-founded, the lack of confidence threatens steadfast moral resolve. That makes the subjective issue for the highest good resolving this anxiety about purity of heart. Taking the next step requires that we have some control of Kant's very difficult concept of the *Gesinnung*.

3 A *Gesinnung* is a maxim, an agent's most fundamental practical principle or rational disposition, "the ultimate subjective ground of the adoption of maxims" (*RGV* 6:25). Its content represents her ordering of two contending incentives or principles – morality and self-love. One's *Gesinnung* is either evil or good; there is no middle ground. Objectively, the moral law *is* fundamental. Subjectively, it has to be made the condition of one's practical life.

Part of what makes the idea of a *Gesinnung* strange and different from our other maxims is that, as the most basic expression of our freedom, it is both adopted and yet not a determination of the will in time (or at a time). Were its adoption to take place at a time, some event would have preceded and partly determined it; it would not then express practical freedom. But it also cannot be adopted for a reason, since nothing could be the source of such a reason if the *Gesinnung* is our most basic principle. And not least, the very idea of a *Gesinnung* as the *one* fundamental principle of a life seems to conflict with the idea that moral change and reform are always possible, even change of the deepest sort.

Here's one way we might think about this. Whatever the source of our reasons, we do not choose reasons in the way that we choose things *for reasons*. Some reasons are given by the conditions of our agency – for Kant, reasons of self-love and of the moral law. This is the work of the predispositions: They set us up to find things good, which then come to be possible reasons or determinants of willing. (Kant speaks of the impossibility of ever losing the incentive for the good [*RGV* 6:46].) But if we get onto reasons by way of our psychology, how could the taking of reasons into a maxim be regarded as timeless? Think of a maxim as representing a course of reasoning about willing – one we believe to be correct. In a sense, every course of reasoning is timeless (e.g. a contradiction is timelessly invalid). A course of reasoning may be manifest at a time, realized or recognized in time, but its correctness is not a function of any act of reasoning. *Subjectively*, adopting either principle (morality or self-love) as the fundamental principle of one's willing is to regard it as timelessly correct. That is why a *Gesinnung* speaks to a whole life: It is a subjectively authoritative and total point of view, addressing all actions one has taken or will take. But the adoption of only one of the principles gets things right: the two options are not on a par. So it is not difficult to see that a great deal is at stake for anyone who finds himself with the anxiety that he may not be who he is devoting himself to being – even, perhaps especially, the best of us. The trials of the *Gesinnung* create no metaphysical doubt that we are practically free agents with autonomy of will. It is because neither phenomenology nor external conformity to law imply correctness of principle that even the best of us will doubt their fundamental goodness. Increased effort or heightened introspection won't touch the problem.

Although doubt that we are fundamentally good is inescapable, if we come to believe that we are not good, that our heart is corrupt, change of heart or moral conversion is possible (*RGV* 6:48).[8] And of course, even the best of us was once not good. Suppose one takes oneself to have seen the light and tried to do whatever it is that gets the principle right. There is still no certainty about what one takes to have happened, or confidence that it will endure (*RGV* 6:51). Again Kant points to the highest good and now more directly *religion* as the source of the help that can get us past this kind of worry, but there is also a warning.

Belief in the highest good cannot cause conversion or change of heart or prove that one's heart is constant. But mistaken belief in the nature of God's contribution can lead us astray. The danger comes from the fact that *reason* "which by nature finds moral labor vexing, now conjures up, under the pretext of natural impotence, all sort of impure religious ideas (among which belongs falsely imputing to God the principle of happiness as the supreme condition of his commands)" (*RGV* 6:51). Such an error would resolve our anxiety, since it is a condition we can surely meet! As would a divine guarantee that God will make us better persons, if we just ask.

The problem is not in the turn to religion as such, but in religious content. *Moral* religion, by contrast with religion of supplication (rogation), demands good works as a condition for God's cooperation [*höhere*

---

[8] This is a very obscure idea. Perhaps the condition necessary to realize that one has gotten onto the wrong principle *is* getting it right? Weakness and frailty would remain, but they pose more of a management problem once the fundamental principle is secure. The language of conversion marks the fact that change in *Gesinnung* is not for any reason in the usual sense.

Mitwirkung] with our efforts (*RGV* 6:52). So the new version of the subjective question is: What kind of divine cooperation with our good works and best efforts could relieve anxiety of the heart without corrupting the will? We of course cannot hope to understand the workings of divine cooperation. Kant says it isn't necessary that we do. What we are given instead is an account of this cooperative relation with God as presented in liberal Christianity. It is the case study for a moral religion that makes proper use of the doctrine of the highest good.[9] Part Two of the *Religion* works this through.

4 Part Two begins with a reminder that virtue is a battle: not, as the Stoics thought, against the inclinations, which "considered in themselves are good," but against a principle of will we have adopted that resists the moral law as our most fundamental maxim (*RGV* 6:58–9). We have no natural understanding of how this battle is fought or won, just as we have no natural understanding of divine cooperation. The remedy moral religion offers is a kind of *typic* or projection of these notions in terms that allow us to have a rational response to the things we cannot directly understand.[10] Instead of the mysterious battle between heart and will, we are directed to think in terms of an "invisible enemy," an evil spirit or tempter outside us.[11] Instead of God as a partner, we are given the Son of God as a prototype. Two moves frame the argument to come. Against past philosophy, we are to see innocence in the body and guilt as flowing from the heart. On behalf of religion, we are to be prepared to interpret its representations, its stories, as modes of access to things beyond our cognitive powers. The hermeneutic is moral: Religious doctrine is relevant only as it is able to typify elements central to our moral labors. The typic of our humanity, for example, a way of having access to the value of the human being as other than a mere created thing, is as a being loved by

---

[9] Kant suggests that there are other moral religions and other adequate conceptions of divine cooperation. Whether from conviction or from strategic concern, he presents liberal Christianity as the most successful.

[10] The resources of Christian theology direct Kant to the terminology of "personification." The use of a typic or schema is recurrent in Kant's thought; it provides a way of making judgment possible where ideas or concepts have no direct application in experience. The most familiar typic is the law of nature formulation of the categorical imperative in the *Groundwork of the Metaphysics of Morals*. We need to be able to tell whether something has the form of law (*simpliciter* or for rational beings as such). We're in no position to say. But we can judge whether something could be a law of nature – whether it fits with other laws; whether its governance is coherent for the things under it. If a principle could not be a law of nature on such grounds, we can say that it does not have the form of law. In general, a typic allows judgment in one domain to yield conclusions in another.

[11] It is a benign representation, Kant argues, since no external tempter would succeed if "we are not in secret agreement with him" (*RGV* 6:60).

224 BARBARA HERMAN

God, proceeding from God's nature for all eternity, represented in his only-begotten Son in whom God loved the world; etc. (*RGV* 6:60–1).[12]

This launches what is surely the hardest part of the *Religion* for secular-minded readers – the Christology. It can hardly be avoided if, as Kant says, it is through practical faith in the idea of the Son of God as a *prototype* of moral perfection that the human being is enabled "to believe and self-assuredly trust" in the possibility of moral goodness or perfection for himself. What follows is a very tentative reconstruction of the main arguments.

A *prototype* is the original design or model from which copies are made. The Son of God is the *prototype* for us, the (other) children of God. Through the prototype's life history we find out what we are designed to be. Whether or not we succeed in living the life we are made for, the *prototype* stands guarantee for its possibility. Though in one sense the *prototype* is a projection or a vivified idea, in the world interpreted through Christian doctrine, he is real. Inside the hermeneutic, we cannot doubt the purity of his heart or his moral force or his constancy. Absolute perfection in the *prototype* would make the idea as good as empty; to be a typic or schema for us, the *prototype* has to live the relevant pieces of a human life, including the lure of self-love and the costs of the moral life. The *prototype* therefore faces temptations and is made to suffer for the sake of others (indeed, *all* others). Through his steadfast good choices, his suffering and his sacrifice, the goodness of the *prototype* has a human form. Sustained by God's love, which is the principle of his being, the *prototype is* recognizable to us as, at the deepest level, good. The effect of the typification is a shift in defaults: Phenomenology is replaced by theology, doubt about an unknowable principle of will is banished by confidence in God's love. (That is: since being loved by God is a typification of rational nature, our inability to regard ourselves as loved, or valued as a rational being, is the theological interpretation of the source of our moral anxiety.)

The detail of our moral anxiety is represented in the theology by the gap between even the best of us and the *prototype*'s strength and purity of character.[13] As Kant sees it, three difficulties need to be overcome to close (or bridge) the gap (here I simply follow the order of the text at *RGV* 6:66ff.). Each of them requires God's cooperation, which we find typified in Christian theology. First, there is the business of our imperfection. We contrast the *prototype*'s simple goodness and our endless striving: We

---

[12] I include the "etc." for the *und so weiter* at the end of the German paragraph – a plain indication of the kind of discussion we are embarked on.

[13] By analogy with moral psychology we are here dealing with what we might call *theological* psychology: what must be assumed true of our personality for us to have our assigned place in the theological story.

are at each instant and always only imperfectly good. The theology gives us warrant to regard our striving as part of an infinite sequence. Our improvement now (for every now) is then not to be regarded as we see it, as still marred by defect, but as God can see it in the prototype, as the germ or seed of perfection, good in its form (we don't fault the sapling for being young). We thereby gain a new view of what we are.

Second, there is the anxiety about the constancy of our disposition. We are right to doubt that we will be constant. Yet, Kant says, we must have confidence in our constancy if we are to persevere (*RGV* 6:68). The best of us wants to believe they have adopted the good principle. We gain typified warrant to believe that given a sufficiently long life of good works, one is entitled to the conjecture that one's fundamental disposition is stably good. How so? The theology confronts the anxiety with the challenge of eternity: In the best of us, with the experience of steady goodness, the idea of eternity induces no fear. Quite the contrary, it offers an arc of life that grounds hope. For the rest of us, if we respond at all, the idea of eternity either rouses conscience and heightens self-criticism or it foretells the misery of endless failure.

Note that we don't need to believe in our immortality or that God knows something about us that we don't. The typified idea of immortality is rather a rite of passage, a test.

The third and greatest difficulty for those who would be good has its source in events before moral conversion (adoption of the correct *Gesinnung*), from the time when even the best of us lacked a good disposition (even if there is no wrongdoing, the human will only becomes a good in time). The problem arises from our inability to disown our own past. In the language of the theology: Even though moral conversion can create a "new man" – one not guilty of anything – the "new man" carries the guilt of the "old man" left behind (*RGV* 6:72ff). If it is not yet clear why there should be a transfer of guilt, it is a bit clearer that if the "new man" *is* guilty for the "old man's" sins, the "new man" will be unable to fully realize the good of his own disposition. The pairing of goodness and guilt is a recipe for despair.

This idea of transferred guilt is not altogether strange. Suppose, in the past, one had wrongfully harmed someone. There might be a debt to be paid, apology and forgiveness negotiated. That would remain true even if one had ceased being someone who could wrongfully harm in that way.[14]

---

[14] We can imagine the shock of the wrongdoing being the cause of conversion. It is yet intelligible to say, "I, who could not harm you, apologize for harming you."

Now assume there had been no wrong-doing only wrong-willing. Suppose that as an adult I realize that misplaced anger at a parent was the driving force of many of my adolescent actions. I would feel bad about this, even if there had not been any bad doings (perhaps I was an obedient and resentful child), and even if I am not now moved by anger. I feel guilt now at not having been a loving child. There is no repair available. My past interferes with my fully inhabiting the present; it is a consequence of being the kind of agent who has a history. One would want release from such a burden. We might begin psychotherapy.

The solution offered in the theology is the very difficult doctrine of "the vicarious substitute" (*RGV* 6:74f).[15] The strategy of interpretation is the same: see if a bit of theology can work as a typified solution to a subjective problem of character. I think it goes this way. The *prototype*, who is himself wholly good (there is no guilt from his past, having been created in God's love), is called to sacrifice for our sins. *His* act provides a "vicarious substitute" for *our* discharging our guilt. It is not quite that he is able to do for us what we cannot do for ourselves, but that he is in a position to offer his suffering, not owed to anyone, as a pure gift. Inside the theology, wrong-willing, the adoption of an evil *Gesinnung*, is a sin against God. We have no power to repair that (it is timelessly wrong, as is the "old man" timelessly who we are). Some sort of penance is owed; nothing we can offer would suffice. As an act of love and of mercy, God receives the suffering freely offered by the *prototype* as a gift, for our sake. From our point of view, it is the gift of grace. It puts us in a position to move beyond our history. But how?

The theological typic adds a new piece to our moral repertoire (it is an addition to the moral imagination, I would say). Taking the *prototype* as our typified guide, it allows the person of good will to regard the "ills and sufferings" that befall anyone in the pursuit of ends as a freely offered gift – a gift from the "new man" on behalf of the "old." The "new man" does not and should not regard the ills and sufferings as something he deserves; he can welcome them as a test and exercise for his reformed disposition, of value to him now because of the wrong-willing of the person he once was and as a discipline to stay the course. Following the idea of vicarious substitution, taking the ills and sufferings as a gift makes it true that the "new man" has left behind the calculus of pleasures and pains that were the marks of his past corrupt principle. *And*, by analogy with God's grace, the

[15] One could see the equally difficult notion of transference in psychoanalytic theory as its secular variant.

Religion and the Highest Good

ills and sufferings can serve for the "old man" as punishment – as paying the debt in a currency the "old man" understands: It was precisely to avoid the burdens of the moral life that he made his fundamental maxim conditional on happiness. The interpretive device thereby allows the good person to address the moral deficit of his past self without drawing the guilt into his present life. This resolves the last piece of the moral anxiety of even the best of us.

I would conjecture that the difficult notion of *grace* functions in the theological typic as the analogue of moral teleology in the *Critique of Practical Reason* account of the highest good – the God-sourced rational ordering of morality and nature that secures the proportionality of virtue and happiness. As I've interpreted it here, it gives the vexed notion of proportionality moral content that it otherwise lacked. Rather than the morally dangerous idea of God supervising a system of rewards and punishment into eternity, it interprets the good person's ills and sufferings so that they do not detract from the happiness such a person can achieve or hope for.[16] The person with a corrupt will, committed to the principle of worldly success as the condition of goodness, is untouched; he remains caught up in contingency and competition with others, and hostage to his past.

To my mind, this development of the idea of proportionality – of the fit between virtue and burden – is one of the signal contributions of the *Religion* to Kant's moral thought. It criticizes the terms of traditional or natural idea of proportionality that prompts the highest good (that we should gain happiness because of virtue and regard the burdens of the virtuous as untoward) – showing that the natural idea carries with it the marks of unreformed character. I don't think the *Critique of Practical Reason* embraces the traditional view; its argument has the task of showing that the abstract idea of the highest good – of some proportionality between virtue and happiness – does not disturb the central argument. It is not until the *Religion* that we learn how to think about proportionality *from within morality*.

5 We are not quite done. The subjective turn to the highest good occurred in Part One of the *Religion* as a response to the moral anxiety of even the best of us to sustain moral self-confidence in the face of the practical and theoretical limits of empirical character. The propensity to

---

[16] It does not alleviate the burdens of accident and circumstance, but it shouldn't do that. It rather offers a new dimension of self-love that comes from the power of free giving.

228   BARBARA HERMAN

evil remains a threat so long as one cares about happiness and tries to make sense of the relations between morality and happiness in a good life. The highest good is supposed to provide an answer involving a turn to religion, and in Part Two Kant shows how an actual religion can bring God into the moral story to make moral character secure, without undermining moral goodness. What remains is to see how this extends to an account of the highest good as a *final end* – a purpose to be realized through our moral action. This is the subject of the third and fourth parts of the *Religion*.[17] There is unfortunately only time for a quick survey of their argument.

We should continue, as Kant does, by looking at what remains a problem for the best of us after the deed of moral conversion that re-orients the heart, and after the resolution of the subjective anxieties. There is the risk of human frailty, being overcome by strong feeling, and the lure of the other loves that make up a person's character and that tempt us to impurity. Even a good person seeks worldly happiness; we live and love socially in ways that make us vulnerable to comparative assessments of worth. The best of us remains "exposed to the assaults of the evil principle" just because he lives among human beings "who will mutually corrupt each other's moral disposition and make one another evil" (*RGV* 6:93–4). The imperfect nature of human projects, the strains and costs of cooperation, the fog of self-confidence, are enough to erode virtue. It adds up. We don't live alone; individual effort is not enough; there is no invisible hand to set things right. Since the threat to human goodness arises from the ways we pursue our *separate* purposes, the solution is a *union* around a common principle: an *ethical community*. (Morality on its own does not give rise to a community; the idea of the *kingdom of ends* gives the objective form of a moral order, not a plan for living together.)

The ethical community as Kant describes it has two defining features – its laws are laws of virtue and it is a church. We are to understand a law of virtue as a command of God. The contrast is with a political order that regulates external action; that is its purpose, and all it can do given the epistemic limits of human judging. Because we cannot know one another's hearts, our law cannot be a law of virtue. No such limit applies to God: He can command where he can judge. So we are able to think of ourselves as in a community of virtue, as "a people of God," whose law commands the heart (*RGV* 6:99).

---

[17] Kant clearly has multiple purposes in mind with these last two parts, and multiple battles to fight about interpretation of religious doctrine and the morally acceptable form of religious institutions. Since this chapter is meant to be about the highest good, I restrict myself to that line of inquiry.

Religion and the Highest Good 229

Second, the ethical community can protect human beings from each other's influence, combating natural tendencies toward "envy, addiction to power, avarice," and avoiding "dissensions from their common goal of goodness" (*RGV* 6:97). It does this by providing a common end that orients the inner life of each member: They together pursue the "preservation of morality by counteracting evil with united forces" (*RGV* 6:94). The organizing principle of the community in the hands of human beings is a *church*, a disciplinary body in the Foucauldian sense: an institution whose practices and texts, its spiritual exercises, serve the law, maintaining the moral order of the inner life of virtue.[18] Whereas the end of the political community is equal freedom (which need be no person's end), the end of the ethical community is the highest good in nature, the improvement of the human race as a common end of all its members. It is an end we can love, and one that organizes our other loves. Indeed, by adding to our loves, it can aim to change human nature. The remainder of the *Religion* sets out the conditions and potential pitfalls of a church that would fulfill this moral purpose.[19]

The overall argument of the *Religion* is that liberal Christianity has both a theology that answers the anxieties of the best of us, and an ecclesiastical church (of worship and text) that creates an ethical community in which we together work toward the highest moral good in nature. Able to win the hearts of those who understand their duty, it answers their need for an ultimate end for moral action which reason can justify.

6 There is a more general lesson we can take away from this immersion in the *Religion*. Some appearances to the contrary, there is serious space in Kant's moral thinking for the *subjective* needs of the human moral person. The issues are not foundational, but they are vital to understanding what morality is for us. Kant's focus on subjectivity is not about the impediments to moral action (those are virtue's concerns). It is about securing our confidence in our moral identity and finding a home for moral life in community with others. Kant thinks religion and the right sort of church can do this. In the next century, others make the same kind of argument in

---

[18] The idea of the ethical community encompasses all people, maybe all finite rational beings, at all times (the church invisible); each visible church is a partial society, a representation or a schema of the ideal (*RGV* 6:96).

[19] Topics range from relation to historical antecedents, to its view of inwardness versus deeds, the role of holy texts, the relations between laity and clergy, the nature of priestcraft; natural versus Christian religion, the threats of religious delusion, creed and conscience, etc. It is worth some study if only because it is one of the few instances we have where Kant evaluates institutions that have a moral purpose.

terms of a progressive history and the right sort of politics.[20] One might almost say: Before the French Revolution the idea of the highest good has to involve religion; after, there is a secular option. It is interesting, though not surprising, that many of the questions that must be answered remain the same. Can we see beyond the limits of individual action to a good we might together be promoting? How do we approach the burdens of staying the course within a conception of a decent human life? How can we make peace with our past transgressions? What is surprising is to discover how clearly Kant saw that the material form of the highest good had to get it right about institutions as well as teleology to make a common highest good possible.[21]

---

[20] Although Kant has the idea of a progressive history, its account is part of an external view of the way a moral history works.

[21] Like so many others, I am grateful to Paul Guyer for his many contributions to the study of Kant's philosophy.

PART IV

Freedom on a Bounded Sphere: Kant's Political Philosophy

CHAPTER 12

Right and Ethics: A Critical Tribute to Paul Guyer

Allen Wood

In this chapter, I mean to pay tribute to my friend and longtime collaborator, Paul Guyer. One of the main ways to pay tribute to philosophers is to argue with them; and that's what I plan to do in this chapter. But that intention does not leave me with too many options. Most of Guyer's writings, especially about Kant, are simply informative, perceptive, and cogently argued. One learns a lot from them about what Kant said, and how it fits together. This is true, as a matter of fact, even in the case of those writings with which I disagree. But there is one interesting topic in Kant interpretation on which Guyer and I do disagree – about which we have disagreed before – and where I think I can say something new in relation to our disagreement.

Kant divides "morals" (*Sitten*) into two parts: right (*Recht*) and ethics (*Ethik*). But Kant does not make it clear how right and ethics relate to each other, or how their treatment together forms a single whole: "morals." Robert Pippin has characterized the two main positions on this question as "derivationist" and "separationist" (Pippin 2006). A *derivationist* is someone who thinks that for Kant, *right is derived from ethics*. A *separationist* is someone who denies this. Pippin would call Guyer's position derivationist, and mine separationist.

Guyer does pose the issue by asking: "Are Kant's principles of right derived from the supreme principle of morality?" and he appears to answer this question in the affirmative (Guyer 2005a:198, 201, 220). So I will let stand the name "derivationist" for Guyer's position, at least until he tells me he rejects it. But I have to object to the term "separationist," if it is supposed to apply to me. The implication of the term is that right and ethics are simply separate, and that's all there is to it. Perhaps this has been the view of some: Julius Ebbinghaus, for instance, or Marcus Willaschek (at least at one time). Fichte does think that right and ethics are separate not only in their foundations, but two separate sciences. But it has never been my interpretation of Kant.

233

Pippin's categories are defective, because they do not include all the options, and they mischaracterize what I regard as the right way to reject what Pippin would call "derivationism." It begs the main question to call a "separationist" anyone who rejects the thesis that right is derived from the supreme principle of morality. This implies that right and ethics are originally one or together; and that anyone who rejects derivationism wants to perpetrate the violent act of separating them. But that assumes that the correct position is derivationism and suggests that the separationist wants to do violence to Kant's practical philosophy by cleaving it in half.

Second, even more misleadingly, calling me a separationist would imply that I want the two bleeding halves, so violently cloven, to remain separate. But I do not in the least believe in separation. My view is that right and ethics have distinct and independent *foundations*. But I want to understand how Kant can justifiably regard them as two parts of a single system of "morals." So my preferred name for my position would be "unificationist." As someone once said (he was lying, and I am not): I am a uniter, not a divider. If my view seems to beg the question in favor of right and ethics being originally separate, then I would admit to this, and take upon myself the task of showing that in their foundations, they are separate. But I do not accept the idea that in Kant's practical philosophy, they should be seen as separate. They are parts of a single whole. I reject the view that they have to be unified through one part (right) being dependent on and derived from the other part (ethics). I think they have to be unified in a different way.

What way? I think they are unified because they share a common concept of *obligation* – regarded as conformity to the universal criterion of reason in all its forms, namely universal law. Right does not originally contain this concept, but comes to share it with ethics when right, which is already grounded independently, borrows this concept of obligation from ethics. But now I am anticipating what can become clear only later.

To those who approach Kant's *Metaphysics of Morals* having first acquainted themselves with Kant's ethics from the *Groundwork*, the derivationist position will seem natural. It brings the domain of right under the heading of the principle Kant searched for and thought he had found and established in that work. So it caters to the long-standing illusion, especially common in Anglophone ethics, that we can fully understand Kant's practical philosophy solely through the *Groundwork*. For the *Groundwork* speaks of right only incidentally and at a single point, in connection with the example of the false promise, when considered in terms of the formula of humanity as end in itself (*GMS* 4:430). About the time Kant wrote the

Groundwork, he also gave the lectures whose transcription is now conventionally called *Naturrecht Feyerabend*. It does introduce right by deriving it from an application of that formula of the moral law (*NF* 27:1319–20). I think the most reasonable interpretation of Kant's views *at that time* is a derivationist one. But I think Kant changed his mind later on, when he saw a problem that could not be solved on that understanding of right. More on that presently.

A derivationist reading also enables us to fit Kant's philosophy of law and politics into the same model we find in many other moral and political philosophers, which Arthur Ripstein has characterized as: "applying general moral principles to the factual circumstances that make political society necessary" (Ripstein 2009:1). Ripstein is correct, however, in insisting that Kant's philosophy of right involves the fundamental rejection of this model. For that reason, and because the *Groundwork* lays the foundations of ethics only, it is not of much help in understanding right, or in finding the unity of the *Metaphysics of Morals*. In fact, it even tends to mislead us in these enterprises.

If we look at some of the most basic claims Kant makes in the *Rechtslehre* about the concept of right and the legislation of right, they not only raise questions for the derivationist position but also threaten the unity of morals, and even call in question whether there can, properly speaking, be any duties of right. Kant speaks of *Rechtspflichte*, yet for Kant all genuine duties are grounded on categorical imperatives (*RL* 6:222–3). It is the mark of a categorical imperative, however, that the obligation imposed by it must depend solely on a pure rational incentive, valid for all rational beings as such (*GMS* 4:414–5, 427–8). Kant distinguishes the legislation of right from that of ethics by saying that with ethical obligations "the law makes duty the incentive," while the legislation of right "does not include the incentive of duty in the law and so admits of an incentive other than the idea of duty itself" (*RL* 6:218–19). So Kant holds that the incentive pertaining to the legislation of right is not a pure rational incentive, but rather consists in the incentives provided by external coercion through a public authority. It would apparently follow that duties of right cannot be (or rest on) categorical imperatives, and therefore cannot, properly speaking, be duties at all. The expression "duty of right" would contain a *contradictio in adjecto*. Derivationists appear to sweep this problem under the rug, claiming in effect that Kant cannot mean what he says, or at any rate that he need not accept what plainly follows from it. By contrast, I want to take this puzzle seriously, and will presently offer a solution to it.

Yet another objection to the derivationist position is that the principle of right does not even directly command us to do anything. It says: "Any action is right if it can coexist with everyone's freedom in accordance with a universal law, or if on its maxim the freedom of choice of each can coexist with everyone's freedom in accordance with a universal law" (*RL* 6:230). This does not tell us to perform actions that are right, or limit our actions to these, but only tells us which actions count as "right." If, as Kant says, there is in addition to the principle of right also a "law of right" commanding us to perform only actions that are right (*RL* 6:231), then Kant also says explicitly that this law "does not expect, much less demand, that I *myself should* limit my freedom to those conditions just for the sake of this obligation; instead, it says only that freedom *is* limited to those conditions in conformity with the idea of it and that it may also be limited through deeds (*tätlich*) by others; and it says this as a postulate that is incapable of further proof" (*RL* 6:231).

Another problem for the derivationist is that Kant also adds later that the principle of right is analytic, whereas the principle of ethics is synthetic (*TL* 6:396). It is far from clear how an analytic principle could need, or even admit of, derivation from a synthetic one. And further, if the principle of right is a "postulate incapable of further proof," then that too seems to preclude its being derived from the principle of morality. Concerning these claims about the analyticity of the principle of right and the concept of a postulate, Guyer has spent considerable effort, and deployed his typical skill and knowledge, in showing that they do not actually preclude the possibility that a proposition that is analytic (or can be considered analytic in one respect) could not also be derived from one that is synthetic, and also that a proposition that is considered a postulate incapable of further proof might not also in another respect admit of some sort of derivation (Guyer 2005a:203–17). I think he establishes these claims in the abstract, as possibilities allowed for by Kant's terminology, but he still falls well short of showing that these possibilities are actually realized in the case of the principle of ethics and the principle of right. I think in fact the principle of right is analytic because it simply analyzes the concept of right, a concept that is independent of the supreme principle of morality. And it is a postulate incapable of further proof because it is not derived from that principle, or from any other principle – but has its own independent foundation in the rational demands of free action.

Guyer admits that "strictly construed, the claim that Kant's universal principle of right is not derived from the Categorical Imperative,

Right and Ethics: A Critical Tribute to Paul Guyer 237

understood as the requirement to act only on principles that can serve as universal law, is correct." But Guyer immediately hastens to add: "However, any broader claim that the principle of right is not derived from the principle of morality, in the sense of the fundamental concept of morality, is surely implausible" (Guyer 2005a:201). This only makes me wonder what broader claim he has in mind, and whether I would be interested in making it. Guyer's writings on Kantian ethics do illuminate this, up to a point. For Guyer's position is that Kant's fundamental principle of morality is equivalent to "freedom," and consists in "the greatest possible use of freedom" (Guyer 2017). Apparently, he wants to claim that "freedom" is the content of the supreme principle of morality and takes those of us who deny derivationism to be denying that right is in any way derived from "freedom." But I find Guyer's talk of "freedom" murky and ambiguous. "Freedom" can mean many different things. Kant distinguishes freedom of the power of choice in a negative sense from freedom of the power of choice in a positive sense (*GMS* 4:447, *KpV* 5:33); both are distinct from the external freedom which is fundamental to the concept of right (*TP* 8:289–90, *RL* 6:237) as well as from "inner freedom" which is an important aspect of ethical virtue (*KpV* 5:161, *TL* 6:406–7). "Freedom" is not a single thing that admits of maximization. I would agree that right is based on freedom (*external* freedom), but that is a sense of "freedom" in which freedom is not an end or value and a sense that precludes any derivation of right from ethics.

Elsewhere, Guyer identifies the "freedom" he has in mind with the formula of humanity as end in itself, on the ground that "humanity" refers to the "*ability to set our own ends and the capacity to realize and successfully pursue them*" (Guyer 2005a:250). Guyer claims that Kantian ethics is based on the "greatest possible use of freedom," an idea he finds in Kant's lectures on ethics from the 1770s and early 1780s. I do find such maximizing talk still in the *Critique of Pure Reason*, in Kant's description of the idea of right as "the *greatest human freedom according to laws that permit the freedom of each to exist together with that of others*" (*KrV* A316/B373). Guyer concedes that such formulations are no longer to be found in Kant's mature (post-1784) ethical writings (Guyer 2017). He obviously attaches far less importance to this point than I do. For it seems to me that a concept of freedom that runs together both the external freedom to pursue our own ends (rather than to have our actions constrained to pursue the ends of others) and the capacity to realize our ends (in effect, the perfection of our talent to pursue these ends, and even the achievement of these

238   ALLEN WOOD

ends – our happiness, or parts of it) is a concept that has confused the
distinct foundations of right and ethics in Kant.

Guyer's "greatest possible freedom" is therefore a vague and indeterminate concept, broader than that which grounds either right or ethics,
properly considered. Ethics rests on ends, but right does not. Thus, to
accept a picture of Kant's supreme principle of morality that rests on
freedom as an end is to miss altogether the distinction between right and
ethics, and their foundations. A telltale sign that Guyer sees Kant's ethical
principle in this encompassing way that misses the distinction between
right and ethics is his claim that "duties of right are simply the coercively
enforceable subset of our duties to preserve humanity" – that is, of our
ethical duties (Guyer 2005a:201). This would seem to fit what Kant says in
the *Groundwork* about the duties corresponding to human rights (*GMS*
4:429–30). But there he is not considering them as coercively enforceable,
only as they are to be regarded from the standpoint of ethics and the inner
constraint of duty. In this passage Guyer also succumbs to the false idea,
correctly rejected by Ripstein, that Kantian right is just the application of
ethics to the conditions that make political life necessary.

We can begin to see the actual nature of Kant's concept of right, and the
problem of the distinction between right and ethics, only if we realize that
the "the coercively enforceable subset of our ethical duties" is for Kant the
empty set. *There are no directly ethical duties that are, or could ever rightfully
be, coercively enforced* (*RL* 6:220, 239). "Strict right, namely, that which is
not mingled with anything ethical, requires only external grounds for
determining choice... If [the concept of right] is to remain pure, the
consciousness [of duty as a ground for determining choice] may not and
cannot be appealed to as an incentive" (*RL* 6:232). Thus, if duties of right
were, as Guyer says, the coercively enforceable subset of our ethical duties,
then there could be no duties of right at all.

This, in my view, is the crucial point Kant already saw at the time of the
Naturrecht Feyerabend, but had not figured out how to accommodate,
consistently with a derivation of right from the principle of ethics.

> Right is nothing other than the law of the equality of action and reaction
> regarding freedom through which my freedom agrees with universal free-
> dom. If someone acts against this universal freedom and the other resists him
> then this resistor acts in conformity with universal freedom and thus right.
> So I have a right to coerce others to comply with right. All of the authors
> have failed to explain this. They have already included it in the definition but
> it is derived from it. – They said right is authorization to coerce, but they
> could not explain how right stands freely in relation to me. (*NF* 27:1335)

Kant himself, insofar as he proposes to derive right from the ethical principle, is one of the authors who have failed to explain how I can have a right to coerce others to comply with right. His immediate solution is to consider all duties ethical but only some of them duties of right:

> Ethics encompasses all duties but right not all. Right considers duties as coercive duties and in accordance with their legality and not in accordance with their morality. *Jus* relates merely to the matter of the action, ethics also to the form, the way in which they are done. In this way it has less than ethics. But on the other side it has more than ethics, namely coercion. This can be applied only to outer actions but not to dispositions as in ethics. (*NF* 27:1338)

But this will not work. For the point is that it is the mark of ethical duties that they rest *only* on an inner, ethical incentive, and cannot be made the object of external coercion. To coerce an ethical duty is always contrary to right, and even a violation of the ethical duty of respect for others. The problem can be solved, therefore, only by realizing that duties of right must have a foundation distinct from ethics, a foundation that carries with it a right to coerce their fulfillment. This is what Kant had come to see by the time he wrote the *Metaphysics of Morals*.

It is of course possible to fulfill duties of right from an ethical incentive. Ethical duties may be coerced, but in cases where coercion by the law or by civil authority fails to obtain, the agent can also fulfill them from ethical motives. Kant therefore says that "duties of right are therefore only indirectly ethical" (*RL* 6:221). No ethical duty as such could ever admit of rightful external enforcement. Coercing people to fulfill ethical duties is always contrary to right. Ethical duties are always grounded on ends: on the existent or self-sufficient end of humanity as end in itself, and on duties of virtue (the ends that are at the same time duties: our own perfection and the happiness of others). But duties of right are not grounded on ends. I think we will see that, as Guyer insists, they can be said to be grounded on *freedom*, but only on *external* freedom, not on freedom considered as an end or a value.

Kant's theory of right is based on a single, simple, powerful, and radical idea: External freedom – independence of the constraining choice of another (*RL* 6:237) – may be limited only when that limitation is required by external freedom itself, as a matter of formal consistency, i.e., according to universal law. The coercion of a rational being cannot be justified for any ethical duty, or for the sake of any end or value, not the highest good, not even for the sake of freedom itself, whenever "freedom" names an end or a value.

No end, however valuable, could ever justify coercing any rational being to promote it. For that end would then be the coercer's, not the end set by the rational being who is coerced. That would subject the coerced to the will of the coercer, violating the rightful external freedom of the one coerced. The coercer's end might, of course, also have *inner* authority for the person coerced, if it is also an end of morality. But no end of morality, however grand or fundamental, could ever override the right of an adult human being to choose those actions that serve the ends which *that* human being has set. This is equally true no matter what those ends are, and even whether the ends are moral or immoral. The coercion of one rational being by another, involving the substitution of the choice of the coercer for that of the one coerced in regard to the actions of the latter, can never be justified, according to the concept of right, by any end or value whatever, or by any ethical duty. Coercion on such a basis would always be wrong or unjust. This follows merely from the concept of right, of which the principle of right is an analysis (*RL* 6:230).

The crucial question – the only question truly about the foundation of right – is this: What could justify the coercion of a rational being? And we must begin by recognizing that for Kant, no moral law, ethical duty, or moral end, not my own perfection or the happiness of others, not humanity as end in itself, not even the highest good, could ever justify coercing a rational being to do anything. Kant seems to me to put the matter most clearly in the following passage:

> One can think of the relation of end to duty in two ways: One can begin with the end and seek out the *maxim* of actions in conformity with the duty or, on the other hand, one can begin with the maxim of actions in conformity with duty and seek out the end that is also a duty. – The *doctrine of right* takes the first way. What end anyone wants to set for his action is left to his free choice. The maxim of his action, however, is determined *a priori*, namely that the freedom of the agent could coexist with the freedom of every other in accordance with a universal law.
>
> But *ethics* takes the opposite way. It cannot begin with the ends that a human being may set himself and in accordance with them prescribe the maxims he is to adopt.... – Hence in ethics the *concept of duty* will lead to ends and will have to establish maxims with respect to ends we *ought* to set ourselves. (*TL* 6:382)

Ethics is both grounded on an end – the end of humanity as end in itself – and it also prescribes the ends we should inwardly constrain ourselves to set. Right, however, places no limit on the ends anyone may set. These may be moral or immoral, as we choose. Right constrains only the *external*

Right and Ethics: A Critical Tribute to Paul Guyer 241

actions we may take toward our ends; it does not do so on the basis of any end, but only on the formal conditions of external freedom – external freedom under universal law.

The basis of right lies in the rational structure of action. An action, by its concept, is something that lies within the power of a rational agent which it can choose as a means to an end it has set: "Rational nature discriminates itself from the rest in that it sets itself an end" (*GMS* 4:437). "That which serves the will as the objective ground of its self-determination is the end... By contrast, what contains merely the ground of the possibility of the action whose effect is the end is called the means" (*GMS* 4:427). Setting an end involves the rational demand to choose the means to it. Therefore, *independently of any end*, we rationally require, as far as is possible consistent with other demands of reason, the external freedom to choose our actions as means to ends *we* have set rather than ends *others* have set. This is a requirement every rational being as such implicitly makes, and must make, on all others; by the same reasoning, it is a requirement every rational being must equally acknowledge as made by others. The equality and mutuality of this requirement thus also determines the content of the qualification "consistent with other demands of reason," that sets the limit to the external freedom I may rationally demand of others, and the external freedom they may rationally demand of me.

The only way I could be completely free of all possible external constraint by the choice of another is if their choices were totally under the coercive power of mine. One person could have total external freedom only if all others with whom that person externally interacted had none. But reason demands that all equally should have external freedom, since by the concept of rational action itself, all equally require it of others. For all to be externally free, therefore, the freedom of all must be coercively restricted. Each of us must submit to external coercion to the extent that this is required for the same external freedom of all others. External freedom, insofar as it stands under this rationally necessary limitation, is what Kant means by the word "right." This limitation does not depend on any end or value: not even the value of "freedom" – when that word designates some value. It depends only on the formal rational requirements of free action itself, when the concept of external freedom is related to a plurality of free rational beings.

Now we can understand the meaning of the Universal Principle of Right, and why it is analytic: It does not command anything, but only explicates the concept of right (external freedom of all). The corresponding *command* would be "the law of right": "Perform only actions that are right." But about this law, as we have seen, Kant hastens to add: "[This law] does not expect, much less demand, that I myself should limit my freedom to those conditions just for the sake of this obligation; instead, it says only that freedom *is* limited to those conditions in conformity with the idea of it and that it may also be limited through deeds (*tätlich*) by others; and it says this as a postulate that is incapable of further proof" (*RL* 6:231). The possibility of "further proof" that is specifically and explicitly being denied here is precisely that of the derivation of the law of right from some ethical obligation, or from any of the ends associated with ethics.

Kant says: "There is only one innate right: Freedom (independence of the constraining choice of another), insofar as it can coexist with the freedom of every other in accordance with a universal law, is the only original right belonging to every human being by virtue of his humanity" (MS 6:237). It is tempting to understand this last phrase as saying that we have the innate right to freedom on account of the value or worth of humanity as end in itself, hence based on the moral law as the Formula of Humanity. But of course that involves reading something into the passage that is simply not there. "Humanity" in Kant's technical sense of the term (the same one used in the Formula of Humanity) is the capacity to set ends according to reason and to choose actions as means to them. We have seen that it is precisely this that is the basis of the rational requirement, independent of any particular end, that every rational being should be externally free, as far as is consistent with other demands of reason, to choose actions as means to ends that rational being has set, and not actions imposed coercively to serve the ends of others.

At times it seems as if Guyer wants to understand all of Kantian moral philosophy, both right and ethics, in terms of "freedom" regarded as a single collective end to be maximized, in the way that utilitarians want to maximize happiness. I doubt that freedom – any kind of freedom, but especially external freedom – admits of any standard of maximization. I doubt this equally in the case of happiness, but that is beside the point for now. One person's specific external freedom to do something always depends on the limitation of the external freedom of others in specific ways, since for Kant freedom means independence from constraint by others. (I've had students ask me if this means external freedom is a "zero sum game," but that's misleading too, since it presupposes that external freedom comes in quantities that can be traded off against one another.) To give me the freedom to do X is for you to be deprived of the freedom to interfere with my doing X. There is no measure of "freedom" that is common to all these instances of it, and instances of the deprivation of

Right and Ethics: A Critical Tribute to Paul Guyer 243

freedom. The question can never be how to increase the *total amount* of external freedom, because that is not even a coherent notion. It is always rather which freedoms are rightful and which are contrary to right. That question is never a matter of maximizing anything; it's a question of deciding which agents should be free from the constraint of which others to do which things.

Perhaps surprisingly, a number of things Guyer himself says suggest quite a different account from this maximizing one – in fact, they suggest something like the very account I am offering. He says, for instance, that "the principle of right is derived from the concept of freedom," and that "The proof of a principle of ethics must appeal beyond the concept of freedom itself to a necessary end of mankind, while the proof of a principle of right need demonstrate only that a relationship between persons is one that is consistent with the concept of freedom itself." Consistency, as I would understand it here, is that some external freedom of mine is consistent with the concept of freedom if there is no one whose freedom it subordinates to mine. The rightful freedom of each of us is that freedom whose protection involves only the limitation of the freedom of others that is necessary if we are all to enjoy *rightful* freedom. This formal mutual consistency is wholly distinct from the pursuit of any end or object of our actions, in particular those ends that ground our ethical duties. Guyer thus sums up: "We arrive at duties of right by considering merely the formal consistency of our use of freedom, while [by contrast] we arrive at ethical duties by considering ... the object, purposiveness or 'matter' of our actions" (Guyer 2005a:219). This gives a wholly correct account of the basis of right.

Such an account, however, could not possibly be derivationist. For the mere concept of external freedom, and the formal consistency of free actions with the external freedom of others, must be distinct from any end or value that might provide an ethical incentive. Guyer thus seems to me to misdescribe his own account when he says, a few pages further on, that principles of right are derived from "the fundamental moral concept of freedom," and hence from "the fundamental principle of morality" (Guyer 2005a:220). For the concept of freedom that pertains to the fundamental principle of morality necessarily involves "the necessary ends of mankind," while the concept of external freedom and its formal consistency, which grounds the principle of right, abstracts from all such ends.

I have just said, as Kant does, that right is independent of all ends. But right does *give rise* to certain ends: It grounds the setting of the end of establishing a condition of right, in which an external authority coercively limits actions to those that are right. It also grounds the end of perfecting an empirical condition of right to bring it closer to the idea of a condition of right. And right may also ground the various political ends set by officials of a state, insofar as these ends tend to the preservation and perfection of a condition of right. Also included here is every end that takes the form of seeking through coercion not to have some specific person interfere with some specific rightful action. These ends do obviously involve making freedom an end, and they are ends that follow from right. But these ends are *grounded* on right; they are not the *ground of* right. The role these ends play in the system of right does not involve right's being grounded freedom as an end, or grounded on any end whatever. We are required to seek the end of a rightful condition because right is binding on us as the rational demand of external freedom under universal law. This is a demand we make independently of any specific end. It is not the case, conversely, that right is binding on us because we are required to seek a condition of right, or the perfection of that condition, or freedom from some specific constraint on a rightful action – or, indeed, on any other end whatever that we might set.

Derivationists always eventually get around to citing the following passage:

> But why is the doctrine of morals [*Sittenlehre (Moral)*] called (especially in Cicero) a doctrine of *duties* and not also a doctrine of *rights*, even though rights have reference to duties? – The reason is this: we are acquainted with our own freedom (from which all moral laws, and so all rights as well as duties proceed) only through the *moral imperative*, which is a proposition commanding duty, from which the capacity for putting others under obligation, that is, the concept of a right, can afterwards be explicated. (*RL* 6:239)

Does this passage say that the legislation of right is grounded on that of ethics? No, it doesn't. Derivationists can think it does only by misunderstanding even the issue it is meant to address. Properly understood, this passage not only doesn't support derivationism but even shows precisely why derivationism has to be the wrong interpretation of Kant's theory of right.

What the passage says is that we *become acquainted with our freedom* from the moral imperative, and this acquaintance is the source of the *concept* of duty or obligation, from which the concept of *a right* is drawn, when it is *afterwards* (*nachher*) explicated through the concept of duty. "Afterwards" is the most important word in the passage for our present purposes. For it means: *after* pure or strict right has already been grounded independently of the concepts of duty or obligation. When, *after* pure or strict right has been grounded on the formal demands of external freedom alone, only *then* can the concept of a right be explicated through the concepts of duty and obligation.

> Strict right, namely, that which is not mingled with anything ethical, requires only external grounds for determining choice... If [the concept of right] is to remain pure, the consciousness [of duty as a ground for determining choice] may not and cannot be appealed to as an incentive. Thus when it is said that a creditor has a right to require his debtor to pay his debt, this does not mean that he can remind the debtor that his reason itself puts him under obligation to perform this; it means instead that coercion which constrains everyone to pay his debts can coexist with the freedom of everyone, including that of debtors, in accordance with universal law. (*RL* 6:232)

As we have just seen, determination of the will on grounds of duty is not strict (or pure) right at all. The passage always cited by the derivationists therefore merely helps to explain how strict right can *afterwards* borrow concepts not proper to right itself, to pure or strict right, but indigenous to ethics: the concepts of *duty* and of *a right* corresponding to duty. The passage, correctly understood, precludes derivationism as a possible account of Kant's theory of right.

A system of right depends on the use of coercion to protect the rightful freedom of others, and Kant claims that the authorization to coerce is contained analytically in the concept of right.

Guyer raises the pertinent question whether Kant can justify the claim that coercion is capable of protecting right, since this would seem to be a contingent empirical claim, and not something derivable from the mere explication of the concept of right (Guyer 2005a:224–5). I think Guyer has located a real problem for Kant here, and that some of Kant's views about justifiable coercion are beset with problems he never adequately addresses. But these problems are not really relevant here. Kant is fully aware that not every infringement of rightful freedom can be prevented by coercion: This is the basis of his treatment of the two species of *ius aequivoca*, the right of equity and the right of necessity (*RL* 6:234–6). Kant's claim is not that we can know *a priori* that *every* rightful external freedom is capable of protection through coercion, but rather we can be certain that no act of coercion can be justified *except* as part of a rightful condition (or to force others to join such a condition). This claim does not require Kant to investigate the empirical details, or causal connections, determining when coercion can protect rightful freedom and when it cannot.

Earlier we asked how, or whether, duties of right can be duties in the strict Kantian sense, that is, categorical imperatives. I think the answer is that strictly speaking they cannot. This was a point appreciated by Ebbinghaus and later by Willaschek. But there are two ways in which duties of right might nevertheless be brought under the concept of a categorical imperative. One way involves considering the duty of right not as a direct duty of right, but as an indirectly ethical duty. When we restrict our actions to what is right not on account of external coercion but from ethical incentives, we may consider these duties as indirectly ethical, and the imperative from which we fulfill them as categorical. The other way involves slightly expanding the concept of a categorical imperative, adapting it to the concept of right. Suppose we think of a categorical imperative not as one associated specifically with the ethical incentive of duty, but instead as any imperative that constrains not by some pre-given end but through an incentive that is directly connected to the constraining imperative itself. Then when the incentive provided by an externally coercive authority is the incentive for restricting our actions to those that are right, we may consider duties of right as categorical imperatives in relation to that coercive incentive. That is the only sense in which imperatives of right as such can be considered categorical imperatives.

This observation enables us to make another important point. To regard right as independent of ethics, and its incentive as rightful external coercion, is not to transform imperatives of right into hypothetical or pragmatic imperatives, as though the authority of right were being reduced to that of finding a means to be as happy as possible, or a means to promote whatever other discretionary ends one might, while living with its demands and threats. This may be how someone would view it who childishly misconceives the nature of rightful coercive authority, just as a superficial person might confuse the rational motive of ethical duty with a desire to avoid guilt feelings or comply with the demands of parental or religious socialization. The motive of duty is nothing like this, however. It is a rational response to the categorical command of reason. Likewise, the rightful authority of the law of a legitimate state is not based on contingent ends, or on hypothetical or pragmatic imperatives. It is simply the unconditional requirement, coercively enforced, that you limit your external freedom to the condition that it be consistent with a like freedom for all under universal law.

Right and Ethics: A Critical Tribute to Paul Guyer   247

Now I think we are in a position to see how we can be *unificationists*. That is, we can understand how right and ethics, though distinct legislations, having distinct and independent foundations, can have enough in common that they can be considered as two parts of a single whole: morals (*Sitten, Moral*). What right and ethics have in common, namely, is the concept of obligation, or "what obligation is: act upon a maxim that can hold as a universal law" (*RL* 6:225). Right is united with ethics insofar as it borrows from ethics the concept of duty, so that the external coercion of right can be represented to those subject to it as a legislation they are obligated, as well as compelled, to respect. In one way, of course, this goes beyond strict right, to which the notion of duty and obligation is not indigenous. But in another way it shows how right and ethics, even though they have distinct foundations, still have something in common. Ethics is grounded on ends that rational beings ought to set as a matter of universal law. Right is grounded on those limitations on external freedom to which all must be subject if everyone is to be externally free according to universal law. This is why Kant considers the Formula of Universal Law, when its application is limited to maxims involving external freedom (rather than maxims involving ends), as also a principle of right (*TP* 8:377).

I suspect that some Kantians become derivationists because they identify the supreme principle of morality with this merely formal requirement, which Kant introduces in his first formulation of the moral law in the *Groundwork*. So when they see that the principle of right demands acting on a maxim consistent with the external freedom of all according to universal law, they think this is merely an application of the moral law, in its first formulation, to questions of external freedom. But it is noteworthy that even in the *Groundwork*, Kant says that we have not entered properly into a metaphysics of morals until we advance to the *second formula* of the moral law, the one that locates the objective ground or motive of the moral law in humanity as *end in itself* (*GMS* 4:426–7). Ethics, as we have seen, is a matter of *ends*; and its supreme principle depends not only on the formal concept of obligation but also on the matter of the law, the end in itself. The same formal concept of obligation, the requirement of universal law, belongs to the principle of right, but it too is not complete apart from the concept of external freedom, which is the necessary requirement every rational being makes on others, limited only by that formal concept as a demand of reason. Universal validity is not a specifically ethical, or even a specifically practical requirement of reason. It is a criterion of all thinking, as Kant sometimes makes explicit. To think at all is to subject one's thought to the norm that its ground could be made the ground of thinking for anyone according to universal law (*WDO* 8:146n)

The derivationist error I have just described, confusing the law of ethics with the mere formal concept of obligation, or even the norm of reason in general, that appears equally, though in different ways, in all thinking, is not an error of which Guyer is guilty. For he insists that the foundation of Kant's system of duties is the end of humanity, and not merely the formal requirement of universal law (Guyer 2005a:250). Guyer has thereby correctly identified the rational foundation of *ethics*. He errs only in thinking that this is also the foundation of right. But right is independent of all ends, and therefore of ethics.

I have often thought that derivationists err not so much because they give the wrong answers to the questions they ask, as because they *do not ask the right questions*. The right questions are: What is the foundation of right? And how can we justify coercion of a rational being? These are quite different from the question: Why is there an ethical incentive for fulfilling duties of right? Which is in effect the question: Why are duties of right also indirectly ethical duties? Clearly some sort of derivation of this incentive from the supreme principle of morality would have to be involved in answering this last question. But it is not involved in justifying coercion or grounding right itself.

Other derivationists correctly note that a condition of right is, on Kant's view, a necessary condition for the culture of human reason and progress toward moral virtue, as well as a condition of the happiness merited by virtuous rational beings, and hence a condition for progress toward the highest good. They seem to think that the foundation of right must consist in the highest and grandest human end that right serves, and then they can't help noticing that this end is grounded on the principle of morality. But they thereby ask the wrong question and miss the foundation of right. The real question is neither of these. It is rather the question: How can the coercion of one rational being by another be justified? Because no ethical duties whatever could be rightfully enforced through coercion, no derivationist answer to this question could ever be correct. The objective goodness of an end, as Kant sees it, however magnificent the end may be, could never justify anyone in coercing another to promote that end.

Guyer seems to be looking in Kant for a single grand fundamental value or end, from which the whole of the metaphysics of morals might be derived. Guyer wants to say that this fundamental value is "freedom," in some grandiose, all-encompassing sense of the word. But we understand

Kant's theory of right better if we think small rather than big. The justification of coercion can have nothing to do with ethics, or ends, or values – not even with *freedom*, whatever we might mean by that profoundly ambiguous word, as long as it is taken to refer to an end or a valuable object. Instead, right is based solely on the formal consistency of external freedom according to universal law. That is wholly independent of ethics, in no sense derived from it.

CHAPTER 13

From Justice to Fairness: Does Kant's Doctrine of Right Imply a Theory of Distributive Justice?[1]

Michael Nance and Jeppe von Platz

1 Introduction

Kant's *Doctrine of Right* gives us a theory of property and argues that as a matter of public right the state has authority to tax to secure its preservation and to support "charitable or pious institutions" (*RL* 6:326), but Kant does not articulate or defend a theory of distributive justice.

The fact that Kant does not articulate a theory of distributive justice has not kept political philosophers from citing Kant as inspiration and support for whatever theory of distributive justice they favor[2] – including those who argue that the notion of distributive justice is itself mistaken.[3] This widespread reliance on Kant invites the question, "Does the *Doctrine of Right* imply a theory of distributive justice?"

To address this question, we discuss Paul Guyer's argument that Kant's *Doctrine of Right* implies, roughly, the principles of distributive justice as found in Rawls's justice as fairness. Guyer's argument is that Kant's theory of property implies a contractualist theory of distributive justice; in turn, this implies that the distribution of property rights must be fair, and that fairness is secured only by something like Rawls's second principle of justice.

---

[1] Earlier drafts of this chapter were presented and discussed at the conference "Nature and Freedom in Kant," Brown University, October 2013, and at a meeting of the DC/Baltimore Kant Workshop in July 2014. We are grateful for the feedback and criticism we received from audience members and workshop participants on these occasions. For her commentary at the Brown conference, we especially thank Marcy Latta. For editorial assistance, we thank Lauren McGillicuddy and Kate Moran. Lastly, we wish to express our gratitude to Paul Guyer for his generosity as a scholar, mentor, and friend.

[2] See, e.g., Rawls 1999:221–7, esp. 226–7; Lomasky 1987:99–100; Barry 1995:31 Tomasi 2012:96–8; Nagel 1991:chapter 5.

[3] Both Hayek and Nozick cite Kant as support even while rejecting that distributive justice is a legitimate political concern. For Hayek's statement of the view that distributive justice is mistaken, see Hayek 1960; for the tie to Kant, see Hayek 1960:160–77. For Nozick's claim that distributive justice is a mistake, see Nozick 1974:chapter 7; for references to Kant, see Nozick 1974:32 and 228.

From Justice to Fairness 251

We have doubts about each step in Guyer's argument. That is, we question whether Kant meant for his theory of property to imply a Rawlsian form of contractualism, whether Kant's contractualism implies fairness, and whether fairness implies the difference principle.

Regarding Kant's relation to contractualism, we hold that, although Kant clearly maintains *a conventionalist view* of property rights, the normative basis of his theory of the *Rechtstaat* contains both contractualist and non-contractualist elements. We argue that Kant's non-contractualist commitments in the *Doctrine of Right* pose problems for a reading of Kant's state of nature as a hypothetical choice situation analogous to Rawls's original position.

Next, we consider the steps of Guyer's argument that move from contractualism to fairness, and from fairness to the difference principle. Guyer's argument draws attention to the fact that the contractualist ideal can be read in two ways. First, the contractualist ideal typically states the requirement that the terms of society must be acceptable to every member of society and identifies the terms that satisfy this requirement. Second, and with greater originality, Guyer argues that on Kant's contractualist view, there are moral constraints on the terms it is permissible to offer other members. Guyer's insight is that one can approach a contractualist argument from two different directions: One can ask what terms are rationally *acceptable*, or one can ask what terms are morally *offerable*. We argue, however, that neither direction gets Guyer to the conclusion he draws. The first direction gets us a principle of mutual advantage, while the second direction gets us a principle of formal equality. Neither direction gets us to a criterion of fairness. Thus, the third step in the argument, from fairness to Rawls's difference principle, also fails.

The outcome is that *Kant's Doctrine of Right* is compatible with, but does not require, a number of principles of distributive justice – including those principles we find in Rawls's justice as fairness. Kant's *Doctrine of Right*, then, does not imply a single theory of distributive justice.[4]

In the next section, we present Guyer's argument. In Sections 3–5, we offer reasons to doubt the main moves in that argument. In Section 6,

---

[4] Thus, we agree with Mary Gregor's claim that "students of Kant will presumably be interested not only in interpreting the text but in trying to develop on the basis of it a theory of distributive justice in the sense of fairness in the distribution of goods and burdens. Kant himself is not concerned with this problem... His concern ... is not with the problem of what distribution of goods would be fair but with the more basic problem of how someone could acquire 'goods' of a certain kind..." (Gregor 1988:762).

252 MICHAEL NANCE AND JEPPE VON PLATZ

we offer some concluding reflections about the relation between liberty and distributive justice that are suggested by our discussion of Guyer's argument.

2 Guyer's Reading: From the Universal Principle of Right to the Difference Principle

Guyer argues that Kant's theory of property as developed in Private Right implies a principle of distributive justice along the lines of Rawls's difference principle.

From the Universal Principle of Right to Kant's Theory of Property

The universal principle of right states: "Any action is right if it can coexist with everyone's freedom in accordance with a universal law, or if on its maxim the freedom of choice of each can coexist with everyone's freedom in accordance with a universal law" (*RL* 6:230). A correlate of the universal principle of right is that every person has an innate right to "*Freedom* (independence from being constrained by another's choice), insofar as it can coexist with the freedom of every other in accordance with a universal law" (*RL* 6:237). The innate right to freedom is the only innate right. All other rights are acquired, meaning that they are established by an act (e.g., a crime or a contract) (*RL* 6:237). Acquired rights are of three kinds (*RL* 6:247–8; 6:259–60): rights to land and objects; rights to the performance of acts by other persons; and rights of authority that allow one person to command another in some respect.

The essence of a property right is a claim to exclusive possession of an object, so that all other persons are required to defer to the claimant's will in regard to said object.[5] Kant's account of the nature of property rights can be helpfully contrasted with that of Locke. Locke famously holds that one acquires a right to a thing by "mixing one's labor" with it. On Locke's view a property right is thus a direct relation between a person and an object.[6] Even if there were no other persons on earth, Locke's position implies that I could still acquire a right to own an object by mixing my labor with it. On Kant's alternative to Locke's account, a right to property is not a relation between the right-holder and the object, but a relation between the will of that person and the wills of all other persons with regard to that object (*RL* 6:260–1, 6:268). Property rights are thus a matter

---

[5] Guyer 2000b:2005a:256; 263.
[6] Guyer 2006b:269. For Locke's chapter on property, see Locke 1960:285–302.

From Justice to Fairness

253

of social convention; that is, of agreement between rational persons about who is entitled to what.

According to Kant, land and objects are originally held in common (*RL* 6:262). This raises the question of how one person can acquire rights of exclusive possession in these in a manner that is consistent with the equal freedom of others.

Guyer finds Kant's ultimate solution to this puzzle of rightful acquisition in the self-same ontology of property that gave rise to the problem.[7] If a claim to exclusive possession could meet with the rational agreement of all those limited by it, then the implied limitation on their freedom is consistent with their will, and so consistent with their freedom. Thus, a unilateral provisional claim to property can be rightful so long as it is such that others could rationally agree to it. Kant holds that such an original acquisition is "provisionally rightful" (*RL* 6:257). An acquisition is conclusively rightful only in the civil condition (*RL* 6:257, 6:264).

Thus, according to Guyer, a property right *factually consists* in the agreement of others to defer to the authority of the owner. As Guyer writes, "a property right consists in a relation *among* wills, *regarding* an object, namely the consent of all those persons who *could* control and use an object that *one* among them *can*" (Guyer 2005b:263). Moreover, a property right *normatively depends* on the possible agreement of other persons. For Guyer, just as the original acquisition of a provisional property right is valid only if others could rationally agree to it, so the origination of property rights in a civil state requires the possible consent of all to those rights (or to the system of rules that defines and maintains those rights). In a slogan, the conclusion that Guyer draws from Kant's account of property in Private Right is that "the ontology of property [that property consists in a relation between wills of persons with regard to an object] demands its morality [that property rights could be agreed to by all affected]" (Guyer 2000e:281).

Since Kant holds that we must have property rights (by the postulate of practical reason with regard to rights, *RL* 6:250), and since (both normatively and factually) we can have these conclusively only in a rightful civil condition, we have a moral obligation to create and maintain a civil condition (a state).[8] The state both keeps track of the distribution of property rights (the state as recorder of deeds), and offers assurance that

---

[7] See especially Guyer 2000b and Guyer 2005a.   [8] Cf. *RL*, sections 42 and 44.

254   MICHAEL NANCE AND JEPPE VON PLATZ

all have sufficient incentives to respect the property rights of others (the state as sheriff).[9]

So far, Guyer's reading has taken us from the moral law to the conclusion that property rights require the possibility of agreement by all those affected by them, both for their normative validity and for their factual efficacy. And Guyer has shown how this conclusion, together with certain facts about human nature and the human condition, entails that we must form a civil condition with the institutions sufficient to secure the innate and acquired (property) rights of all.

At this point, Guyer has not identified the principle of distributive justice that ought to guide the design and activities of the state with respect to property and related economic institutions. The next three steps in Guyer's argument are meant to identify the sort of principle of distributive justice that Kant's doctrine of right implies.

From Kant's Theory of Property to Contractualism

According to Guyer, property rights normatively require that all affected by them could agree to them or to the system of rules and institutions that sustain them. Agreement can be either forced or free (Guyer 2000b:238). Since "unprovoked threat or use of force ... would violate the innate right to freedom ... of anyone on whom it was exercised" (Guyer 2000b:249), the right to property can "be grounded only in the freely and rationally given consent of those whose deference is needed."[10] While it is permissible to use force to create the needed assurance that property rights will be respected, the agreement required by the normative dimension of property rights cannot be forced; Guyer concludes that "for any system of property rights to be morally acceptable, all affected by that system must be able to freely consent to it" (Guyer 2006b:270).

Since we have a duty of right to create a system of public right that institutes, tracks, and secures property rights, it follows that we have a duty to create a system of public right that could be freely agreed to by all those affected by it.

---

[9] Cf. Guyer 2005a:239–40. Kant defines "state" at *RL* 6:313.

[10] Guyer 2005b:249. In "Life, Liberty, and Property," Guyer specifies that coercion to ensure agreement on a claim to property right could not "be justified in the only way that coercion can be justified, as a hindrance to a hindrance to freedom" (Guyer 2000e:281).

Thus, Kant's doctrine of right and theory of property imply three claims: 1) we are morally required to create and maintain a state that defines and secures for all a system of property rights; 2) this system of property rights must be constituted so that all affected could freely agree to it; thus, 3) we are morally required to create and maintain a state where the distribution of property rights could be freely agreed to by all.

It follows that Kant's theory of right and property together imply a contractualist approach to distributive justice: "on Kant's view, property cannot exist at all except by means of agreement, so a social contract or proviso of distributive justice cannot be merely added to already existing property rights; it is inherent in the very idea of rightful or morally acceptable property" (Guyer 2006b:271).

From Contractualism to Fairness

Guyer's next move is to assert that a system of property rights can be freely agreed to by all only if it is fair to all: "a reasonable person will consent to a system of property rights only if he sees it as sufficiently *fair*... So, if a *rightful* system of property must be consistent with the universality of external freedom, and reasonable persons would only freely consent to a system of property that meets some minimal standard of fairness, then a rightful system of property must meet some such standard" (Guyer 2005b:264).

From Fairness to the Difference Principle

Guyer suggests that the minimal standard of fairness is the one articulated by Rawls's difference principle: "Rawls's difference principle is a plausible interpretation of the conditions under which it would be morally permissible to demand the agreement of others to a system of property and rational for them to consent to it" (Guyer 2000e:281). Depending on the specifics of the contract situation (like relative bargaining power, knowledge, and interests of the consenting parties), it might be rational to consent to principles other than the difference principle, but Guyer suggests that even if it might be rational to consent to other principles, other principles do not satisfy the moral requirements on what persons can demand that others consent to (and so cannot be permissibly offered as terms of distributive justice): "even if the difference principle does not follow from pragmatic considerations alone, it could be argued to follow from the moral constraints on demanding the consent of others to one's property claims" (Guyer 2000e:281).

Guyer thus concludes that "Kant is committed to the conclusion that there can be external or public legislation enforcing the right to property, but only under conditions of equality like those defined by Rawls's second principle of justice" (Guyer 2000e:281). Since we must have a system of public legislation enforcing the right to property, it follows that Kant's theory of justice not only permits but *requires* that we implement Rawls's second principle of justice (or something close to it) (Guyer 2000e:266).

3 From Conventionalism to Contractualism?

In this section, we argue that Kant's Doctrine of Right involves significant non-contractualist normative commitments, and that these non-contractualist elements of Kant's view pose problems for Guyer's Rawlsian contractualist reading of the *Doctrine of Right*.

As we have seen, Guyer argues that property rights require the agreement of others both normatively and factually: normatively, because a property right limits the freedom of others and so is impermissible by the universal principle of right unless it can meet with their agreement; factually, because to have a property right implies that other persons actually tend to defer to one's will with respect to the object as a matter of social convention. If most others do not uphold the convention, then one does not actually have a right. So Guyer's interpretation combines a conventionalist factual account of property with a contractualist normative account.

It is tempting to think that in the case of property rights, conventionalism *implies* contractualism. After all, if property rights are a matter of tacit or explicit agreement among persons (that is, if property rights are conventions), it is quite natural to suppose that the moral justification for the convention of property must be explained in terms of the fairness or rationality of the persons' agreement. That is, it is natural to suppose that the moral status of a convention must be analyzed in contractualist terms. Guyer himself seems to invite such a view when he writes that "the ontology of property demands its morality" (Guyer 2000e:281).

However, there is no necessary connection between conventionalism as a factual or ontological account of property rights and contractualism as a normative account of property rights. Consider Hume's theory of property. Like Kant, Hume holds that there are no natural rights to property in the Lockean sense. Instead, property rights are simply a matter of human

From Justice to Fairness

convention or custom.[11] And Hume holds that our property conventions are morally justified. But Hume's account of the normative justification of the convention of property is decidedly non-contractualist. Hume argues that the convention of property is justified because of its beneficial consequences for human societies, not because of any agreement, whether tacit, actual, or rationally possible.[12] Thus, Hume's account of property illustrates that conventionalism about property does not imply contractualism about property.

Of course, Guyer does not think that conventionalism by itself implies contractualism. Guyer's contractualism instead arises from the conjunction of conventionalism with Guyer's contractualist analysis of Kant's theory of external freedom. On Guyer's argument, consent to the institution of property is either forced or free, and since the use of force is permissible only when it hinders a hindrance to freedom, force cannot permissibly be used to secure consent to a system of property rights. Thus, property rights require the free and rational consent of those whose freedom is limited by them.

This argument is too quick. The second premise of Guyer's argument assumes that forcing someone to give her consent to a system of property rights cannot itself be a hindrance to a hindrance to freedom. But in the *Doctrine of Right*, Kant argues that we can force others to enter into a civil condition with us, even against their will, because to remain in the state of nature is wrong (*RL* 6:256, 6:257, 6:307–8). Remaining in the state of nature is wrong because it hinders the secure and universally consistent use of external freedom. Therefore, we have a duty of right to give our consent to the institution of a civil condition, which establishes a system of property rights.[13] Thus, forcing someone to consent to a scheme of property rights can be justified as a hindrance to a hindrance to freedom, for withholding consent to such a scheme can itself be a hindrance to the exercise of external freedom.[14]

---

[11] See Hume 1998:93–4.

[12] For the positive thesis that the rules of justice are morally justified by their consequences, see *Enquiry* pp. 83–9. For the negative thesis, that justice does not depend on a social contract, see Hume 1985:465–87.

[13] The civil condition, for Kant, is equivalent to a society governed by the united general will. Thus, we could also say that we have a duty of right to consent to the authority of the united general will.

[14] Kant's theory of right thus does not rely solely on hypothetically rational consent for its normative foundation. It also relies on *normative consent*: consent that we *ought* to give. Cf. David Estlund's notion of normative consent, Estlund 2008:10 and chapter VII. If Kant's theory of right relies on normative consent, then some of the normative work is accomplished, not by the social contract itself, but by the prior duty to give one's consent.

This outcome is important, for three reasons. First, it contradicts a key premise of Guyer's argument: that we cannot rightfully force others to give their consent to the establishment of a property regime. Second, it points to an important non-contractualist source of normativity in Kant's theory of private right: the duty to exit the state of nature, which Kant derives from non-contractualist premises.[15]

Third, it points to a fundamental disanalogy between Rawls's original position and Kant's state of nature. For Rawls, there is no duty to reach an agreement in the original position, and no authorization to coerce others to agree. Kant's state of nature, by contrast, exhibits both of these features: There is a duty of right to form a civil state with others, and there is an authorization to coerce others to join with one in forming such a state. Guyer's move from conventionalism to (Rawlsian) contractualism, in other words, is complicated by Kant's endorsement of a prior, coercively enforceable, non-contractualist duty to exit the state of nature and form a civil state. Guyer's contractualist reading does not sufficiently take account of the hybrid character of Kant's view of the normative foundations of the *Rechtstaat*, which involves both contractualist and non-contractualist elements.

Guyer might reply to our argument by granting that, on Kant's view, others may be coerced into joining or respecting a system of property rights, but insisting that one can coerce others only if that system of property rights is *rightful*. And the rightfulness of a system of property rights, Guyer could argue, depends on whether the system is such that free and rational persons *could* consent to it. If and only if the system of property rights is rightful in this sense – if hypothetical free and rational persons could or would accept it – does the system of property rights uphold the external freedom of all. Only in such a system can actual persons legitimately be coerced into compliance.[16]

This response raises the question, to which we return in the next section, of the legitimacy conditions for a rightful Kantian system of property rights. We agree that, for Kant, not just any system of property rights counts as rightful, and that individuals in Kant's state of nature may not rightfully force others to join them in establishing a non-rightful civil condition (which would not really be a civil condition at all). But we

---

[15] Cf. Kersting 1983 and Varden 2008.
[16] Cf. Guyer 2006b: "... we have the responsibility even prior to or in the absence of a well-functioning state to make only property claims that could be fairly enforced against others and to coerce them only into a state that would maintain a fair system of property rights."

From Justice to Fairness 259

disagree that, for Kant, the relevant legitimacy condition is that a scheme of property rights must meet the high threshold of Rawls's second principle of justice. Individuals in Kant's state of nature may rightfully coerce others to enter into less egalitarian regimes of property rights, and those who refuse to consent to such regimes do wrong. We make the case for these claims in the following two sections.

4 From Contractualism to Fairness?

After arguing for a contractualist reading of Kant's theory of property, Guyer's next step is to maintain that free consent can be expected only where the terms of agreement are fair to all parties and that Kant's theory of justice, therefore, implies that the distribution of property rights must be fair to all. Although we have cast doubt on the idea that, for Kant, a legitimate state can be based only on unforced consent, we grant that assumption for the sake of argument in this section and the next. We then argue that even on this assumption, Kant's theory of property does not imply a Rawlsian conception of distributive justice.

It would be somewhat surprising if Kant's universal principle of right together with a few facts about human nature and the human condition implied a principle of distributive fairness. Guyer's argument is that, on Kantian premises, liberty implies equality, so that one "cannot subsume the right to property under a principle of liberty akin to Rawls's first principle of justice without also acknowledging something very much like Rawls's second principle" (Guyer 2000e:282). This move is controversial, and not one that Rawls would endorse. With regard to the apparent conflict between liberty and equality, Rawls rejects that either can be derived from the other; rather, liberty (the basic liberties) and equality (of opportunity and the difference principle) together present the basic terms of cooperation appropriate for a democratic society.

Moreover, it is notable that Rawls did not argue from contractualism to fairness, but from fairness to contractualism. Rawls's idea is that if we conceive of society as a system of social cooperation between free and equal persons, then we must find a way to fairly distribute the benefits and burdens among the cooperators. He then moves from the need for principles that secure distributive fairness to contractualism as the way to identify these principles.

Of course, Guyer's aim is not to discuss Rawls, so Guyer could shrug off these worries as insignificant: The point remains that free consent can be expected only to fair terms. But is that true? It seems there are many

260   MICHAEL NANCE AND JEPPE VON PLATZ

examples of free (and informed) consent to unfair terms. When the indigent consent to harsh terms of employment, is that not free consent to unfair terms?

Guyer might reply that such consent is not free, since the circumstances force the choice. But then it seems that Guyer relies on concepts of coercion and freedom different from those found in Kant. For Kant, coercion is a relation between persons and the freedom that is the subject of the universal principle of right is freedom from those limitations persons impose on each other.[17] So, if someone cannot meet her needs due to misfortune, and she therefore consents to unfair terms of cooperation with others, then we cannot by Kant's concept of freedom say that her consent is not free or that she was forced to consent to these terms. No person forced her, and her consent is based on the benefits agreement brings and so is rational. She freely and rationally consented to terms that are unfair insofar as they exploit her situation. And that, of course, is partly the point of Rawls's original position: Free consent is indicative of fairness only if the parties are situated as equals and ignorant of facts that they might use to offer terms that favor those they represent.

So, it is not the case that people cannot freely and rationally consent to unfair terms of agreement. Any free and rational agreement must in some sense benefit all the agreeing parties, but not all mutually advantageous agreements are fair.

How about the other direction of Guyer's argument – the direction that appeals to what it is morally permissible to offer as terms of agreement, rather than what terms others can freely consent to? If we follow this direction, Guyer's argument is: (i) the system of property must be structured in accordance with terms to which all could freely agree; (ii) it is morally impermissible to offer unfair terms of agreement; so (iii) the system of property must be structured in accordance with terms that are fair to all.

---

[17] As Kant puts it, external freedom involves being *sui iuris*, being "one's own master" (*RL* 6:238). Furthermore, in his statement of the innate right to freedom, Kant glosses freedom as "independence from being constrained by another's choice," which makes clear that external freedom is about relations between persons (*RL* 6:237). Our reading of Kant's notion of being *sui iuris* focuses on an ideal of freedom as non-interference, not on a more demanding notion of freedom as non-domination. It could be argued that being *sui iuris* requires a background of relative economic equality to eliminate arbitrary power relations among private citizens, but that argument would go beyond anything suggested in Kant's text. Kant seems to hold that formal equality, and perhaps certain basic rights to one's "most necessary natural needs" (*RL* 6:326), are sufficient to establish one's status as *sui iuris*.

From Justice to Fairness 261

The problem with this argument is that when Kant discusses the moral restrictions on the terms that we can offer others, the restriction he identifies is not fairness, but consistency or reciprocity:

> When I declare (by word or deed), I will that something external is to be mine, I thereby declare that everyone else is under obligation to refrain from using that object of my choice... This claim involves, however, acknowledging that I in turn am under obligation to every other to refrain from using what is externally his; for the obligation here arises from a universal rule having to do with external rightful relations... the universality, and with it the reciprocity, of obligation arises from a universal rule. (*RL* 6:255)

What Kant says here is that a claim to property rights must acknowledge the equal entitlement of others to claim property rights. This consistency requirement does not, however, entail anything about the *content* of the rights of others.

The requirement of consistency can be elaborated in terms of the equality that Kant frequently says is one of the three defining properties of republican citizenship (the other two are freedom and independence).[18] This is "equality as a subject" and it means that, with the exception of the head of state, "Each member of a commonwealth has coercive rights against every other" (*TP* 8:291). Kant makes clear that this formal equality of citizenship "is quite consistent with the greatest inequality in terms of the quantity and degree of their possessions ... and in rights generally (of which there can be many) relatively to others" (*TP* 8:292). The equality in question, in other words, is an equal right to have rights and to have one's rights enforced. Citizens cannot claim a right to have rights that others could not have, and no person "can rightfully bind another to something without also being subject to a law by which he in turn *can* be bound in the same way by the other."[19]

The equality that Kant affirms thus turns out to have little to do with Rawlsian equality or a principle of substantive fairness, but is instead a formal equality which means that (apart from the head of state) there can be no distinctions between citizens when it comes to the right to have rights and to have one's rights protected by the state: "all are equal to one another as subjects; for, no one of them can coerce any other except through public law ... no one can lose this authorization to coerce (and so to have a right against others) except by his own crime" (*TP* 8:292).

---

[18] Compare *ZeF* 8:349–50; *TP* 290–4; *RL* 6:314.
[19] *ZeF* 8:350n, likewise in *RL*: no person has a "superior with the moral capacity to bind him as a matter of right in a way that he could not in turn bind the other" (*RL* 6:314).

262   MICHAEL NANCE AND JEPPE VON PLATZ

Thus, though Guyer is correct that Kant thinks that there are moral restrictions on the terms of agreement we could offer others, and that these restrictions imply a standard for the system of property we should institute in a civil condition, the requirement that Kant affirms is not one of fairness, but one of formal equality. This requirement rules out a scenario where some are formally excluded from ownership rights, but the requirement does not get us to an egalitarian (or prioritarian) principle of distributive justice.

Guyer's distinction between the two directions that a contractualist argument can take is important. And, in fact, we have shown that this is a substantive distinction, producing different requirements of distributive justice based on which direction we follow. If we follow the direction of what terms persons can freely and rationally agree to, we get a principle of mutual advantage. If we follow the direction of what terms persons can permissibly offer as terms of free agreement, we get a principle of formal equality. Yet neither of the directions gets us to a principle of fairness.

5 From Fairness to the Difference Principle

The final step in Guyer's argument aims to show that only the difference principle (or something like it) satisfies the requirement of fairness.

Guyer does not offer much of an argument that the difference principle is required by the principles of Kant's theory of justice. He again suggests that the argument would proceed from the moral requirements on what terms of agreement one can offer others as terms of society, rather than relying on what those agreeing to the terms could freely consent to. But, as we have already indicated, it is not clear why it is impermissible to offer any other terms of agreement than the difference principle. Guyer acknowledges that his argument here is incomplete:

> [E]ven if the difference principle does not follow from pragmatic considerations alone, it could be argued to follow from the moral constraints on demanding the consent of others to one's property claims. I do not attempt to pursue this issue further. Let us just stipulate that Kant has established in a general way that one can neither reasonably expect nor reasonably demand to establish a property right of one's own without the consent of others, and that they will give that consent only if they see the system of property rights thereby implied as in their own best interest as well. In other words, one has a right to property as an exercise of one's own freedom, but only under the condition that one is willing to concede an analogous right to property to others. (Guyer 2000e:282)

From Justice to Fairness   263

This is an interesting passage. In addition to admitting that his argument is incomplete, Guyer here returns to the argumentative strategy of asking what terms persons could freely consent to (not what terms they could permissibly offer), and then states the two principles of distributive justice that we have suggested are implied by the sort of contractualism that Guyer finds in Kant, namely, the principle that the system of property rights must be in the interest of all, and, second, the principle of formal equality.[20]

Moreover, a closer look at Guyer's interpretation as it is expounded across various writings reveals that he finds support for multiple principles of distributive justice that could be freely consented to or permissibly offered by all in Kant's writings.

The first principle is the minimal principle of formal equality of access to rights. This criterion is grounded in a claim of reciprocity: Those claiming property rights must be willing to grant the same rights to others who satisfy the relevant and non-discriminatory legal criteria.[21] This principle is consistent with any number of distributions of benefits and burdens, even distributions where some are worse off than they would be without the system of property rights or distributions where they have less than they need to sustain a decent existence.

The second principle is that the system of property rights must be to the benefit of all: "it will be in our interest to agree freely to a property claim when the system of property rights within which such a claim is being made promises all of the participants in it some reasonable level of access to its benefits."[22] The term "benefit" is relative, but at least every person must be better off with the system of property rights than they would be without it. The most straightforward interpretation of this requirement is that the system of property must make everyone better off than they would be in the state of nature.

Guyer suggests a third principle of distributive justice: the sufficientarian principle that all persons must have at least enough resources to lead a decent life: "the right to an opportunity to property sufficient to maintain existence or an equivalent that can produce the same result provides a minimum standard for the rational acceptability of any system of property

---

[20] As we discuss, there is an ambiguity in Guyer's claim that one must extend to others an "analogous right" to property. "Analogous" could be construed materially or formally. We have argued that Kant is concerned with formally equal rights, not with materially equal rights.

[21] Guyer 2000e:282.

[22] Guyer 2000b:239. Likewise: "the system of property rights must work for the benefit of all" (2006b:271).

rights, where the rational acceptability of such a system is in turn a necessary condition of its morality."[23]

A fourth principle that Guyer suggests is that the system of property rights works better than any realistic alternative in securing the ends of those affected by it: "any system of property rights . . . must . . . [be seen as] at least working better than any realistic alternative" (Guyer 2006b:270). It is not immediately clear how we should interpret this principle (best by what standard?). But a reasonable interpretation would be that no person's interests can be sacrificed to better satisfy the interests of others.[24] An alternative interpretation yields a tempered utilitarianism (maximizing aggregate preference satisfaction combined with a guaranteed minimum sufficient for decent living), though Guyer does not himself suggest this interpretation.

Finally, we reach the principle that Guyer argues is required by Kant's doctrine of right: the principle that the system should be designed to maximize the position of the least well off. It seems plausible that this principle could be freely agreed to by all, and that it could be permissibly offered as terms of agreement. This shows that the principle is compatible with the contractualism that Guyer finds in Kant, but not that it is required by it.

Are any of these principles required by Guyer's Kantian contractualism? It depends on the direction of the question: Are we asking what people could freely consent to or what terms people could reasonably (morally) ask others to consent to?

If we ask the first question, what people could freely and rationally consent to, it seems that people could freely consent to any principle that makes them better off. Thus, the second of the principles we listed, the principle that all must be better off with the system of property than they would be in a state of nature, is required.

If we ask the second question, what terms people can morally offer as terms of agreement, it seems clear that on Kant's view reciprocity demands formal equality, so that the system must provide an equal right to have property rights (but not rights to equal property).

---

[23] Guyer 2000b:254. Kant provides support for a sufficientarian reading in his discussion of redistributive taxation, *RL* 6:325–6; though it should be noted that 1) this passage is from Public Right, not Private Right, and 2) Kant does not allude to the property theory he developed in Private Right to support his argument for redistribution.

[24] Perhaps that is what Guyer means when he writes that "a system of property rights can be freely agreed to by rational beings only if it is equitable to some suitable degree."

From Justice to Fairness 265

None of the other principles are required – no matter the direction of the argument. The other principles are all principles that persons could freely consent to if the alternative is a state of nature (no stable system of property). Conversely, we do not see any Kantian reasons why offering the other principles as terms of agreement is morally prohibited.

6 Conclusion: Liberty and Distributive Justice

One consequence of our argument is that the Doctrine of Right does not single out any principle or set of principles as *required* for distributive justice.

In Section 3, we cast doubt on Guyer's Rawlsian interpretation of Kant's state of nature. But even granting that part of Guyer's argument, we argued in Sections 4–5 that Guyer's interpretation does not establish that Rawls's difference principle is required by Kant's Doctrine of Right. Leaving aside the question of whether Guyer's interpretation is faithful to Kant's text, we showed that it does establish two minimal requirements that any system of property rights must satisfy. First, if, as Guyer argues, a system of property rights must be one to which all could freely and rationally consent, then everyone must be better off in that system than they would be without any system (i.e., in a state of nature). Second, if the system of property rights must be one that all could permissibly offer others as terms of agreement, then the system must respect formal equality, so that all affected by it have the same rights of access to property rights.

If these are the only two requirements of distributive justice that follow from Guyer's interpretation of Kant (no matter the direction of the contractualist argument), then Guyer's reading of the Doctrine of Right is compatible with a number of principles of distributive justice. Many principles satisfy these two requirements, and many principles that do not satisfy them could be conjoined to them. Thus, sufficientarianism, tempered utilitarianism, varieties of egalitarianism where all are better off than in the state of nature, and the difference principle are all compatible with Guyer's Kant.[25]

That Guyer's view is compatible with a number of principles of distributive justice does not mean that it is toothless. The two distributive

---

[25] Furthermore, although Kant himself develops his property theory as a theory of specifically *private* property, nothing in Kant's view seems to us to rule out the possibility of social ownership (socialism). Since modern socialism did not develop until the nineteenth century, it is no surprise that Kant does not address this possibility.

requirements that follow from Guyer's reading rule out varieties of pure consequentialism, since, first, pure consequentialism might leave some worse off than they would be in a state of nature if necessary to maximize the good, and, second, pure consequentialism allows only a conditional commitment to formal equality. Guyer's Kantian contractualism also seems to rule out varieties of Nozickean libertarianism, meaning theories of distributive justice that (i) reject the very notion of a system of public property rights apart from the natural rights that persons have independently of the state; and, therefore, (ii) permit any distribution of property rights that actually results from free transactions (or if all past wrongdoings have been corrected). Nozickean schemes therefore (iii) deny that a system of property rights can be measured by whether it benefits those affected by it. So, though Nozickean libertarianism accepts formal equality, Kant would reject it because (i) it relies on a mistaken theory of property, (ii) it has a mistaken view of the state (rejecting the idea that the state must be governed by a general will rather than the sum of unilateral and bilateral wills), and (iii) it rejects that the justice of a system can be measured by whether those affected by it benefit or not, and so does not require that all are better off than they would be in the state of nature.

All of these remarks have referred to the consequences of Kant's view for distributive justice *on Guyer's reading*. But since we disagree with one of the premises of Guyer's interpretation – that on Kant's view consent to a property scheme cannot be forced – there is still a question about the implications of Kant's view for distributive justice *on our reading*. As discussed in Section 4, we accept that a notion of reciprocity is at the core of Kant's idea of a civil condition, and therefore accept that Kant's view entails formal equality – each person must have an equal right to have property rights. However, things are murkier regarding the first consequence of Guyer's interpretation – that a system of property rights must, for Kant, be to the advantage of all. The case for this requirement that we discussed in Section 4 depends on Guyer's assumption that people must freely accept the terms of social cooperation. But this is precisely the assumption that we called into question in Section 3. Can our reading provide a separate Kantian route to this seemingly quite plausible conclusion?

We have suggested that, for Kant, consent to a scheme of property rights need not be free for the reasons we offered in Section 3, but it still must be rational. And the requirement of mutual advantage can be regarded as following from the nature of a rational agreement – a rational

From Justice to Fairness

agreement must be in the interest of each party. This suggestion finds some support in Kant's texts. The basis for the duty to exit the state of nature is the postulate of practical reason with regard to rights, which holds that objects must be useable in the interest of human freedom. And it is plausible that all will be better off within a regime of property rights that allows for the stable use of objects than they would be within the state of nature, for a regime of enforceable property rights and contracts makes possible new modes of economic production and cooperation.[26] Thus the rational agreement to exit the state of nature can be expected to be mutually advantageous.

On Guyer's interpretation and on our own, then, two requirements governing distributive justice follow from Kant's Doctrine of Right: the requirement of formal equality, and the requirement of mutual advantage. Neither requirement individually, nor the conjunction of the two requirements, entails a specific conception of distributive justice.

Finally, we draw attention to two ways that the conclusion that Kant's theory of justice is compatible with a number of principles of distributive justice. This is an interesting, non-trivial conclusion.

First, since many have argued that Kant supports their particular theory of distributive justice – Rawls, Nozick, and others mention Kant's moral philosophy as a source of their theories (and anti-theories) of distributive justice – it is remarkable that Kant's theory of justice actually leaves distributive justice underdetermined. Since we agree with Guyer that Kant meant his theory of justice to be implied by (and to be the only one implied by) his moral philosophy, we have reason to doubt those who argue that Kant's moral or political philosophy implies their favored theory of distributive justice.

Second, Kant's political philosophy works from a single and widely accepted principle of equal liberty: the principle that, from the perspective of justice, every person is and ought to be at liberty to decide what to do for themselves, as long as what they do is consistent with the equal liberty of others. Kant's theory of justice unfolds from this basic principle, the correlative innate right to freedom, and a few facts about human nature

---

[26] Kant also suggests at *RL* 6:326 some rudiments of a welfare state that would ensure that all citizens have their "most necessary natural needs" met, which again suggests that all will be better off within the civil state than they would be without it.

and the human condition. Many political philosophies accept Kant's basic principle and the facts he works with. If our argument is correct, attempts to derive a theory of distributive justice simply from the principle of equal liberty and the facts that Kant works with fail and will continue to fail, since these Kantian materials do not decide the question.

Postscript
Nature and Freedom in Kant's Practical Philosophy
Paul Guyer

1 Bridging the Gulf

In 1790, Kant stated that a third *Critique* was necessary in order to bridge the "incalculable gulf fixed between the domain of the concept of nature, as the sensible, and the domain of the concept of freedom, as the supersensible," for although no transition from the former to the latter is possible "by means of the theoretical use of reason," nevertheless the latter, the supersensible domain of freedom, "*should* have an influence on the former, namely the concept of reason should make the end that is imposed by its law real in the sensible world" (*KU* 5:176). Since his announcement of the doctrine of transcendental idealism in the inaugural dissertation of 1770, Kant had held that we could have no theoretical insight into the nature of the "supersensible," that is, objects beyond the reach of our senses, thus no *knowledge* about how any things are in themselves beyond our assurance of the fact that something affects us with the representations that we synthesize into our experience of our empirical selves moving through an empirical world in space and time, that is, the realm of appearance. But he had also held since the publication of the first edition of the *Critique of Pure Reason* in 1781 that we can form rational *beliefs* about the supersensible on practical rather than theoretical grounds, and moreover that on practical grounds we are led "inexorably" to the idea of "the purposive unity of all things that constitute this great whole, in accordance with universal laws of nature," that is, to the idea of a *natural* world that nevertheless "must be represented as having arisen out of an idea if it is to be in agreement with that use of reason without which we would hold ourselves unworthy of reason, namely the moral use. . ."

> All research into nature is thereby directed toward the form of a system of ends, and becomes, in its fullest extension, physico-theology. This, however, since it arises from moral order as a unity which is grounded in the essence of freedom and not contingently founded through external

commands, brings the purposiveness of nature down to grounds that must be inseparably connected *a priori* to the inner possibility of things, and thereby leads to a *transcendental theology* that takes the ideal of the highest ontological perfection as a principle of systematic unity, which connects all things in accordance with universal and necessary laws of nature, since they all have their origin in the absolute necessity of a single original being. (*KrV* A815–16/B843–4)

Already in 1781, then, Kant had maintained that practical reason requires us to conceive of the world of nature as grounded "in the absolute necessity of a single original being" whose purpose is the realization of a morally perfect world in nature and who has determined the laws of nature so that such a world can be realized, or so that the "purposive unity" of a morally perfect world can be realized in the "great whole" of nature "in accordance with universal laws of nature." Since we humans are to be moral agents, presumably we are not to be mere pawns in this realization, moved around by the will of God rather than by our own. Rather, Kant's idea must be that the realization of the moral ideal in the natural world is to come about *through* our efforts as moral agents, freely obeying the moral law that we impose upon ourselves but at the same time acting in accordance with natural laws. It is, of course, transcendental idealism that allows him to maintain this position: We can be free as we are in ourselves yet determined by laws of nature in the realm of appearance.

The gulf between the domains of nature and freedom would thus seem to have been bridged in the first *Critique*, so the question naturally arises, why is this question raised again in the third *Critique*, and what does the third add to Kant's previous position? The *Critique of the Power of Judgment* is divided into two parts, the critiques of the aesthetic and teleological powers of judgment. The first adds to what Kant had previously argued primarily the claims, in the field of empirical moral psychology, that fine art especially can make moral ideas vivid to us and that aesthetic experience in general can be conducive to moral conduct. The critique of teleological judgment adds above all the argument that it is not only morality that requires us to conceive of the natural world as a purposive unity grounded in a necessary being outside of that world but also our attempt to comprehend "organized beings," that is, organisms: This is the argument that we can only comprehend the "internal purposiveness" of organisms but also the "external purposiveness" of the natural world as a whole to the thought of which our experience of the former naturally leads us as the product of an extramundane designer, although we must also recognize that this is only a "regulative" ideal grounded in

Nature and Freedom in Kant's Practical Philosophy

"reflective" rather than "determinant" judgment. But I will argue here that the third *Critique* does not represent a fundamental change in Kant's overall conception of the relation between our freedom and our nature: Throughout the critical decade, he holds that there is a gulf between these two realms, yet throughout the decade he also holds that it can be bridged in a variety of ways.

In this postscript I will review the chief bridges between the domains of freedom and nature that Kant had already thrown over the gulf between them within his moral philosophy (although I use "already" tendentiously, as I will allow myself to refer to the *Metaphysics of Morals* and *Religion within the Bounds of Mere Nature*, which were both published after 1790, as well as to the *Groundwork for the Metaphysics of Morals* and the *Critique of Practical Reason*, which were published before, and the lectures on ethics, which were not published by Kant at all.) I have three bridges in mind. First, although Kant might make it seem as if morality requires of us only a good will, something that might be regarded as an entirely internal intention and that could, given Kant's metaphysics, be regarded as an act of the noumenal will – "intelligible character," as Kant calls it in the first *Critique* (e.g., A551/B579) – the specific duties morality requires of us are duties to act as embodied beings in the physical world. In particular, the *freedom to set our own ends* that must be preserved and promoted by morality (e.g., *GMS* 4:430) cannot be regarded as something entirely mental that is unaffected by our possibilities for external action, but is interdependent with the latter. Second, although once again the decision to act morally, or to make the moral law one's fundamental maxim (*RGV* 6:35–6), might seem to be something entirely internal and noumenal, Kant makes it clear that not only must such a decision be reflected in an agent's actions in nature and even in the laws of nature, but also that an agent's implementation of her moral will is affected by external and natural conditions. And third, although Kant initially describes the "moral world" as something that can be fully realized only in the noumenal realm, he ultimately makes it clear in his conception of the "complete object" of morality, the highest good, that the moral world must in fact be realized in the natural world.

I have discussed all of these issues in previous papers. Here I want to integrate my previous arguments into a systematic interpretation of Kant's bridge from freedom to nature. The conclusion to be drawn from this review is that although there are important developments in Kant's conception of the relation between freedom and nature from the beginning of the 1780s into the 1790s, above all in his commitment to the postulate of

272 PAUL GUYER

the immortality of the human soul, bridging the gulf between freedom and nature is by no means a new project of the third *Critique*, but what Kant had been attempting to do throughout the critical philosophy.

2 Setting and Pursuing Ends

In at least one passage, Kant suggests that the most fundamental formulation of the categorical imperative, because it is the "ground" of the others (*GMS* 4:428), is the Formula of Humanity as an End in Itself, the imperative "So act that you use humanity, whether in your own person or in the person of any other, always as an end, never merely as a means" (*GMS* 4:429). Since he subsequently defines humanity as the "capacity to set oneself an end – any end whatsoever" (*TL* 6:392), this entails that the fundamental requirement of morality is to treat the capacity to set ends, whether in one's own person or in the person of any other, always as an end, never merely as a means. Since setting an end is an exercise of freedom, *choosing* to try to satisfy a desire rather than simply being *acted upon* by a desire, this in turn means that the fundamental principle of morality is to treat freedom, whether in oneself or in any other, always as an end and never merely as a means. In other words, freedom itself is to be preserved and promoted, not treated as a mere means to some other end or good. Kant's formulation in the *Groundwork* is therefore equivalent to his statement in his lectures on ethics, formulated without his technical conception of humanity in order to be accessible to his teen-aged students, that freedom "has to be restricted, not, though, by other properties and faculties, but by itself," so that "the greatest use of freedom," its use "consistent with itself," is the "highest *principium* of life," the "*principium* of all duties," and the "essential ends of mankind" (*Collins* 27:346). Of course, the requirement to always treat freedom as an end, in oneself and in all others, means that in the end one cannot use one's own humanity to set any end whatsoever, after all – consistent with this principle one can set only those ends that are compatible with one's own continued freedom to set ends and with the freedom of all others to set their own ends, subject to the same condition. But the crucial point is that it is only the status of humanity as an end in itself that sets limits on everyone's use of their own humanity, not anything else.

Now it might seem as if setting an end and thus exercising one's humanity is an entirely internal and in Kant's metaphysics therefore noumenal or intelligible action, not an action that takes place in the phenomenal world and can be impinged upon by external conditions.

Nature and Freedom in Kant's Practical Philosophy   273

But a little reflection shows that cannot be the case. If my setting one end can impinge upon my own future freedom to set other ends or on the freedom of others to set their own ends, it can only be because my act of following through on my setting an end now – by acting, in time, and with my body – can impinge upon my capacity to set ends later, and because my setting an end now – again, that is, acting to realize it, in time, and with my body – can impinge upon someone else's freedom to set ends, now or later. A few examples will make this clear. If I make it my end to commit suicide now – and successfully carry out this end – that will destroy my freedom to set ends later, for what would have otherwise been the rest of my life. If I make it my end now to make a false promise to you, and act upon this end, that will compromise your ability to make your own reasonable choice of ends later. If I make it my end to get drunk now, and do so, that will compromise my ability to set my own ends freely and rationally for some hours to come, and if I further choose to drive I might get into an accident that will temporarily impair or permanently destroy my further freedom to set my own ends or that of someone else. One person's choice of ends can impair or undermine her own further ability to set ends or that of others only because setting ends does not take place entirely within an internal bubble of intention, but naturally has consequences in the physical world of moving bodies. And even if we distinguish between setting an end and acting so as to realize it, considering the former internal and only the latter external, the latter will impinge upon my own future freedom even to set ends or that of others.

These obvious cases are in fact all cases of perfect duties of omission, duties to refrain from various kinds of actions injurious to oneself or others that are in fact injurious to the humanity or freedom of self or others. Imperfect duties of commission toward self and others require a subtler analysis. Kant describes these in the *Groundwork* as the duties to develop one's own capacities, "since they serve [one] and are given to him for all sorts of possible purposes" (*GMS* 4:423), and the duty to contribute to the happiness of others by trying, "as far as [one] can, to further the ends of others" (*GMS* 4:430), the latter on the ground that a will that rejected the maxim that people should assist each other in cases of need "would conflict with itself" since it "would rob [the agent] himself of all hope of the assistance he wishes for himself" (*GMS* 4:423). In the *Metaphysics of Morals*, these two kinds of duty are named the "ends that are also duties" to promote "one's own perfection" and "the happiness of others" (*TL* 6:386–7), and each is treated as a genus under which several more specific duties are subsumed. The duty of self-perfection includes the duty to

274 PAUL GUYER

perfect one's moral capacities, including conscience and self-knowledge (sections 13–14) as well as one's natural bodily and intellectual capacities, "powers of spirit, mind, and body" (section 19, 6:444), and the duty to promote the happiness of others is divided into the duties of "love" and "respect," the former comprising "beneficence, gratitude, and sympathy" (section 29, 6:452) and the latter requiring the avoidance of "arrogance, defamation, and ridicule" (section 42, 6:365). The latter are really perfect duties not to injure the dignity of others rather than imperfect duties to promote their happiness, and are presumably included among the duties of virtue because they are not suitable for coercive, juridical enforcement and are therefore not to be included among the duties of right. And the duty to self to perfect the moral capacities of conscience and self-knowledge also seems like a special case, a sort of meta-duty to perfect one's capacity to recognize one's other duties rather than a first-order duty to perfect capacities necessary for the achievement of "all sorts of ends" as the duty to self was originally described in the *Groundwork*.

These cases aside, it might seem natural to think that the duties to develop one's own natural abilities and to assist others in the realization of their ends are necessary in order to facilitate the *realization* of the ends that oneself and others have freely set, and that if duties to be so grounded are to be considered *part* of the duty to treat humanity as an end, that must be because humanity is the two-part ability to set *and effectively pursue* ends. But Kant never defines humanity this way. And there is a way to understand the duty to treat humanity as the capacity just to set ends, or as the freedom to set ends, which does not require this amplification. In the *Groundwork*'s account of *hypothetical* imperatives, Kant treats it as a general canon of practical reason, not a canon of specifically pure practical or moral reason, that to will the *end* is also to will the (or a sufficient) *means* to that end: "Whoever wills the end also wills (insofar as reason has decisive influence on his actions) the indispensably necessary means to it that are within his power" (*GMS* 4:417). But such a premise allows for both *modus ponens* and *modus tollens* inferences. That is, it entails that if you will some end and there is some sufficient means to it available to you, then you should (*ceteris paribus*) rationally will that means; but it also entails that if you *would* will some end but there is no sufficient means to it available to you, *then you cannot rationally will that end after all*. As the canon of rationality on which both such kinds of inference depend is entirely general, it does not itself specify what could make means unavailable: Means to a proposed end might be naturally unavailable to you, physically impossible or emotionally unpalatable, or they might be morally

Nature and Freedom in Kant's Practical Philosophy

unavailable to you, something you are not morally willing to do even though it might be the only means to an end that you regard as morally permissible or maybe even, other things being equal, morally mandatory (except in such a case, other things are not equal). But whatever the reason, if you cannot will the means, you cannot rationally will the end. And that in turn means that if you have *voluntarily* made possible means to an end unavailable, for example you have voluntarily chosen not to cultivate a physical or mental capacity that if developed could have allowed you to achieve some end of your own or assist another to achieve some end of hers, or if you have *voluntarily* refused to help another achieve some end when you could have done so, then you have *voluntarily* compromised the freedom of yourself or another to *set that end* rationally. That is to say, you have minimized rather than maximized the freedom of yourself or another.

So the failure to provide means compromises the freedom to set ends, and the ability to pursue ends effectively does not have to be treated as a separate component of humanity. Even if humanity is defined just as the freedom to set ends, failure to develop necessary means to (morally) possible ends directly limits the freedom to set ends, the range of ends that oneself or others can rationally set, and thereby is a failure to treat humanity as an end in itself. Kant does not spell this out, nor does he spell out the further point that such a failure is presumably motivated by some non-moral desire or inclination, in which case one's omission can be seen as a means to gratifying that desire or inclination and as treating one's humanity as a mere means to that gratification rather than as an end in itself. Likewise, refusal to help another when one could is presumably motivated by the choice to gratify some non-moral desire or inclination of one's own, and can be counted as treating the other, including her own capacity to set ends, as a mere means to one's own gratification. So the voluntary failure to develop one's own talents and to render assistance to others can be understood as treating humanity merely as a means rather than an end.

The general point here is that setting ends cannot be regarded as a purely mental act that can go on unrestricted by external, natural conditions. Rather, one's capacity to set ends rationally is either restricted or enhanced by one's natural condition, though that itself reflects one's prior choices at least in part – of course, one's abilities and therefore the extent of one's freedom to set ends rationally can also be affected by many factors other than one's own choices, such as accidents of birth, the choices of others, and so on. The duties of self-perfection and the promotion of the happiness of others are, as Kant himself makes clear, always duties to promote these ends as far as is possible – for example, one must try, but must *only* try, "as far as he can, to further the ends of others" (*GMS* 4:430). This only clarifies that the act of setting ends does not take place in some purely mental space, but in the natural world, and in this regard there is already a bridge between the domain of freedom and the domain of nature.

The interrelation of the two domains is evident in Kant's fullest explication of our duties in the *Metaphysics of Morals* and the lectures on ethics. First, the argument of the former is that although the fundamental principle of morality is entirely *a priori* and valid for all rational beings, what kinds of duties that principle entails for us human beings depends upon the natural conditions of our existence, that we are embodied creatures inhabiting the surface of a terraqueous sphere. That we have bodies that depend on other bodies, both non-human and human, for their continued existence and efficacy, and that as embodied creatures we need cultivation and education, are the natural facts that determine that we can fulfill the fundamental principle of morality only through the duties of right and duties of virtue that Kant enumerates. The duties of right are the subset of our perfect duties to others that are properly coercively enforceable, and they arise from the fact that as embodied beings with the kinds of bodies that we have we need access to the produce of the earth and the seas. That is why we must collectively regulate access to the land and sea, in the form of property rights, and more generally collectively determine and enforce the conditions under which we can use the bodies and goods of others for our own purposes. If we did not have bodies that can interact with and impinge upon those of others, and if this interaction did not take place on a naturally undivided surface any point of which can be reached from any other, we would not have duties of right, or at least not the specific duties that we have. Similarly, the duties of virtue also depend upon the natural facts of our embodiment as the conditions under which our agency can be exercised. As we have seen, our duties of virtue fall under the two great headings of the duties of self-perfection and of the promotion of happiness of others. If we were not the kinds of creatures whose mental and physical capabilities can be weakened by the neglect or abuse of our bodies, for example by gluttony and drunkenness, we would not have the negative duties to self that we do have, and if our mental and physical capabilities did not develop only gradually and with effort, we would not have the positive duties of self-cultivation and -education that we do have. Likewise, if our personal abilities and resources were not so limited that we predictably need the assistance of others to realize our ends, and even to fulfill our duties to ourselves, such as the duty to educate

Nature and Freedom in Kant's Practical Philosophy 277

ourselves, then we would not have the duties of love or of mutual assistance. Again, if the natural circumstances of our existence were different, we might have different duties of virtue, but not the ones we do have. Kant's entire doctrine of duties presupposes that we exercise our freedom in the domain of nature.

I have just mentioned Kant's contrast between duties of right and duties of virtue. The latter should actually be subsumed under a broader class, that of ethical duties, because in addition to the specific duties of self-perfection and promotion of the happiness of others, our non-juridically enforceable duties also include the general duty to act out of respect for the moral law and to develop virtue as the "fortitude" or strength of will to do so (*TL* 6:380). That it needs effort to act out of respect for the moral law and that we must develop the strength of will to do so are facts about us as natural rather than purely rational beings. According to transcendental idealism, it is within our power to choose to act in accordance with the moral law at any time, even if this involves overcoming a standing disposition to evil and even a prior choice to subordinate acting on the moral law to acting out of self-love – this is the argument of Part One of Kant's *Religion within the Boundaries of Mere Reason* (see especially *RGV* 6:35–7). But according to Kant's "moral anthropology," the noumenal decision to be moral has to be implemented through the natural or "subjective conditions that hinder people or help them in *fulfilling* the laws of a metaphysics of morals" (*TL* 6:217). Kant expands upon this point in the Introduction to the Doctrine of Virtue in the *Metaphysics of Morals*. Here he argues that there are "natural predispositions of the mind (*praedispositio*) for being affected by the concept of duty . . . which every human being has, and it is by virtue of them that he can be put under obligation" (*TL* 6:399). It cannot be considered a duty to *have* or *acquire* these dispositions from scratch, because without them we cannot try to fulfill duty at all – here is a place at which Kant tacitly appeals to the premise that "ought implies can." But it is our duty to *cultivate* and *strengthen* these "natural predispositions," because it is part of our nature that these dispositions, like our other capabilities, are initially present only as it were in germ and need to be cultivated in order to be efficacious when we need them to be so.

Kant's further explication of this claim emphasizes the natural character of these predispositions. For what he argues is that "Every determination of choice proceeds *from the representation of a possible action to* the deed through the feeling of pleasure or displeasure, taking an interest in the action" (*TL* 6:399). That we proceed from the determination of the will to

278   PAUL GUYER

action through a feeling of pleasure is a fact about us as natural beings, not as purely rational beings. Kant then details four kinds of morally efficacious feelings of pleasure or displeasure that we human beings have. The first is "moral feeling" in general, which is "consciousness of obligation" in general, presumably pleasure at the thought of doing what is morally required and pain at the thought of violating duty, although Kant does not make this explicit (*TL* 6:399–400). The second is "conscience," which Kant defines as "practical reason holding the human being's duty before him for his acquittal or condemnation in every case that comes under a law" (Section 12b, 6:400). This does not seem like a kind of feeling at all, but perhaps Kant is assuming that acquittal must feel pleasant and condemnation painful. To keep conscience from collapsing into moral feeling in general, perhaps we should also assume that Kant means here what he elsewhere classifies as *conscientia consequens*, "judging" conscience, that is, "the examination of past actions," which may include the "twinge of remorse" in the case of an immoral action but presumably also a feeling of pleasure in the case of a moral action, rather than *conscientia antecedens*, "examining" conscience, which considers whether a proposed action would be right or wrong (*Vigil* 27:615; the feeling of pleasure at a past action of one's own that is both morally correct and done out of respect for the moral law could be what Kant calls "contentment," *Zufriedenheit*, at *KpV*, 5:118). Either way, the difference between conscience and mere understanding seems to be that while the latter concerns only a "general proposition," the former "is addressed to a *factum*," that is, a particular action proposed in particular circumstances, but also that while understanding may be considered apart from our natural condition, conscience reflects the fact that it is our nature to accompany our judgments of morality or immorality with feelings. Finally, Kant introduces two more specific "natural predispositions," the love of others (later recast as "sympathetic" feeling) and self-esteem, which are presumably meant to be proximate causes for actions fulfilling our duties of virtue to others and self respectively. And Kant's claim about all of these is that, first, they are part of the mechanism by means of which morally requisite action, even if required by a fundamental maxim chosen by the noumenal will, is effected in the phenomenal world, and, second, that given our nature in the phenomenal world, they must be cultivated and strengthened by various techniques, just as our other mental as well as bodily capabilities must be. In a word, Kant's moral anthropology presupposes that we are moral agents acting in a natural world. He assumes a bridge between the domains of nature and freedom throughout this moral anthropology.

3 Noumenal and Phenomenal Freedom

The brief allusion in the previous paragraph to Kant's theory of noumenal choice and its phenomenal effect needs to be more fully discussed. For Kant, the category of causality, defined as succession in accordance with a rule (*KrV*, A144/B183, A202/B247), is dependent upon time as our transcendentally ideal form of intuition and thus not applicable to things as they are in themselves. Yet from the outset of the argument for transcendental idealism he assumes that the mind is "affected with" sensible intuitions by something other than itself, even though the argument will conclude that we cannot characterize the affecting thing in spatio-temporal terms. There seems to be a blatant contradiction between these two claims. Moreover, if the first is true, it seems to create a gulf between the domains of freedom and nature that must indeed be unbridgeable: The idea of free decisions in the noumenal world causing actions in the phenomenal world would seem incoherent. However, although there has been a longstanding debate about the intelligibility of "noumenal causation," the solution to this problem is easy: What Kant should have included in the table of *categories*, as the correlate to the logical function of hypothetical judgment, is the general concept of *ground and consequence*, and he should have included the *temporal* category of causation as succession in accordance with a rule only on the table of *schemata*, which is supposed to consist of temporal correlates to the categories that allow them to be applied to our (spatio-)temporal intuitions (*KrV*, A138–9/B177–8). This move, required by Kant's own most fundamental principles, would have allowed him to speak coherently of the noumenal will as *grounding* phenomenal action without calling that causation, and of course without allowing that we can have *knowledge* of such noumenal grounding except on *practical* grounds and insofar as required for practical purposes (*KrV*, Bxxix-xxx).

In any case, throughout the 1780s, thus prior to the third *Critique*, Kant argued that we are entitled to consider the noumenal determination of the will as the ground of our actions in the phenomenal world, and that this is the condition of the possibility of and our responsibility for acting in accordance with the moral law. In the Third Antinomy of the *Critique of Pure Reason*, Kant argues that the apparent contradiction between the thesis that "Causality in accordance with laws of nature is not the only one from which all the appearances of the world can be derived" and the antithesis that "There is no freedom, but everything in the world happens solely in accordance with laws of nature" (*KrV*, A444–5/B472–3) can be

PAUL GUYER

resolved by the possibility that "empirical causality itself, without the least interruption of its connection with natural causes, could nevertheless be an effect of a causality that is not empirical, but rather intelligible, i.e., an original action of a cause in regard to appearances, which to that extent is not appearance" but outside the series of appearances (*KrV*, A544/B572). In such passages, Kant continues to bedevil his argument by speaking of noumenal *causality*, but we can save him from himself by translating into terms of noumenal *grounding*. In the first instance, this possibility makes room for a conception of God as the ground of the entire series of appearances that is itself outside that series, but it also makes room for a conception of human will as intelligible and outside the series of the appearances of a person's actions but that is nevertheless the ground of that action. The human will considered as noumenon would then be the ground of the human's actions without being the *subsequent effect of any antecedent cause*. Kant characterizes the noumenal will of an agent as its "intelligible character" and considers this the ground of its "empirical character," its characteristic pattern of conduct in the phenomenal world. Of course, Kant insists that we have only the "general concept" of intelligible character, not actual cognition of it, but nevertheless he takes this to make room for human freedom:

> But in its intelligible character (even though we can have nothing more than merely the general concept of it), this subject would nevertheless have to be declared free of all influences of sensibility and determination by appearances; and since, in it, insofar as it is a *noumenon*, nothing *happens*, thus no alteration requiring a dynamical time-determination is encountered in its actions, this active being would to this extent be free of all the natural necessity present solely in the world of sense. Of it one would say quite correctly that it begins its effects in the sensible world *from itself*, without its action beginning *in it* itself; and this would hold without allowing effects in the world of sense to begin from themselves, because in this world they are always determined beforehand by empirical conditions in the preceding time, but only by means of the empirical character (which is a mere appearance of the intelligible character)... (*KrV*, A541/B569)

Kant presents all this as a conceptual possibility rather than as theoretical cognition, thus he is content in the first *Critique* to "stop at this point and assume [that] it is at least possible that reason does actually have causality in regard to appearances" (*KrV*, A548–9/B577–8) (once again speaking of noumenal causality when he should say noumenal grounding).

Apart from the problem of how this possibility might be transformed into knowledge, Kant's resolution of the Third Antinomy raises the

Nature and Freedom in Kant's Practical Philosophy

problem of how the noumenal efficacy of individual human wills could be compatible with the status of God as the noumenal ground of the entire phenomenal world – the age-old theological problem of the compatibility of the freedom of the human will with divine omnipotence. Kant makes little attempt to solve this problem in any of his published works, although he discusses it in his lectures on metaphysics and philosophical theology. But Kant does devote much effort in the *Groundwork* and the *Critique of Practical Reason* to transforming the conceptual possibility of human noumenal freedom into a kind of cognition on practical grounds, what he calls in his unsubmitted drafts from the early 1790s for an essay on the *Real Progress of Metaphysics in Germany since the Times of Leibniz and Wolff* "practico-dogmatic" knowledge. In the *Groundwork*, Kant argues that a being that conceives of itself as free must also conceive of itself as subject to the moral law, but in order not to merely assume that we are actually subject to the moral law we must prove that we are actually free (*GMS* 4:447–50). He then argues that the application of the distinction between appearance and thing in itself, which even "the commonest understanding can make" (!), to the self, entails that "the human being cannot claim to cognize what he is in himself through the cognizance he has by mere inner sensation" (*GMS* 4:451), which is subject to temporality and therefore to determinism, but also is what makes it possible that "a human being really finds in himself a capacity by which he distinguishes from all other things, even from himself insofar as he is affected by objects, and that is *reason*," which is in turn "pure self-activity." Thus Kant claims that our cognition of our own reason also gives us cognition of our freedom "*as intelligence*" or as a "being belonging to the intelligible world," with which "*autonomy*" and with that the "the universal principle of morality" is "inseparably combined" (*GMS* 4:452). Kant does not explain how we have knowledge of the "self-activity" of reason as noumenal, as opposed to the mere form of reason, which could apply to anything, but he seems confident that we do. And this bridges the gulf between noumenal and the phenomenal, or the domains of freedom and nature.

That the Kant of the *Groundwork* does not see any problem about bridging the gulf between freedom and nature through the noumenal will's determination of the action of the phenomenal self is also demonstrated by what seems a perverse twist in its argument. The identification of the noumenal reality that is the ground of our phenomenal reality with pure, self-active reason and the latter with autonomy, governed by the moral law, would seem to imply that our noumenal will must be fully moral and that our phenomenal will must fully reflect that. There would seem to be no room for freely willed but immoral action on this account. But no sooner has Kant concluded his argument that "the world of understanding contains the ground of the world of sense and so too of its law" (*GMS* 4:453), which would seem to imply that the laws of the world of sense must be consistent with those of the world of understanding (here meaning reason), than he introduces the idea of a possible *conflict* between the laws of the sensible and intelligible worlds, or of nature and freedom. This is the centerpiece of his answer to the question "How is a Categorical Imperative Possible?" (*GMS* 4:453), which is clearly intended to be his explanation of how the transcendental idealist argument for our obligation under the moral law just completed in Section III of the *Groundwork* answers the question originally raised in Section II (*GMS* 4:419–20). Yet this explanation seems to undercut the argument just given because instead of describing the moral law as the *ground* of the laws of sensible nature, it describes the moral law as a categorical imperative for us precisely because of the possibility of a *conflict* between the law of a pure rational will and the laws of our actual sensible wills:

> And so categorical imperatives are possible by this: that the idea of freedom makes me a member of an intelligible world and consequently, if I were only this, all my actions *would* always be in conformity with the autonomy of the will; but since at the same time I intuit myself as a member of the world of sense, they *ought* to be in conformity with it; and this *categorical* ought represents a synthetic proposition *a priori*, since to my will affected by sensible desires there is added the idea of the same will but belonging to the world of understanding – a will pure and practical of itself, which contains the supreme condition, in accordance with reason, of the former will... (*GMS* 4:454)

On this account, the moral law becomes an ideal or norm to which the human being subject to the law of nature *should* and *can* aspire, but it is not the real, underlying *causal law* of the human being who appears in the sensible world. The moral law presents itself to such a being precisely because he *should* but *does not necessarily* act in conformity with it. Nevertheless, the fact that Kant takes it that the sensible human being *can* act in accordance with the moral law shows that he does not believe the gulf between the law of freedom and the laws of nature to be unbridgeable; he just does not believe that this gulf is *necessarily* or automatically bridged.

In 1788, Johann August Heinrich Ulrich would press against Kant the objection that leaps out from these final pages of the *Groundwork*, namely that if the moral law were really the causal law of the noumenal will there would be no possibility of immoral action. One might think that Kant's

Critique of Practical Reason, also published in 1788 but not any part of Kant's original critical program, was motivated by the need to resolve this issue and rebut Ulrich's objection. However, the second *Critique* was completed by the end of 1787, thus before Kant could have seen Ulrich's work, to which he did not in fact reply until 1792, when he published the essay on radical evil that would become Part One of *Religion within the Boundaries of Mere Reason* in 1793. Instead, the second *Critique* seems to have been motivated by several other concerns, the first of which is apparently doubt about the argument of the *first* half of Section III of the *Groundwork*, that is, the argument that we can infer that the moral law is truly binding upon us from our insight into the self-activity of reason and thus into our freedom. Kant now argues that "the moral law cannot be proved by any deduction" (*KpV* 5:47) and that consciousness of it must be considered "a fact of reason because one cannot ferret it out from any antecedent data of reason" (*KpV* 5:31), but that instead the reality of our freedom may be inferred from the fact of our obligation under the moral law: "something different and quite paradoxical takes the place of this vainly sought deduction of the moral principle, namely that the moral principle conversely itself serves as the principle of the deduction of ... the faculty of freedom" (*KpV* 5:47). Now, it has seemed to many that this deduction of freedom from the moral law proceeds by means of the intermediate premise that "ought implies can," for Kant's *empirical confirmation* of his inference turns on the claim that one "judges ... that he can do something because he is aware that he ought to do it" (*KpV* 5:30), and Kant repeats this sort of formulation more than half-a-dozen times in the first two parts of the *Religion*. An inference to freedom via "ought implies can" would have the advantage of avoiding the Ulrich problem, even if that problem has not been explicitly raised, for the simple reason that while "ought" implies "can," "can" does not imply "does." However, Kant's fundamental argument for freedom in the second *Critique* does not actually avoid the problem, because this argument is that our consciousness of the *necessity* of the moral law implies the existence of *pure* reason, and that "The concept of a pure will arises from" our consciousness of our pure reason, just as our "consciousness of a pure understanding arises from" our awareness of the "pure theoretical principles" and to their "setting aside of all empirical conditions" (*KpV* 5:30). This argument depends on an assumption of identity or at least immediate connection between pure practical reason, as the source of moral law, and pure will, which does raise what would become the Ulrich problem again: If the pure will and pure practical reason are identical, and if we really do have a pure

284 PAUL GUYER

will, then how could we ever will contrary to what the moral law requires? The *Critique of Practical Reason* has no more answer to this question than does the *Groundwork*.

Nevertheless, the second *Critique* does assume throughout that the pure or noumenal will, whether or not it could freely will anything immoral, is the ground of all of an agent's phenomenal choices and actions, and thus that there is no unbridgeable gulf between the domains of freedom and nature. Although Kant does not repeat the first *Critique*'s terminology of "intelligible" and "empirical" character, he explicitly refers to that work in the "Critical Elucidation of the Analytic of Pure Practical Reason," where he states that "one must recall what was said in the *Critique of Pure Reason* or follows from it." This is that "the natural necessity which" *apparently* "cannot coexist with the freedom of the subject attaches merely to the determinations of a thing which stands under the conditions of time and so only to the determinations of the acting subject as appearance." However, even though everything about the empirical subject seems determined by natural causes, in fact it is due to its character and choice as a thing in itself:

> But the very same subject, being on the other side conscious of himself as a thing in itself, also views his existence *insofar as it does not stand under conditions of time* and himself as determinable only through laws that he gives himself through reason; and in this existence of his nothing is, for him, antecedent to the determination of his will, but every action – and in general every determination of his existence changing conformably with inner sense, even the whole sequence of his existence as a sensible being – is to be regarded in the consciousness of his intelligible existence as nothing but the consequence and never as the determining ground of his causality as a *noumenon*. (*KpV* 5:97–8)

How the noumenal self might be free to choose contrary to the moral law remains unexplained, but what is not in doubt is that the determination of the noumenal will is entirely responsible for the agent's "character as a phenomenon." The laws of phenomenal nature, at least of the phenomenal nature of any agent, must simply be assumed to be consistent with and indeed determined by its noumenal will. There is no gulf between its freedom and its nature.

As suggested, Kant would finally address the Ulrich problem in *Religion within the Boundaries of Mere Reason* – and then he just slashes through it like a Gordian knot. He now rejects the second *Critique*'s identity of pure practical reason and the noumenal will by means of a firm distinction

Nature and Freedom in Kant's Practical Philosophy 285

between *Wille* as the former and *Willkür* or the power of choice as the latter and conceives of the freedom of the latter as "radical" precisely in the sense that it is an inscrutable freedom to choose either good or evil, in the form of choosing whether to subordinate self-love to the moral law or the moral law to self-love. Kant was not the first to take up the Ulrich problem; Carl Christian Erhard Schmid in 1790 and Karl Leonhard Reinhold in 1792 both replied with what are essentially their own versions of a distinction between *Wille* and *Willkür*, in their terms a distinction between reason as the source of moral law and the free choice whether or not to accept it. Kant's response in the *Religion* is typical of him, for he does not admit that there is any problem with his previous position or acknowledge that he is revising it; he just repeatedly states that if something is one's duty, then "however evil a human being has been right up to the moment of an impending free action," "he must therefore be capable of it" (*RGV* 6:42; see also 45, 47, 49n., 50, 62, 66) as if this had always been his sole argument for freedom of the will and a sufficient argument for it. However, what Kant does now clearly assert, in contrast to anything in his previous treatments, is that freedom can only be the ability to choose either of two alternatives, in the moral case to choose between good and evil, and remains the power to choose one alternative for the future even when one has chosen the other in the past. Since Kant takes desires and a disposition to satisfy them under the name of self-love to be an inelimin-able part of human nature, which must be subordinated to morality but cannot be simply extirpated, he defines all moral choice as at bottom that between subordinating self-love to morality, making acting as self-love suggests conditional upon the satisfaction of the demands of morality, which is the choice of the good, or subordinating morality to self-love, making acting in compliance with the demands of morality conditional upon the consistency of that with self-love, which is evil. He thus calls evil an "inversion" of the proper order of our principles, and then states:

> If a propensity to this [inversion] does lie in human nature, then there is in the human being a natural propensity to evil; and this propensity itself is morally evil, since it must ultimately be sought in a free power of choice [*Willkür*], and hence is imputable. This evil is *radical*, since it corrupts the ground of all maxims; as natural propensity, it is also not to be *extirpated* through human forces, for this could only happen through good maxims – something that cannot take place if the subjective supreme ground of all maxims is pre-supposed to be corrupted. Yet it must equally be possible to *overcome* this evil, for it is found in the human being as acting freely. (*RGV* 6:37).

PAUL GUYER

Evil does not lie in choosing some self-serving maxims while accepting other, morally acceptable maxims, but in an underlying willingness to subordinate morality to self-love. Thus it cannot be overcome one individual maxim at time, but only by a reversal of fundamental maxim, by undertaking a commitment to subordinate self-love to morality whenever and however that is necessary. Kant's explicit point in the present passage is then that if evil is to be imputable, that is, if we are to be held responsible for it, it must be the product of a free choice, which is one that could have gone the other way as well; but if that is the case, then we remain free to reverse the choice and convert from evil to good. The choice of evil must be radical in the sense that it perverts all our particular maxims, but the choice of good must likewise be radical in that it moralizes all our particular maxims, and freedom itself must be radical in the sense that it is the ability to choose either of these alternatives.

Now it might seem that if freedom must be lodged in a *noumenal* faculty of choice not subject to time and the determinism that is the necessary condition of time-determination, as Kant had earlier argued and certainly presupposes in the *Religion*, then it must be fallacious for him to speak of a *sequence* of free choices, *first* a choice of evil *followed* by a choice of good (or for that matter, the opposite sequence, since that too must be allowed by radical freedom). It might seem that in the timeless realm of the noumenal, the free will could only have a single choice, which the entire, enduring empirical character of the phenomenal agent must unfailingly reflect, as the second *Critique* had suggested. Some of Kant's successors, such as Arthur Schopenhauer, interpreted him this way. But what would actually be fallacious would be to infer that because the noumenal self is non-temporal it can choose only once, because that would assume that our temporal way of representing change is the only kind of multiplicity there can be. All that we can conclude is that we cannot really understand the possibility of a multiplicity of choices at the noumenal level in our ordinary, phenomenal temporal terms, but that nevertheless the "ought implies can" principle and our continuing obligation to become good even when we have previously been evil requires rational belief in the possibility of such multiplicity. At the same time, since our imagination and therefore our powers of description are constrained by our forms of intuition, we have no way to refer to this multiplicity except in our ordinary, temporal terms. So we must go ahead and speak of free will and the possibility of moral conversion in terms of a sequence of choices, a change of heart, although we know that such terms cannot literally describe the noumenal will.

Nature and Freedom in Kant's Practical Philosophy

But in all of this Kant continues to assume that our phenomenal character will reflect our noumenal choice of fundamental maxim, whichever that is and however often it undergoes the noumenal equivalent of change. In fact, Kant revives the terminology of the first *Critique* and once again speaks of empirical and intelligible character (*RGV* 6:37). So he does not, any more than previously, suppose that there is an unbridgeable gulf between the domain of freedom and the domain of nature. He does add one consideration to his earlier view of the relation between intelligible and empirical character, however. This is that because the empirical is temporal, and time presents itself to us as an indefinitely extendable sequence, so must the empirical character of goodness present itself to us in the form of an indefinitely extendable but never completed *progress* from evil to good even though change of heart from evil to good can be complete and, as it were although not literally, instantaneous. He writes:

> In our estimation, since we are unavoidably restricted to temporal conditions in our conceptions of the relationship of cause to effect, the [empirical] deed, as a continuous advance *in infinitum* from a defective good to something better, always remains defective, so that we are bound to consider the good as it appears to us, i.e., according to the [empirical] *deed*, as *at each instant* [*jederzeit*] inadequate to a holy law. But because of the [intelligible] *disposition* from which it derives and which transcends the senses, we can think of the infinite progress of the good towards conformity with the law as being judged by him who scrutinizes the heart (through his pure intellectual intuition) to be a perfected whole even with respect to the deed (the conduct of life). And so notwithstanding his permanent deficiency, a human being can still expect to be pleasing to God after all [*überhaupt*], at whatever point in time his existence be cut short. (*RGV*, 6:67)

This passage is remarkable. For one, although Kant does not acknowledge this, it undercuts his previous arguments for the postulate of immortality as necessary for the perfection of human virtue (see especially *KpV* 5:122) by supposing that a change of heart from evil to good can be complete (and recognized to be so by God if not by us) at any point. Again, the point of completion of the conversion at the noumenal level cannot be literally temporal, although we have no other way of talking about it, but at least both empirical and intelligible agents can now be considered finite. So we do not have the problem of trying to correlate a phenomenal existence that is finite in duration with a noumenal one that is in some sense, although not a literally temporal one, infinite, and that will no doubt reduce the challenge of bridging the gulf between the domain of nature and freedom.

288   PAUL GUYER

The second striking point about this passage is that it does not say precisely why the progress of the empirical character (the "deed") from evil to good must always be imperfect. The reason could be substantive or merely epistemological. In the latter case, the problem would be that since an agent's true motivation, if noumenal, must be inscrutable to him, and since actions motivated by self-love can always be in outward conformity with the requirements of morality, no number of apparently moral actions, over no matter how long a period, can provide conclusive evidence that the agent has made a change of heart from evil to good. But in the former case, the problem would be that an agent's noumenal conversion from evil to good is never completely efficacious in the phenomenal world, that for some reason the quality of the agent's deed never quite catches up to the quality of his fundamental maxim.

The first of these worries would seem reasonable enough; indeed, even on an entirely naturalistic model of human action, which does not transpose the choice of fundamental maxim to an inscrutable noumenal realm, that we can never be sure of the real motivation of our actions seems plausible, and would seem to be a salutary warning against moral self-satisfaction. The second worry seems more problematic: Given Kant's insistence in the first two *Critiques* that intelligible character must be the sufficient ground of phenomenal character, it is hard to understand how empirical character could not fully reflect intelligible character. However, if we were to adopt the model into which Kant seems to slip in the second half of Section III of the *Groundwork*, namely that the moral law is an ideal for us as sensible beings but that as sensible beings there is always a struggle in us between reason and inclination, or in the terms of the *Religion* between morality and self-love, then we could understand why our empirical character is never completely moral, at best always on the way to being moral: The possibility of a struggle, or of a relapse into self-love even if we seem to have completely conquered it, is always there.

On such a view, there would be no unbridgeable gulf between freedom and nature, although it might be a more thoroughly naturalistic view than Kant ever intended: Moral choice itself would be phenomenal rather than noumenal, and with that Kant's confidence of our freedom of the will would be out the window. There would be no bridge between the phenomenal and the noumenal, but a location of moral choice in the empirical worlds as the only one there is – which however would leave no room for freedom on Kant's understanding of freedom. So this cannot be Kant's intended position, although then it remains difficult to see why the

Nature and Freedom in Kant's Practical Philosophy   289

moral progress of the empirical agent must be substantively and not merely epistemologically imperfect.

This conclusion might be a good point at which to conclude this postscript. But I want to discuss one more topic relevant to bridging the gulf between nature and freedom, namely Kant's treatment of the highest good.

4   The Highest Good

It might appear that in its treatment of the highest good the third *Critique* really does bridge a gulf between the domains of freedom and nature that was left open by the earlier critiques. In those works Kant may seem to have deferred any possible realization of the highest good to a non-natural realm, while in the Doctrine of Method of the Critique of the Power of Teleological Judgment, he seems to argue that the realization of the highest good must be possible entirely within the realm of nature. But both sides of this story are more complicated than initially appears.

Kant introduces the concept of the highest good in the Canon of Pure Reason in the Doctrine of Method of the first *Critique*. He begins with the idea of a "moral world," the world "as it *can* be in accordance with the *freedom* of rational beings and *should* be in accordance with the necessary laws of *morality*" (*KrV* A808/B836). In such a world, "a system of happiness proportionately combined with morality can also be thought as necessary, since freedom, partly moved and partly restricted by moral laws, would itself be the cause of the general happiness, and rational beings, under the guidance of such principles, would themselves be the authors of their own enduring welfare and at the same time that of others" (*KrV* A809/B838). Kant does not explain precisely why under optimal circumstances the morality of all agents would also produce their welfare and happiness, although since he does not suppose that morality is directly aimed at happiness such an explanation is needed. The explanation must lie in the fact that even though happiness is not the direct object of morality, in the kingdom of ends that is, in which each person is treated as an end in him- or herself and the permissible ends of each are all promoted (*GMS* 4:433), the greatest morally possible intra- and interpersonal happiness would in fact result. But the important point for our present purposes is that the moral world, as one in which general morality leads to general happiness, seems to be one that could be realized in the natural world, indeed one that could only be realized in the natural world, since "Happiness is the satisfaction of all of our inclinations" (*KrV* A806/B834) and our inclinations (or more properly desires, since inclinations are a subset of desires, namely those that have become entrenched) exist only in the natural world. However, Kant also holds that "this system of self-rewarding morality is only an idea," because no one can count on everyone else being moral (*KrV* A810/B838). So, apparently in order to maintain their "resolve" (*KrV* A813/B841), those agents who are fully committed to morality must allow themselves the rational belief in "God and a future life" as the conditions of possibility for the realization of the moral world: What does not seem likely to happen in the natural world must be able to be thought to be possible in another, non-natural world. In his first statement of this claim, Kant does not make it clear whether this belief will be that in a future life God will make sure that *everyone* is moral, from which the general welfare and happiness will result, or will make sure that the efforts *only of those who do choose to act morally* will be accompanied with *their own* happiness. When Kant subsequently says that for the "complete good … he who has not conducted himself so as to be unworthy of happiness must be able to hope to partake of it" (*KrV* A813/B841), he might seem to point to the latter interpretation. But even that statement is compatible with the possibility that a moral agent might be rewarded with happiness in a divinely governed future life only if in that life everyone in fact acts morally. Either way, however, it seems as if the realization of the highest good must be deferred to a future, non-natural life, thus that there is a considerable gulf between the realm of nature and that of morality.

In its Dialectic, the *Critique of Practical Reason* provides Kant's most extended treatment of the highest good, and thus might be thought to provide Kant's most coherent treatment of the topic. In fact, this treatment verges on incoherence. On the one hand, Kant is firm that for human beings "*complete conformity* of dispositions with the moral law," as "the supreme condition of the highest good," "can only be found in an *endless progress*," which is in turn "possible only on the presupposition of the *existence* and personality of the same rational being continuing *endlessly* (which is called the immortality of the soul)" (*KpV* 5:122). Since the perfection of morality should be the condition of the complete realization of happiness, if the former must be deferred to a non-natural life then so should the latter. Then Kant's conception of the locus for the realization of the highest good in the second *Critique* would be identical with that in the first. On the other hand, however, Kant is insistent in the second *Critique* that God is postulated as the author or cause of *nature*, namely a nature in

Nature and Freedom in Kant's Practical Philosophy

which the complete realization of the highest good is possible. The highest good will consist in a "necessary connection between the morality and the proportionate happiness of a being belonging to the world as part of it and hence dependent upon it, who for that reason cannot by his will be a cause of this nature and, as far as his happiness is concerned, cannot by his own powers make it harmonize thoroughly with his practical principles" (*KpV* 5:124). This suggests that the highest good consists in the realization of happiness for any individual agent who is completely moral, not in the general happiness dependent on the morality of all; and this might seem like something that should also be expected only in a future, non-natural life. However, in case the references to "the world" and "this nature" just quoted were not already clear enough, Kant continues:

> The existence of a cause of all nature, distinct from nature, which contains the ground of this connection, namely of the exact correspondence of happiness with morality, is also *postulated*. However, this supreme cause is to contain the ground of the correspondence of nature not merely with a law of the will of rational beings but with the representation of this *law*, so far as they make it the *supreme determining ground of the will*, and consequently not merely with morals in their form but also with their morality as their determining ground, that is, with their moral disposition. Therefore, the highest good in the world is possible only insofar as a supreme cause of nature having a causality in keeping with the moral disposition is assumed. (*KpV* 5:125)

Here Kant claims that God must be postulated as the author *of nature* so that the accompaniment of morality with happiness *in nature* can be assumed. This claim is reasonable insofar as happiness seems to be a necessarily natural condition, but it is problematic because it either withdraws the previous claim that the moral disposition of agents can be perfected only in non-natural, immortal life or else allows that the realization of happiness may *precede* the perfection of the moral disposition. But either way, Kant's postulation of God as the author of a *nature* that is consistent with morality shows that he does not assume that there is an unbridgeable gulf between the domains of freedom and nature: He assumes that our efforts to be moral can be efficacious in nature, bringing about our happiness, although only because the laws of nature are divinely underwritten to be consistent with the moral law. That is to say, Kant does not suppose that we must hope for a miraculous intervention in the laws of nature, otherwise indifferent to our happiness, but rather that we must believe that the laws of nature themselves make possible the realization of the highest good.

That the laws of nature might be reasonably considered as if intended to bring about human happiness under any circumstances seems to be explicitly denied in the Doctrine of Method of the Critique of the Power of Teleological Judgment: "it is so far from being the case that nature has made the human being its special favorite and favored him with beneficence above all other animals, that it has rather spared him just as little as any other animal from its destructive effects," and "even if the most beneficent nature outside of us had made the happiness of our species its end, that end would not be attained in a system of nature upon the earth, because the nature inside of us is not receptive to that" (*KU* section 83, 5:430). However, this is only a preliminary statement, a preliminary challenge to teleological judgment rather than a conclusive rejection of it, although to be sure what Kant will defend is a conception of teleological judgment as reflective and regulative rather than determinant and constitutive. Kant goes on to answer this challenge in two steps. The first is to argue that even if human happiness does not seem to be a likely product of nature, human *discipline* can be achieved in nature, and discipline, which "consists in the liberation of the will from the despotism of desires" (*KU* 5:432), is at least a necessary condition for the realization of morality and thus of the highest good, although, it should also be noted, of a morality that is assumed from the outset to have to be able to be efficacious within nature and for that reason to have to overcome wanton desires. But, second, Kant goes on to describe the highest good, "**happiness** – under the objective condition of the concordance of humans with the law of **morality**, as the worthiness to be happy" (*KU* section 87, 4:450), as something that we must be able to believe to be possible *in nature* and that calls for a "moral proof of the existence of God" insofar as it "compels our rational judging to go beyond the world and to seek an intelligent supreme principle for that relation of nature to what is moral in us, in order to represent nature as purposive even in relation to the morally internal legislation and its possible execution" (*GMS* 4:448). In other words, once we have allowed for the possibility of rational belief in the existence of God outside of but as the ground of nature (which of course requires transcendental idealism), we can also believe, in spite of initial appearances otherwise, that the laws of nature are purposive with respect to our moral goal after all. Once again, there is no unbridgeable gulf between the domains of nature and freedom.

This is not an innovation in the third *Critique*, however, but very much the same argument that Kant offered in the exposition of the postulate of the existence of God in the second, although now within the framework of a general theory of reflective and regulative judgment. Nevertheless, two changes in the third *Critique* may be noted, one of which might be thought of as bringing the domains of nature and freedom even closer together than before, but the other of which might be regarded as still maintaining some distance between them. First, Kant offers no argument in the third *Critique* that complete conformity of the human will to the moral law would require immortality, indeed he offers no argument for immortality at all, although he still leaves open its theoretical possibility (*KU* section 89, 4:460). In this regard the third *Critique* eliminates a non-naturalistic moment still present in the second. The second point, however, is that although, as we have seen, Kant does hold that discipline of the desires, as a necessary condition of morality, is something that can be achieved within nature, consistently with and by means of its own laws, he does not in fact reduce human freedom to mere discipline. He continues to maintain that the moral law is not given by nature, by our "supersensible" freedom, and that our ability to determine our will in accordance with the moral law is likewise a "supersensible faculty" of freedom. (Kant does not yet assume the clear distinction between *Wille* as pure practical reason and *Willkür* as the noumenally free faculty to choose whether or not to act in accordance with pure reason that we will just two years later.) Kant writes:

> Now we have in the world only a single sort of beings whose causality is teleological, i.e., aimed at ends and yet at the same time so constituted that the law in accordance with which they have to determine ends is represented by themselves as unconditioned and independent of natural conditions but yet as necessary in itself. The being of this sort is the human being, though considered as noumenon: the only natural being in which we can nevertheless cognize, on the basis of its own constitution, a supersensible faculty (*freedom*) and even the law of the causality together with the object that it can set for itself as the highest end (the highest good in the world). (*KU* section 84, 5:435)

The laws of nature allow for the development of discipline, but only the noumenally free human being can impose the moral law and its attendant end of the highest good upon itself and choose to use the discipline that nature makes available to it in order to realize the morality and the highest good. The laws of nature make it possible to bridge the gulf between freedom of nature, but they cannot bridge the gulf by themselves.

That there is a gulf between the domains of nature and freedom but that this gulf can be bridged was thus not a new idea in the third *Critique*, but something that Kant maintained, although with variations, throughout the

294 PAUL GUYER

critical decade from 1781 to 1790 (and beyond, into his final, uncompleted work). The fundamental end to be preserved and promoted by morality, our humanity as our freedom to set our own ends, might seem to be something entirely mental and potentially noumenal and non-natural; but the scope of our freedom to set ends, the range of ends that we can rationally set for ourselves, can be either promoted or compromised by external, natural conditions, and that is why we have the specific duties that we have. The choice of each of us whether or not to set his or her own ends in accordance with the moral law might seem like something non-natural and noumenal, but Kant always assumes that it must be brought to bear upon the natural world and that the laws of the natural world must at least be consistent with the exercise of the free will within that world. And, although Kant's thought about the highest good undergoes twists and turns throughout the critical decade, it always assumes at least one element, namely happiness, that seems most plausibly realized only within the natural world, but another, namely moral disposition, which is not entirely of the natural world but must be efficacious within it. So Kant always assumes a gulf between nature and freedom, but never an unbridgeable gulf.

Bibliography

Allison, Henry E. 1996. "Autonomy and Spontaneity in the Self," in *Idealism and Freedom: Essays on Kant's Theoretical and Practical Philosophy*. Cambridge: Cambridge University Press, 1996: 129–42.

2001. *Kant's Theory of Taste*. Cambridge: Cambridge University Press.

2004. *Kant's Transcendental Idealism: An Interpretation and Defense*, revised ed. New Haven: Yale University Press.

2011. *Kant's Groundwork for the Metaphysics of Morals: A Commentary*. Oxford: Oxford University Press.

Ameriks, Karl 2003. "Kant's Transcendental Deduction as a Regressive Argument," in *Interpreting Kant's Critiques*. Oxford: Oxford University Press: 51–66.

2012. *Kant's Elliptical Path*. Oxford: Oxford University Press.

Arendt, Hannah 1992. *Lectures on Kant's Political Philosophy*. Chicago: University of Chicago Press.

Astington, Jane Wilde 1994. *The Child's Discovery of the Mind*. London: Fontana Press.

Barry, Brian 1995. *Justice as Impartiality*. Oxford: Oxford University Press.

Baumgarten, A. G. 2011. *Metaphysica/Metaphysik*, Günter Gawlick and Lothar Kreimendahl (trans. and eds.). Stuttgart-Bad Cannstatt: Fromann-Holzboog.

Baxley, Anne Margaret 2015. *Kant's Theory of Virtue*. Cambridge: Cambridge University Press.

Beck, Lewis White 1969. *Early German Philosophy: Kant and His Predecessors*. Cambridge: Belknap Press.

2002. "Did the Sage of Königsberg Have No Dreams?" in Hoke Robinson (ed.), *Lewis White Beck: Selected Essays on Kant*. Rochester: University of Rochester Press: 85–102.

Berger, Larissa 2015. "Der 'Zirkel' im Dritten Abschnitt der *Grundlegung*," in Dieter Schönecker (ed.), *Kants Begründung von Freiheit und Moral in Grundlegung III*. Münster: Mentis: 9–81.

Bittner, Rüdiger 1996. "What is Enlightenment?" in James Schmidt (ed.), *What is Enlightenment? Eighteenth Century Answers and Twentieth Century Questions*. Berkeley: University of California Press: 345–58.

Brandt, Reinhard 2007. *Die Bestimmung des Menschen bei Kant*. Frankfurt: Felix Meiner.

Bibliography

Bratman, M. E. 1989. "Intention and Personal policies," in J. E. Tomberlin (ed.), *Philosophical Perspectives: Philosophy of Mind and Action Theory*, vol. 3. Atascadero, CA: Ridgeview Publishing.

Bräuer, Juliane, Joseph Call, and Michael Tomasello, 2006. "Are Apes Really Inequity Averse?" *Proceedings of the Royal Society B* 273:3123–8.

2009. "Are Apes Inequity Averse? New Data on the Token-Exchange Paradigm," *American Journal of Primatology* 71:175–81.

Brosnan, Sarah F. and Frans B. M. de Waal 2003. "Monkeys Reject Unequal Pay," *Nature* 425: 297–9.

Browning, Christopher 1992. *Ordinary Men: Reserve Police Battalion 101 and the Final Solution in Poland*. New York: Harper.

Bushnell, I. W. R. 2001. "Mother's Face Recognition in Newborn Infants: Learning and Memory," *Infant and Child Development* 10: 67–74.

Caygill, Howard 1995. *A Kant Dictionary*. Oxford: Wiley-Blackwell.

Darwall, Stephen 1977. "Two Kinds of Respect," *Ethics* 88: 36–49.

Das Chatterjee, Nilanjana 2016. *Man–Elephant Conflict: A Case Study from Forests in West Bengal, India*. New York: Springer.

Dean, Richard 2006. *The Value of Humanity in Kant's Moral Theory*. Oxford: Clarendon Press.

2009. "The Formula of Humanity as an End in Itself," in Thomas Hill (ed.), *The Blackwell Guide to Kant's Ethics*. Malden: Blackwell: 83–101.

2013. "Humanity as an Idea, as an Ideal, and as an End in Itself," *Kantian Review* 18: 171–95.

de Boer, Karin 2016. "Categories versus Schemata: Kant's Two-Aspect Theory of Pure Concepts and His Critique of Wolffian Metaphysics," *Journal of the History of Philosophy* 54: 441–68.

Deligiorgi, Katerina 2012. *The Scope of Autonomy: Kant and the Morality of Freedom*. Oxford: Oxford University Press.

Denis, Lara 2011a. "Freedom, Primacy, and Perfect Duties to Oneself," in Lara Denis (ed.), *Kant's Metaphysics of Morals: A Critical Guide*. Cambridge: Cambridge University Press: 170–91.

(ed.), 2011b. *Kant's Metaphysics of Morals: A Critical Guide*. Cambridge: Cambridge University Press.

Dobe, Jennifer 2010. "Kant's Common Sense and the Strategy for a Deduction," *Journal of Aesthetics and Art Criticism* 68: 48–60.

Doris, John M. 2002. *Lack of Character: Personality and Moral Behavior*. Cambridge: Cambridge University Press.

Dunham, Barrows 1933. *A Study of Kant's Aesthetics*. Princeton: Princeton University Press.

Dyck, Corey 2011. "Kant's Transcendental Deduction and the Ghosts of Kant and Hume," *British Journal for the History of Philosophy* 19: 473–96.

2014. *Kant and Rational Psychology*. Oxford: Oxford University Press.

Esser, Andrea M. 2013. "The Inner Court of Conscience, Moral Self-Knowledge, and the Proper Object of Duty," in Andreas Trampota et al. (eds.), *Kants "Tugendlehre."* Berlin: de Gruyter.

Bibliography

Estlund, David 2008. *Democratic Authority: A Philosophical Framework.* Princeton: Princeton University Press.

Flikschuh, Katrin 2012. "Personal Autonomy and Public Authority," in Sensen 2012 (ed.): 169–89.

Forman, David 2012. "Kant on Moral Freedom and Moral Slavery," *Kantian Review* 17: 1–32.

Formosa, Paul 2013. "Is Kant a Moral Constructivist or a Moral Realist?" *European Journal of Philosophy* 21: 170–96.

Frierson, Patrick 2014. *Kant's Empirical Psychology.* Cambridge: Cambridge University Press.

Gibson, James J. 2015. *The Ecological Approach to Visual Perception.* New York: Psychology Press.

Ginsborg, Hannah 1997. "Lawfulness Without a Law: Kant on the Free Play of Imagination and Understanding," *Philosophical Topics* 25: 37–81.

Gottsched, J. C. 1762. *Erste Gründe der gesammten Weltweissheit*, 7th ed. Leipzig: Breitkopf. Reprinted in Christian Wolff, *Gesammelte Werke*, Pt. 3, vols. 20.1–20.2. Hildesheim: Olms, 1983.

Greenberg, Robert 2001. *Kant's Theory of A Priori Knowledge.* University Park: Pennsylvania State University Press.

Gregor, Mary 1988. "Kant's Theory of Property," *The Review of Metaphysics* 41: 757–87.

Gregor, Mary and Jens Timmermann 2012 (trans. and eds.). *Immanuel Kant, Groundwork of the Metaphysics of Morals.* Cambridge: Cambridge University Press.

Grenberg, Jeanine 2011. "What is the Enemy of Virtue?" in Denis 2011 (ed.): 152–69.

Guyer, Paul 1979. *Kant and the Claims of Taste.* Cambridge: Cambridge University Press.

1987. *Kant and the Claims of Knowledge.* Cambridge: Cambridge University Press.

1992. "The Transcendental Deduction of the Categories," in Paul Guyer (ed.), *The Cambridge Companion to Kant.* Cambridge: Cambridge University Press: 123–60.

1995. "Os Simbolos Da Liberdade Na Estetica Kantiana," *o que nos faz pensar* 9: 73–92.

1996a. "Duty and Inclination," in Guyer 1996b: 335–94.

1996b. *Kant and the Experience of Freedom.* Cambridge: Cambridge University Press.

1996c. "Nature, Art, and Autonomy," in Guyer 1996b: 229–74.

1996d. "The Value of Agency," *Ethics* 106: 404–23.

1998. "The Value of Reason and the Value of Freedom," *Ethics* 109: 22–35.

2000a. "Freedom as the Inner Value of the World," in Guyer 2000c: 96–128.

2000b. "Kantian Foundations for Liberalism," in Guyer 2000c: 235–61.

2000c. *Kant on Freedom, Law and Happiness.* Cambridge: Cambridge University Press.

298   *Bibliography*

2000d. "Kant's Morality of Law and Morality of Freedom," in Guyer 2000c: 129–71.

2000e. "Life, Liberty, Property," in Guyer 2000c: 262–86.

2001. "Space, Time, and the Categories: The Project of the Transcendental Deduction," in R. Schumacher (ed.), *Idealismus als Theorie der Repräsentation?* Paderborn: Mentis: 313–38.

2005a. "Kant's Deductions of the Principles of Right," in Guyer 2005c: 198–242.

2005b. "Kant's System of Duties," in Guyer 2005c: 243–74.

2005c. *Kant's System of Nature and Freedom.* Oxford: Oxford University Press.

2006a. "Aesthetics and Cognition in Kant's Critical Philosophy," in R. Kukla 2011 (ed.): 162–93.

2006b. *Kant.* New York: Routledge.

2007a. *Kant's* Groundwork for the Metaphysics of Morals*: A Reader's Guide.* New York: Continuum.

2007b. "Naturalistic and Transcendental Moments in Kant's Moral Philosophy," *Inquiry: An Interdisciplinary Journal of Philosophy* 50: 444–64.

2007c. "Perfection, Autonomy, and Heautonomy: The Path of Reason from Wolff to Kant," in Jürgen Stolzenburg and Oliver-Pierre Rudolph (eds.), *Christian Wolff und die europäishe Aufklärung: Akten des. 1. Internationalen Christian-Wolff-Kongress.* Hildesheim: Olms: 299–322.

2009a. "The Harmony of the Faculties in Recent Books on the *Critique of the Power of Judgment,*" *Journal of Aesthetics and Art Criticism* 67: 201–21.

2009b. "Problems with Freedom: Kant's Argument in Groundwork III and Its Subsequent Emendations," in Jens Timmermann (ed.), *Groundwork for the Metaphysics of Morals: A Critical Guide.* Cambridge: Cambridge University Press: 176–202.

2010. "The Deduction of the Categories: The Metaphysical and Transcendental Deductions," in Paul Guyer (ed.), *The Cambridge Companion to Kant's Critique of Pure Reason.* Cambridge: Cambridge University Press: 118–50.

2012. "Progress Toward Autonomy," in Sensen 2012 (ed.).

2016. "Proving Ourselves Free," in *Virtues of Freedom: Selected Essays on Kant.* Oxford: Oxford University Press: 146–163.

2017. "Setting and Pursuing Ends: Internal and External Freedom," in *The Virtues of Freedom: Selected Essays on Kant.* Oxford: Oxford University Press: 87–104.

Guyer, Paul and Henry E. Allison 2011. "Dialogue: Paul Guyer and Henry Allison on Allison's *Theory of Taste,*" in R. Kukla 2011 (ed.): 111–37.

de Haan, Michelle, Olivier Pascalis, and Mark H. Johnson 2002. "Specialization of Neural Mechanisms Underlying Face Recognition in Human Infants," *Journal of Cognitive Neuroscience* 14:199–209.

Hayek, Friedrich A. 1960. *The Constitution of Liberty.* Chicago: The University of Chicago Press.

1967. "The Principles of a Liberal Social Order," in Friedrich A. Hayek (ed.), *Studies in Philosophy, Politics, and Economics.* Chicago: The University of Chicago Press, 1967: 160–77.

Bibliography

Hegel, G. W. F. 1988. *Faith and Knowledge*, Walter Cerf and H. S. Harris (trans. and eds.). Albany: SUNY Press.

Henrich, Dieter 1982. "The Proof-Structure of Kant's Transcendental Deduction," in Ralph C. S. Walker (ed.), *Kant on Pure Reason*. Oxford: Oxford University Press: 66–81.

Herman, Barbara 1984. "Mutual Aid and Respect for Persons," *Ethics* 94: 577–602.
   1993. *The Practice of Moral Judgement*. Cambridge, MA: Harvard University Press.

Hill, Thomas E. and Arnulf Zweig 2002. "Editor's Introduction," in *Groundwork of the Metaphysics of Morals*, Thomas E. Hill, Jr., and Arnulf Zweig (eds.), Oxford: Oxford University Press.

Hills, Allison 2008. "Kantian Value Realism," *Ratio* 21: 182–200.

Hume, David 1998. *An Enquiry concerning the Principles of Morals*. Tom Beauchamp (ed.). New York: Oxford University Press.
   1985. "Of the Original Contract," in Eugene F. Miller (ed.), *Essays: Moral, Political and Literary*. Indianapolis: Liberty Fund.

Jensen, K., B. Hare, J. Call, and M. Tomasello 2006. "Chimpanzees Are Self-Regarding Maximizers in a Food Acquisition Task," *Proceedings of the Royal Society* 273: 1013–21.

Johnson, Robert N. 2007. "Value and Autonomy in Kantian Ethics," in Russ Shafer-Landau (ed.), *Oxford Studies in Metaethics*. Oxford: Oxford University Press: 133–48.
   2011. *Self-Improvement: An Essay in Kantian Ethics*. Oxford: Oxford University Press.

Kersting, Wolfgang 1983. "Kant und der staatsphilosophische Kontraktualismus," *Allgemeine Zeitschrift für Philosophie* 8: 1–26.

Kitcher, Patricia 2017a. "A Kantian Argument for the Formula of Humanity," *Kant-Studien* 108(2): 218–46.
   2017b. "A Kantian Critique of Transparency," in Anil Gomes and Andrew Stephenson (eds.), *Kant and the Philosophy of Mind: Perception, Reason, and the Self*. Oxford: Oxford University Press: 158–72.

Korsgaard, Christine 1990. *The Standpoint of Practical Reason*. New York: Garland.
   1996a. *Creating the Kingdom of Ends*. New York: Cambridge University Press.
   1996b. "Kant's Formula of Humanity," in Korsgaard 1996a: 106–32.
   1996c. *The Sources of Normativity*. Cambridge: Cambridge University Press.
   1999. "Self-Constitution in the Ethics of Plato and Kant," *Journal of Ethics* 3: 1–29.

Kuehn, Manfred 1997. "The Wolffian Background of Kant's Transcendental Deduction," in Patricia Easton (ed.), *Logic and the Workings of the Mind: The Logic of Ideas and Faculty Psychology in Early Modern Philosophy*. Atascadero, CA: Ridgeview: 229–50.

Kukla, Rebecca (ed.) 2011. *Aesthetics and Cognition in Kant's Critical Philosophy*. Cambridge: Cambridge University Press.

Larmore, Charles 2011. "Kant and the Meanings of Autonomy," *Internationales Jahrbuch des Deutschen Idealismus/International Yearbook of German Idealism* 9: 3–21.

Bibliography

Laywine, Alison 1993. *Kant's Early Metaphysics and the Origins of the Critical Philosophy*. Atascadero, CA: Ridgeview Press.

Leblan, Vincent 2016. "Territorial and Land-Use Rights Perspectives on Human-Chimpanzee-Elephant Coexistence in West Africa (Guinea, Guinea-Bissau, Senegal, Nineteenth to Twenty-First Centuries)," *Primates* 57:359–66.

Liszkowski, U., M. Carpenter, A. Henning, T. Striano, and M. Tomasello 2004. "Twelve-Month-Olds Point to Share Attention and Interest," *Developmental Science* 7:297–307.

Locke, John 1960. *Two Treatises of Government*, Peter Laslett, (ed.). Cambridge: Cambridge University Press.

Lomasky, Loren 1987. *Persons, Rights, and the Moral Community*. New York: Oxford University Press.

Longuenesse, Béatrice 1998. *Kant and the Capacity to Judge*. Princeton: Princeton University Press.

 2005. *Kant on the Human Standpoint*. Cambridge: Cambridge University Press.

 2006. "Kant on A Priori Concepts: The Metaphysical Deduction of the Categories," in Paul Guyer (ed.), *Cambridge Companion to Kant and Modern Philosophy*. Cambridge: Cambridge University Press: 129–68.

 2007. *Hegel's Critique of Metaphysics*. Cambridge: Cambridge University Press.

Louden, Robert 2011. *Kant's Human Being*. New York: Oxford University Press.

Ludovici, C. G. 1737–8. *Entwurf einer vollständigen Historie der Wolffschen Philosophie*, 3 vols. Leipzig: Löwe.

Mackie, J. L. 1977. *Ethics: Inventing Right and Wrong*. Middlesex: Penguin.

Matthews, Patricia 1997. *The Significance of Beauty: Kant on Feeling and the System of the Mind*. Boston: Kluwer Academic Publishers.

Mehler, Jacques, Peter Jusczyk, Gislaine Lambertz, Nilofor Halsted, Josiane Bertancine, and Claudine Amiel-Tilson 2002. "A Precursor of Language Acquisition in Young Infants," in Gerry T. M. Altmann, (ed.), in *Psycholinguistics: Critical Concepts in Psychology*, vol. 4. London: Routledge: 25–60.

Meier, G. F. 1765. *Metaphysik*, 4 vols. Halle: Gebauer. Reprinted in Christian Wolff, *Gesammelte Werke*, Pt. 3, vols. 108.1–108.4. Hildesheim: Olms, 2007.

Mensch, Jennifer 2007. "The Key to All Metaphysics: Kant's Letter to Herz, 1772," *Kantian Review* 12: 109–27.

Milgram, Stanley 1963. "Behavioral Study of Obedience," *Journal of Abnormal and Social Psychology* 67: 371–8.

Moll, H. and M. Tomasello 2007. "Cooperation and Human Cognition: The Vygotskian Intelligence Hypothesis," *Philosophical Transactions of the Royal Society B* 362: 639–48.

Mondloch, Catherine J. et al. 1999. "Face Perception During Early Infancy," *Psychological Science* 10:419–22.

Munzel, G. Felicitas 2012. *Kant's Conception of Pedagogy*. Evanston: Northwestern University Press.

Nagel, Thomas 1991. *Equality and Partiality*. New York: Oxford University Press.

Nozick, Robert 1974. *Anarchy, State, and Utopia*. New York: Basic Books.

Bibliography

O'Neill, Onora 1975. *Acting on Principle: An Essay on Kantian Ethics*. New York: Columbia University Press.

1989. *Constructions of Reason*. Cambridge: Cambridge University Press.

2002. "Constructivism in Rawls and Kant," in Samuel Freeman (ed.), *The Cambridge Companion to Rawls*. Cambridge: Cambridge University Press: 347–67.

2013. "Postscript: Heteronomy as the Clue to Kantian Autonomy," in Oliver Sensen (ed.), *Kant on Moral Autonomy*. Cambridge: Cambridge University Press: 282–7.

Pascalis, Olivier, Michelle de Haan, and Charles Nelson 2002. "Is Face processing Species-Specific During the First Year of Life," *Science* 296: 1321–3.

Paton, H. J. 1936. *Kant's Metaphysics of Experience*. London: G. Allen and Unwin.

Pippin, Robert 1987. "Kant on the Spontaneity of Mind," *Canadian Journal of Philosophy* 17: 449–75.

2006. "Mine and Thine? The Kantian State," in Paul Guyer (ed.), *The Cambridge Companion to Kant and Modern Philosophy*. Cambridge: Cambridge University Press: 416–46.

2013. "Reason's Form," in Karl Ameriks (ed.), *The Impact of Idealism. The Legacy of Post-Kantian German Thought, vol. 1: Philosophy and Natural Sciences*. Cambridge: Cambridge University Press: 373–94.

Pluhar, Werner (trans.) 1996. *Immanuel Kant. Critique of Pure Reason: Unified Edition*. Indianapolis: Hackett.

Prauss, Gerold 1989. "Für sich selber praktische Vernunft," in Otfried Höffe (ed.), *Grundlegung zur Metaphysik der Sitten: Ein kooperativer Kommentar*. Frankfurt: Klostermann: 253–63.

Prichard, H. A. 1912. "Does Moral Philosophy Rest on a Mistake?" *Mind*, 21: 21–37.

Pufendorf, Samuel 2003. *On the Whole Duty of Man*, Andrew Tooke (trans.), Ian Hunter and David Saunders (eds.). Indianapolis: Liberty Fund.

Rauscher, Frederick 2002. "Kant's Moral Anti-Realism," *Journal of the History of Philosophy* 40: 477–99.

2007. "'God' Without God: Kant's Postulate," *Kant e-Prints* 2: 27–62.

2015. *Naturalism and Realism in Kant's Ethics*. Cambridge: Cambridge University Press.

Rawls, John 1978. "Remarks on Kant's Ethics." Unpublished lecture.

1989. "Themes in Kant's Moral Philosophy," in Eckart Förster (ed.), *Kant's Transcendental Deductions*. Stanford: Stanford University Press.

1999. *A Theory of Justice: Revised Edition*. Cambridge, MA: Belknap Press.

2000. *Lectures on the History of Moral Philosophy*. Barbara Herman (ed.). Cambridge, MA: Harvard University Press.

Reddy, Vasudevi 2010. *How Infants Know Minds*. Cambridge, MA: Harvard University Press.

Ripstein, Arthur 2009. *Force and Freedom: Kant's Legal and Political Philosophy*. Cambridge, MA: Harvard University Press.

Roche, Andrew 2010. "Kant's Principle of Sense," *British Journal for the History of Philosophy* 18: 663–91.

Bibliography

Rohlf, Michael 2013. "Promissory Notes: Kant's Argument for Transcendental Idealism," in S. Bacin, A. Ferrarin, C. La Rocca, and M. Ruffing (eds.), *Kant und die Philosophie in weltbürgerlicher Absicht: Akten des XI. Kant-Kongresses 2010.* Berlin: Walter De Gruyter: 371–82.

Rosenkoetter, Timothy 2009. "Truth Criteria and the Very Project of a Transcendental Logic," *Archiv für Geschichte der Philosophie* 91: 193–236.

Samuels, C. A. et al. 1994, "Facial Aesthetics: Babies Prefer Attractiveness to Symmetry" *Perception* 23: 823–31.

Sayre-McCord, Geoffrey 1988. "The Many Moral Realisms," in Geoffrey Sayre-McCord (ed.), *Essays on Moral Realism*. Ithaca: Cornell University Press: 1–23.

Schapiro, Lisa 2009. "The Nature of Inclination," *Ethics* 119: 229–56.

Schönecker, Dieter 2013. "'A Free Will and a Will Under the Moral Law are the Same': Kant's Concept of Autonomy and His Thesis of Analyticity in Groundwork III," in *Sensen* 2011: 225–45.

Sensen, Oliver 2011. *Kant on Human Dignity*. Berlin: Walter De Gruyter.

(ed.), 2012. *Kant on Moral Autonomy*. Cambridge: Cambridge University Press.

Silk, J. B., S. F. Brosnan, J. Vonk, J. Henrich, D. J. Povinelli, A. S. Richardson, S. P. Lambeth, J. Mascaro, and S. J. Schapiro 2005. "Chimpanzees Are Indifferent to the Welfare of Unrelated Group Members," *Nature* 437:1357–9.

Smith, Norman Kemp 1918. *A Commentary on Kant's* Critique of Pure Reason. London: MacMillan and Company.

Stern, Robert 2011. *Understanding Moral Obligation: Kant, Hegel, Kierkegaard.* Cambridge: Cambridge University Press.

Sticker, Martin 2017. "When the Reflective Watch Dog Barks: Conscience and Self-Deception in Kant," *Journal of Value Inquiry* 51: 85–104.

Sturm, Thomas 2001. "Kant on Empirical Psychology: How Not to Investigate the Human Mind," in Eric Watkins (ed.), *Kant and the Sciences*. Oxford: Oxford University Press.

Sukumar, Raman 2003. *The Living Elephants: Evolutionary Ecology, Behavior, and Conservation*. New York: Oxford University Press.

Thorpe, Lucas 2006. "What is the Point of Studying Ethics According to Kant?" *Journal of Value Inquiry* 40: 461–5.

2011. "Autonomy and Community," in Lucas Thorpe and Charlton Payne (eds.), *Kant and the Concept of Community, A North American Kant Society Special Volume.* Rochester: University of Rochester Press.

2010. "Is Kant's Realm of Ends a Unum per Se? Aquinas, Suárez, Leibniz and Kant on Composition," *British Journal of the History of Philosophy* 18: 461–85.

2013. "One Community or Many? Community and Interaction in Kant: From Logic to Politics via Metaphysics and Ethics," in Howard Williams, Sorin Baiasu, and Sami Pihlström (eds.), *Politics and Metaphysics in Kant*. Cardiff: University of Wales Press.

Timmermann, Jens 2007. *Kant's* Groundwork of the Metaphysics of Morals*: A Commentary*. Cambridge: Cambridge University Press.

Bibliography

2009. "Acting from Duty: Inclination, Reason, and Moral Worth," in Jens Timmermann (ed.), Kant's Groundwork for the Metaphysics of Morals: A Critical Guide. Cambridge: Cambridge University Press.

Tolley, Clinton 2012. "The Generality of Kant's Transcendental Logic," *Journal of the History of Philosophy* 50: 417–46.

Tomasello, Michael 2008. *Origin of Human Communication*. Cambridge, MA: MIT Press.

Tomasello, Michael, Malinda Carpenter, Josep Call, Tanya Behne, and Henrike Moll 2005. "Understanding and Sharing Intentions: The Origins of Cultural Cognition," *Behavioral and Brain Sciences* 28: 675–735.

Tomasi, John 2012. *Free Market Fairness*. Princeton: Princeton University Press.

Tonelli, Georgio 1974. "Leibniz on Innate Ideas and the Earl Reactions to the Publication of the *Noveaux Essais* (1765)," *Journal of the History of Philosophy* 12: 437–54.

Varden, Helga 2008. "Kant's Non-Voluntarist Conception of Political Obligation," *Kantian Review* 13: 1–45.

Vespers, Achim 2015. "*Bedürfniß*," in Marcus Willaschek, Jürgen Stolzenberg, Georg Mohr, and Stefano Bacin (eds.), *Kant-Lexikon*. Berlin: de Gruyter.

Vouloumanos, P. A. and J. F. Werker 2007. "Listening to Language at Birth: Evidence For a Bias For Speech in Neonates," *Developmental Science* 10: 159–64.

de Waal, Frans. 1989. "Food Sharing and Reciprocal Obligations Among Chimpanzees," *Journal of Human Evolution* 18: 433–59.

1997. "The Chimpanzee's Service Economy: Food for Grooming," *Evolution and Human Behavior* 18: 375–86.

Ware, Owen 2009. "The Duty of Self-Knowledge," *Philosophy and Phenomenological Research* 79: 671–98.

Warneken, F., and M. Tomasello 2006. "Altruistic Helping in Human Infants and Young Chimpanzees," *Science* 31: 1301–3.

2007. "Helping and Co-Operation at 14 Months of Age," *Infancy* 11: 271–94.

Watkins, Eric 2002. "Kant's Transcendental Idealism and the Categories," *History of Philosophy Quarterly* 19: 191–215.

Watkins, Eric and William Fitzpatrick 2002. "O'Neill and Korsgaard on the Construction of Normativity," *Journal of Value Inquiry* 36: 349–67.

Waxman, Wayne 2005. *Kant and the Empiricists: Understanding Understanding.* Oxford: Oxford University Press.

2008. "Kant's Humean Solution to Hume's Problem," in Daniel Garber and Béatrice Longuenesse (eds.), *Kant and the Early Modern*. Princeton: Princeton University Press: 172–92.

Wenzel, Christian 2005. *Introduction to Kant's Aesthetics*. Malden: Blackwell.

Wolff, Christian 1736. *Philosophia prima seu Ontologia*, 2nd ed. Frankfurt and Leipzig: Regner. Reprinted in Christian Wolff, *Gesammelte Werke*, Pt. 2, vol. 3. Hildesheim: Olms, 1962.

1738. *Psychologia empirica*, 2nd ed. Frankfurt am Main: Regner. In Christian Wolff, *Gesammelte Werke*, Pt. 2, vol. 5. Hildesheim: Olms, 1968.

304   Bibliography

1740. *Der vernüfftigen Gedanken von Gott, der Welt und der Seele des Menschen, auch allen Dinge überhaupt, anderer Theil, bestehend aus ausführlichen Anmerkungen,* 4th ed. Frankfurt am Main: Andreä and Hort. Reprinted in Christian Wolff, *Gesammelte Werke,* Pt. 1, vol. 3. Hildesheim: Olms, 1983.

1740. *Discurses praeliminaris de philosophia in genere.* In *Philosophia rationalis, sive Logica,* 3rd ed. Frankfurt am Main: Regner. Reprinted in Christian Wolff, *Gesammelte Werke,* Pt. 2, vols. 1–2. Hildesheim: Olms, 1983.

1751. *Vernüfftige Gedanken von Gott, der Welt und der Seele des Menschen, auch allen Dinge überhaupt,* 11th ed. Halle: Regner. Reprinted in ChristianWolff, Gesammelte Werke, Pt. 1, vol. 2. Hildesheim: Olms, 1983.

1754. *Vernüftige Gedanken von den Kräften des menschlichen Verstandes und ihrem Gebrauch in Erknänntnis der Wahrheit,* 14th ed. Halle: Regner. Reprinted in ChristianWolff, *Gesammelte Werke,* Pt. 1, vol. 1. Hildesheim: Olms, 1965.

Wolff, R. P. 1963. *Kant's Theory of Mental Activity.* Cambridge, MA: Harvard University Press.

Wood, Allen 1999. *Kant's Ethical Thought.* Cambridge: Cambridge University Press.

2001. "The Moral Law as a System of Formulas," in Hans-Friederich Fulda and Jürgen Stolzenberg (eds.), *Architektonik und System in der Philosophie Kants.* Hamburg: Felix Meiner: 287–306.

2003. "Kant and the Problem of Human Nature," in Brian Jacobs and Patrick Kain (eds.), *Essays on Kant's Anthropology.* Cambridge: Cambridge University Press: 38–59.

2006. "The Supreme Principle of Morality," in Paul Guyer, (ed.), *The Cambridge Companion to Kant and Modern Philosophy.* Cambridge: Cambridge University Press: 342–80.

2008. *Kantian Ethics.* Cambridge: Cambridge University Press.

Wuerth, Julian 2011. "Moving Beyond Kant's Account of Agency in the *Grounding,*" in Wuerth and Jost 2011 (eds.): 147–63.

Wuerth, Julian and Jost, Lawrence (eds.) 2011. *Perfecting Virtue: New Essays on Kantian Ethics and Virtue Ethics.* Cambridge: Cambridge University Press.

Wuerth, Julian and Jost, Lawrence 2013. "Sense and Sensibility in Kant's Practical Agent: Against the Intellectualism of Korsgaard and Sidgwick." *European Journal of Philosophy* 21: 1–36.

2014. *Kant on Mind, Action, and Ethics.* Oxford: Oxford University Press.

Zinkin, Melissa 2006. "Intensive Magnitudes and the Normativity of Taste," in Rebecca Kukla (ed.), *Aesthetics and Cognition in Kant's Critical Philosophy.* Cambridge: Cambridge University Press: 138–61.

Zuckert, Rachel 2002. "A New Look at Kant's Theory of Pleasure," *Journal of Aesthetics and Art Criticism* 60: 239–52.

2007. *Kant on Beauty and Biology.* Cambridge: Cambridge University Press.

Index

absolute value, 186, 197–8
  as formal ranking, 165
acquired right, 252
aesthetic presuppositions, 123–4, 271–7
affordance (social), 116–17
agency, 189
agreeable, 68, 80, 83
Allison, Henry, 42, 45, 54–5, 58, 62, 64, 67, 71, 75–6, 81–2
altruism, 134–5
apperception, 22, 52, 58, 62–3, 157
  and unity of space and time, 52
  objective unity of, 26
apprehension, 21–3
Arendt, Hannah, 67
Astington, Janet, 128–9
autocracy, 204, 211
autonomy, 2, 6–7, 93, 96, 108, 157, 171, 175–6, 218, 222, 281

Baumgarten, Alexander, 36, 142
beatitude (*Seligkeit*), 200, 203
  and independence, 203
  word origin, 204
Beck, Lewis White, 53–4
beneficence, 101–2, 274
Berger, Larissa, 97
Bittner, Rüdiger, 192
blame, 193
Bratman, Michael, 114
Browning, Christopher, 124
Bushnell, I., 128

capacity for morality, 5, 110
categorical imperative, 235
  and duties of right, 246
  formal character, 165
  in civil condition. *See also* formula of autonomy, formula of humanity, formula of universal law, formula of the realm of ends

categories, 1, 3, 30–8, 40, 66
  as conditions of self-consciousness, 55
  and content (*Inhalt*), 43–4
  and intellectual origin, 41–2
  objective validity of, 64
  and sensibility, 31
  and sensible intuition, 42
  and Transcendental Deduction, 52, 64
  vs. schematized categories, 45
causality, 279
change of heart, 222, 286–8
character, 195, 218
choice (*Willkür*), 193
Christology, 224–7
CI-procedure, 144, 146
civil condition, 253, 266
coercion, 8, 238, 245, *See also* hindrance principle
cognition, 69, 71
  empirical cognition, 13
  of freedom, 281
  objects of, 13
  and role of consciousness, 95
compatibilism, 173–5, 188–90
concepts, 37, *See also* categories
  and Christian Wolff, 35–6
conscience, 211–12, 278
constructivism, 6, 145–54
contentment, 207–10, 278
contractualism, 9, 251, 256–9
conventionalism, 9, 256–9

Darwall, Stephen, 104
Dean, Richard, 84–5, 112
Deduction of Judgments of Taste, 68, 70, 72–4, 76–7
definitions, 48–9
despondency, 209–11
determination, 171–3
  epistemological vs. causal sense, 172
  formal vs. normative sense, 172

Index

developmental psychology, 6, 126–36
difference principle, 9, 250–5, 259, 262
dignity, 152, 156
disposition (*Gesinnung*), 221–2
distributive justice, 2, 9, 250–1, 259
  and consent, 260, 263
Doris, John, 124
duties of virtue, 276
dynamical principles, 63

Ebbinghaus, Julius, 233, 246
Elimination of Sensibility Procedure, 6, 137,
  144–5
empirical judgment, 13–16
  content and form, 14
  objective validity of, 13
end-setting, 241, *See also* freedom
  and natural conditions, 275
  willing necessary means, 274
enlightenment, 191
Epicurus, 139, 141
equality, 259
  in civil condition, 261
  formal equality, 263–4, 266
Estlund, David, 257
ethical community
  as church, 8, 217, 228

fact of reason, 98–9, 157, 162, 283
faculty of desire, 152
Fichte, Johann Gottlieb, 173, 233
Flikschuh, Katrin, 191
formal equality. *See* equality
formal intuitions
  and time-determinations, 59
formula of autonomy, 113, 182, 187
formula of humanity, 5, 90–2, 100–2, 113, 145,
  149, 162, 165, 234, 237, 272
  and containing others' ends, 101–2
  and highest good, 104–5
  and infant development, 133–4
  and intrinsic worth, 93
formula of the kingdom of ends, 165
formula of universal law, 91, 113, 145
  as a principle of right, 247
  validity of, 93–4, 96
freedom, 175–6
  acting under idea of, 158
  as causality, 188
  as end-setting capacity, 10, 271
  equality of external freedom, 241
  external freedom, 239
  and happiness, 89–90
  and human nature, 85
  as independence from alien influence,
    97

as innate right, 9, 242, 252
and intelligible character, 280
and intrinsic worth, 92
as "inner value of the world," 6, 155
lending idea of, 5, 94, 96
and nature, 9, 269–70
noumenal and phenomenal, 278–9
and principle of right, 237
and relation to moral law, 89
and validity of moral law, 94
Frierson, Patrick, 122, 196

Garve, Christian, 103, 142
geometry, 50
Gibson, James, 116
Ginsborg, Hannah, 83
God, 215, 222, 224–5
  as author of nature, 290, *See also* practical
    postulates
  and grace, 226
  as ground of phenomenal world, 281
good will, 112, 125, 138, 144–5
Gottsched, Johann Christoph, 36
grace, 227
grounds of morality, 139
guilt
  of "new man," 225
Guyer, Paul, 9, 52–3, 58, 62, 67, 69, 72, 78–84,
    89–92, 110, 118, 120–2, 125, 155, 158–9,
    164, 233, 236–8, 242–3, 245, 248, 250,
    252, 257

happiness, 2, 139
  and laws of nature, 292
  as necessary end for human beings, 215
  and relation to morality, 141
harmonious play, 68–72, 74–7, 80, *See also*
    pleasure
  temporal structure, 77
harmony of the faculties, 79
Helvetius, Claude, 139, 141
Henrich, Dieter, 53
Herder, Johann Gottfried, 192
Herman, Barbara, 102, 112
heteronomy, 157, 185, 187–9
highest good, 2, 5, 8, 10, 90, 102–6, 141, 214,
    271, 289
  and change of heart, 222
  and formula of humanity, 104–5
  and happiness, 102–3
  and immortality of the soul, 103
  proportionality between virtue and happiness,
    214, 289
  as realizable in natural world, 289
  in *Religion Within the Boundaries of Mere
    Reason*, 216

Index

307

Hill, Thomas, 112
hindrance principle, 257, *See also* coercion
Hobbes, Thomas, 140
holy will, 125, 215
human nature
  determinable through freedom, 85
  and principle of taste, 67
humanity, 90–2, 161, 197, 199
  and absolute value, 162
  as capacity for morality, 112
  as capacity to set ends, 92, 111–12, 272
  criteria for recognizing, 119–20
  as "end in itself," 163
  and joint cooperative activity, 114
  as necessary end, 162, 164
  and principle of taste, 85
  as possession of a good will, 112
  and rational nature, 111
  and social affordances, 116–17
  scope of, 108–10, 116
  value of, 162
Hume, David, 256
Hutcheson, Francis, 139

imagination, 1, 67, 80, *See also* transcendental
    imagination
  attunement with understanding, 5, 71
immortality. *See* practical postulates
imperfect duty, 273–4
inclination, 2, 7, 151, 195–9, 205, 211
  and relationship with need, 200–2
independence, 7, 203
  as ideal, 206
infant development, 126–36
  and formula of humanity, 133–4
innate right to freedom. *See* freedom
intrinsic worth, 91–3, 157
intuition, 14, 25, 27, 53–4
  and imagination, 26

joint cooperative activity, 114–16, 126, 130–3
joy, 212–13
judgments of beauty, 71, 82
  basis of, 68
judgments of taste
  agreement in, 75
  basis of, 80
  and feeling, 80
  pure, 72–3

kingdom of ends. *See* realm of ends
Korsgaard, Christine, 6, 92, 111, 138, 149–54, 197

Larmore, Charles, 182, 191
Leibniz, G. W., 173
libertarianism, 266

Liszkowski, U., 131
Locke, John, 252
Longuenesse, Béatrice, 4, 56–9
love of others, 278
luxury, 202

Mackie, J. L., 147
Mandeville, Bernard, 139, 141
manifold of intuition, 13, 27
mathematics, 48, 51, 64
  mathematical principles, 61–3
Meier, Georg Friedrich, 37
mercy, 121, 125–6
metaphysical deduction, 14–17
metaphysical exposition, 49
miserliness, 209–11
Moll, H., 115
Montaigne, Michel de, 140
Moore, G.E., 153
moral anxiety, 8, 204, 206, 208, 211–12, 221,
    224, *See also* moral misery
moral character. *See* character
moral feeling, 278
moral goodness, 139
  vs. prudential goodness, 138–45
moral ideal, 270
moral idealism, 156, *See also* constructivism
moral law
  as causal law, 282
  consciousness of, 97–8
  necessity of, 138, 140, 144, 180
moral misery, 207, 211, *See also* moral anxiety
moral realism, 6, 144–5, 147, 156, 158–9
  transcendental vs. empirical, 157
moral reliabilism, 5, 111
moral status, 110
  and aesthetic presuppositions, 123–4
  attribution of, 5, 120
  of non-human animals, 134–6
  scope of, 108–10, 116
moral value
  as formal ordering, 6, 163
  not intrinsic property, 159
morals (*Sitten*), 8, 233, 247

need, 7, 198–203, 211
  and relationship with inclination, 200–2
  true needs, 102, 202–3
noumenal will, 280
Nozick, Robert, 266

O'Neill, Onora, 112, 146, 148
object constitution, 17
  and transcendental imagination, 13
obligation, 8, 142, 234, 247
original position, 146, 258

Index

perfectionism, 142–3, 147
Piaget, Jean, 127
Pippin, Robert, 233
pleasure, 69–71
  and harmonious play, 69, 79
  as intentional feeling, 83
  and play of faculties, 75
  and self-consciousness, 83
  and universal communicability, 83
  as universally communicable, 80
  universal valdity in judgments of taste, 78
  universally communicable feeling, 71
practical postulates, 160–1, 215, 272, 287, 293
practical reason, 161, 269
  and ontology, 159, 162
  as *Wille*, 184–5
predispositions to the good, 218
Prichard, H. A., 138, 150–1
principle of aesthetic judgment. *See* principle of
  judgments of taste
principle of judgments of taste, 4, 66, 71, 74–5
  normative function, 82
  universally shared, 68, 73–4
principle of right, 2, 8, 252
  as analytic, 236, 241
  and freedom, 237
propensity to evil, 218–19, 285
  in heart, not will, 220
property right, 250, 252–4, 276
  as mutual agreement, 253
  requires consent, 254–5, 257
public use of reason, 191
pure concepts of the understanding.
  See categories
pure judgments of taste. *See* judgments of taste
purposive unity, 269–70
purposiveness
  internal and external, 270

radical evil, 217–18, 285–6
rational intuitionism, 145
Rawls, John, 9, 112, 118, 144–8, 214, 250–1,
  255–6, 258–9
realm of appearance, 269
realm of ends, 113, 181
Reddy, Vasudevi, 130
Reinhold, Karl Leonhard, 285
religion, 8, 216, 222–3, 228, 230
right. *See also* principle of right
  and coercion, 238, 245, 274, 276
  cannot begin with ends, 240
  as giving rise to ends, 243
  and incentives, 235
  and obligation, 236
  and relation to ethics, 233–6, 247
right of equity, 245

right of necessity, 245
Ripstein, Arthur, 235, 238
Rosenkoetter, Timothy, 44
Rousseau, Jean-Jacques, 173, 192, 203

Sayre-McCord, Geofrey, 156
schematism, 45, 60, 119, *See also* categories
Schmid, Carl Christian Erhard, 285
Schönecker, Dieter, 93
Schopenhauer, Arthur, 286
Schulz, J. H., 190
Searle, John, 116
self-deception, 210–11
self-esteem, 278
selfhood, 173–4
sensation, 18–19
  and imagination, 19–21
Sensen, Oliver, 160
sensible representations, 15–16
Shaftesbury, 3rd Earl of, 139
shared cooperative activity. *See* joint cooperative
  activity
skepticism, 55
space and time
  representations as singular, 52
Spalding, J. J., 173
spontaneity, 1–2
spontaneity of the understanding, 31, 37, 47
state of nature
  duty to exit, 257
  vs. original position, 258
Sticker, Martin, 124
Stoicism, 141, 207, 215, 223
Sturm, Thomas, 122
summum bonum. See highest good

taxation, 250, 264
things in themselves, 55, 161
third antinomy, 163, 279–80
time determination, 59–60
Timmermann, Jens, 91, 197
Tomasello, Michael, 113–16, 131–2
Transcendental Aesthetic, 49
  and transcendental idealism, 49
Transcendental Deduction, 4, 51
  and categories, 52, 64
Transcendental Exposition, 49
transcendental idealism, 4, 49, 51, 65, 270, 277,
  279
  Kant's argument for, 51
  and Transcendental Aesthetic, 49
  and Transcendental Deduction, 52
transcendental imagination, 3, 16–17
  and aesthetic contemplation, 28
  and object constitution, 13
  and perception, 25–6

Index

transcendental synthesis of imagination, 57
  vs. empirical synthesis, 59

Ulrich, Johann August Heinrich, 282
understanding. *See also* spontaneity of the understanding
  attunement with imagination, 71
  and Christian Wolff, 33–7
  as capacity to judge, 37, 39
  and imagination, 23, 25
  and sensibility, 30, 39
unity. *See also* purposive unity
  need for, 66–7
unity of apperception. *See* apperception
universal principle of right. *See* principle of right

virtue, 195, 205, 223, 277
Vouloumanos, P., 129

Werker, J., 129
will
  vs. *Willkür*, 285
will (*Wille*), 178–9, 187, 193
  and practical reason, 184–5
  and universal law, 181
  vs. *Willkür*, 179
Willaschek, Marcus, 233, 246
Wizenmann. Thomas, 201
Wolff, Christian, 3, 30–3, 143
Wood, Allen, 85, 92, 112, 123

Zinkin, Melissa, 69, 70, 85
Zuckert, Rachel, 67, 69, 74